On9 93358 WEN

Literature after 9/11

Routledge Studies in Contemporary Literature

1. Literature after 9/11
Edited by Ann Keniston and
Jeanne Follansbee Quinn

Literature after 9/11

**Edited by Ann Keniston and
Jeanne Follansbee Quinn**

Routledge
Taylor & Francis Group
New York   London

First published 2008
by Routledge
270 Madison Ave, New York, NY 10016

Simultaneously published in the UK
by Routledge
2 Park Square, Milton Park, Abingdon, Oxon OX14 4RN

Routledge is an imprint of the Taylor & Francis Group, an informa business

Transferred to Digital Printing 2010

© 2008 Taylor & Francis

Typeset in Sabon by IBT Global.

Library of Congress Cataloging in Publication Data

Literature after 9/11 / edited by Ann Keniston and Jeanne Follansbee Quinn.
p. cm. -- (Routledge studies in contemporary literature)
Includes bibliographical references and index.
ISBN-13: 978-0-415-96252-0 (acid-free paper)
ISBN-10: 0-415-96252-8 (acid-free paper)
1. American literature—21st century—History and criticism. 2. September 11 Terrorist Attacks, 2001—Influence. 3. September 11 Terrorist Attacks, 2001, in literature. 4. September 11 Terrorist Attacks, 2001, in art. 5. Terrorism in literature. 6. Psychic trauma in literature. 7. Politics and literature—United States—History—21st century. I. Keniston, Ann, 1961– II. Quinn, Jeanne Follansbee, 1956– III. Title: Literature after nine eleven.
PS231.S47L57 2008
820.9'35873931—dc22
2008006812

ISBN10: 0-415-96252-8 (hbk)
ISBN10: 0-415-88398-9 (pbk)

ISBN13: 978-0-415-96252-0 (hbk)
ISBN13: 978-0-415-88398-6 (pbk)

To our children,
Jeremy and Paul Novak
and
Martin and Karen Quinn

Brooklyn Heights Promenade, November 3, 2001, Lorie Novak

Contents

List of Figures   ix
Acknowledgments   xi

Introduction
   Representing 9/11: Literature and Resistance   1
   ANN KENISTON AND JEANNE FOLLANSBEE QUINN

PART 1
Experiencing 9/11: Time, Trauma, and the
Incommensurable Event

1   Portraits of Grief: Telling Details and the New Genres
    of Testimony   19
    NANCY K. MILLER

2   Foer, Spiegelman, and 9/11's Timely Traumas   42
    MITCHUM HUEHLS

3   Graphic Implosion: Politics, Time, and Value in
    Post-9/11 Comics   60
    SIMON COOPER AND PAUL ATKINSON

4   "Sometimes things disappear": Absence and Mutability
    in Colson Whitehead's *The Colossus of New York*   82
    STEPHANIE LI

5   Witnessing 9/11: Art Spiegelman and the Persistence
    of Trauma   99
    RICHARD GLEJZER

PART 2
9/11 Politics and Representation

6   Seeing Terror, Feeling Art: Public and Private in
    Post-9/11 Literature   123
    MICHAEL ROTHBERG

7   "We're Not a Friggin' Girl Band": September 11, Masculinity, and the British-American Relationship in David Hare's *Stuff Happens* and Ian McEwan's *Saturday*   143
    REBECCA CARPENTER

8   "We're the Culture That Cried Wolf": Discourse and Terrorism in Chuck Palahniuk's *Lullaby*   161
    LANCE RUBIN

9   Still Life: 9/11's Falling Bodies   180
    LAURA FROST

PART 3
9/11 and the Literary Tradition

10 Telling It Like It Isn't   209
    DAVID SIMPSON

11 *Portraits 9/11/01:* The *New York Times* and the Pornography of Grief   224
    SIMON STOW

12 Theater after 9/11   242
    ROBERT BRUSTEIN

13 Real Planes and Imaginary Towers: Philip Roth's *The Plot Against America* as 9/11 Prosthetic Screen   246
    CHARLES LEWIS

14 Precocious Testimony: Poetry and the Uncommemorable   261
    JEFFREY GRAY

Afterword
    Imagination and Monstrosity   285
    ROBERT PINSKY

Contributors   291
Index   295

List of Figures

Frontispiece *Brooklyn Heights Promenade, November 3, 2001,*
  Lorie Novak.   vi

1.1   *Grand Central Station Memorial Wall, October 24, 2002,*
        Lorie Novak.   20

1.2   *Requiem for September 11, detail,* Tatana Kellner.   30

1.3   *Requiem for September 11, detail,* Tatana Kellner.   32

1.4   *Hudson River Park, November 27, 2001,* Lorie Novak.   33

1.5   *Grand Central Station Memorial Wall, October 24, 2002,*
        Lorie Novak.   34

3.1a   *The Amazing Spider-Man,* issue #36 © 2001, John
        Romita, Jr., art, and J. Michael Straczynski, text.   64

3.1b   *The Amazing Spider-Man,* issue #36 © 2001, John
        Romita, Jr., art, and J. Michael Straczynski, text.   65

3.2   Published by Dark Horse Comics, Inc.   76

5.1   From *In the Shadow of No Towers* by Art Spiegelman.   103

5.2   From *In the Shadow of No Towers* by Art Spiegelman.   105

5.3   From *In the Shadow of No Towers* by Art Spiegelman.   106

5.4   From *In the Shadow of No Towers* by Art Spiegelman.   112

5.5   From *In the Shadow of No Towers* by Art Spiegelman.   114

5.6   From *In the Shadow of No Towers* by Art Spiegelman.   115

9.1   *Tumbling Woman,* 38" x 72" x 48," bronze, 2001–2002,
        Eric Fischl.   182

9.2   *World Trade Center Jumper* © 2001, Lyle Owerko.   184

9.3   Detail, *World Trade Center Jumper* © 2001, Lyle Owerko.   192

9.4   *Soaring Spirit*, John Mavroudis and Owen Smith.   197

9.5   *Soaring Spirit*, John Mavroudis and Owen Smith.   198

Acknowledgments

We are grateful to the extraordinary imagination and diligence of the contributors to this volume, whose creative and original responses to 9/11 literature have shaped a new area of study.

Eric Stottlemyer conscientiously and cheerfully checked citations, formatted the manuscript, and followed up on editorial questions of all kinds. Jake Segal reviewed the manuscript and compiled the index. Andy Romig and Lauren Mulcahy scanned files and provided invaluable technical support as we compiled the manuscript.

We benefited from many conversations with colleagues at the University of Nevada, Reno, the University of North Carolina, Greensboro, and Harvard, and at panels at the Modern Language Association and American Literature Association conferences in 2005 and 2007. Special thanks to Aaron Santesso for first encouraging this collection.

The editors gratefully acknowledge financial support from the UNR Junior Faculty Research Grant Program, the UNR College of Liberal Arts Scholarly and Creative Activities Grant Program, and the Harvard Faculty Research Fund.

We dedicate this book to our children, Jeremy and Paul Novak and Martin and Karen Quinn, in gratitude for the ways they compelled us to think about the meaning of 9/11 for the generation growing up in the shadow of no towers and for their capacity to remind us of what persists amid cataclysmic events.

We also acknowledge permission to reprint the following texts and images:

From *Colossus of New York: A City in Thirteen Parts* by Colson White-head, copyright © 2003 by Colson Whitehead. Used by permission of Doubleday, a division of Random House, Inc.

First published in *Colossus of New York: A City in Thirteen Parts* and reprinted by permission of Colson Whitehead and Aragi, Inc.

From *In the Shadow of No Towers* by Art Spiegelman, copyright © 2004 by Art Spiegleman. Used by permission of Pantheon Books, a division of Random House, Inc.

From *In the Shadow of No Towers* by Art Spiegelman, copyright © 2004 by Art Spiegleman, reprinted with permission of the Wylie Agency, Inc.

"Four November 9ths" by Anne-Marie Levine. Used by permission of the author. The poem originally appeared in *Poetry after 9/11: An Anthology of New York Poets* (Melville House 2002).

"first writing since" by Suheir Hammad. Reprinted from *Trauma at Home: After 9/11* edited by Judith Greenberg by permission of the University of Nebraska Press. Copyright © 2003 by the Board of Regents of the University of Nebraska.

From "October Rendezvous," from *Burnt Island: Three* Suites by D. Nurkse, copyright © 2005 by D. Nurkse. Used by permission of Alfred A. Knopf, a division of Random House, Inc.

From *Lullaby: A Novel* by Chuck Palahniuk, copyright © 2002 by Chuck Palahniuk. Used by permission of Doubleday, a division of Random House, Inc.

From *Lullaby: A Novel* by Chuck Palahniuk, copyright © 2002 by Chuck Palahniuk. Reprinted by permission of Donadio & Olson, Inc.

Eric Fischl. "Tumbling Woman." 38" by 72" by 48." Bronze. 2001–2001. Courtesy: Mary Boone Gallery, New York. (MBG#8425)

"Soaring Spirit." Image by John Mavroudis and Owen Smith. Used by permission of the artists.

"World Trade Center Jumper." Photograph by Lyle Owerko. Lyle Owerko © 2001.

Excerpt from *Monologue of a Dog*, copyright © 2002 by Wislawa Szymborska, English translation copyright © 2006 by Harcourt, Inc., reprinted by permission of the publisher.

From *The Plot against America* by Philip Roth. Copyright © 2004 by Philip Roth, reprinted with permission of The Wylie Agency.

"Curse," excerpts from "Luggage," "Advice to the Players," and "Heart Beat" from *Star Dust* by Frank Bidart. Copyright © 2005 by Frank Bidart. Reprinted by permission of Farrar, Straus and Giroux, LLC.

From David Rigsbee, *Sonnets to Hamlet*. Used by permission of the author.

Excerpt from "When the Towers Fell," from *Strong is Your Hold: Poems* by Galway Kinnell. Copyright © 2006 by Galway Kinnell. Reprinted by permission of Houghton Mifflin Company. All rights reserved.

Excerpt from "When the Towers Fell," from *Strong is Your Hold: Poems* by Galway Kinnell. Copyright © 2006 by Galway Kinnell. Bloodaxe Books 2006.

Baraka, Amiri. *Somebody Blew Up America & Other Poems*. Philipsburg: House of Nehesi Publishers, 2004.

From di Prima, Diane, "Notes toward a Poem of Revolution." Allen Cohen and Clive Matson, eds. *An Eye for an Eye Makes the Whole World Blind: Poets on 9/11* (Regent 2002).

"The Badlands" from *Birthday Letters* by Ted Hughes. Copyright © 1998 by Ted Hughes. Reprinted by permission of Farrar, Straus and Giroux, LLC.

"The Badlands" from *Birthday Letters* by Ted Hughes. Copyright © 1998 by Ted Hughes. Reprinted by permission of Faber and Faber Ltd.

"War" from *The Singing* by C. K. Williams. Copyright © 2003 by C. K. Williams. Reprinted by permission of Farrar, Straus and Giroux, LLC.

"War" from C. K. Williams, *Collected Poems*. Bloodaxe Books, 2006.

From Sam Hamill, Ed. *Poets Against the War*. Reprinted by permission of Nation Books, a member of Perseus Books Group.

From "Easter 1916" by W. B. Yeats. Used by permission of A. P. Watt Ltd. On behalf of Gráinne Yeats.

From "Souvenir of the Ancient World" by Carlos Drummond de Andrade. Translated by Mark Strand. Copyright © 1976 by Mark Strand. Used by permission of the author.

"Curse" from *Star Dust* by Frank Bidart. Copyright © 2005 by Frank Bidart. Reprinted by permission of Frank Bidart.

Versions of Chapters 1, 6, and 12 were published previously. We acknowledge permission to reprint them here.

Michael Rothberg, "'There is no poetry in this': Writing, Trauma, and Home." Reprinted from *Trauma at Home: After 9/11* edited by Judith

Greenberg by permission of the University of Nebraska Press. Copyright © 2003 by the Board of Regents of the University of Nebraska.

Nancy K. Miller, "Portraits of Grief: Telling Details and Testimony of Trauma" in *differences*, Volume 14, no. 3, pp. 112–135. Copyright, 2003, Brown University and *differences: A Journal of Feminist Cultural Studies.* All rights reserved. Use by permission of the publisher.

Robert Brustein. "Theater After 9/11." *The New Republic,* October 3, 2005.

Introduction

Representing 9/11:
Literature and Resistance

Ann Keniston and
Jeanne Follansbee Quinn

The World Trade Center (WTC), like any famous skyscraper, was both real and imaginary. It was a commercial and tourist center, occupied every day by tens of thousands. As two of the tallest buildings in the world, the towers also stood for American power and commerce, and for capitalism more generally. After their destruction on September 11, 2001, these roles—what literary studies might call the literal and the figurative—remained, but their relationship changed: the material reality or "fact" of the destruction of the towers has itself been overwhelming, but this destruction has increasingly been understood and represented through a range of complex symbolic formations.

The competing demands of utility and symbol have been particularly acute in the ongoing and contentious debates about the buildings and memorials to be erected at Ground Zero. The 9/11 Memorial, for example, is at once a symbolic space—a place to recall the towers, the dead, and the effects of their absence—and something like an actual graveyard, but one whose dead bodies are unrecognizable and unrecoverable. Throughout such debates, there remains a desire to be true—to the calamity itself, to the feelings of the victims' families, to the collective need to mourn. But 9/11 itself, or more exactly its capacity to be understood in different ways, also obstructs such desires: no one wants 9/11 to be misrepresented, politicized, co-opted, or distorted. Yet, it seems difficult not to do just this.

While such problems are not literary, the tension between the symbolic suggestiveness of the WTC and the fact of its destruction is central to many literary texts written in the wake of 9/11. (Literary representations of 9/11 focus almost exclusively on events in New York City. The destruction of the Pentagon and the crash in Shanksville, PA, while suggestive for film makers, have not proven as interesting to writers.) Art Spiegelman's influential 2004 graphic novel *In the Shadow of No Towers* enacts the tension between the literal and the figurative quite starkly. On the one hand, the book is bound to the experience of 9/11 and its aftermath; its words and images recount Spiegelman's physical and emotional responses on that day and afterward. But it also remains separate from this lived experience:

Spiegelman explicitly interrogates the "facts" and "reality" of what happened, and the text's distinctive visual and verbal repetitions insist on its status as an imaginative representation of lived experience. Spiegelman's work thus insists—and it is similar in this way to much 9/11 literature—on the space between the real and the imagined, between image and trope, and between the private realm of memory and the public realm of history. 9/11 literature impels us to see these spaces even as it forces them together; it consistently uses the literal to deconstruct the symbolic and the reverse. It thus offers a kind of partial, awkward bridge between life and language. To adapt a term that Charles Lewis's chapter in this volume draws from Philip Roth's *The Plot Against America,* 9/11 literature works as a prosthesis, an awkward substitute for and attempt to compensate for the unrepresentable absence effected by 9/11 itself.

If literature expresses what remains unrepresentable about 9/11, it also raises persistent questions about how we interpret and represent 9/11, questions precipitated by debates within and outside the United States about the "war on terror." In the years after the attacks of September 11, 2001, with early national unity dissipated and global sympathy foundering in the wake of the U.S. invasion of Iraq, American perspective on the attacks has continued to evolve. Suspicion about the Bush administration's attempts to link Iraq, Al Qaeda, and September 11—coupled with an enduring sense of mourning for the losses of that day—have led to political and historical frameworks for 9/11 that go beyond the initially articulated binary of "us" and "them." This struggle to speak about the meaning of 9/11 is reflected in the highly varied and ever-growing range of literary responses considered in this volume. Fiction and poetry by prominent writers, including Don DeLillo, Ian McEwan, Philip Roth, John Updike, Louise Glück, Frank Bidart, and Robert Pinsky, have contributed to and complicated on-going conversations among political commentators and cultural critics about the meaning and uses of 9/11. By placing literary texts within this cultural and political context, *Literature after 9/11* defines literature's perspective on 9/11, as well as on the relationship between politics and aesthetics, and between history and narrative.

The chapters in *Literature after 9/11* examine the ways that literature has participated in the larger cultural process of representing and interpreting the events of September 11, 2001, while also revealing the difficulties of doing so when cataclysmic events are still so recent. The questions that organize *Literature after 9/11* emerge from the literature itself; as the chapters show, literary works reframe and focus the meaning of 9/11 by employing representational strategies that emphasize the desire for (and construction of) meaning, and that dramatize the continuing resonance of 9/11 in the collective life of the United States and beyond. As the contributions to *Literature after 9/11* suggest, we can read texts as diverse as Claire Messud's social satire *The Emperor's Children,* Art Spiegelman's graphic novel *In the Shadow of No Towers,* and Philip Roth's fascist allegory *The*

Plot Against America as involved in a broadly similar task: offering critiques of and challenges to political discourses that seek to simplify or fix the meaning of 9/11.

The volume does not offer a single point of view on 9/11; instead, its chapters define a new body of literature—literature *after* 9/11—that reveals the instability of 9/11 as an event and the ways that literature contests 9/11's co-option for narrowly political ends. Because the literary works examined here engage self-reflexively with frameworks for interpreting 9/11—as well as with attempts to represent the events themselves—the chapters in *Literature after 9/11* depict a passage from raw experience to representation. In short, the works examined in *Literature after 9/11* reveal the tension between private experience and the necessarily social means for representing it. By defining "literature" broadly and by including chapters by scholars from a range of different disciplines, *Literature after 9/11* demonstrates the connection between "literature" and the narratives that have shaped public debate about the meaning of 9/11.

Collectively, these chapters refuse to interpret 9/11 *either* as a rupture with the past *or* as continuous with (and even anticipated by) earlier historical events. Instead, the time elapsed since 9/11 provides the contributors to *Literature after 9/11* with a unique vantage point for tracing a more complex alternative: while the initial experience of 9/11 seemed unprecedented and cataclysmic, the experience of incommensurability generated a culture-wide need for explanatory narratives, not simply as a means for countering the trauma, but as a means for refusing incommensurability, prompting attempts to place 9/11 into an historical framework. We might say, then, that the history of literary representations of 9/11 can be characterized by the *transition* from narratives of rupture to narratives of continuity.

The history of literature written about and after 9/11 can also be seen, at least in part, as a sequence of genres. That is, shorter forms appeared first—essays, brief personal reminiscences, and poetry. It took several years longer for novels and full-length memoirs to appear. Early works often attempted directly to capture and convey the events of 9/11 and emotional responses to the events; as time has passed, the approach to the attacks has become more nuanced. 9/11 has come to seem less what these works are about than an event to which they refer, one element among many. At the same time, 9/11 has given rise to a number of hybrid forms, including the *New York Times*'s "Portraits of Grief," and to new kinds of images and iconography in written texts, graphic novels, and traditional comic books.

The earliest writings about 9/11 include poems published online by non-professional and often anonymous poets. Often formally conventional, they attempt to bridge the gap between personal loss and a larger political meaning. The 2002 poetry collection edited by Allen Cohen and Clive Matson, *An Eye for an Eye Makes the Whole World Blind: Poets on 9/11,* for example, consciously attempted, as its editor claims, to set forth through poetry "a . . . historical record of these monumental events" that was "different" from that put forth by the "corporate controlled media, presidency, and congress [*sic*]" (i). Sam Hamill's 2003 anthology *Poets Against the War* and the voluminous website from which its poems were selected celebrates its "rising tide of voices" which "the Bush people" failed to "quell" (viii).

While these poems confirm the notion that poetry defines and makes public private and often subversive feelings, poems written later by "professional" poets have been quite different. Many of these poems move falteringly, relying less on assertion than on allusion and citation. Galway Kinnell's "When the Towers Fell," discussed by Jeffrey Gray, stitches together lines from a range of texts in an enactment of the difficulty of speaking about the attacks; Robert Pinsky's "Anniversary" does something similar, and a number of poems attempt to imagine or adopt the position of the "other," J. D. McClatchy's "Jihad" and Frank Bidart's "Curse" among them. These poems tend to begin with a sense of the dangers of identification and speech.

Narrative and dramatic responses to 9/11, including mainstream comics, *avant garde* comix, memoir, plays, and novels, have similarly shifted focus since September 11, 2001. Like the first poems after 9/11, early narratives and plays grappled with representing 9/11, but as distance from the events has increased, later texts have registered the reverberations of 9/11, framing representations of the events, if they are depicted at all, within narratives that are weighted towards depicting their aftermath. We can see this shift in the move from one of the first plays about September 11, Anne Nelson's "The Guys" (2001), which dramatizes the efforts by a New York fire fighter to write eulogies for those who died in the WTC, to David Hare's 2004 play, "Stuff Happens," which satirizes the appropriation of 9/11 by the Bush administration in the run-up to the Iraq War. Similarly, Frederic Beigbeder's novel *Windows on the World* (2004), which is based on *102 Minutes: The Untold Story of the Fight to Survive Inside the Twin Towers,* a journalistic reconstruction of events inside the Twin Towers by Jim Dwyer and Kevin Flynn, depicts events in the WTC on September 11, while Don DeLillo's *Falling Man* (2007) incorporates 9/11 into a larger story about its effects on a survivor and his family.

The transition from 2004's *Windows on the World* to 2007's *Falling Man* demonstrates another feature of 9/11 narratives that distinguish them from the poetry written about and after 9/11. Whereas the initial poems tended to be formally conventional, the first novels about 9/11 featured formal innovations—self-reflexive meta-narratives, disrupted temporality, multiple viewpoints. Later novels have tended to be more formally conservative, yet these more straightforward narratives grapple with more complex representational challenges, often combining exploration of the subjectivities of characters living "in the shadow of no towers"—to use Spiegelman's phrase—with dramatization of contested interpretations of 9/11. *Windows on the World,* while formally innovative, is chronologically conservative. The novel combines two alternating narratives: the minute-by-minute imagined experience of a father and two sons trapped in the restaurant Windows on the World on the morning of September 11, 2001, and the self-reflexive record of Beigbeder's experience watching the towers fall on television in Paris that autumn day. The novel begins at 8:30 a.m. and ends at 10:29 a.m., one minute after the North Tower collapses. While the structure of the novel allows the narrator to reflect on the experience of virtual witness (watching the events on television), its primary thread centers on what it might have been like to die that morning in the North Tower.

While Beigbeder employs self-reflexive strategies to foreground the gap between direct witness and representation, Don DeLillo's *Falling Man,* published in 2007, employs a more straightforward—but temporally and spatially disrupted—narrative to dramatize the effects of 9/11 on a survivor from the South Tower and his family. The novel opens in the moments immediately after the North Tower collapses, as the protagonist flees the destruction in Lower Manhattan, and it ends with a harrowing account of the first plane hitting the towers. Between these two scenes, the narrative follows the lives of the survivor, Keith, and his family in the immediate aftermath of the attacks and then skips to three years afterward to show how 9/11 continues to reverberate in their lives. But the novel also loops back to their earlier experiences and to that of an another character, Hammad, as he trains with Muhammad Atta for the 9/11 attacks. The novel's temporal shifts allow DeLillo to represent the effects of the attacks on the characters, but they also dramatize how the survivors remember and integrate the experience into their lives. By leaving his representation of the attack itself until the end of the book, DeLillo suggests that we cannot understand the events of 9/11 except retrospectively and that memories are fragile and need constantly to be reiterated in order to be made meaningful. The novel leads us inexorably (and inevitably) to the chaos of the morning of September 11, and it leaves us there, recognizing the profound uncertainty precipitated by the attacks, as it connects the survivors and the terrorist, the past and the present.

As this publication history highlights tensions between direct and indirect representations of 9/11, it also raises questions about the aesthetics of representing 9/11 at all. Such questions are, broadly speaking, the purview of the three parts of *Literature after 9/11.* What does it mean to have witnessed and to recall an event that felt incommensurable, inaccessible, and incomprehensible? Is it possible to speak in a voice that exceeds the personal, to use a public voice, to launch a political critique in literature? What form can such a literature take, negotiating as it must between the event itself and the dictates of genre, tradition, and the impulse to find an audience? How, in brief, does literature after 9/11 represent the possibility of witness, the political or public sphere, and its own literary status?

* * * * *

The towers' destruction intensified the sense of both compulsory and disrupted witness that had always been associated with them: the tourist's stable, if unconventional, gaze from the top of the towers was both replicated and refused in the towers' spectacular absence. The chapters in Part One of *Literature after 9/11* suggest that the 9/11 attacks compelled writers to chronicle what happened; all the literary works considered in these chapters take place in New York City after the attacks, and all consider the attacks quite directly. Yet these works often openly interrogate the mechanisms and ethics of witness itself. Part One as a whole represents 9/11 not only as a physical disaster but as a fundamental challenge to notions of time, witness, loss, and privacy. And while all these chapters explore the incommensurability of 9/11, they also interrogate this incommensurability, tracing the ways different authors locate 9/11 alongside or within a range of contexts.

9/11 literature thus reveals the impossibility of knowing or conveying what actually occurred on that day. Richard Glejzer's chapter, "Witnessing 9/11: Art Spiegelman and the Persistence of Trauma," offers perhaps the most direct example of this challenge to conventional notions of witness: Glejzer claims that Spiegelman's *In the Shadow of No Towers* locates itself during a preliminary, unformed "time before eventness takes hold," "the moment of witness before testimony." Refusing the kind of chronological or psychological distance that characterized his earlier, far more mediated *Maus,* Spiegelman shows, in Glejzer's terms, "that trauma persists in the temporal disruption itself." As a result, *In the Shadow* "is a text fundamentally about the very failure of all representation to give substance to the act of bearing witness." As the repeated image of "the glowing North Tower about to collapse" makes clear, "the image 'interrupts' his narrative while also marking the return of the event: 'trauma piles upon trauma.'"

While Spiegelman, in Glejzer's reading, challenges witness through the unmediated intensity of his proximity to the events of 9/11 themselves, Stephanie Li's "'Sometimes Things Disappear': Absence and Mutability in Colson Whitehead's *The Colossus of New York*," reveals the failure of witness in a very different way: Whitehead alludes to but does not describe the World Trade Center's destruction. By celebrating New York's mutability, he renders the need to bear witness superfluous. In Li's terms, Whitehead "manipulates absence"—an amorphous, nonspecific, inevitable phenomenon—"to avoid a confrontation with actual loss," the particular, historical, geographical loss of the towers. Whitehead's embrace of a collective New Yorker identity, albeit one characterized by individual isolation, functions paradoxically: "it is absence that unites New York." Yet Li finds within Whitehead's text a number of ruptures and inconsistencies of voice and perspective that in some ways resemble those located by Glejzer in *In the Shadow* and that complicate Whitehead's apparent assertion that witness is unnecessary. While Li sees in Whitehead's indirectness "a degree of narrative subterfuge," she also implies that the text's gaps gesture toward the loss he refuses to name. In this way, Whitehead complicates the notion of collective identity in ways that recall Spiegelman's more violent refusal of sanctioned narratives of 9/11.

Whereas Spiegelman's repetition of a single traumatic moment reveals the ways 9/11 disrupted chronology, Whitehead's repetitive, regenerative notion of time permits the recovery or refashioning of what is absent. In this way, both Glejzer and Li suggest that any discussion of 9/11's challenges to witnessing (to the experience of being there and knowing what occurred) also requires a discussion of the ways 9/11 affected chronology and memory. That we refer to "9/11" marks, as Simon Cooper and Paul Atkinson's chapter notes, the centrality of time to our understanding of the events of that day. Temporal concerns are also, of course, arguably the central purview of literature: while we read texts from beginning to end, literature also complicates chronology through flashback, anticipation, and other strategies. The recurrent discussions of problems, manipulations, and distortions of chronology in Part One suggest that such concerns are crucial to the attempt to chronicle 9/11. These issues seem particularly central to comics and the graphic novel form, perhaps because traditional comics are both insistently chronological—one cell follows another—and, as Cooper and Atkinson point out, ungrounded, since they rarely refer to historical events.

Freud's notion of *Nachträglichkeit* or the tendency of traumatic events to be assimilated not at the moment of their occurrence but later, often through repetition and reenactment, is central to Mitchum Huehls's claim in "Foer, Spiegelman, and 9/11's Timely Traumas" that Spiegelman's *In the Shadow* and Jonathan Safran Foer's novel *Extremely Loud & Incredibly Close* "attempt . . . to mend the relationship between temporal experience and consciousness." Both works create what Huehls calls "new temporal forms," which enable the texts and their narrators to gain distance from the "temporally traumatic effects" of 9/11. Huehls examines the ways that the trauma *of* 9/11 becomes a distinctively *textual* trauma, enacted and also resolved through practices that exceed both the conventionally chronological and the conventionally literary. The novel culminates with what Huehls calls a reversal of time: the narrator, Oskar, converts a static image—a photograph of a man falling from the towers—into a "flip-book" represented at the end of the novel, which creates a "cinematic, real-time performance of motion," enabling the man to "fall" upward and granting "Oskar the illusion of reversing time, while also insisting on a process-based, real-time solution to healing." In contrast, Huehls argues, Spiegelman imposes the static onto the dynamic: the comix format divides actions into discrete, static images. For Huehls, this strategy functions quite differently from Glejzer's reading; these temporal manipulations enable Spiegelman to link "timelessness . . . and timeliness" in ways that create a "safe space" in which he can resolve "the conflict . . . between personal and public" notions of time. Like Foer's manipulations of time, according to Huehls, Spiegelman's enable a movement toward knowledge.

A related temporal dislocation is present in the mainstream comics analyzed by Cooper and Atkinson in "Graphic Implosion: Politics, Time, and Value in Post-9/11 Comics," but to quite different effects. Comics are generally both chronological and historically ungrounded, but comics about 9/11 tend to stop time. According to Cooper and Atkinson, such temporal disruptions function in deeply conservative ways, eradicating the possibility of political understanding and action. Thus, for example, when Spider-Man stands motionless, surveying the devastation of Ground Zero but unable to intervene to remedy the situation, we identify with his position as transcendent observer and, like him, become powerless, able to see but not feel horror and grief. Something similar is at work in a different group of comics often featuring child protagonists, which seem to embrace "the liberal ideals of tolerance and diversity" yet refuse to acknowledge true cultural difference.

As Part One's chapters explore 9/11's disruptions both of conventional ways of marking witness ("I saw this") and memory ("This is what happened"), they also link 9/11 and its representations to other events. Echoing Jean Baudrillard's oft-cited remark that "we have dreamt of this event" (5), the chapters in Part One describe a pattern in which analogies are made between 9/11 and other calamities and then disrupted. This tendency is perhaps most explicit in Whitehead's *The Colossus of New York,* which in Li's reading naturalizes loss by chronicling its recurrence: 9/11 becomes not a unique rupture but something consistent with past events, or at least with past ruptures. The focus of Nancy K. Miller's discussion in "Portraits of Grief: Telling Details and the New Genres of Testimony" is more explicitly textual: Miller both locates the *New York Times* "Portraits of Grief" "within recognizable conventions, within what we might call an ethics of mourning," and suggests that memorialization practices themselves evolve. The "Portraits" accomplish this evolution through a recourse to visual images that are far less textually disruptive than those considered by Glejzer, Huehls, and Cooper and Atkinson; for Miller, the model of the snapshot—based in this case on the actual snapshots of 9/11 victims posted on flyers throughout New York City—enables a new mode of writing, one that draws more from the offhand, spontaneous anecdote than from the more formal obituary. By borrowing from the private, the "Portraits" redefine public discourse. Yet for Miller this combination opens the "Portraits" to some of the same problems identified by Cooper and Atkinson in apparently liberal comics: by insisting on a narrow range of acceptable responses to 9/11, the "Portraits" "render taboo the expression of certain kinds of emotion in the public domain"—especially ambivalence about the dead—as well as the expression of empathy over the suffering of non-Americans.

While Miller, like Li, establishes a context for the losses of 9/11, other chapters reveal more radical temporal disruptions. Superhero comics, Cooper and Atkinson argue, insist on 9/11 as an extreme rupture, "the beginning of a new age," which requires the creation of an entirely new calendar or notion of chronology. Glejzer and Huehls read Spiegelman's inclusion of old comics and newspaper headlines in *In the Shadow* as a way both of inventing analogies to 9/11 and of complicating them. These earlier comics for Huehls "represent a safe temporality" that rescues Spiegelman from "the suspended timelessness of his post-9/11 world." For Glejzer, however, their presence is more disruptive: they "mark . . . a return of the event" by "prefigur[ing]" it; the images ultimately "fail . . . to bear the weight of his vision." The effect, both authors suggest, is indeterminacy: Spiegelman, like many of the authors discussed in Part One, is impelled to make analogies to other events, revealing both that 9/11 cannot stand alone and that it cannot be assimilated.

Pairing a helpless superhero like Spider-Man with depictions of innocent children jeopardized by terrorism in other graphic narratives allows Cooper and Atkinson to make plain the relationship between ideology and witness, a connection that marks the transition between Part One and Part Two of *Literature after 9/11*. While Part One concentrates on the formal problems of representing the experience of witnessing 9/11, Part Two's chapters focus explicitly on the politics of representation, showing how literary works interpret 9/11 and revealing the ways that interpretation is always ideological. As Cooper and Atkinson show, even stories that position us as observers invite us to identify with a particular view of September 11. In the examples they analyze, we become witnesses who see but are unable to feel or act. A similar failure to feel, as Michael Rothberg argues in his chapter in Part Two, isolates us in our private loss, preventing us from placing 9/11 into history and leaving us unable to see the crucial connections between personal experiences of loss and public responses to 9/11. Rothberg's argument about the need to historicize 9/11 underscores two key themes in the chapters of Part Two: the danger of incommensurability and the crucial work of literature—and especially narrative—in bridging the private and public realms. The works in Part Two challenge accounts that cast 9/11 as a wholly unique event, and in moving away from the direct representation of 9/11, these works expose the ideologies that drive acts of interpretation. These texts suggest the power of narrative to restore temporal disruptions, to counter the suspension of history that visual representation sometimes invites, and to restore the links between private memory and public history.

The chapters in Part Two explore the connection between the private and public by mapping the relationships between witness, feeling, and interpretation. In "Seeing Terror, Feeling Art: Public and Private in Post-9/11 Literature," Rothberg argues that literature can help us integrate subjective experience with global history. Rothberg opens with a reading of Don DeLillo's prescient 1991 novel, *Mao II,* which represents terrorism as "a public act that defines its success or failure by its ability to penetrate into the private sphere." By beginning with a novel about terrorism written *before* 9/11, Rothberg refuses to isolate 9/11 as he foregrounds the attempt to reconcile the historical with the personal. Similarly, Rothberg reads DeLillo's 2001 essay "In the Ruins of the Future" and post-9/11 poetry by Anne-Marie Levine, D. Nurkse, and Suheir Hammad as emblematic in their reconnection of feeling and seeing. While lyric poetry and the personal essay seem to reinforce the subjective experiences of witness explored in Part One, Rothberg demonstrates how, by exploring the differences between "us" and "them," between "individual" and "collective" histories, and between "seeing" and "feeling," these authors undermine the structuring binaries essential to the "war on terror" and offer a "rooted cosmopolitanism" as "a post-secular alternative."

Mao II depicts terrorism as a global spectacle played repeatedly on television screens all over the world, a theme that recurs in many of the post-9/11 works examined in Part Two. DeLillo's exploration of the endless spectacle of terrorism anticipates Jean Baudrillard's *The Spirit of Terrorism* and Slavoj Žižek's *Welcome to the Desert of the Real: Five Essays on September 11 and Related Dates,* which inform many of the chapters in Part Two. Baudrillard and Žižek insist on the inevitability of Americans' attempts to isolate 9/11 from history (a view with which Cooper and Atkinson in Part One and David Simpson in Part Three concur). Both Baudrillard and Žižek critique assertions of the incommensurability of 9/11 given our constant reconsumption of the spectacle of the towers' fall and the ubiquity of popular cultural representations of similar disasters in Hollywood films. One of the central claims of Part Two, however, is that we need not be trapped by such consumption; rather, these chapters counteract the reification of 9/11 that occurs through spectacle by exposing the ideology underlying visual representations of 9/11 and the politics of spectacle itself. Literary texts, they claim, resist reifying 9/11 when they re-narrate it.

Through this focus on narrative's capacity to reintegrate 9/11 into history, the literary texts examined in Part Two challenge accounts of traumatic witness that privilege image over story. If the chapters in Part One use trauma theory to probe the etiology of witness, those in Part Two explore the limitations of trauma theory by critiquing its exclusive emphasis on the private. Laura Frost's chapter, "Still Life: 9/11's Falling Bodies" directly challenges recent trauma theorists who insist that still photographs help people resolve trauma by "arresting time." By placing Foer's treatment of the falling man in *Extremely Loud & Incredibly Close* in relation to representations of the same image in poetry, sculpture, and film, Frost shows that Foer's novel questions "photography's efficacy to resolve the trauma of the falling people" even as the novel's protagonist attempts to memorialize his father's death by collecting images of the falling man in his notebook. Frost suggests that this image complicates attempts to work through the trauma of 9/11: it captures what is uncertain in the public record about the identities of the falling people and what is unknowable about the experience of the victims who died in the buildings' collapse. In a reading quite different from that of Huehls in Part One, Frost argues that Foer's novel both represents narrative time and reinscribes the discontinuous time of the photograph as a repetition compulsion: a dynamic closer to disavowal than healing.

Frost's reading of the falling man centers on the ways that fiction, as a diachronic form, facilitates our understanding and interpretation of traumatic events like 9/11 by placing them into history. Frost, like Rothberg, positions literature (and, in Frost's chapter, more specifically, narrative) against spectacle, suggesting that aesthetic forms resist mass cultural representations that evacuate history and emphasize incommensurability. Lance Rubin pursues a similar line of argument, suggesting that Chuck Palahniuk's 2002 novel *Lullaby*, by subverting the conventions of genre fiction—in this case horror fiction—reveals the ideological construction of "official" narratives about 9/11. In "'We're the Culture that Cried Wolf': Discourse and Terrorism in Chuck Palahniuk's *Lullaby*," Rubin reads Palahniuk's novel as "an allegorical exploration of the power of language and the battle to shape the discursive framework of the so-called 'war on terror'" and reveals a connection between acts of terrorism and the forms of language used to describe and explain those acts. In the world of Palahniuk's novel, language—particularly language disseminated by the mass media—operates as a form of symbolic violence that renders spectators passive and atrophies their critical faculties. Rubin places *Lullaby* into the context of attempts by the Bush administration and the national media to eliminate critical voices in the debates after 9/11, and he demonstrates how Palahniuk's rewriting of horror fiction offers a solution to post-9/11 censorship.

By tracing how *Lullaby* represents both the linguistic violence of government narratives and the agency of transgressive fiction, Rubin marks the emphasis in Part Two on literature that takes up interpretations of 9/11. *Lullaby, Extremely Loud & Incredibly Close, Mao II*, and the poems and essay Rothberg examines in his chapter all suggest that the meaning of 9/11 is neither self-evident nor contained in any single image or political account. Rather, these works attempt to unsettle readers and unfix meanings in order to produce critical frameworks for interpreting 9/11. While Rothberg, Frost, and Rubin provide broad accounts of the ideological workings of narrative in 9/11 literature, Rebecca Carpenter delineates the ways that preexisting narratives contribute to the construction of critical frameworks for understanding the "war on terror." In "'We're Not a Friggin' Girl Band': September 11, Masculinity, and the British-American Relationship in David Hare's *Stuff Happens* and Ian McEwan's *Saturday*," Carpenter explores the ways that gendered terms are used to denote the relationship between the United States and Great Britain in two post-9/11 works by British writers. Carpenter's comparison centers on how the metaphors of femininity and castration in Hare's 2004 play and the representation of masculinity in McEwan's 2005 novel signify the waning of British political power during the lead-up to the war in Iraq. Anxieties about this decline, Carpenter argues, echo longstanding anxieties about Great Britain's relationship with the United States that reach back to the Suez Crisis of 1956. Carpenter juxtaposes Hare's send-up of Blair's emasculation in the face of American cowboyism with McEwan's cerebral, reasonable protagonist,

Henry Perowne, arguing that these texts not only critique the masculinist swagger of what Carpenter calls "the Machiavellian neo-cons," but also demonstrate attempts to "re-masculinize" the British commitment to international principles and reasoned debate.

As the chapters in Parts One and Two demonstrate, representing 9/11 raises crucial questions about the relationship between historical events and literary form. Several works in Parts One and Two—including those discussed by Huehls, Miller, Frost, and Rubin—directly consider form, genre, and literary conventions; these earlier discussions emphasize the creation of generically hybrid works about 9/11. The chapters in Part Three reveal a different pattern, one in which 9/11 is described within more conventional genres, including lyric poetry, realistic novels, and drama. The works considered in Part Three are also less directly "about"—to adapt the terms in Charles Lewis's chapter—than "after" 9/11; they were mostly written at least several years after 2001. Perhaps as a result of this chronological distance, Part Three's chapters comment more directly on reception, audience, and the role of literature itself.

While several chapters in Part Three consider works that do not focus explicitly on 9/11, their point is not that 9/11 is irrelevant to these works but that their indirectness comments on the difficulties of representing 9/11's impact. In "Real Planes and Imaginary Towers: Philip Roth's *The Plot Against America* as 9/11 Prosthetic Screen," Charles Lewis reads Philip Roth's counterfactual novel, set long before 2001, not as a "pasteboard allegory" of 9/11 but rather as an assertion that fiction offers a useful, because indirect, way of setting forth historical analogies. Lewis reads the novel as "a kind of 9/11 replacement narrative, in which the reader encounters [the] familiar topography [of 9/11] projected onto the fictional screen . . . of an imagined past." Central to Lewis's reading of the novel is the slipperiness implied by the image of the screen, as well as by the novel's recurrent images of breakages, amputations, truncations, and blurrings. This imagery of rupture and partial repair, Lewis argues, articulates the displacement and replacement enacted by the novel, which offers "a prosthetic screen, a substitute surface that both registers the traumatic consequence of [9/11] and stands in as the projected realization of it." Fiction, Lewis argues, offers Roth the most accurate way to convey not 9/11 but its instabilities.

David Simpson's chapter makes a related argument about two different post-9/11 novels. In "Telling It Like It Isn't," Simpson considers directly the broader question of how literature—and in particular fiction—should address an event like 9/11: is explicit and graphic detail more accurate, emotionally true, and affecting than an indirectness that risks normalizing, even trivializing, catastrophe? Simpson argues that neither John Updike's coming of age/midlife crisis novel *The Terrorist* nor Claire Messud's "social satire" *The Emperor's Children* looks head-on at 9/11 nor subjects the reader to graphic details of destruction and death; instead, both sidestep catastrophe. While this strategy risks replicating the reductive "suspicio[n]" of "the ideological mainstream" about "the rhetoric of 9/11 as a world-changing event," neither novel takes a clear ideological stand. This evasiveness can be read in two different and conflicting ways, either as a "tribute to the resilience of ordinary life or [as] a more damning indictment of the sheer indifference—and self-centeredness—of the homeland mainstream."

As Simpson suggests, the tendency to evade the horrors of 9/11 is often linked with "formal . . . and thematic . . . conservati[sm]." Like Lewis, Simpson suggests that the conservatism of the novel form permits 9/11 to be normalized—if a conventional novel can be written after 9/11, how bad could the attacks have been?—but also destabilized—is fiction the most "accurate" way of conveying an experience that itself resembles fiction? Jeffrey Gray's reading of several post-9/11 American poems in "Precocious Testimony: Poetry and the Uncommemorable" begins with a question similar to Simpson's: was 9/11 a rupture, and if so does it require plain, direct, accurate poetry? Through a reading of several post-9/11 poems, Gray identifies a linguistic mode that recalls a far older, "indeed Paleolithic" tradition of poetry with "sources . . . in divination, repetition, and prophecy." Such poetry expresses not the certainty that Gray associates with poems that confront 9/11 directly, but rather the condition of not-knowing, along with "the problems of making." It also sets forth an alternate view of temporality that is "diachronic . . . rather than . . . synchronic," establishing a distinctively textual mode of remembering that binds 9/11 to something beyond the representation of what actually occurred. Poetry's evocation of its own generic prehistory offers a paradoxical challenge to what Gray calls "the aesthetics and poetic practice of most of the past century."

Whereas Part One's chapters often emphasize obstructions to individual or private memory, Gray and several other authors in Part Three argue that it is not only possible but necessary to recall earlier forms and texts. Perhaps the most dramatic reading of this kind is Simon Stow's association of the *New York Times*'s "Portraits of Grief" with an apparently very different and historically distinct tradition, the elegiac flute songs performed by *pornai* or classical Athenian prostitutes. Simpson argues that many authors writing about disasters steer clear of graphic details "to avoid pornographic stimulation." But in "*Portraits 9/11/01: The New York Times* and the Pornography of Grief," Stow employs the same term to come to a conclusion about the "Portraits" very different from Miller's discussion of them in Part One: the "Portraits" function pornographically, undermining through an excess of subjectivity the democratic impulses that they apparently champion. By individualizing the dead and—more crucially—by foregrounding the production of individual, isolated, and endless grief in the reader, the "Portraits" impel a voyeurism antithetical to the restraint necessary to democracy.

The effects of representations of 9/11 on a particular audience are also central to Robert Brustein's chapter, "Theater After 9/11." Brustein ends with the claim that the "pity and terror" audiences may feel in response to theatrical representations of 9/11 and its aftermath are "not incompatible with a night on the town." Brustein's overview of the ways theater has responded, and failed to respond, to 9/11 and the war in Iraq insists that art offers an "opportunity to provide some understanding of our predicament." Through "escapis[t]," "obscurantis[t]," and "witless" productions, commercial theater has missed the opportunity to respond to its audience's post-9/11 needs, although off-Broadway theater, including a number of plays written before the attacks, has, Brustein claims, done better, "prob[ing] into the social and political issues of the time" in ways that have helped audiences disillusioned with the contemporary American political process.

Brustein's claims about the importance of audience reaction reverberate with Stow's claim that the "Portraits" are flawed because they require an individual, isolated response and thus valorize separation, passivity, and voyeurism. Lewis's reading of Roth's novel privileges another kind of reciprocity, that between the novel's plot and its cultural function, and Gray's champions poetry's capacity to "perform" something that is both "timeless" and "real." Read together, these chapters insist on literature's capacity, through performance of various kinds, to speak to its audience. This recurrent theme also draws attention to the shared assumption among the chapters in Part Three that literature offers a way beyond binary thinking (beyond the opposition, for example, between transparent and mystical language, or between graphic details and their absence) not because it is entertaining or titillating but because, unlike journalism and jingoism, it refuses familiar sentiments. Because literature is difficult, indirect, and allusive, because it mixes verisimilitude with imagination, the literal with the symbolic, it can express something of the complexity of 9/11. The chapters here, then—and the negative example of the "Portraits" as read by Stow confirms this idea—evince, in the end, a faith in literature's capacity to expose, but not resolve, problems that resonate for its audience.

This central issue—what might be called the salutary intransigence of literature—enables the chapters of Part Three, and indeed of the book as a whole, partway to transcend the rubric under which we have grouped them: these *are* discussions of literature after 9/11, but they are also discussions of the relations between literature, catastrophe, memory, politics, and history more generally. The fact that Robert Pinsky's Afterword, "Imagination and Monstrosity," like the chapters by Rothberg, Brustein, Gray, and Simpson, considers works written before 9/11 that anticipate or seem to respond to it, is part of the point. Pinsky's meditation on the ways that culture mutates disaster into artifact or art, just as it mutates the actual Hiroshima into the imagined Godzilla, crystallizes the transformations, alterations, and distortions effected by literature. These transformations recall the terms with which we began this Introduction: the disaster remains itself even as it is symbolically co-opted and changed, rendered metaphorical. Literature after 9/11, through its resistance to co-option, paradoxically complicates and even transcends the events of a single day. And, as Pinsky says, we rely on patient readers, like the contributors to this book, to render visible these transformations.

WORKS CITED

Baudrillard, Jean. *The Spirit of Terrorism and Other Essays*. Trans. Chris Turner. New York: Verso, 2003.

Cohen, Allen and Clive Matson, eds. *An Eye for an Eye Makes the Whole World Blind: Poets on 9/11*. Oakland, CA: Regent, 2002.

Hamill, Sam, ed. *Poets Against the War*. New York: Thunder Mouth, 2003.

Part I

Experiencing 9/11

Time, Trauma, and the
Incommensurable Event

1 Portraits of Grief
Telling Details and the
New Genres of Testimony

Nancy K. Miller

In the summer of 2002, Times Books published a volume containing the 1,910 "Portraits of Grief" that had appeared in the *New York Times* between September 15 and December 31, 2001. The 1,910 stories that readers had consumed in the newspaper along with their daily breakfast or their morning commute were now compiled into a manageable archive and filed in alphabetical order. Rescued from the ephemera of the daily paper and the fluctuations of the Internet, the "Portraits" finally came to rest between hard covers.[1] In the prefatory material to the volume, editors and reporters characterize the work they did in creating this popular and much-remarked-on journalism. Their commentary both describes how the genre came into being and provides a frame through which the "Portraits" should be read.

Almost immediately after the disaster of September 11, 2001, the frantic search for missing persons took the form of flyers identifying the missing. These home-made artifacts were hurriedly pasted onto walls, mailboxes, lampposts, and phone booths, papering the walls of bus shelters and train stations. In addition to detailed physical descriptions, the flyers typically included photographs of the loved ones, almost always smiling. (see Figure 1.1.) As the hope of finding survivors faded, the distinction between the missing and the dead began to blur. It is no doubt for this reason that as of the second day of reporting, the original title of the series, "Among the Missing," with its implicit hope of recovery disappeared to become "Portraits of Grief." Given their spontaneous and multiple origins, the flyers varied widely in size, style, and presentation. The newsprint versions of necessity were uniform. As in a high school yearbook, everyone memorialized was given equal space and equal treatment.

How could readers be made to care daily about the individual dead who, unlike the subjects of traditional *New York Times* obituaries, were neither eminent nor glamorous? At the one-month anniversary of the profiles, an editorial titled "Among the Missing" analyzed the newspaper's attempts to master the civilian trauma. Faced with the massive numbers of victims, the editors pondered the best strategy for identifying the singularity of each life within the constraints of the form: "Each profile is only a snapshot, a single

Figure 1.1 Grand Central Station Memorial Wall, October 24, 2002, Lorie Novak.

still frame lifted from the unrecountable complexity of a lived life" (D12). On the first day of reporting the losses, the metaphor of photography had also figured—recalling the effect of the flyers: "Snapshots of Their Lives, With Family and at Work" ran the headline (A11).

In the Introduction to the volume, Janny Scott, the reporter chiefly responsible for the earliest coverage of the victims, makes explicit the connection between the "Portraits" and the flyers, the verbal and the visual. "We began," she explains,

> dialing the phone numbers on the flyers. What we wanted were stories, anecdotes, tiny but telling details that seemed to reveal something true and essential about how each person lived. . . . The profiles . . . were closer to snapshots—concise, impressionistic, their power at least as much emotional as intellectual. And they were utterly democratic. (ix)

Scott continues to make the analogy to the visual medium as she looks for a metaphor to render the vast undertaking. "Like a panoramic photograph, the project gathered everyone it could and attempted to bring each one fleetingly into focus" (ix). Howell Raines, the *Times*'s executive editor, also embraces the discourse of photography in his Foreword to the volume: "I'm convinced," he states, "that the core of the portraits' appeal lies in our metropolitan desk's decision to cast these stories as snapshots of lives interrupted as they were being actively lived, rather than in the traditional obituary form." Most of the people who died would not have been the subjects of the traditional obituaries, he observes, a "powerful storytelling format in itself . . . entirely appropriate to the task of recording the key facts of prominent (or notorious) lives" (vii).

In these statements that self-consciously define the newspaper's project, the visual trumps the verbal, almost as though the "newspaper of record" found itself at a loss for words, words suddenly seeming inadequate to the task of representing what makes an individual life a life, unable to convey its emotional truth. If not the classic obituary, then what? What shape to give to the stories? In the face of collective disaster, whose scale strained the imagination, the anecdote was seized upon as a mode suited to rendering the familiar acts of ordinary life. Like the snapshot, the anecdote, through the brevity of its narrative, catches life in its everyday dimensions. Like the snapshot, the anecdote's appeal resides in its ability to carry both life and death, present and past: what once *was* but recalled to memory somehow *still is*.

Let's return now to the language of reporter Janny Scott's account of how the portrait genre was invented. "What we wanted," she said, were "stories, anecdotes, tiny but telling details that seemed to reveal something true and essential about how each person lived." The anecdote here is set up in apposition to the detail, but the two are not interchangeable; their relationship is not reversible. The effective anecdote requires details; but details by themselves do not necessarily add up to an anecdote. Nonetheless, in the slippery discourse about the "Portraits," it is no easy matter to separate anecdote from detail. The anecdote might even be said to serve as a telling detail in a life's interrupted story.

In January 2002, the *New Yorker* devoted a column to the portraits, fleshing out some of the back story on the reporting and the reporters. Here (unlike Howell Raines's recourse to the snapshot metaphor), the portrait of portrait making, as it were, retains its narrative function. Once again, the creation of the "Portraits"—the subject of some fascination—is retold . . . to a reporter. And again, the anecdote alternates with the detail but also introduces other generic references into a by-now familiar story: the birth of a genre. The reporters placed phone calls to the numbers displayed on the flyers in order to "glean details about the lives of a few hundred among the thousands of individuals who had disappeared." The "Portraits" here are characterized as "mini-profiles" and the first batch of them as vignettes—"twenty vignettes, averaging less than two hundred words each." The "Portraits" are further described as "sketches"—picking up the pictorial code—"sketches that revealed an emblematic, usually endearing anecdote or character trait" (Singer 30). In this context, the "Portraits" conform to the dictionary definition of the anecdote: "[A] usually short narrative of an interesting, amusing, or curious incident, often biographical and generally characterized by human interest" (*Webster's*). The anecdote has the right dimensions for evoking a brief life, which was mainly the case among the dead on September 11.

Editorial self-consciousness about the genre was immediate. For if the "Portraits" sprang up spontaneously, their production was not unsupervised. One month into the daily practice (around the time of the newspaper's editorial, "Among the Missing," referred to earlier), a memo was circulated "admonishing contributors to avoid certain tropes." Reporters were encouraged to "reach for illuminating details" beyond the "bond traders who loved their wife and kids," the perks of "the Cantor Fitzgerald guys," and "how the deceased was such a devoted student of 'The Simpsons' or Bruce Springsteen" (Singer 31). Jan Hoffman, a reporter who turned in a large number of the "Portraits," says that what got to her on the phone with the survivors ("I have never wept so much while working," she confesses), was "the crispness of their memories, the way they described these poignant, funny, heroic moments." As she reflects upon the forensics of eliciting responses, Hoffman explains her methods: you have to listen patiently "until you have that click where you can see the person and how they moved on the planet" (31). The desirable response for the "Portraits of Grief," we might say, supplies narrative DNA.

Here is an example from a set of "Portraits" published in early December 2002 about Steven Schlag:

> When a neighbor was in her third pregnancy and uncomfortably late, Mr. Schlag, 41, a partner with Cantor Fitzgerald who lived in Franklin Lakes, N.J., whipped up his chicken cacciatore, which had helped his wife go into labor. (It didn't do the trick for the neighbor.) And when a friend was scheduled for cancer surgery on Sept. 11, 2001, Mrs. Schlag

recalled, her husband bought two copies of the bicyclist Lance Armstrong's autobiography and told his friend, "We're both going to read this, and you're going to get through it." (B54)

An internal gloss of the "Portrait" by the widow generates its title: "She related a trademark attitude of his," the reporter observed, "which she and their three children. . . . are trying to live by now. 'Strangers would come up to him when he was skiing and ask, "How are the conditions at the top?"' she said. 'He'd always say, "It's 88 and sunny."' "That was his favorite saying."'" That saying became the newspaper's caption.

Tied to family and friends, beloved of coworkers, the victims were also smiling in the memory of those who survived them, not just in the snapshots. Nonetheless, traces of sadness of course punctuate the mourners' narratives, and often provide an underlying sense of irony. Here's one other from December 2002 about Kevin Prior, "'I'm always coming home.'" Like so many of the "Portraits," this one is a love story.

> Firefighter Prior's cheerful hardheadedness surfaced again in 2001 atop a mountain in Ireland, the couple's ancestral home. They both wanted to take a rock home from the peak back to New York, but each claimed to have found the perfect one. So they wound up taking both. When Firefighter Prior died in the World Trade Center, Ms. Noone [his fiancée] was glad they had two rocks. She kept one and put the other in his coffin. (B54)

If you have attended a funeral lately, or watched one on television, these anecdotes will sound familiar. Like the subject of the eulogy, the subject of the portrait always appears in a good, often humorous, light—and the story told, like the desirable details the reporters typically sought for, is meant to illuminate that something "true and essential," Mr. Schlag's "trademark attitude." The trademark reveals something good, like virtue, often civic, or at least domestic. Not every single "Portrait" is organized anecdotally. Sometimes the details are not harnessed to a narrative. Rather, they provide points of entry into character: personality traits, habits, quirks, hobbies, mottoes, that are cumulative in effect but not shaped into a story. Almost all have a catchy signoff, however, that summarizes the victims and what they meant to the ones left behind in a kind of anecdotal degree zero, where nouns lack their verbs: "He was my plumber, my electrician, my seamstress," a widow concludes. "My everything, really" (B54).

Like the eulogy, by giving formal dimensions to suffering, the "Portraits of Grief" create a coherent public persona to fit the event, and one that also serves to protect both the victim and the mourners from the display of unsuitable emotions. The genre takes the private person into the public arena within recognizable conventions, within what we might call an ethics of mourning: the "emblematic" anecdote is "endearing" not damning.

What feels new about the portrait as genre, of course, is the fact that for the vast majority these private lives were not destined for the public space of the newspaper. In its etymology *anecdote* means unpublished—"items of unpublished or secret history or biography" (*Webster's*). By passing through the scrim of the "Portraits of Grief," the anecdote becomes what it was not meant to be: a public document. We are left with a paradox: the anecdotes extracted by the reporters were meant to bring the dead back to life—or at least to keep them alive—in the memories of the living. Is an anecdote still an anecdote once it is published? Or, in the end, are the "Portraits" really informal obituaries, and not a new genre after all?

In *Nicomachean Ethics*, Aristotle wonders about the "praise accorded to happiness" (27). Praise, he writes, "is proper to virtue or excellence, because it is excellence that makes men capable of performing noble deeds." But then he goes on to add: "Eulogies, on the other hand, are appropriate for achievements of the body as well as of the mind. However, a detailed analysis of this subject is perhaps rather the business of those who have made a study of eulogies" (28–29). In the winter of 2002, I went to a play that had been created in the immediate aftermath of 9/11, Anne Nelson's *The Guys*, that staged the relation of the anecdote to the eulogy. A fire fighter feels overwhelmed by the number of eulogies he has to deliver at the funerals of the men from his company he has lost. He finds himself speechless with pain. A writer—a middle-aged woman—volunteers to help him put his anguish into words. He needs to figure out what to say "for them, for the families." And he wants to describe the fireman in such a way that the families and the other men will "recognize" him. "Tell me about him," the woman says. And the captain provides details—"the Waldorf salad for the church picnic," the fireman's "work, church, home" motto—scraps of memory, details, that the writer shapes into anecdotes. When one of the portraits makes the man seem too much of a hero and not sufficiently "human," the captain objects—"he sounds too perfect." What's his flaw, then? "He was a perfectionist!" When the captain reads aloud the portraits the writer has devised, he has delivered the eulogy.

Unlike the obituary, which presents life in the past tense like a plot that has come to its end, the anecdote, however narrative in form, remains closer to the structure of human character—which is probably why it is a staple of the eulogy. Paradoxically, perhaps, and for this reason, the anecdote feels timeless, life-like—alive with what's always uniquely true of an individual—and why it fits a life that is too short to have discovered the shape of its own, singular plot. Nonetheless, incorporated into the "Portraits," as in a eulogy, the anecdote is necessarily also a memento mori bearing a different message. It says: remember that one of the perfect rocks ended up in a coffin, having met the one plot that fits all and that therefore cannot be avoided.

I want now to pick up the thread of the "tiny but telling details" that reporter Janny Scott explained were the key to unlocking the mystery of an individual life, the details that would "reveal something true and essential about how each person lived." This is reporter Jan Hoffman's "click" of discovery, or perhaps, changing registers, the *punctum* of Roland Barthes. If we re-enlist the metaphor of photography that, as we saw earlier, made the snapshot the visual analog of the portrait, then we might say that the "Portraits" as a genre belong to the domain of what Barthes in *Camera Lucida* famously called the photographic *studium,* "that very wide field of unconcerned desire," whereas the "telling" detail resembles the *punctum,* "that accident which pricks me (but also bruises me, is poignant to me)" (27). Although Barthes, we know, argues that the *studium* is a result of the photographer's intentions, and the *punctum* a spectator's purely subjective reaction to an element that punctures or punctuates the *studium,* we can, for purposes of argument, bracket the question of intention to deal with the effect—and the affect—of the *punctum.* For Barthes, we know, the *punctum* is the detail that grabs him as viewer, that "attracts or distresses" (40). For Naomi Schor reading Barthes, the detail is also, she emphasizes, Proustian, that is, associated with the "valorization of involuntary memory" (90). As Barthes declares, the effect of the *punctum* is not to be understood through intellectual effort: "No analysis would be of any use to me"; he goes on, however, to add in a parenthesis, "(but perhaps memory sometimes would)" (42). The reporters consciously press the mourners, newly placed in the role of biographers, for their memories. When the memories bubble up to the surface they provide the reporters with the unexpected but much desired details needed to create a portrait that in turn captures the life—that "something true and essential about how each person lived." The memories prompted by questions are not strictly speaking "involuntary"; but in the combination of the terms "crispness" and "poignant" used by the reporter, we feel the effects of something *punctum*-like, the kind of homely detail that doesn't belong, for instance, to the discourse of the *studium,* of the official obituary. (We do not know what details caused Susan Sontag, an eminent Barthesian, to cry, as was reported, when she read the "Portraits" every morning [Scott, "Closing" B6].)

The "telling details" would be out of place in the narrative of publicly acknowledged accomplishment. Still, if the "Portraits" seem to reveal this essential truth because of the detail's power to deliver the truth of personality, can we trust that performance? Or, should we heed Schor's warning about investing the "detail with a truth-bearing function" (7)? Returning to the matter of our perception, rather than the reportorial production, of the details in the "Portrait," if we are moved, does this mean that we are moved because we've been given entry into the truth of another person's life, or because it makes a good story? Put another way, just because we are "pricked" by, say, the rock in the coffin or the chicken cacciatore recipe, should we believe that we've had access to the whole story and that it's all true? I've been struck by the overwhelming public acceptance of the genre, the assumption among journalists and readers that the anecdotes and details have delivered the truth of the beloved victim. And I've also been unable to keep myself from wondering about the stories the details *aren't* telling.

Interviewed live near the World Trade Center as events were unfolding, Rudolph Giuliani, the mayor of New York City, urged people in the area to leave the site of the disaster and "go north." For many of us living uptown who witnessed the events solely on television, it almost felt as though we were inhabitants of another city. But a young woman who lived in my building, and who had served on the co-op board, died on September 11. Although I did not know Karen Klitzman (by all accounts a remarkable person), along with neighbors I attended a memorial service in celebration of her life that her family had organized at a local synagogue; it seemed a small if inadequate gesture toward sharing in the communal grief. I found it strange and indeed poignant to see her face for the first time when her "Portrait" was published in the newspaper shortly after the service. Like most of the victims, in the snapshot that accompanied the "Portrait," Karen Klitzman was smiling.

In September 2002, the day before the first anniversary, Karen Klitzman's brother, Robert, a psychiatrist, published a personal essay in the Health and Fitness section of the *Times*. He described his painful and confused reaction to his sister's death: "I saw what I had been taught but never experienced or understood as much as now: that the grief over the loss of an ambivalent relationship can be far harder than the grief would be otherwise." After narrating the various strategies he employed to allay the pain he was feeling—from anti-depressants to seeing a psychic—he concluded: "The difficulties were far more complicated and long-lasting than I would ever have imagined; closure has been far more elusive." Only when another sister told him she was going to say that Karen "was not perfect but that we loved her anyway" was he able to compose a eulogy (F5). The codes of idealization in the "Portraits of Grief" render taboo the expression of certain kinds of emotions in the public domain. Another survivor is quoted in the *Times* the day after the anniversary on that very subject: "'My brother was a selfish, arrogant guy,' one man said, 'but you can't say that because my 87-year-old mother will be reading this.' Secrets about the victim," the reporter goes on to observe, "character flaws gnaw and tear at the survivors, who struggle over whether and how to acknowledge them" (Hoffman B9).

The coverage of the first anniversary was organized as a kind of calendar of grief, describing symptoms from the initial psychic blows in the immediate aftermath to the mood of the summer of 2002. The commentary for January/February raises the problem of the truth in the "Portraits" for the first time since the creation of the genre: "As survivors realize, there are many truths about a victim. . . . While many families are satisfied by the published sketches of the victim, others are offended and pained. Some feel guilty for not having been sufficiently articulate when they talked about their loved ones" (Hoffman B9). But of course as readers standing outside the circle of intimate loss, we have no way of gauging the emotional, not to say factual, accuracy of the "Portraits" in relation to the experience. We are confronted with the texts, the narratives, what almost instantly became the *studium* of the new genre. "By now, many families have created a public narrative of their victim. The tales feel oft-repeated, laminated" (Hoffman B9). We can only guess by what's reported elsewhere about family feuds whose details have been suppressed or edited out. Is the suppression of ambivalence in the "Portraits" and comparable forums—along with other emotions tinged with negativity like anger and resentment—really the best way to carry out the process of memorialization?[2] Not surprisingly, when the Discovery Channel selected the subjects of their televised portraits— the video version of the newspaper narratives—they chose individuals who loved, or wished to appear in public saying that they loved, the ones they lost unambivalently. I confess. I did tear up watching this program. I felt overcome—wrung out, actually—by the display of so much love. Being me, I suspended critical judgment and instead envied their emotions, the happiness of their families despite their loss, and felt not just like a bad survivor but a poor human being.[3]

After a long hiatus, a fresh installment of the "Portraits" appeared on Sunday March 9, 2003. One, about Thomas Patrick Knox, took as its theme the challenge of accounting for feelings of overwhelming loss while defining the specificity of the victim. This is how it begins:

> With Tommy Knox it was often the little things. The way he put the toothpaste on his wife's toothbrush when he got up before her, almost every day. He'd leave it on the vanity ready for her before he left his home in Hoboken for his job as a broker at Cantor Fitzgerald. (B36)

The toothpaste on the toothbrush is the quintessential prosaic detail, the ultimate fact of everyday life, the metonymy of the domestic fable, and often the summary of couple strife: putting or not putting the cap back on the tube, squeezing the tube from the bottom or the top, or worst of all, squishing it in the middle. Here the toothpaste pre-squeezed onto the toothbrush is the mark of suave consideration for the other, the proof of love. If this is not a "telling" detail in the narrative universe of the *Times* "Portraits," what is?; for it tells the story of what worked in the marriage, and to the extent that the "Portraits" are meant to represent something larger than an individual, they are crafted to serve as the microcosm of family life, of community values, of a valiant, though wounded, America. The domestic detail of the toothbrush comes to stand for the intimacy of the home, and the home for the nation's public life: the home front against the incursions of terrorism. The detail as the index of loss—the toothpaste on the toothbrush, the minute and the familiar—embodies that which we cherish against that which is foreign and terrifying, that which protects against the war on terror. In measuring disaster, the smaller the marker, the bigger the loss, seems to be the rule of incommensurability (Robert Klitzman, on visiting his sister's apartment after her death: "I took her toothpaste, indented by her fingers, but as I used it up, felt sad again." [F5]).

The "Portraits" of March 9, 2003, are not based on the sharp immediacy of memory but rather are shaped by the distilled temporality of recollection.[4] What Nancy Knox remembers, she says, are "I guess all the little things. . . . All these little, special things that made Tommy who he was and made us all love him" (B36). Like the emotional calculus that figures individual loss through "the little things," what adds up in the affective economy of the detail only appears to be a paradox: the loss is so great that the only way to bring it to language is to think small, cutting it down to size. You accede to the big through the little: the "telling detail" testifies to the big whole, the hole left by the disappearance of the loved one within the global identity of victim. Thus, in an article reporting on discussions of what form the memorial to September 11 should take, which drew on an analogy to the United States Holocaust Memorial Museum's display of a mountain of abandoned shoes, the headline read: "Remembering the Little Things." If, as the article suggests, the shoes are "the most vivid reminders of the terror and the hope of survival, of panic and the uniquely individual scale of that monumental tragedy" (B35), we can wonder what "little things" from the dust and rubble will come to stand for September 11.[5]

In the months following September 11, as they appeared daily in the newspaper, the "Portraits"—lives captured in miniature—relying as they did on anecdotes, often served as the little things that provided the footprint of human scale—and of community. What will become of the newspaper experience of reading the "Portraits"? In an article titled "Horror Pictures" in which he discussed the difference between publishing war photographs in the newspaper and in books, John Berger (writing in July 1972 during the Vietnam War) made the following observation: "There is a sense in which a newspaper belongs to the events it records, it is part of the same process, the same flux: it bears the same stains. A book stays clean and is meant to outlive its meaning" (194).[6] Eventually, the newspaper stopped publishing the "Portraits." The volume will remain in the homes of the victims' families, in libraries, and in the museum that will one day be created in relation to the memorial.

Beyond the pedagogy of the archive, remembrance will take other forms of historical preservation. Tatana Kellner, an artist known for her work connected to Holocaust memorialization, has created an installation for a gallery in Buffalo that makes use of the "Portraits" as they appeared in the newspaper. Her project, *Requiem for September 11,* was displayed on the Web in the fall of 2002. (see Figure 1.2.) The artwork consists of forty-five banners, sixteen feet long by four feet wide, spaced two feet apart. The banners were designed to fill the open atrium of the Market Arcade Building in Buffalo—a nineteenth-century retail building. On the website,

Kellner describes the impulse behind the project as a response to reading the "Portraits" in the newspaper:

> For the past 4 months I have been reading, cutting out and re-assembling the "Portraits of Grief" pages from the *New York Times*. This is my way of "doing something, anything" about this national tragedy. As I read the sketches I cry and laugh and am saddened by so many lives cut short. I'm struck by the youth of the victims and their apparent normalcy. These were not captains of industry, but ordinary people aspiring to the good life.
>
> What speaks to me most are the victims' faces, mostly smiling in snapshots of happy times. I plan to transform this material into a large scale installation which will be a memorial to the victims of the September 11th tragedy: Each victim will be represented by a photograph, name and a byline describing the person. The images will be screen printed on a multi fiber fabric using the devore process, the resulting images will appear ghost like. What I hope to accomplish is to put a human face on numbers that are unfathomable to most of us. (Kellner)

Kellner's assemblage features the actual snapshots that accompanied the "Portraits" in the newspaper. The smiling faces belong to a life that is no more, the past tense of "happy times." In this work, the texts of the "Portraits" disappear (sometimes marked by blanks), their prior existence signaled by the caption that served as the title of the "Portrait" and that shares in the euphoric register of the snapshot: "Fat Cigar and Time for Fun," "The Big Kid of the Family," to cite the captions of the very first portraits, of Timothy G. Byrne and John G. Scharf, as they appeared in the original installment, "Snapshots of Their Lives with Family and at Work" (A11).

As the journalists involved in the project sought to come to grips with the numbers (the "interminable registry of the missing" ["After the Attacks" A11]), they tried to refashion in narrative the life lost to language; to find a story to go with the name (above the headline announcing the new feature, the mention "The Names" appeared in small caps). Paradoxically, Kellner pays homage to the verbal portraits that emerged from the desperate information the flyers supplied by eliminating the text, keeping instead the visual imprint of the face. Of the "endearing anecdotes" that formed the body of the "Portraits," Kellner retains the irony of the smile of "happy times" and the caption: like the smile, a synecdoche of the portrait's narrative. Through her emphasis on the physical layout of "Portraits" as they appeared in the *Times,* however, Kellner preserves even as she transforms the ephemera of the newspaper. Enlarging the images and names of the victims with a photocopier, she transfers the pages of newspaper onto a silkscreen and then onto the banners of fabric. The verbal "Portraits" pass into another kind of text, another cultural register. The names of the September 11 victims are listed alphabetically (as they are in the volume of

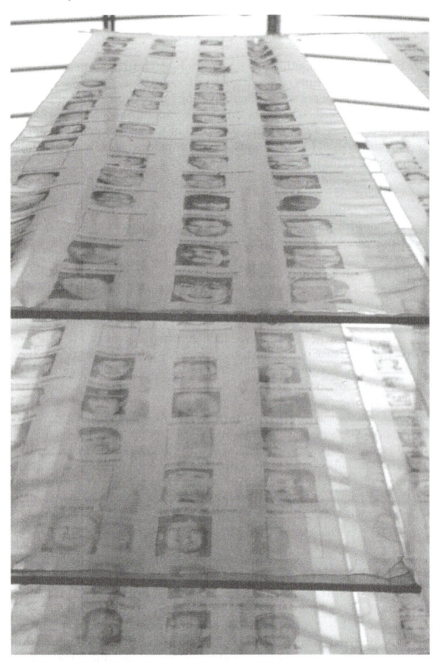

Figure 1.2 Requiem for September 11, detail. Installed at the Market Arcade, Buffalo, NY, September 11–December 20, 2002. Silk screen on organza, 45 panels, each panel 16.5 feet x 4 feet, Tatana Kellner.

published *Portraits*), followed by those of the Pentagon and Shanksville. Here, though, the logic of scale that operated in the "Portraits" representation of emotional devastation that we saw earlier is reversed: by their size, the banners make big what was little, as intimate loss expands to occupy the space of a public building, as the one comes to stand in for the many, the individual name for the collective story. The solitary experience of reading the small print of the newspaper becomes a form of shared large-type public viewing. In the process of that transformation, Kellner also restores the work of countermemory performed by the flyers that documented the many faces of loss. In *Requiem for September 11* the smiling faces on the banners created from the newspaper "Portraits" evoke the flyers produced in the immediate wake of the disaster. (see Figure 1.3.) The banners hang one by one, recognizing each individual. But the transparent sheets of fabric also allow the viewer to look through the layers and, along with the face of the victim, simultaneously receive the impact of the images that follow immediately behind—the succession of the dead. The banners float like the melancholy ghosts of the lost and disappeared.

Larry Harris's ten-minute play, *Totems of the Fall,* created in the wake of September 11, also works the boundaries between past and present, erasure and connection, as actors representing "the photographs and Xeroxes of the missing" are brought briefly to language, returning from the dead. "In general," Harris indicates in the script, "the photographs depict happy moments" (Harris).[7] But assembled at the wall belonging to St. Vincent's Hospital at the corner of Seventh Avenue and Eleventh Street, in a vast collage of despair and hope juxtaposed (and then preserved under glass), the photographs on the flyers also carry the mark of death—of happiness that *was.* A pedestrian arrives carrying flowers, deposits the flowers and card, looks at the photographs which in Harris's play are arranged in a tableau and which begin to speak, one by one. The ordinary people in the photographs affixed to the wall of remembrance are no more and no less than their particularity; a young woman on the brink of a new romance, an older man, self-conscious about his chins in a photo ID, a new dad holding his six-month-old son, a fireman come briefly to life in the time of a camera flash. The testimony to their loss constituted by the play's gestures—neighbors and passers-by depositing cards, messages, candles, in a word, totems—reenacts as theater the testimony to loss that had already begun in post-September 11 daily life. Remember me, each says, as terrible noise returns them all to silence, and the speechless photographs reabsorb the voices of the dead.

Photographer Lorie Novak, who is known for her work on the complex relations between snapshots, memory, and politics, took photographs of the flyers and improvised memorials that sprung up throughout the city, especially downtown. "Placed near the site as public memorials," she writes, "the photographs also become portals to speak to the dead" (94), exactly what is staged in *Totems of the Fall*. Her photographs record

*Figure 1.3 Requiem for September 11, detail. Installed at the Market Arcade, Buffalo, NY, September 11–December 20, 2002. Silk screen on organza, 45 panels, each panel 16.5 feet x 4 feet,*Tatana Kellner.

the life of the snapshots on the flyers as the images become texts—family and friends sign them like a yearbook or the cast on a broken leg—and as they begin inexorably to erode from the effects of the weather and the passage of time.[8] (see Figure 1.4.) Novak's photographs bring

Figure 1.4 Hudson River Park, November 27, 2001, Lorie Novak.

into relief the clumsy details of the homemade artifact: the corners of the tape affixing the flyers to the walls (like children's drawings pasted onto refrigerator doors) start to curl up and wrinkle. For me, the tape carries the *punctum,* as the happy faces on tattered flyers become the perverse measure of the pain of loss.

Figure 1.5 Grand Central Station Memorial Wall, October 24, 2002, Lorie Novak.

When survivors convert the images into texts, they bring their personal grief into the open. Several of Novak's images eerily identify the places where "messages to the deceased . . . make private messages public" (94). In certain cases, the survivors have returned to the original flyer, even months later, to add information as well as expressions of love, including the dates when the body was found and buried. This return is the unbreakable link between flyer and event, and to the productivity of the original (even if, paradox of postmodern cliché, the original is a photocopy).[9] (see Figure 1.5.) In much the same way, since the anniversaries of September 11, we have witnessed a significant reworking of the border between private suffering and public reckoning.

As survivors seek different kinds of recognition and compensation for their loss, the portrait continues to play a role in the production of public testimony. I want to follow here the reportorial afterlife of the portrait genre—the reliance on detail, anecdote, and narrative in various reenactments of traumatic memorialization. In October 2002, the *Times* reported the production of narratives by families applying to the Victim Compensation Fund: "minibiographies about the dead, based on interviews, photos or videotapes." The journalist David Chen suggests that economic incentive—the wish to increase the amount of the award for emotional suffering—is not the only motive behind the narratives (especially since Kenneth Feinberg, the special master in charge of the fund, indicated that his flexibility in deciding on the awards would be in the area of economic and not emotional compensation): "the real value," Chen speculates, "may lie in their timeless and therapeutic resonance in telling the full story of life, love and loss, beyond cold, raw numbers" ("Families" B1). In certain cases, the narratives include the last words of the victim left in a voicemail message. Like the original "missing" posters, these individual creations taken together will constitute an archive both of "what happened in the doomed buildings on Sept. 11, and what the people who died there meant to their families" (Chen, "Families" B1). As with the "Portraits of Grief," each minibiography becomes a synecdoche for the lost whole. The "Portraits" worked, Alan Singer observes in the *New Yorker,* by "reducing to human scale, the immeasurable dimensions of September 11th while rendering, in a different sense, the incomprehensible totality of what had been lost" (30). Survivors who want their loved ones to count must become authors in their own right, not merely the subjects of journalistic solicitation. They have been forced to learn not only how to manage their suffering but how to turn its implications to good account. It is unlikely, however, that these portraits will escape the push toward idealization that we encountered in the newspaper "Portraits"; after all, the families—and their lawyers—are trying to make a case for the value of the life that was lost in the disaster to prove that their loved one "was a special person" (Chen, "Families" B6). In this sense, following the model of the "Portraits," the minibiographies provide not so much the "whole truth" that we swear by in court, but the partial, emotional, perhaps literary truth of what makes the person you love special to you.[10]

Finally, like the piercing visual detail of the Barthesian *punctum,* the memorializing narrative also demonstrates a wounding temporal dimension. And like the snapshots of the flyers, or the anecdotes that punctuate the eulogy, or the "Portraits of Grief," the power of these new portraits derives from the fact that they inevitably bear the signature of death in the future, as well as life now. This is the newspaper account of one of the post-anniversary videos:

> As she watched her husband's life unfold on the screen, Mrs. Van Auken crumpled tissue after tissue to dab away the tears. "It's ripping your heart out," she said. "But I'm glad I'm doing this, because it's something you'll have forever." Then, almost as abruptly as it began, the video was over. And for the next minute or so, no one said anything. (Chen, "Beyond" B6)

It is perhaps the way trauma binds us to a temporality that by definition we do not master that supplies the true measure of its pain. Six months after watching the video biography of her husband, Mrs. Van Auken testified at the first—by all accounts highly emotional—day of hearings held by the National Commission on Terrorist Attacks Upon the United States, March 31, 2003. Her photograph, along with that of another widow whose husband worked at Cantor Fitzgerald and a Port Authority police officer, appears below the article (Chen, "Beyond" B15). Although her testimony is not quoted, the tormented expression on Mrs. Van Auken's sorrowful face speaks volumes. Her head is tilted to one side like a Modigliani portrait and a single, glistening tear begins to slide from beneath her lower lid, pointing toward her cheekbone.

Unlike the victims, in photographs the survivors do not smile.

* * *

Christie McDonald examines the "Portraits of Grief" in the context of the Iraq War, arguing persuasively in the spring of 2003 that the "Portraits" have a different effect when read retrospectively, in the early stages of the war.[11] This is one of the crucial ways in which the disaster at the World Trade Center has been pulled into a national narrative not immediately visible in the direct aftermath of the event. A parent who had lost his son, a firefighter and former marine, at the Twin Towers, held up a sign that read: "HE WOULD BE SAFER IN IRAQ THAN HE WAS AT THE WTC ON 9/11!" At the hearings described above, Mindy Kleinberg, the other widow mentioned, "mixed personal anguish over the death of her husband . . . as well as a detailed summary of her own research into the shortcomings of American intelligence. . . . Afterward, some of the family members . . . expressed a queasiness over whether their words would stick, or whether political considerations would eventually erode their concerns" (Chen, "Beyond," B15).

The coverage of the soldiers who were killed and wounded in the war demonstrated some of the same features that the "Portraits of Grief" did, but because the soldiers had chosen the military, their deaths could not be described with the same underlying sense of injustice (without making the soldiers seem unpatriotic). In the reporting on the first deaths, under the heading "The First to Fall," photographs of victims' relatives were shown— often in a fairly large format—with the relatives holding photographs of their lost loved ones, mostly smiling in happier times. In their emphasis on human interest and personality—"He Was Like a Magnet"—the portraits showed distinct similarities to the "Portraits of Grief"; they evoked the World Trade Center photos in the use of touching anecdotes, and the attention to the intensity of family bonds emerged when American casualties occurred after the war was supposed to be over (Halbfinger B11). When she heard that her twenty-three-year-old grandson had died jumping into a canal to save his comrades, one soldier's grandmother said: "We have a lake here too, and if he would have seen someone fall in there, he would have been right in after them" (Davey A11). Many of the men killed in the war—those whose photos are not taken in uniform are mainly smiling too—were as young as, if not younger than, the civilians killed at the World Trade Center. This kind of coverage was not sustained, however, and never became a distinct feature of the newspaper.

It is also the case that no comparable attention was paid to the individuality of those killed by Americans, first in Afghanistan and then Iraq. As Howard Zinn wrote in *The Nation,* "In contrast with the vignettes about the victims featured in the *New York Times,* there are few available details about the dead men, women and children in Afghanistan" (16). As the war persisted, however, there were glimmers of journalistic self-consciousness about the enemy—beyond the sheer numbers of casualties. For example, the *Times* produced a photo-essay late in December 2005 titled "The Face and Voice of Civilian Sacrifice in Iraq" that showed several images of civilians with captions testifying to their suffering. "Their portraits and their stories compel attention, not because they have endured worse than others, but because their miseries are so commonplace, because they stand for what thousands of Iraqi families have endured, directly or through ties of community and tribe. In his or her own way, each of these survivors is a totem for all . . ." (Burns A18). A more characteristic example of war reporting is a long article occasioned by the American body count, "3,000 Deaths in Iraq, Countless Tears at Home," accompanied by a two-page spread of head shots of the dead military, as well as "Portrait"-like vignettes (Alvarez and Lehren A1).

In December 2006, I collaborated with two colleagues, Jay Prosser and Geoffrey Batchen, to produce a symposium at the CUNY Graduate Center called "Picturing Atrocity: Photography in Crisis." In conjunction with the event, Batchen, an art historian, led a doctoral seminar on photographic representations of atrocity that culminated in an exhibit in the lobby of the Graduate Center. The students created fourteen new "Portraits of Grief" based on the model of the "Portraits" that had appeared in the *New York Times.* Here, each "Portrait" took as its subject an Iraqi civilian, often a very young person, killed in the war. The descriptions of dead Iraqis were similar in style and tone to those of the Americans lost in the World Trade Center disaster, citing hobbies and personality traits and quoting family members, with one crucial difference: the specific manner of death: "Ali Rekaad was killed, along with his mother, father, sisters and two younger brothers, by an American helicopter gunship that bombed their tent at Makr al-Deeb, Al-Anbar Province, at 2:45 a.m. on May 19, 2004."[12] In this fatally telling detail, the "Portrait" both evokes the American template and presents the other side of the aftermath of September 11. Perhaps one day, when the Iraq War is over, readers of the *New York Times* will have a more complex picture of grief.

NOTES

1. I presented a version of this chapter at a symposium in memory of Naomi Schor held at the Pembroke Center, Brown University, entitled "The Lure of the Detail: Critical Reading Today." Some of the papers were published in an issue of the journal *differences*, of which Schor had been a co-founder (Fall 2003). Her death came so close to September 11, 2001, that I inevitably thought of her—and the shock created by sudden loss—as I meditated about the "Portraits of Grief." I also wrote about the "Portraits" for *Trauma at Home: After 9/11*, a collection edited by Judith Greenberg, before the *Times* volume appeared. Traces of the thinking that shaped that essay ("Reporting the Disaster") remain in this piece.

2. There is a striking absence in the "Portraits" of political anger having to do with safety conditions at the World Trade Center, governmental handling of security, and all issues related to the national context of the event. A small number of relatives of victims (fifty representing thirty-five victims) formed a group called "Sept. 11 Families for Peaceful Tomorrows" with the goal of promoting an anti-war agenda. A woman who lost her brother, a man whose rescue efforts were lauded in public by Bush, said that "she didn't feel honored. She felt as if she'd been punched in the stomach" (Haberman B1). The politics of loss has surfaced in the arena of economic compensation and also in that of public recognition. As the commission on the design of the memorial considers the entries, various groups press their demands for representation. Some felt that "everyone who died should be treated equally" (following the principle of the "Portraits"); others did not. The president of the Uniformed Firefighters Association stated in the *Times*: "We are not going to let people say that what we did on 9/11 was the same as everybody else. . . . Because it wasn't" (Lipton B47). The struggle over recognition has continued in every aspect of the rebuilding of Ground Zero: preserving the "footprint" of the towers, and in particular a debate over the matter of the names. How should the victims be identified, and where? Should ages be mentioned? Rank? Affiliation? (Dunlap B2).

3. Still, the videos were surprising in other ways. One focused on a gay male couple, unusual given the heavily heterosexual and familial model of the mourning families. Another dealt with a young woman, Jacqueline Donovan, whose portrait is not found in the volume. The calendar of grief picks her up, though. "Sturdier relatives can see their loved ones in the clear light of life, rather than a halo of death. 'These stories make Jackie sound like a party animal,' said Jacqueline Donovan's father, James. 'Well, she was'" (Hoffman B9).

4. Despite the difference that time can make in mourning, the later "Portraits" echo the figures of speech we saw in the earlier ones. Here, a very young

Russian woman talks about losing her husband of one year, and how even in December 2001, she believed that he would be found: "I even had a tiny hope in October 2002." In March 2003, she is finally willing to speak to the reporters, sounding very much like the widow I quoted earlier, whose testimony was closer to the event but was still after the first anniversary: "All I need to say is: He was my everything. That is very important to me to say" ("Alexandre Ivantsov" B36).

5. On memorialization and scale, see Hirsch and Spitzer, and Yaeger. On problems of visualization and scale, the aftermath of September 11, and the Holocaust, see Spiegelman.

6. The article, published in a magazine, *New Society,* was collected under the title "Photographs of Agony" in *About Looking,* but this quotation does not appear in it.

7. *Totems of the Fall* was written in response to a call from Nicola Sheara, Artistic Director of TheatreSounds, for plays related to the events of 9/11. Under Sheara's direction, *WANTED* (as it was originally titled) was read in October 2001 in Kingston, New York as part of a memorial evening and later in Rhinebeck, New York as a benefit for Hudson Valley firemen.

8. Through a strange coincidence, this snapshot features a victim whose "Portrait" I described in a previous essay on the reporting of September 11. The photograph of Andrew Stern (on the right) is signed by his wife and children (Novak 94). I felt as though Novak and I separately had both come to "know" the same person.

9. Novak was fascinated, she said, by the fact that "the families altered the original missing posters rather than replacing them with new memorials. It is as if the missing poster was a stand in for the deceased" (Novak "Email").

10. The lawyers involved in the proceedings take the task of constructing a persuasive narrative as seriously as the survivors. Maura V. Laffan is quoted as saying that she "has been thinking about Faulkner, Henry James and others 'who have looked very closely at the human condition,' because the narratives are 'probably the most important pieces that I'll ever write'" (Chen, "Families" B6).

11. Letters to the editor also made the connection between the war and the politics of the genre—here in relation to American troops. One outraged woman writes, wondering whether it was time for you to resurrect your "Portraits of Grief," which you published for the World Trade Center Victims. This time you can call it "Portraits of Courage," highlighting the men and women killed in Iraq and Afghanistan. Just because President Bush does not publicly mourn them, why shouldn't the American people have the opportunity to know who they are on a more personal level, and mourn their wasted lives. (Lehmann A26) And another, lamenting the government policy in Iraq: "Bring back your 'Portraits of Grief' so that once more, the human face of a life lived marks the notice of a confirmed casualty" (Kenney A24).

12. See Holmberg's review, "Portraits of Outrage."

WORKS CITED

"Aleksandr Ivantsov: 'He Was My Everything.'" *New York Times* 9 Mar. 2003: B36.

Alvarez, Lizette, and Andrew Lehren. "3,000 Deaths in Iraq, Countless Tears at Home." *New York Times* 1 Jan. 2007: A1.

"Among the Missing." Editorial. *New York Times* 14 Oct. 2001: D12.

"Anecdote." *Webster's Third New International Dictionary,* 1968.

Aristotle. *Nicomachean Ethics*. Trans. Martin Oswald. Indianapolis: Bobbs-Merrill, 1962.

Barthes, Roland. *Camera Lucida: Reflections on Photography*. Trans. Richard Howard. New York: Hill, 1994.

Berger, John. *About Looking*. New York: Pantheon, 1980.

———. "Horror Pictures." *New Society* 27 (1972): 194–95.

Burns, John F. "The Face and Voice of Civilian Sacrifice in Iraq." *New York Times* 26 Dec. 2005: A18.

Chen, David W. "Beyond Numbers, 9/11 Panel Hears Families' Anguish." *New York Times* 1 Apr. 2003: A1+.

———. "Families Humanize 9/11 Aid Forms." *New York Times* 26 Oct. 2002: B1+.

Davey, Monica. "As the Fighting Continues, Some Back Home Wonder, 'Why Are People Dying?'" *New York Times* 2 June 2003: A11.

Dunlap, David W. "Still the Question of Displaying the Names of 9/11." *New York Times* 11 Jan. 2007: B2.

Greenberg, Judith, ed. *Trauma at Home: After 9/11*. Lincoln: U of Nebraska P, 2003.

Haberman, Clyde. "Swords, Plowshares, and 9/11 Steel." *New York Times* 7 Jan. 2003: B1.

Halbfinger, David M. "Overseas, the Inevitable; At Home, a Grim Ritual." *New York Times* 24 Mar. 2003: B11.

Hirsch, Marianne, and Leo Spitzer. "Testimonial Objects: Memory, Gender, and Transmission." *Poetics Today* 27 (2006): 353–83.

Hoffman, Jan. "For the Families, a Long Year's Journey into Grief, and Back Again." *New York Times* 12 Sept. 2002: B9.

Holmberg, Ryan. "Portraits of Outrage: Picturing Atrocity: Photography in Crisis." *Afterimage* 33.5 (2006): 36–39.

"John G. Scharf: The Big Kid of the Family." *New York Times* 15 Sept. 2001: A11.

Kellner, Tatana. *Requiem for September 11ᵗʰ*. 21 Feb. 2003. http://www.cepagallery.org/exhibitions/sept11.02/kellner.pdf .

Kenney, Barbara Allen. "Taking the Temperature on Iraq." *New York Times* 16 Sept. 2003: A24.

"Kevin Prior: 'I'm Always Coming Home.'" *New York Times* 8 Dec. 2002: B54.

Klitzman, Robert. "When Grief Takes Hold of the Body." *New York Times* 10 Sept. 2002: F5.

Lehmann, Gail. "The President and the Mourning." *New York Times* 6 Nov. 2003: A26.

Lipton, Eric. "At Firefighter's Funeral, Mayor Says 9/11 Memorial Should Identify Rescuers." *New York Times* 8 June 2003: B47.

McDonald, Christie. "Grieving through Portraits." Conf. on the Lure of the Detail: Critical Reading Today. Pembroke Center, Brown University. 5 Apr. 2003.

Miller, Nancy K. "Reporting the Disaster." Greenberg 39–47.

Nelson, Anne. *The Guys*. Flea Theater, New York City. 2001–02.

Novak, Lorie. Email to the author. 22 Nov. 2002.

———. "Photographs." Greenberg 87–94.

Portraits: 9/11/01: The Collected "Portraits of Grief" from the New York Times. New York: Times Books / Henry Holt, 2002.

Raines, Howell. "Foreword." *Portraits* vii–viii.

"Remembering the Little Things: Older Monuments Guide Planner of Sept. 11 Memorial." *New York Times* 13 Oct. 2002: B35.

Schor, Naomi. *Reading in Detail: Aesthetics and the Feminine*. New York: Methuen, 1987.

Scott, Janny. "Closing a Scrapbook Full of Life and Sorrow." *New York Times* 31 Dec. 2001: B6.

———. "Introduction." *Portraits* ix–x.

Singer, Mark. "Talk of the Town: Grief Desk." *New Yorker* 14 Jan. 2002: 30–31.

"Snapshots of Their Lives with Family and at Work." *New York Times* 15 Sept. 2001: A11.

Spiegelman, Art. *In the Shadow of No Towers*. New York: Pantheon, 2004.

"Steven Schlag. 'It's 88 and Sunny.'" *New York Times* 8 Dec. 2002: B54.

Totems of the Fall. By Larry Harris. Dir. Rochele Tillman. Perf. Jeanine T. Abraham, Eric Kaiser, Margaux Laskey, Vivian Meisner, Miguel Parga, Dayna Steinfeld, Jonathan Reuning, and Matt Boethin. Intar, New York City. Nov. 2002.

"Timothy G. Byrne: Fat Cigar and Time for Fun." *New York Times* 15 Sept. 2001: A11.

Yaeger, Patricia. "Rubble as Archive, or 9/11 as Dust, Debris, and Bodily Vanishing." Greenberg 187–94.

Zinn, Howard. "The Others." *The Nation* 11 Feb. 2002: 16–20.

2 Foer, Spiegelman, and 9/11's Timely Traumas

Mitchum Huehls

> [T]he *"time" in the time of trauma . . . is not simply one moment in history during which trauma appears prevalent. The "time of trauma" or "trauma's time" also refers to a radical change in the way we understand the relationship . . . between time and consciousness, of [trauma's] effects not only on the present, but the past, and—most strikingly—the future.*
>
> —Aimee Pozorski, "Trauma's Time"

In his 1895 *Project for a Scientific Psychology,* Freud introduced the concept *Nachträglichkeit,* perhaps best translated as "afterward-ness," to describe the specifically temporal nature of trauma.[1] Because consciousness cannot absorb the traumatic event in the moment of its occurrence, Freud suggests that the time of the original event inflects all future times, thereby skewing temporal experience in general. Trauma is thus not of a moment, but instead spans an individual's temporal continuum, constituting her past, present, and future. Commonly registering September 11, 2001, as just such an affront to individual temporal experience, both Jonathan Safran Foer's *Extremely Loud & Incredibly Close* and Art Spiegelman's *In the Shadow of No Towers* chronicle different attempts to mend the relationship between temporal experience and consciousness. To prevent the skewed time of trauma from dominating their interactions with the world, each text's protagonist must identify new temporal forms—new ways of incorporating time into his understanding of the world—that will move him beyond 9/11's temporally traumatic effects.

A common image from the two texts—that of a man falling from a tower before its collapse—reveals the specific version of temporal understanding each seeks. Oskar Schell, Foer's nine-year-old narrator whose father died in the attacks, keeps a collage-like journal entitled *Stuff That Happened to Me* into which he has taped a series of photographs of the man in various stages of descent. At the novel's conclusion, Oskar removes the images from his book and re-inserts them in reverse order, so that when the pages are flipped forward, the man defies fate and flies safely into the building. Foer then includes these images as the final 15 pages of his own work, bringing their cinematic temporality to the reader's own fingertips and making the novel performatively coextensive with Oskar's journal. Spiegelman also enlists this provocative image, depicting himself as the man jumping out of the tower. To capture the temporal experience of falling, however, he superimposes five drawings of himself, in various stages of descent, over an image of one tower. Upon landing, the Spiegelman figure becomes Happy Hooligan, a historical cartoon character. As each human figure indexes a different moment in time, Spiegelman here represents the event's temporality rather than performing it.

This difference between performance and representation also inflects the debate over the timing of U.S. intelligence both before and after the 9/11 attacks. Fueled by the logic of dot connecting, the recriminations concerning who knew what when about 9/11 lent credence to Condoleezza Rice's warning, just a year later, that any delay in action against Iraq only increased the likelihood that "the smoking gun would be a mushroom cloud" (CNN). Desperate to avoid another 9/11, Rice's rhetoric represents the Bush administration's search for its own new form of temporal understanding. Rather than waiting for the dots to coalesce into an intelligible representation of an attack, she implies that the United States must act in real time, if not sooner, a belief that led the Bush administration to embrace the immanent temporality of performance and eschew the retroactive temporality of representation. Because Foer's literary performances and Spiegelman's historical representations deploy these same temporal forms, linking them directly to personal traumas of 9/11, their texts productively illuminate the very challenges facing an administration operating in a newly temporalized political sphere. Specifically, the performative logic of Foer's novel reveals the challenges that attend any attempt to gain knowledge in real time, while Spiegelman's representational embrace of history suggests that waiting for after-the-fact knowledge does not guarantee disaster and might even mitigate performance's inclination to leap before looking. Taken together, then, these two texts allegorize the U.S. struggle to manage its own timely traumas since 9/11.

On one level, the difference between these performative and representational portrayals of falling's temporal arc are a function of genre: Spiegelman composed his 10-page series of comix in single-page installments for the German newspaper *Die Ziet,* a format not conducive to a flip-book's mobile illusions.[2] Nevertheless, Foer and Spieglman's disparate treatments of the falling-man image also point to the particular form of temporal experience each believes will counter 9/11's skewing of time. Because 9/11 reorients his entire existence around the moment his father died, Oskar thinks he will be healed if he can reverse time. While this reversal is clearly just so much wishful thinking, its temporal form—the flip-book's cinematic, real-time performance of motion—proves crucial to Oskar's healing process. He must relegate the event to the past by embracing time's forward progress into the future, an argument his therapist implicitly makes when he asks Oskar if he has noticed any hairs on his scrotum. If hormones, not 9/11, were causing Oskar's emotional distress, then his life would in fact be moving forward, not back. Sympathetic to Oskar's sense that his "dad died the most horrible death that anyone ever could invent," Foer's filmic portrayal of the falling man thus allows Oskar the illusion of reversing time, while also insisting on a process-based, real-time solution to healing (201).

"[R]eeling on that faultline where World History and Personal History collide," this same forward motion will not remedy Spiegelman's temporal problems, which instead require the realignment of public and personal times (Introduction). While Spiegelman's personal sense of time "stands still at the moment of trauma" (2), the government responds rapidly and aggressively with wars in Afghanistan and Iraq, a disjunction nicely captured in his suspicion that the nation's "'leaders' are reading the book of Revelations" while he reads "the paranoid science fiction of Philip K. Dick" (7). Given the discrepancy between the apocalyptically committed government and the individual paralyzed by paranoia, Spiegelman looks for a version of time that unites the personal and the public, kick-starting the personal with time's forward motion while slowing down what he sees as public time's death-driven acceleration. In his treatment of the falling-man image, therefore, Spiegelman puts himself in the place of the anonymous figure, personalizing this globally disseminated image and superimposing the personal on the public. Furthermore, reproducing his image five times over brings a semblance of temporal motion to the timeless isolation of his personal experience of the attacks, while the public aspect of the event pauses a moment in the solitary form of the looming tower. At least representationally, then, the temporal discrepancy between the personal and the public are brought into a tentative alignment that the accompanying narrative reinforces. For instance, Spiegelman identifies a parallel between globally published accounts of people jumping from the towers and the underreported local story of New Yorkers who have more metaphorically "landed in the street" "in the economic dislocation that has followed since that day" (6). Here he analogizes the images that he witnessed personally with the widely disseminated public images that threaten to preempt his understanding of the event and its aftermath. Finally, Spiegelman uses history to achieve this temporal alignment as the Happy Hooligan character simultaneously embodies the final stage of Spiegelman's fall from the tower and a hobo sitting among garbage on the city street. This historical representation thus allows Spiegelman to experience stopped personal time and moving public time simultaneously and without conflict; history here represents the only "place" where he is safe from the time of 9/11's trauma.

As I suggested earlier, achieving and inhabiting these healing forms of temporal experience entails mending the rift between time and consciousness—developing a better way to incorporate time into the process of knowing. Such temporalized knowledge is hard to come by, however, because it is a knowledge *of* time that must also be acquired *in* time. In an essay appearing just months after the attacks, Don DeLillo wrestles with this complicated relationship among time, trauma, and representation: after the first plane hit the building, it gradually "became possible for us to absorb this, barely. But when the towers fell. When the rolling smoke began moving downward, floor to floor. This was so vast and terrible that it was outside imagining even as it happened. We could not catch up with it" (39). Even as time moved the violent events forward, the human experience of them lagged behind, as DeLillo's incomplete sentences haltingly perform. DeLillo contends that months later, "We seem pressed for time, all of us. Time is scarcer now. There is a sense of compression, plans made hurriedly, time forced and distorted"(39). While suggesting that the aesthetic can play some role in "catching up" with this time lag, DeLillo also warns against certain representational modes: "The event itself has no purchase on the mercies of analogy or simile. We have to take the shock and horror as it is" (39). Here DeLillo calls for a form of representation that does not reduce the temporal experience of the event in the way that analogy or simile might.[3]

The challenge here involves the best way to unite time and knowledge without compromising one for the other. Phenomenology has consistently revealed the paradox at the heart of any such analysis of temporal experience, suggesting that one can either have stable knowledge and a compromised sense of time or a replete temporal experience with compromised knowledge of that experience.[4] The point is not that such phenomenological pursuits are misguided, simply that they are representationally challenged, forced to choose between the performative, which embraces time at the expense of meaning and understanding, and the representational, which stabilizes meaning at the expense of time.

Using images to produce and elicit forms of temporal experience might initially seem counter-intuitive. After all, images, particularly the still photographs included in Foer's text, represent stable and self-contained slivers of time. Functioning by analogy and simile, they tend to reduce, hypostatize, and impose meaning on a constantly moving reality better captured through cinema's diachronic form. My readings will nevertheless suggest that Foer's novel and Spiegelman's comix successfully overcome this reductive aspect of images, enlisting them to portray specifically temporal forms of knowing. Advocating a contingent and fully temporalized mode of knowing as the best antidote for Oskar's trauma, Foer privileges process over content and uses images performatively. Seeking a realignment of his personal and public times that does not require Oskar's turn to real-time experience, Spiegelman's images can represent a healing version of temporal experience without having to perform it. Consequently, Spiegelman imports history into his present where its union of timelessness (history as something eternal and always with us) and timeliness (history as a domain where action occurs and events transpire) provides him the safe space required to negotiate the conflict he experiences between personal and private times.

As I have already noted, these texts not only highlight the specifically temporal challenges 9/11 has posed to individuals, but they also point more broadly to a general shift from spatial to temporal logics occurring on the level of U.S. foreign policy, as the Bush administration struggles, just like Oskar and Spiegelman, to make sense of its place in a post-9/11 world. As George W. Bush highlighted on September 14, 2001, the attacks established time as the requisite paradigm for understanding our new global reality: "The conflict was begun on the timing and terms of others; it will end in a way and at an hour, of our choosing." While the Cold War, dominated by spatial metaphors of dominoes, walls, and curtains, sought to control territory (Berlin, Korea, Cuba, Vietnam, Central America, and even outer space), our current "war on terror" needs to control time. And from the war against Iraq to curtailing civil liberties under the Patriot Act and detaining "enemy combatants" at Guantanamo Bay without due process, preemption has defined the Bush administration's primary relation to time. While preemption removes us from time's gradual unfolding—from its "due process"—it does so not by stopping time but by accelerating it, by determining the future before it has a chance to occur.

As Richard Posner implies in his review of *The 9/11 Commission Report,* however, preemption may evade or trump the problem of gaining knowledge in real time, but it certainly does not solve it. He concludes instead that the main lesson we should take from 9/11 is the simple truth "that it is almost impossible to take effective action to prevent something that hasn't occurred previously" (9). Indeed, as Donald Rumsfeld's frustrated musings about "known knowns," "known unknowns," and "unknown unknowns" demonstrate, the timely thinking that this post-9/11 paradigm shift demands is more complex than U.S. preemption has allowed. Known knowns belong to the past, and known unknowns are easily and legally preempted under the international legal doctrine of imminent threat. As Posner points out, however, the future is not populated with known unknowns; rather, it explodes with unknown unknowns, as the United States, which did not know that it did not know that Iraq did not have weapons of mass destruction, learned the hard way.

But as Foer's novel suggests, it is not clear that there are any good options when it comes to unknown unknowns. Trapped in the paradox of time and knowledge, Oskar and the Bush administration can either act in real-time with compromised knowledge, or they can stabilize their knowledge but risk acting too late. Instead of compromising, the government chose preemption, and Oskar chooses to obsess over the moment of his father's death. Given this parallel between Oskar's fear of an unknown and uncontrollable future and the nation's similar terror, Foer's novel proves particularly useful for examining the feasibility of pursuing knowledge in real time. While Foer's text ultimately advocates a form of real-time knowledge acquisition that would be too dangerous as foreign intelligence policy, I will argue that Spiegelman's text does in fact respond productively to preemption, identifying historical time as an alternative to the Faustian choice of acting without knowing and knowing without acting that currently plagues U.S. foreign policy decisions.

Fixated on the moment of impact, Oskar chooses secure knowledge over action in his attempt to come to terms with his father's death. Perhaps this is because his trauma does not stem simply from his father's death, but from the horror of not knowing that his father was about to die. Oskar recounts his experience of being sent home from school on the morning of 9/11: "I opened the apartment door, put down my bag, and took off my shoes, like everything was wonderful, because I didn't know that in reality everything was actually horrible, because how could I?" (68). It is this radically unknown unknown that traumatizes Oskar and fuels his desire to fill the hole in his knowledge of the event. Tracing his attempt to gain symbolic understanding, the novel's plot follows Oskar's search for the lock that matches a key he finds in his father's closet after 9/11. The key is in an envelope with the word "Black" written on it. Believing that "the lock was between [him] and [his] Dad," Oskar methodically visits every "Black" listed in the phone book, interrogating each about the key (52).

A quaint story, but the novel also suggests that this symbolic reunion with his father is impossible. Using DeLillo's language, we might say that the symbol is not strong enough to carry the weight of the event; symbolic language cannot find an adequate substitute for the event that will make its meaning and significance clear, even if that symbol is a present absence like a lock. For the key to unlock the lock would be for Oskar to inhabit the moment of his father's death, to understand the logic of that traumatic instant. Instead he can only come "incredibly close" to the event, as he is when he visualizes himself in a building hit by a plane: "I imagined the last second, when I would see the pilot's face, who would be a terrorist. I imagined us looking each other in the eyes when the nose of the plane was one millimeter from the building" (244). Indeed, when Oskar finally meets the man who owns the matching lock, Oskar declines to open it.

The key/lock plot clearly indicates the nature of Oskar's response to 9/11 and its aftermath: the more he knows about the event, the more secure he will feel in his post-9/11 world. After calculating that he could visit each of the 216 Blacks listed in the phone book in three years, for example, Oskar reveals, "I couldn't survive three years without knowing," and he cancels his weekend French lessons, allowing him to "know everything" in just one and a half years (51). Related to his epistemophilia, Oskar invents fantastic devices—skyscrapers with movable parts, a portable pocket that holds people, a birdseed shirt that attracts birds to help people fly—intended to reduce all unknown contingencies to a known and manageable form. Like the symbolic search for the lock, however, these inventions preempt future death but preclude him from living his life, as Oskar's observation that he compulsively invents whenever he feels insecure indicates (234).

Finally, Oskar also stabilizes his relationship to his world with representational photography. Photographs are scattered throughout *Extremely
Loud*, frequently depicting a person or scene described in adjacent text,
as when a picture of Abby Black, the woman whose husband owns the
matching lock, faces the page on which Oskar narrates taking the picture.
Such photos are comingled with others that Oskar clearly did not take, but
which also illustrate some aspect of adjacent text. (His pictures only appear
in the chapters he narrates, not in those containing his grandfather's journal or his grandmother's letters.) Most performatively, at one point Oskar
shows us some of the pictures collected in *Stuff That Happened to Me*.
He narrates from his bed, "I flipped through it for a while, wishing that I
would finally fall asleep," and then the next 15 pages contain images from
his book, after which he resumes his narrative, telling us that he "got out
of bed" (52–68). Although they loosely chronicle the events in Oskar's life,
all of these interpolated pictures also have a symbolic register that exceeds
their ostensibly documentary function. This is why he photographs the
back of Abby Black's head. If he were truly just accumulating "stuff that
happened to him," we would see her putting her hand in front of her face
as she did when Oskar tried to take her picture. Instead, Oskar tells us, "I
thought of a different picture I could take, which would be more truthful,
anyway" (99).

Suffering the traumas of a different horror, Oskar's grandfather stopped
speaking shortly after living through the Dresden fire bombings, and he
keeps a daybook in which he writes messages to people along with unsent
letters to his son explaining "Why I'm Not Where You Are." Like Oskar,
the grandfather also takes photos, but his are purely documentary. After
the war he began photographing everything he owned, right down to the
doorknobs in his apartment, and these pictures are inserted into his journal. While Oskar's pictures aim at a deeper truth, the grandfather's pictures have no meaning beyond the object they represent. They are, in effect,
ontological substitutes—proof of existence for a hypothetical insurance
adjuster of the future. Like Oskar's photos, these also enhance the performativity of the grandfather's chapters, which even reproduce the visual
appearance of the daybook's pages so that some pages have only a few
words on them while others have text flush to the margins.

Both of these photographic styles, Oskar's, which aims at symbolic depth,
and the grandfather's, which aims at encyclopedic breadth, unsuccessfully
heal their respective traumas. Just as Oskar's symbolic search for the lock
cannot replace his father's violent absence, and just as his inventions come
at the expense of his mental and emotional stability in the present, so too
do these photographs run from rather than embrace the contingencies of
temporal experience that define the original trauma. That is, the Dresden
bombings and 9/11 were so sublimely horrific because they were unknown
unknowns, and no amount of inventing, symbolizing, or accruing can possess that central emptiness. Indeed, the novel argues that these characters

should be trying to live, not trying to know, which is why they only exhibit true knowledge when they are not thinking. For example, describing his first sexual encounter with his first love, Anna, Oskar's grandfather relates, "[W]ithout any experience I knew what to do . . . as if the information had been coiled within me like a spring, everything that was happening had happened before and would happen again" (127). Similarly, the grandmother evinces needs that exceed her logical knowledge of them: "What does it mean to need a child? One morning I awoke and understood the hole in the middle of me. . . . I couldn't explain it. The need came before explanations" (177). Tellingly, Oskar experiences such knowledge just once during his search, while standing outside the door of the Black who owns the lock that matches his key: "I didn't believe in being able to know what's going to happen before it happens, but for some reason I knew I had to get inside her apartment" (91).

But if these images prevent Oskar and his grandfather from achieving the kind of intuitive knowledge just described, do they function similarly for the novel's readers? Or, to ask the question that David Palumbo-Liu poses for all acts of imaginative creation post-9/11: do they reclaim the future and incorporate time in a way that addresses 9/11's temporal traumas, or do they become "manic," succumbing to the imagination's "self-generating frenzy, unchecked by the otherness of the external world" (158)? Almost unanimously, book reviewers have pronounced Foer's inventiveness as pathological and compulsive as Oskar's:

> The avant-garde tool kit, developed way back when to disassemble established attitudes and cut through rusty sentiments, has now become the best means, it seems, for restoring them and propping them up. No traditional story could put forward the tritenesses that Foer reshuffles, folds, cuts into strips, seals in seven separate envelopes and then, astonishingly, makes whole, causing the audience to ooh and aah over notions that used to make it groan. (Kirn 2)

Perhaps. But if we give Foer the benefit of the doubt for just a moment, we might see that there is something productively odd about this slew of formal techniques: they all grasp after the performative without ever fully achieving it; they are quasi-performative. For example, when meeting with Abby, Oskar leaves his business card, which Foer reproduces in the text, performing the event for his readers. And yet, the reproduced card is just a square with text in it; some words are italicized and some are capitalized, but the font on the card is identical to the novel's and in no way looks like a business card. The same problem arises with the grandfather's daybook, which performatively recreates the spatial layout of each page but retains the novel's font. This may seem like quibbling, but other pages in the novel do achieve a more consistent performativity: those containing different handwriting styles printed in various colors purport to be, as much as possible, the actual papers Oskar finds at the art supply store (47–49). In other words, these fully performative pages require that we ask why other such moments do not measure up or adhere to the same logic.

A clue might come when we notice that some of the pages in the grandfather's daybook performatively deliver the precise message he wrote at that moment, as when a question to a passerby, "Excuse me, do you know what time it is?" interrupts a letter to his son (111–13). At other times, however, the pages recording these single-line snippets of conversation are part of the letter to his son, included as representations of something that he had previously written in the daybook. For example, an early letter explains the daybook's function: "I would take the book to bed with me and read through the pages of my life:" (18). The next nine pages after the colon then exemplify what he would read: "I want two rolls"; "Help"; or "Ha ha ha!" (19–27). After representing enough examples, the letter finally continues, only to be interrupted by a photo of a doorknob, a moment that heightens rather than undermines the chapter's performativity. The grandfather's daybook thus reveals that the text's overall performativity breaks down because sometimes it claims actually *to be* the thing that we are reading about (e.g., the colored handwriting or Oskar's book) while at other times it seems merely content *to represent* that thing (e.g., the cards, letters, and elements of the grandfather's letters). This same equivocation between representing and being marks the difference between Oskar's and his grandfather's photographs, and it also plagues the photographs themselves. In Oskar's symbolic aesthetic, the pictured object refers us to something "more truthful," and yet these same photos, intended to be deeply symbolic and representational, are also performative when they appear in *Stuff That Happened to Me*. In the grandfather's documentary aesthetic, the photos function as ontological substitutes for the pictured objects, and yet, in a book about a boy searching for a lock, the photos of doorknobs and locks are deeply symbolic. Therefore, both in the novel's photographs and in its overall performativity, there is an equivocation: sometimes a thing is what it is, and at other times it represents something other than itself. Lacking an internal and consistent logic, this undecidability has given reviewers good cause to chastise Foer. And yet, I would like to entertain the possibility that such undecidability might be the point.

After all, this is the very lesson that Oskar's father seeks to impress upon him in their game of "Reconnaissance Expedition"—a game in which he would give Oskar clues and instructions to decode and perform. During one game, Oskar gleans that Central Park holds the clue that will help him solve his mission, but after digging up various objects in the park, he struggles to determine which are clues (i.e., representations) and which are just things. Oskar then wonders if perhaps this undecidability is itself a clue, a notion that is reinforced when plotting the found objects on a map of Central Park leads him to realize that he "could connect the dots to make . . . almost anything [he] wanted" (10). Oskar complains to his father, "But if you don't tell me anything, how can I ever be right?" "How could you ever be wrong?" his father replies (9).

Indeed, readers could make almost anything they wanted out of the "avant-garde toolkit" Foer empties into his novel. But what might first appear as crude and sloppy writing instead proves to be Foer's finest performance of them all: the irresolvable equivocation between performance and representation governs the entire process of reading his novel. That is, the novel offers a second level of performance, a meta-performance, which differs significantly from the performance of ontological substitution that the grandfather's photos enact. The performances internal to the text, which I have described as quasi-performative, are static and removed from time because some form of representational knowledge always intercedes. Of course, such intermittent performance is not a failure as much as it is symptomatic of a world in which leaving oneself open to a radically contingent future could lead to certain death. As such, Oskar and his grandfather will always compromise their performances for knowledge; they will always hedge their bets to protect themselves from the threat of unknown unknowns.

However, these compromises do not prevent Foer from insisting on the value of gaining knowledge in real time and charging head-first into those unknown unknowns, which is precisely the form of knowledge acquisition that the novel's meta-performance—its performance of the equivocation between performance and representation—demands of its readers. If the static performativity of the grandfather's photos, aiming merely to be the thing they represent, produces known knowns, while the symbolic logic of Oskar's photos, aiming at a truth beyond the thing they represent, provide known unknowns, then the contingent logic required to apprehend the conflicted relationship between the two brings us fully into the temporal challenges of post-9/11 unknown unknowns. When we know either what we know or what we do not know, our knowledge is stable and removed from the flow of time. Because unknown unknowns are unknown precisely because of the future's radical contingency, however, if we embrace the formal incoherence of Foer's novel and allow that we do not know what we do not know about the aim and function of his "avant-garde toolkit," then readerly knowledge becomes temporalized.

Of course, Oskar's own journey also proves to be a contingent search for unknown unknowns, but he does not realize it, perhaps because realizing it would make it no longer so. Instead, Oskar characterizes his search as a quest for a known unknown, as he does when he complains, "I don't know a single thing that I didn't know six months ago. And actually I have negative knowledge because I skipped all of those French classes with Marcel" (255). Knowing what he does not know implies that he knows what will solve his problems but currently lacks that thing. But Oskar does not find the thing that he thinks he lost: his connection to his father. Instead, Oskar gains a different kind of knowledge, a different kind of connection—to the city, to his mother, and to his grandparents—that he did not even know he was missing. At the novel's conclusion we finally learn that Oskar's father bought a vase from an estate sale and never even knew about the key, and the man holding the sale only learned after the fact that the vase held the key to his now-deceased father's safe-deposit box (two unknown unknowns). Although Oskar does not reconnect to his father, his search allows Mr. Black to connect to his, yet another unknown unknown articulated through Oskar's speculation that Mr. Black's posters searching for the man who bought the vase may have hung next to the posters Oskar's mother hung searching for her husband after 9/11 (299).

Finally, in addition to the text's internally conflicted performativity, the reciprocal interaction among the novel's interlocking chapters also channels readers into their own contingent search for knowledge. Although Oskar's, the grandfather's, and the grandmother's chapters recount different events, one chapter's story frequently intersects with and appears in the other chapters, making the reading experience an analeptic and proleptic whirl. Early in Oskar's narrative, for example, he describes his grandmother writing a message to him on the window of her apartment across the street, but in one of the grandfather's chapters appearing much later in the novel, we learn that the message was actually for him. In effect, when we read Oskar's account of this scene, we do not know what we do not know, which is that the grandfather had just returned to town and was trying to move back into the apartment. Like two posters unwittingly searching for the same person, there are always relevant events transpiring concurrent to the events being narrated, but they remain unknown unknowns to readers until we go through the *process* of reading. Readers are perpetually recontextualizing their knowledge of the text while the general unreliability of each of the three narrators ensures that they never land on a stable or true understanding of the narrated events. This in turn intimately links the reading experience to time's passing and ensures that our knowledge of the text is only ever associative and contingent, produced from the juxtaposition of the three chapter types, which refuse to be reduced to a coherently unified story just as the text's performativity resists any overarching logic. Foer thus asks his readers to focus on processes of understanding rather than on the specifics of novelistic content. Of course, as Walter Kirn notes in his review, Oskar could have learned that "searching" is more valuable than "finding" if he had simply gone to the docks and talked to Jonathan Livingston Seagull. However, Kirn's caustic criticism of Foer's maudlin message not only ignores its provocative formal enactment, but also fails to recognize how deeply such apparently pithy problems have vexed our nation ever since 9/11 forced us to think in time.

If Foer's novel posits a performatively cinematic real-time as an ideal temporal mode for knowing and healing 9/11's timely traumas, it also reveals that adopting this mode comes with great risks: formal incoherence, an unknown and thus potentially dangerous future, and an equivocal relation to the world and its objects. These are precisely the risks that the Bush administration has refused to take, choosing instead to manage risk with a policy of preemption that is coherent, known, and unequivocal. But does the relationship between time and knowledge only offer these two, all-or-nothing options? Art Spiegelman's *In the Shadow of No Towers* suggests not, and it does so by establishing a unique relationship to history that Spiegelman uses to withstand the government's aggressively preemptive logic.

In some respects, Spiegelman's temporal experience of the 9/11 attacks is remarkably similar to Oskar's. Just as his father's death prevents Oskar from moving on with his life, Spiegelman's personal experience of time's passage stopped on 9/11. And just as Oskar compulsively invents, Spiegelman, depicting himself with a bald eagle hanging around his neck, observes that more than five months after the attacks he must "compulsively retell the calamities of September 11th to anyone who'll still listen" (2). On the other hand, with some loving nudges from his mother and his therapist, Oskar remains free to reanimate his temporal experience at his own pace while Spiegelman's imbrication in the public sphere causes him to feel that the U.S. government is forcing time's reanimation on him. Thus, a public counter-discourse heckles his compulsive retelling: the bald eagle hanging around his neck represents not just the weight of the trauma grinding his personal sense of time to a halt, but also the government's insistence that the nation move forward in time as it squawks, "Everything's changed!" and "Go out and shop!" (2).

Spiegelman portrays his paralyzed experience of time as both an anxious waiting and an obsessive fixation on the events of 9/11. In a strip on the text's first page, he depicts his sense of suspended time as a case of "waiting for the next shoe to drop." In this sequence a man noisily takes off a shoe after a night of drinking. Alarmed at the calamity the first shoe causes, he silently places the second shoe on the floor and drifts off to sleep while his downstairs neighbors anxiously wait for the other shoe to drop (1). Similarly representing his inability to think beyond the morning of the attacks, the next page reveals a "Missing" poster for Spiegelman's brain, claiming that it was "last seen in Lower Manhattan, mid-September 2001" (2). Later in the text, his fixation on the moment of trauma turns into paranoia and a general obsession with the news. Noting that "he totally *lost* it way back then, after 9/11," we see Spiegelman surfing the Internet until 2 AM, looking for information about the attacks, only to go to bed and watch CNN's coverage of various 9/11 conspiracy theories (8).

Of course, just because Spiegelman's sense of time effectively stopped on 9/11 does not mean that the world followed suit: "Amazing how time flies when it stands still," he observes on a page marking the first anniversary of the attacks (4). Problematically, however, violence conspicuously marks the "flying time" of world events. For instance, the "other shoe" drops twice over, once as "Jihad brand footware" falling from the sky onto the frightened masses below (1), and later as a rain of cowboy boots that coincides with the 2004 Republican presidential convention held in New York City (10). That the other shoe belongs to both the terrorists and the Republicans nicely captures Spiegelman's sense that the Bush administration hijacked the hijackings for its own purposes, leaving him "equally terrorized by Al-Qaeda and by his own government." To convey this dual terror, Spiegelman draws himself sleeping at his drawing board while, to his left, a terrorist suspends a bloody knife above his neck, and to his right, George W. Bush holds a gun to his head. While Spiegelman sleepily inhabits his frozen personal time, reliving "his ringside seat to that day's disaster yet again," his waking entrance into the public sphere will clearly be a violent one, as it was for a young woman he overheard at a Tribeca party (2). The woman was mugged the previous night while walking home, an event that she interprets as a positive development since it indicates that "things are finally getting back to normal" (9).

Spiegelman initially believed that re-entering time's forward flow would be peaceful rather than violent, that "Ground Zero" would become "Year Zero" and that a "globe" rather than "provincial American flags" would "sprout out of the embers" of the attacks (Introduction and 7). But such hopes were dashed the moment the administration acted before it knew what it was doing, simultaneously preempting global good will and Spiegelman's personal healing process. Before preemption, Spiegelman thought his comix would entail "sorting through [his] grief and putting it into boxes," and he intended to represent very personal aspects of 9/11 and its aftermath: seeing the tower before it fell, driving to retrieve his son from school, forbidding his daughter to wear red, white, and blue, as school officials requested days after the attack. But as "the world hustled forward" and "the government began to . . . hurtle America into a colonialist adventure in Iraq," he was confronted with "[n]ew traumas [that] began competing with still-fresh wounds and the nature of [his] project began to mutate" (Introduction). Thus in the fourth installment of the series, a sequence of snapshot-like frames neatly contain the personal story of picking up his daughter from school after the attacks, but flying above and outside these boxes, George W. Bush and Dick Cheney straddle a large bald eagle as Bush yells, "Let's roll!" and Cheney slices the eagle's neck with a box cutter (4). Finally, preemption's tendency to accelerate time—to precipitate an event sooner than it would otherwise occur—also threatens to make his comix obsolete before they are even published. Noting the labor-intensive process of creating comix, he quips, "[o]ne has to assume that one will live forever to make them" (Introduction). Convinced that he might not live to see next week, however, "forever" is precisely the kind of time that he does not have. Hence, the representational burden of Spiegelman's text: how can he slow down his experience of public time and reanimate his personal time when those two times are so mutually antagonistic?

The text's final pages do indicate that he achieves a semblance of reconciliation between these competing temporalities. On a page dated more than one and a half years after the attacks, Spiegelman writes, "Time passes. He can think about himself in the first person again, but deep inside the towers still burn" (8). Also, on the text's final page, Spiegelman notes that "even anxious New Yorkers eventually run out of adrenaline and—. . . you go back to thinking that you **might** live forever after all" (10). Finally, in the last frames of the book, a glowing image of the towers that serves as the "pivotal image" of Spiegelman's personal 9/11 experience and appears on every page, fades nearly to black beneath the claim that the towers "seem to get smaller every day" (10). Of course, these successes are highly qualified: he uses the third person to assert his ability to think about himself in the first person; the towers still burn inside; he only "might" live forever; and the glowing tower fades nearly to black, but not all the way.

So how has Spiegelman achieved these qualified successes in the midst of an onslaught of public and political events that threaten permanently to preempt his personal experience of time, leaving it stagnant and frozen at the "moment of trauma"? In her insightful reading of *Maus*, Erin McGlothlin argues that its meta-artistic moments—when Spiegelman draws himself struggling to draw *Maus*—represent a temporal domain where he retreats to work out the vexed relation between his present and his father's past. McGlothlin identifies three interlocking stories in *Maus*, each with its own temporality: the past Holocaust, the present father-son relationship, and the meta-artistic story about *Maus*'s production, occurring in what McGlothlin via Spiegelman dubs the "super-present." This "super-present" allows Spiegelman to "reflect on his project" from a safe "narrative time in which nothing exactly happens, but in which the complexities and contradictions that relate to the other narrative levels are exposed" (186).

In the Shadow, which also recounts a family trauma and tells three stories (Spiegelman's personal 9/11 experience, the global politics surrounding the event and its aftermath, and the production of the text itself), also cultivates a safe temporal space from which Spiegelman can reconcile the conflict between personal and public time. However, unlike *Maus* where each story has its own place in time, here all three stories occur simultaneously in the present. In *Maus II,* Spiegelman famously draws himself at his drawing board with a pile of dead bodies/Holocaust victims on the floor (41). While gruesome and haunting, the past from which these bodies come does not immediately threaten Spiegelman in the super-present. However, when he appears at his drawing board in his 9/11 text, the terrorist's sword and Bush's handgun reveal that the meta-artistic level is no longer safe. In *Maus,* where his father "bleeds history," the trauma lies in the past, and he representationally escapes into the super-present; in this current work, where the traumatic event is unavoidably present, history becomes a time to escape to, rather than a trauma to run from.

Because he does not need the coextensive relationship between time and knowledge that Oskar requires, Spiegelman's text never aims to *perform* its temporality as Foer's does. Instead Spiegelman incorporates historical cartoon characters into his own work to represent a safe temporality in which personal and public times are reconciled. Importing the past into the present, he draws the present as history, but not as the history of some unknown future; instead, this present is the past before the future ever makes it so. In a brief introduction to the cartoons included in the appendix, Spiegelman explains why he turned to old cartoon characters to render his present as past:

> The only cultural artifacts that could get past my defenses to flood my eyes and brain with something other than images of burning towers were old comic strips; vital, unpretentious ephemera from the optimistic dawn of the 20th century. That they were made with so much skill and verve but never intended to last past the day they appeared in the newspaper gave them poignancy; they were just right for an end-of-the-world moment. (unpaginated)

To the extent that they belong to their day of publication which is also the day of their extinction, these cartoons are timely and mortal; but to the extent that they are "ghosts" that continue to "haunt" Spiegelman, they are timeless and eternal (8). In other words, they offer a temporality in which the timely and the timeless are not at odds with each other; their poignancy derives from their unstable ephemerality, not from any attempt to impose meaning by simile or analogy, as a photographic image might. As history, they are alive and animated but also immune to the anxious fear of the next shoe's dropping.

Literally encasing the temporal traumas of Spiegelman's present, the text's title page and the appendix also present historical materials that point to history's eternal timelessness. The title page reproduces a newspaper from September 11, 1901, five days after President McKinley was shot and three days before he died, with headlines attesting to history's eternal return: "President's Wound Reopened" and "Emma Goldman in Jail Charged with Conspiracy." The historical repetitions are clear: the wounding of the President and 9/11's wounding of the nation; using the shooting to imprison anarchists indiscriminately and using 9/11 to curtail civil liberties. The comics in the appendix reveal similar parallels: "The War Scare in Hogan's Alley" depicts a group of rag-tag children recruited to fight England; a comic from 1902 portrays two German children, Hans and Fritz, the Katzenjammer Kids, who trick two innocent American boys into planting a bomb under their grandpa while he recites the Declaration of Independence; a "Little Nemo in Slumberland" cartoon shows giant children strolling around Lower Manhattan, knocking over buildings roughly where the World Trade Center would later stand; and a "Bringing Up Father" strip from 1921 shows "father" traveling in Pisa where he interferes with Italy's infrastructure by propping up the Leaning Tower.

Accompanying the eternal timelessness born of history's self-repetitions, Spiegelman accesses history's timeliness when he replaces the characters in his story (usually himself) with characters from old comics. Occurring most frequently in scenes of intense emotional distress, he asks them to live through events in his life that he, stuck and fixated on the moment of trauma, does not have the time to experience. For example, before Spiegelman and his wife see the tower, they appear as ordinary Manhattanites, but in the next frame, after seeing the tower burning, they are transformed into the Katzenjammer Kids, renamed the "Tower Twins" (2). After retrieving their daughter, they reappear human; but in depicting the feeling that the Iraq invasion made their lives more dangerous, Spiegelman again draws himself and his wife as the twins. In representing the emotional tension 9/11 brought to their marriage, Spiegelman portrays himself and his wife as characters from "Bringing up Father" (8), and he appears as Happy Hooligan after his fall from the tower (6) and again while participating in a sham interview for Tom Brokaw's tribute to 9/11 (10). While Spiegelman's mind remains lost in the suspended timelessness of his post-9/11 world, these historical cartoon characters intervene to embody and personify his experiences. Paradoxically, if he drew himself living through these events, he could not draw the events, because the individual living through the events is entirely unmoored from the very temporality required to represent the sequence of events in the first place. Coming out of the past, the historical characters provide the experiential temporality required to get through the event sequences. When combined with the timelessness of history's repetitions, these historical comics offer Spiegelman a safe temporality from which to approach the timely trauma of his immediate present.

Finally, we can see this union of the timeless and the temporal in Spiegelman's manipulation of the flexible format of these single-page comix. On each of the ten pages, multi-framed strip sequences recounting events transpiring over time overlay single-frame drawings depicting different timeless states of being. For example, a drawing of several people with their heads in the sand, an advertisement for the "Ostrich Party," depicts the general condition of political consciousness in the United States (5); a single-frame fire–and–brimstone image depicts the "inner demons" roiling a homeless woman (6); an image of interlocking red hawks and blue doves, flanked by a skeleton and the grim reaper, represents a potentially violent divide in the United States electorate (7); and a disturbing drawing of Spiegelman jack hammering into his own skull intrudes into a boxed strip sequence in which he diagnoses his own paranoia and neurotic depression (8). Each of these single-frame drawings establishes the general underlying condition of the more fully temporalized events transpiring in the surrounding strip sequences. A few pages take this union of the timeless and the temporal a step further, presenting a full-page background image—the long shadow of the Twin Towers (2), a blown–up image of the Tower Twins (4), and fire engulfing the towers (10)—that subtends the animated events represented on each page. Representing the qualified healing captured in Spiegelman's observation that "most New Yorkers seem to have picked up the rhythms of daily life . . . but right under the surface, we're all still just a bunch of stunned pigeons," Spiegelman's use of historical cartoons, along with his formal layering of different temporalities, effectively unite the timeless and the temporal in a historical vision that facilitates his realignment of personal and public times (8).

Having completed the final installment of *In the Shadow*, Spiegelman observes in the introduction that ideas once deemed too extreme to print in mainstream media outlets—like the notion that George W. Bush has hurt the United States more than the terrorists have—began gaining more popular currency. Once the world came around to his point of view, Spiegelman realizes that he was ahead of his time rather than behind it, and his sense of disconnection and alienation begins to fade. Although his tone suggests a certain amount of personal satisfaction about this turn of events, he also strikes a facetious note, suggesting such anticipatory modes of knowledge, regardless of who deploys them, are not wholly desirable. After all, Spiegelman would have presumably preferred that his apocalyptic vision of the Bush administration be incorrect. Better instead to avoid preemption's hurtling temporality by turning to history, a turn that both Congress and the public at large have made by debating the degree to which Iraq is like Vietnam. Like Spiegelman, these debates deploy history to mitigate the forward-march of what many fear is a war without end. But Spiegelman's text also reveals that we need not wait for preemption before countering it with historical time. The past cannot only disarm preemption, it can also offer its own solution to the paradox of time and knowledge, as it suggests that we need not immediately succumb to the lose-lose choice between acting without knowing and knowing without acting. Instead, like Spiegelman in his moment of trauma, we can look to the past for the histories that best personify us, making our present both more alive and less out of control than it would otherwise be.

NOTES

1. For an elaboration of Freud's ideas on the temporality of trauma, see *Beyond the Pleasure Principle*, Laplanche, and Caruth.
2. Following Spiegelman's lead, "comix" refers to his work and "comics" refers to the reproductions of historical material included in the appendix.
3. See Abel for a reading of DeLillo's essay that treats its cinematic temporality as an alternative to "simile and analogy."
4. For examples of this impasse in phenomenology, see Bergson's distinction between intuition and intellect in *Creative Evolution*; Heidegger's "Letter on Humanism," which describes the limits of his *Being and Time*; Deleuze's *Logic of Sense* on the struggle to represent "Aionic" time; and Ricouer's third volume of *Time and Narrative* on the inherent "aporicity" of any phenomenology of temporality.

WORKS CITED

Abel, Marco. "'In the Ruins of the Future': Literature, Images, and the Rhetoric of Seeing 9/11." *PMLA* 118 (2003): 1236–50.

Bergson, Henri. *Creative Evolution*. Trans. Arthur Mitchell. Westport, CT: Greenwood P, 1975.

Bush, George. "Bush's Speech at the National Cathedral." *Free Republic* 14 Sept. 2001. 29 May 2007 http://www.freerepublic.com/focus/f-news/523290/posts.

Caruth, Cathy. *Unclaimed Experience: Trauma, Narrative, and History*. Baltimore: Johns Hopkins UP, 1996.

CNN. "Top Bush officials push case against Saddam." *CNN.com/insidepolitics* 8 Sept. 2002. 29 May 2007 http://archives.cnn.com/2002/ALLPOLITICS/09/08/iraq.debate.

Deleuze, Gilles. *The Logic of Sense*. Trans. Mark Lester. New York: Columbia UP, 1990.

DeLillo, Don. "In the Ruins of the Future." *Harper's Magazine* 303 (December 2001): 33–40.

Foer, Jonathan Safran. *Extremely Loud & Incredibly Close*. Boston: Houghton Mifflin, 2005.

Heidegger, Martin. "Letter on Humanism." *Basic Writings*. Ed. David Krell. San Francisco: Harper Collins, 1977.

Kirn, Walter. "Everything is Included." *New York Times Book Review* 3 April 2005.

Laplanche, Jean. "An Interview with Jean Laplanche." By Cathy Caruth. *Postmodern Culture* 11.2 (2001) http://www3.iath.virginia.edu/pmc/.

———. "Notes on Afterwardness." *Essays on Otherness*. Ed. John Fletcher. New York: Routledge, 1998. 260–65.

McGlothlin, Erin. "No Time Like the Present: Narrative and Time in Art Spiegelman's *Maus*." *Narrative* 11 (2003): 177–98.

Palumbo-Liu, David. "Preemption, Perpetual War, and the Future of the Imagination." *boundary 2* 33 (2006): 151–69.

Posner, Richard. "The 9/11 Report: A Dissent." *New York Times Book Review* 29 Aug. 2004: 1 and 9–11.

Pozorski, Aimee. "Trauma's Time." *Connecticut Review* 28 (2006): 71–76.

Ricoeur, Paul. *Time and Narrative*. Vol. 3. Trans. Kathleen McLaughlin, David Pellauer, and Kathleen Blamey. Chicago: U of Chicago P, 1984.

Rumsfeld, Donald. "Press Conference by U.S. Secretary of Defense." *NATO* 6 June 2002. 29 May 2007 http://www.nato.int/docu/speech/2002/s020606g.htm.

Spiegelman, Art. *In the Shadow of No Towers*. New York: Pantheon, 2004.

———. *Maus II: And Here My Troubles Began*. New York: Pantheon, 1991.

3 Graphic Implosion
Politics, Time, and Value in Post-9/11 Comics

Simon Cooper and Paul Atkinson

Why analyze comic books (including comics, graphic novels, and graphic short stories) in relation to September 11, 2001? Of course such narratives, with their own distinctive representational strategies and aesthetic forms, are worth examining as a "response" in their own right, but in the case of 9/11 other issues make comic books a compelling case for study: for instance, the uncanny resemblance between the starkly rendered political landscape of the "war on terror" and the moral universe of the mainstream comic book. The Bush administration's depiction of a Manichean post-9/11 world of heroes and villains has sounded at times like a classic comic book scenario. Indeed, if superhero comics are replete with the logic of the vigilante, this same logic also came to mark the way the U.S. administration would govern after the attacks on the World Trade Center.[1] In this sense the generally conservative morality underpinning the comic book universe was echoed in the 9/11 public rhetoric raising the question: would comic books post-9/11 continue to operate in the same way? Given the degree of self-reflexivity that the genre had developed, especially since the 1980s, how would comic books react to a world that seemed increasingly to resemble its own fantasized constructions? The introduction of an extra-diegetic event into the world of the comic book also entails the convergence of mythological and historical worlds. Generally, serialized comic books (and superhero comics especially) are predicated upon the exclusion of history in the sense that characters cannot directly intervene in history.[2] As Umberto Eco observes with respect to *Superman,* if the genre incorporates historical events, the narrative risks exhausting itself due to the limitations imposed by the unchangeable events (123). For comics to include directly events such as 9/11 involves a shift where the comic universe is linked to a non-diegetic historical progression that stretches the compatibility of historical and mythological environments. In a genre predicated upon heroes who consistently save cities from disaster, how might comics respond to a situation where such heroes failed or were absent?

In this article we examine the central themes in a number of mainstream comic books,[3] in particular the two volumes of *9–11—Artists Respond* and issue 36 of *Amazing Spider-Man* and to a lesser extent the collections *A Moment of Silence* and *Heroes*.[4] The first part of the article introduces general themes of memorialization and representation in post-9/11 comic books. Using the work of Derrida and others to register the particular paradoxes and limits to "marking a date in history," we explore tensions within comic books as they attempt to attribute an absolute singularity to an event that marks itself as "beyond comprehension," yet whose images of urban destruction are all too familiar to comic book readers. At the center of this tension stands the superhero, examined primarily in a reading of *Amazing Spider-Man #36,* who is unable to intervene directly but allows for the event to be both registered and incomprehensible though a transcendental act of "witnessing." The second part of the article deals largely with the stories collected in *9/11—Artists Respond* and explores the tension between the representation of the liberal ideals of tolerance and diversity and the formal and narrative limitations that work against them. While many of the stories are concerned with representing the reactions and responses of "ordinary" New York citizens, and run counter to the generic pursuit of justice and punishment, we argue that they close down the possibility of difference and diversity at the same time that they attempt to represent and celebrate such ideals. This is considered as part of a more widespread "intolerant liberalism," noted by writers such as Stanley Fish (2006) and Slavoj Žižek ("A Plea" 2002), that marked the political and cultural context post-9/11.

Despite the differences in terms of their subjects, we argue that these comics are governed by a similar approach that idealizes the heterogeneous traditions of U.S. culture and society, but in a way that fails to engage with the significance of contemporary cultural difference. The superhero comics cannot help but function within a conservative economy where the superhero figure bears the burden of the suffering of the community, but does so in a singular voice which stands in for the collective other. Jarret Lovell argues that many superheroes, such as Superman, are "group servants" dedicated to upholding the moral values of the community (165). Conversely, since many of the comics focus on the citizens of New York, these stories ought to allow for a range of perspectives, but they actually mirror the voice of the superhero. Ultimately both these discourses, the superhero as transcendent witness and the invocation of a liberal imaginary, work to frame 9/11 so as to preclude politically and historically embedded interpretations of these events.

THE SUPERHERO AS TRANSCENDENT WITNESS TO 9/11

In an extended interview with Giovanna Borradori, Jacques Derrida argues that in an analysis of 9/11 we must first ask what it means to *"fait date,"* "to mark a date in history" (85). This is important to the analysis of post-9/11 comic books because so many were produced as responses, where the writers and artists felt they must act immediately to register the historical significance of the event. The event is always conceived within the framework of a discursive response and not as an object in itself. The form of the event and its significance depend on the nature of the response and the temporal boundaries erected around it—a national event marking the end of American innocence, an international event incorporating notions of global capitalism, a community event, or indeed a media event. If we focus on the media, the event is shaped by the temporal rhythms of the news as an ongoing spectacle over and above issues of suffering or the place of the United States in a global political context. For Derrida, one of the defining characteristics of an historical event is that it is "unprecedented," for if it was prefigured then its status as an historical turning point would be brought into question—there must be some level of "immediacy":

> "To mark a date in history" presupposes, in any case, that "something" comes or happens for the first and last time, "something" that we do not yet really know how to identify, determine, recognize, or analyze but that should remain from here on in unforgettable: an ineffaceable event in the shared archive of a universal calendar, that is, a *supposedly* universal calendar. (86)

In other words, we should question what it means to conceptualize the historical event as a singularity, which in the case of 9/11 is underpinned by the use of a date in lieu of a name. The date testifies to a degree of uncertainty as to the form and nature of the event (86), which is, in part, due to the diffuse form of the attack, dispersed across the country unlike the locatable Pearl Harbor bombardment. To name an event by a date is both to separate it from the continuity of history, for this date can be applied to no other event in a "universal calendar," as well as to ritualize and memorialize the event in annual remembrance days. Simon Jenkins, in the *Guardian*, calls the media's response to 9/11 "anniversary journalism" (15). This looking forward to understand the present is a key feature of many of the comic books, but it is most notable in Paul Levitz's graphic story "Tradition," where we are transported into the future specified by the exact date "Sunset, 9/21/11." A woman and child listen to the mobile phone message of someone we assume to be the dead husband. This message is framed by another event, the lighting of the Yahrzeit candle, and the two are brought together in the final caption "Tradition new and old" (*Artists Remember* 45). In this context, the present event (the loss of life) requires the invocation of the universal in the phrase "time immemorial" where the present historical conditions are erased in the name of a "universal calendar."

This positioning of September 11 in a "universal calendar" is also a feature of issue 36 of *Amazing Spider-Man* written by J. Michael Straczynski, but, in contrast to stories such as "Tradition," this occurs within the temporal framework of the comic book series and its universe. The decision to devote an issue to the destruction of the Twin Towers was not made by the writers but by the publisher who decided this was one event that required a response. *Spider-Man* was chosen because it is based in New York and the then-current writer

Straczynski was asked to write it. He thought that the task would be impossible, but nevertheless he sent a script only twenty-four hours after he received the request (Yarbrough par. 6). The structure of the issue's representation is guided both by the extra-diegetic decision to respond by the New York-based Marvel Comics and by the requirement to explain adequately the narrative rupture to a serialized audience. Straczynski's solution is to situate the event as the beginning of a new age and, in its singularity, to separate it from both the serialized narrative and a concrete socio-political context.

The visual structure of *Spider-Man* is integral to this process, as it isolates the event through the articulation of a visual space specific to September 11, a narrative Ground Zero or year one. The opening page is largely black and contains in its center the uncaptioned text, "We interrupt our regularly scheduled program to bring you the following Special Bulletin" and in the lower corner the captioned text "Longitude 74 degrees, 0 minutes, 23 seconds west. Latitude, 40 degrees, 42 minutes, 51 seconds north . . . follow the sound of sirens" (1). This captioned text, which we soon discover to be the voice of Spider-Man,[5] uses the exact coordinates to situate the event in terms of a spatial absolute. In doing so, the destruction of the towers is construed as a global event rather than as one specific to a community or to a lived place, such as Canal Street. Moreover, the text registers the event as the point of reference for all other events, and Spider-Man, in uttering such words, is one of the first to recognize its significance. It is a statement of presence which serves as the starting point for a larger historical notion of time, rationalized in terms of abstract dates and calendar times (Ricoeur 154). The spatial description situates Spider-Man at the event and carries the connotations of documentary evidence; he is not only present but his statements are important as acts of reportage. In contrast, the uncaptioned text in conjunction with the black panel sets up the boundaries of a temporal absolute. Time in comic books is largely indicated by the sequence of panels and a black panel on the first page prepares the reader for what is about to be seen, a point before time and the event, broadly interpreted as the *ex nihilo* of creation. If the black panel appeared in the middle of a page, it could represent night, the death of a character, or a general pause or break in the narrative, but when placed in the beginning it separates issue 36 from the *Amazing Spider-Man* series, the "regularly scheduled program," and introduces the event as a singularity. The broadcasting schedule also serves as a metaphor for the flow of history which is ruptured due to the magnitude of the event. The artifice of the broadcasting schedule is highlighted by the lack of further reference in the text and by its contrast with the actual coverage of the event, where televisions were filled with images of the planes hitting—a relentless presence rather than an absence.

The opening blank screen gives way, with the turn of the page, to the comic's most extraordinary image, a splash page depicting Ground Zero shortly after the collapse of the towers (see Figure 3.1). The burning wreck fills the double-page spread, and the dust frames rather than obscures Spider-Man's view of the disaster. The artist John Romita, Jr., creates an image

Figure 3.1a The Amazing Spider-Man, issue #36 © 2001, John Romita, Jr., art, and J. Michael Straczynski, text

Figure 3.1b The Amazing Spider-Man, issue #36 © 2001, John Romita, Jr., art, and J. Michael Straczynski, text

that is worthy of the event[6] in that it pushes the visual limits of the page and arrests the narrative. The splash page fashions the exceptional event through its emphasis on the spectacle rather than narrative movement, and because its impact depends on the turn of the page—the borderline between visibility and invisibility—it is one of the few visual devices in the comic book that can truly deliver the unforeseen image. This is in marked contrast to the typical process of comic book reading where the eye roams across the page and glances at the comic's immediate future in a continuous process of pro-tension. The visual impact is further emphasized by the long description of the spatial coordinates on page one, which forces the reader to pause before turning the page. When the page is turned, the viewer stops, and the action is complete because the double page spread does not contain the narrative and temporal markers of the gutter and panel. Time is enclosed within the page as Spider-Man looks in horror at what is before him, and for the reader this extended time of visual contemplation opens up the space of memorial-ization. This is also a feature of the single-page spreads in *Heroes,* many of which use the diagonal lines of the Twin Towers' reinforcements to draw the eye to the center of the image. It is only the voice of Spider-Man, discreetly presented in captions at the foot of the page, that gently directs the reader away from the image, with the wide spacing of the captions ensuring that the eye's movement across the page is slow and reverential.

One of the features of the comic book is the separation between text and image, and in *Amazing Spider-Man* #36 this is manifest as a tension between two modes of representation. The text accompanying the splash page positions Spider-Man as a witness to the scene and following the ini-tial exclamation, "God," reveals the superhero's thoughts: "some things are beyond words. . . . Beyond comprehension. . . . Beyond forgiveness" (2–3). These words mirror Straczynski's account of writing the comic: "Ever since the events surrounding the WTC, I have said little because [. . .] I simply didn't have the words and didn't know where to look for them" (Yarbrough par. 3). Nevertheless the words came in the form of Spider-Man's extended reflection on the events—a grandiose collection of thoughts resembling the overburdened speeches of Straczynski's *Babylon 5.* Interestingly, it is in speech, not the image, that the comic book invokes the unspeakable as a supplement to the plenitude of the image, or spectacle. The words, however, seem out of place in a superhero comic where images of destruction are com-mon (the burnt-out city, the destroyed planet, the threatened monument, etc.) and, within the genre, are certainly not "beyond comprehension."

In the broader context of New York City, the event was imaginable because, as John Bird states, New York is one of the world's most visualiz-able cities not only because of its size and monumental architecture, but also because of the vast number of films and television series that use it as a backdrop. Moreover, the destruction of New York and the Twin Towers has been pre-empted by being represented in many such texts (86). For Slavoj Žižek, the destruction of the towers was aestheticized both by the

terrorists, who aimed to create a media event, and by the style of the televised coverage which had much in common with film and disaster movies
(11). The New York based author Siri Hustvedt concurs with Žižek and
states that the attacks conform to the "thrilling spectacle[s]" envisioned
by Hollywood, but adds, "We could all imagine it. It's the fact of it that
annihilated the fantasy" (par. 11). This theme is explored in a number
of the post-9/11 comic books, including the story "The Real Thing" by
the veteran New York comic writer and artist Will Eisner, where a group
of Hollywood producers gather in an office close to the Twin Towers. In
response to one suggestion that the Empire State Building should be used as
the site of a disaster, the head of the group states: "Oh, gawd! Not a King
Kong thing! We need reality here! . . . Special effects stuff, everybody's
got! . . . What sells in the real thing!" On the subsequent page the group
is rendered silent as they look out the office window at the burning Twin
Towers (17–18). Eisner returns to this theme with his story "Reality 9/11"
in *9–11: Emergency Relief,* where a man covered in dust sits slumped in
his armchair watching Ground Zero on a broken and bleeding television
(45). "Reality" in each of these cases has that particular quality of rendering the viewer silent, and silence even serves as the premise for one of the
Marvel volumes, *A Moment of Silence.* In this collection, the graphic stories are told with images because, according to the editor, there is too much
"meaningless chatter," and it is more "fitting to tell the story of real heroes
with nothing but depictions of their selfless deeds" and to "Judge people
by what they do, not by what they say" (37). In this case it is heroism that
is beyond words and only truly understood in an image. What is interesting in these examples, and there are many more embodying this theme,[7]
is that the visual is posited as something that exceeds representation but
only through the negation of another medium—the comic book image is
not-film, not-television, not-"meaningless chatter." In each case the representational structure of the comic book is ignored.

In all of these examples, the real is posited in the narrative structure
or in the editor's comments, but in *Amazing Spider-Man #36* the real is
asserted through the contrast of word and image, where the comic book
shows and then denies the comprehensibility of what is seen. Jan Baetens
argues that comic books must decide whether to show or hide an object,
but a written text, through the mechanism of negation, can both negate
and affirm an object in the same utterance and thus invoke the unspeakable or unknowable (par. 3). In post-9/11 comic books, the text negates
and imposes a logic of the unspeakable on the witnessed and affirmed
image of the collapsing towers; the images are not sufficiently unspeakable since they only serve to reimagine an existing media spectacle. In
Mo Willems' "Walking the Williamsburg Bridge to Work," the protagonist, on witnessing the attacks, has his inability to speak noted in three
speech balloons, two of which contain ellipses and the other the negation "can't be" (100–01). The character is not speaking, but the act of

not speaking is affirmed through the speech balloons, which means that the incomprehensibility of the event is twice removed from the image. In short, the incomprehension is made comprehensible on the level of the text and is added to the generically comprehensible image.[8] Even if it is accepted that September 11 was unforeseen or incomprehensible, this can only be depicted indirectly in the comic book.

The conventions used to express the singularity and exceptionalism of September 11, however, are not necessarily specific to the comic book medium but may be derived from a wider culture of memorialization. Andreas Huyssen argues that since the 1980s, there has been a "globalization" of "memory culture" with the Holocaust serving as a "universal trope" that erases the particular details of a range of traumatic events, including Kosovo (13–14).[9] Barbie Zelizer argues that to bear witness was an integral feature of General Eisenhower's opening up of the concentration camps to photographers. One of the key tropes of this photography was images of people "bearing witness" to various images from the camps which extended to "people looking at photographic exhibits of the atrocities" (53). The act of witnessing was transmuted into a moral act, "the ultimate public response, in that it signified a level of responsibility on the part of the publics who had until then largely been unresponsive" (53–54). In the depiction of September 11 there was a reduplication of the many types of witnessing and this distinguished it from other human atrocities including those in Rwanda and Cambodia (54). In addition to the lack of actual images of human carnage,

> the photographic aesthetic had four main parts, each depicted repeatedly: the site of the attack—primarily the World Trade Center; people witnessing the site of the attack; people witnessing the site of the attack without depiction of the site itself; and people viewing depictions of the site of the attack (primarily photographs) or taking photographs themselves. (Zelizer 57)

Some of the first shots were of locals such as fire fighters gazing at the ruins but over the coming months this came to include a long list of dignitaries bearing witness, each of which was documented in the papers (60). In the post-9/11 comic books these conventions are reproduced and in many the act of bearing witness is invested in a single figure, the superhero, who heroically witnesses on behalf of the whole population.[10] The first third of *Amazing Spider-Man #36* has the superhero witnessing Ground Zero from a range of vantage points with the captions, similar to a voice-over in film, stating his inability to understand what he sees. In *Heroes*, the opening image depicts the Hulk on his knees weeping while holding a fireman's cap (Quesada 1). The Silver Surfer witnesses a flash on the surface of the earth and a weeping Captain America is superimposed on the burning New York skyline (3, 7). In *9–11—The World's Finest Comic Book Writers & Artists Tell Stories to*

Remember, Jimmy Olsen stands looking up to the sky in a state of shock, holding his camera but not yet ready to take a photo (173). On the cover of the same volume, Superman stands with Krypton reverentially looking up at a large image depicting a range of rescue workers, and all Superman can say is "wow." In addition to the superhero references, there are many drawings of the various memorials, fire fighters weeping and images of people gazing at the "missing" posters or watching the events on television.

All of these images of bearing witness share a common lineage, but those of superheroes should be distinguished because they represent a departure from the conventions of the superhero genre. To see superheroes standing solemn before a disaster is in marked contrast to the usual representations of superheroes intervening in moments of crisis. The act of witnessing is the only form of action because the superheroes could not intervene in an event that has already occurred. Mourning and witnessing become heroic acts where the anguished expressions and muscular stances of these exceptional figures serve as indexical signs marking out the event in history, making it truly singular. In this context the superhero is not open to the tragedy, as something that is truly unforeseeable or beyond words. In one image by Carlos Pacheco, we see a group of superheroes, including Captain America and Thor, holding candles with heads bowed. The captioned text by Kurt Busiek reads: "And There Came a Day. A Day Unlike Any Other . . . when Earth's mightiest heroes found themselves united against a common threat" (Quesada 13). The subsequent text informs us that the words were originally applied to the Avengers but now can be used to describe the fire fighters; there is little doubt, due to their prominence in the image, that they must also apply to the superheroes. In another image, Captain America is weeping on his knees, but his contrapposto stance and the raising of his arms by the fire fighters transforms his anguish into a heroic gesture.

In *Amazing Spider-Man #36,* the protagonist and other heroes from the Marvel universe only act in the form of helping out fire fighters or small children. For the most part, they stand defiantly looking at the ruins in a state of mourning. Importantly, they do not speak, and it is only Spider-Man who provides the commentary that joins the present act of witnessing with the trans-historical heroic gesture. The superhero is posited not as a figure for this one time, attendant on the event, but for all time both as the will of the people and the personification of an American mythos. When asked by one of the injured why it happened Spider-Man does not directly reply, but his voice over provides the response: "My God, why? I have seen other worlds, other spaces. I have walked with Gods and wept with angels. But to my shame I have no answers" (Straczynski 15). The figure of Spider-Man is projected across the whole of a fictional history, rather than localized as a citizen of New York, where his role is to indicate the importance of the event. In a subsequent passage, the hero's voice accompanies a series of images heroically portraying ordinary citizens: "In such days as these are heroes born. Not heroes such as ourselves. The true heroes of the Twenty-First century. You, the human being singular. You, who are nobler than you know and stronger than you think. You the heroes of this moment chosen out of history" (20). Spider-Man must stand outside history, looking on the "universal calendar," in order to recognize fully the exceptionalism of the present. This relegation of the superhero to history's witness provides a false testimony because it adds nothing to what the readers have already witnessed in photographs or on television. What it does do is obliquely answer the question asked in many of the comic books, including *Amazing Spider-Man #36*, "Where were you! How could you let this happen?" (4).[11] In other words, where were the gods when we needed them—a question that has been asked repeatedly in relation to many of the world's worst tragedies. This question cannot be answered sufficiently due to the separation of the fictional and non-fictional worlds but, in the guise of history's witness, the superheroes can still be seen to act through projecting themselves beyond the present as both universal memory and a universal will. Post-9/11 comics direct the reader away from speculation on *"what will happen,"* through a redefinition of what has already happened. In *Amazing Spider-Man #36*, it is all about situating the hero relative to the event, putting him in place, rather than describing his role in changing events. When Spider-Man states: "You cannot see us for the dust, but we are here. . . . You cannot hear us for the cries, but we are here" (8), the voice renders the heroes non-present but in conjunction with the images, makes them omnipresent. There is both a negation and an affirmation, for the mythological heroes are always here but are never here in the sense that they can act upon the present or change an event. The superheroes are shrouded by the dust and viewed only by a few and are, consequently, largely invisible at Ground Zero.

In most of the post-9/11 superhero comics, the extra-diegetic space of Ground Zero is incorporated into the diegetic space of the comic with the effect of eliding the difference between the two worlds. Richard Reynolds argues that historical continuity, both in the sense of chronological story development and its relationship with non-diegetic historical events, is generally subordinate to the "metatextual structural continuity" in which the character's actions remain consistent with the unity of the mythological universe (45). The "reality" of the fictional universe depends on its consistency and even in these comics incorporating the events of 9/11 continuity remains paramount. One way of ensuring this continuity is restricting the focus of the superhero comic books to interaction with anonymous figures, the general heroes and victims who occupy the site in popular mythology. There are certainly no instances of Superman or Spider-Man chatting with George W. Bush or Mayor Giuliani about the present destruction or future courses of action. This limitation is clearly examined in Steven T. Seagle's story (art by Duncan Rouleau and Aaron Sowd) "Unreal," where Superman reflects on his various abilities—"I can defy the laws of gravity. I can ignore the principles of physics" (15)—with each statement accompanied by an image of the hero in action. These heroic claims, however, are followed by the lament, "But unfortunately . . . the one thing I can not do . . . is break free from the fictional pages where I live and breathe . . . become real during times of crisis" (16). The image zooms out to reveal a young boy reading the comic while a fire fighter carries him from the burning wreckage of the Twin Towers—an impossibility. The fictional Superman salutes the fire fighter with the words "a world fortunately protected by heroes of its own" (16). In this example and many others, the fictional and non-fictional worlds are joined in the figure of the hero with numerous images depicting the superheroes passing the baton to the new heroes, the rescue workers. The most typical image of this type is J. Scott Campbell and Hi-Fi's image of various Marvel figures lifting up the arms of the rescue workers in a gesture of respect (Campbell and Hi-Fi 23). There is a celebration of the moment of transformation when real life heroes must replace those of the mythic universe, the comic book writers' ultimate homage. In a page by Tim Sale, a young boy dressed in a Superman t-shirt runs into a phone booth and emerges wearing an FDNY t-shirt (Levitz 70). The transformation is complete with the readers also accepting the movement from the mythic figure of the superhero to the localized fire fighter. Marvel tried to cash in on this shift in cultural value with a serialized comic about rescue workers called *The Call Of Duty,* but it was not very popular and remained in print only for a couple of years.

FROM SUPERHERO TO CITIZEN: THE CULTURAL CONTRADICTIONS OF A LIBERAL RESPONSE

In the change of narrative focus from the superhero to the firefighter the figure of the child remains. The child stands on the threshold of two ways of viewing the world, looking to the past with the weight of history and looking to the future with hope (Nyberg 182). If the child chooses not to look back, he is tied to a present that is wholly innocent, a liberal imaginary that is yet to feel the force of anti-liberal sentiment. This is a liberalism of innocence rather than reasoned tolerance, ethical judgment, or celebrated difference. There is no understanding of diversity or difference because the past is occluded, and all that remains is a present governed by good intentions.

The tropes of revenge and violence, normally endemic to the superhero comic, were often avoided in responses to 9/11 in their considered attempts to both incorporate and memorialize 9/11 as a singular event. The limited agency of the superhero figure provides a means of mythologizing 9/11 and rendering it, at least within this cultural sphere, as unanalyzable and disconnected from politics and history. However, many of the graphic stories in the mainstream collections represent 9/11 not so much in terms of an epic passivity but through a series of little narratives incorporating the perspectives of New York citizens. This section explores how other mainstream comic book writers respond to 9/11 through a contradictory liberal imaginary and outside the framework of the superhero. Such an imaginary invokes the ideals of tolerance, diversity, and difference, but only at a superficial level, and indeed often reduces the radical potential of such difference. In particular the *9–11—Artists Respond* anthology contains many stories that avoid themes normally central to the genre, and in their place it is possible to identify several features common to most of the contributions, in particular, a tension between an appeal to openness at a thematic level and a closing down of difference at a formal level. First, many of the stories resort to allegorical modes and restage Biblical narratives such as the "Fall" and the "Tower of Babel." In one story there is a reworking of an Aesop's fable, while in another an alien intelligence visits a traumatized nation and inspires its citizens to adopt the values of tolerance, love for country, world peace and so on. Second, many stories appeal to the values of pluralism and multiculturalism *but in a highly specific way* that works to close down, rather than promote difference. Third, the protagonists of these graphic stories are predominantly children, whose acts of witnessing construct a particular spectator position that prevents political reflection on the events.

In *Artists Respond* the multicultural composition of New York is repeatedly alluded to—whether in the form of children of various ethnicities witnessing the burning towers, stories of the background of 9/11 victims and survivors, images of Middle Eastern shopkeepers handing out sweets to children, or in fire fighters rescuing victims from different racial backgrounds. This invocation of diversity is, however, often undercut through the use of allegorical frameworks. By alluding to Biblical stories, Aesop's fables, and science-fiction utopias, the narratives in *Artists Respond* elide the historical specificity of cultural difference. If 9/11 can be framed in terms of a metaphoric and Biblically-derived cycle of drought and renewal, as told by Mira Freedman in "Jeremiah 17" (*Artists Respond* 112–13), or the United States can be personified as a humble elephant (*Artists Remember* 177–80), or if rescue workers hoist a flag on top of a pile of rubble in a pose identical to the iconic image of soldiers at Iwo Jima (Mason 144), then the act of interpretation, of understanding, is to a degree foreclosed because it has already been pre-empted. In relying on allegorical modes of storytelling these narratives work to limit the possibilities of difference by asking us to see one thing as the repetition of another (Murray 16). In this context, the allegory works to suppress historical and political differences, the causal framework underpinning an event, in order to point out similarities. The similarities are rarely structural but instead refer to the importance of the events in popular and local cultural memory. Iwo Jima is chosen because of its nationalist resonance rather than featuring other, more appropriate examples, such as the attempt to destroy the British Houses of Parliament by Guy Fawkes. There is also a visual resonance that allows for the easy substitution of types, a fabled elephant for the nation, and fire fighters for soldiers. The connotations of one are mapped onto the other without a process of negotiation, explanation, or analysis. This is the dehistoricization of time through pastiche, which relies on the connotative force of a visual and popular imaginary to mark the place of the event in history rather than relying on the grand gesture of a heroic figure.

In contrast are those graphic stories which work metonymically rather than metaphorically. In metonymy, one sign is substituted for another based on contiguity or association; this kind of substitution has the capacity to destabilize the sign because the sign is never fixed within any given context. In the case of 9/11, metonymy shifts the focus away from the meaning of the event, in *itself*, to an exploration of context. In *Artists Respond* the main example of metonymical narrative is Alan Moore and Melinda Gebbie's "This is Information" (185–90).[12] The narrative differs substantially in both form and content because it works through association rather than linear progression, the series of even panels across each page give no priority to any particular image or idea (thus avoiding the trap of fetishization or overdetermination). The narrative moves across different times and places and is one of the only treatments of 9/11 to go outside of New York—moving to the UK and Europe, to the painting of Guernica in the Spanish Civil War, to the medieval crusades, to Afghanistan. This historical movement also serves to critique the claims of singularity because 9/11 is relativized among a collection of important historical events—it no longer stands alone in time immemorial. The narrative moves through its associative techniques from history to politics to mythology and back again, and the meaning slips from the private to the public, from the Crusades to the war on terror, from suffering to humor. Moore and Gebbie are also the only writers in the collection to reflexively comment on the implication of "comic book morality" (189) in the war on terror—drawing Osama bin Laden (a figure almost entirely absent from other contributions) as a Bond villain.[13] In fact the final panel of the story contains one of the most powerful images drawn in response to 9/11—as the hand of a survivor reaches within the rubble to grasp a seemingly alive hand of a dead victim. This powerful image of connection with the dead, coming as it does at the end of a whole series of interpretative possibilities, suggests that we honor the dead and ourselves by not foreclosing on the meaning of 9/11, by thinking through other wars and struggles in history, and by working through the significance of events at a number of levels, rather than remaining fixed within a single perspective.

Outside of the opposition between history and myth, other stories attempt to depict the ideals of difference and pluralism more directly but usually in the form of an idealized present. These stories involve images of a cross-section of New York citizens depicted as either witnesses to the WTC attacks, victims of them, or part of the larger background that led to the current greatness of America. For example, part of a story by Brian McDonald and Brian O'Connell (*Artists Respond* 100) depicts a scene of ethnically diverse faces floating in space staring back at the viewer with blank expressions. This disembodied representation of ethnic diversity is drawn against an evenly spaced white background and connotes a bland and unthreatening form of difference one robbed not only of bodies and ground, but also of history and agency. The image suspends these abstract figures, which stand for our diversity and tolerance, in an eternal present where they do nothing and ask nothing from us except provide an easily consumed form of multiculturalism. These figures can only represent the nation as a collective—a unitary image and an image of unity—and, consequently, they are deprived of the right to speak, that is, to speak differently.

A very similar image forms the subject of Eric Powel's contribution (*Artists Respond* 7). Here a series of ethnically diverse and disembodied subjects solemnly gaze out from beneath an American flag while a lone fire fighter looks on, effectively cementing the familiar dichotomy of multicultural passivity and singular heroic activity in the form of the ubiquitous rescue worker. Other examples include the untitled story by Steve Niles and Paul Lee, where subjects from diverse ethnic backgrounds are shown in almost identical postures, first witnessing the attacks, then being rescued and comforted (*Artists Respond* 155–58). Peter Pachoumis provides a similar collection of diverse and disembodied faces gazing above at the destruction (*Artists Respond* 66). In "Ground Zero: A dream I had on Sep 9, 2001," Al Davison depicts a cross-section of children who emerge from various scenes of destruction and chaos to gather in a circle and witness a giant flowering tree emerge from the urban ruin (*Artists Respond* 188–89). The children's universality and sameness-in-difference is revealed though drawing them within equally-spaced frames and wearing similar expressions. The final scene, where the children gather around the tree, reduces them to abstract figures forming part of a circle, their own stories and contexts are subsumed within this new symbolic universalism. In the joyous and naïve world of the children, there is no past only an ahistorical understanding of the principles of liberalism.

This invocation of abstract difference connects with a wider cultural context, which Stanley Fish calls the "liberal religion." Fish argues that contemporary Western culture is one where "everything is permitted, but nothing is to be taken seriously." This kind of hollow pluralism functions as a new morality, "the morality of a withdrawal from morality in any strong insistent form." Tolerance is possible only to the extent that one is not forced to take the other seriously. When the other reacts in a way that confronts the liberal subject directly—say in the case of riots following the publication of cartoons in Denmark depicting the prophet as a terrorist—one finds instead an aggressive intolerance toward the other. Thus, tolerance is only possible if it costs the self nothing. The "others" depicted in *Artists Respond* as disembodied faces, passive witnesses, or victims are figures that the reader does not have to confront fully.

This "thinned out" ideal of tolerance can be connected to other political struggles over the memorialization of 9/11. Part of the cultural component of one plan for Ground Zero was a new museum called the "International Freedom Center," which would tell the story of struggles for freedom at other times and in other cultures. This met with widespread resistance from particular lobby groups and some families of victims who felt that such a display diluted the message of the Ground Zero memorial. Political pressure was put on the Governor who agreed to scrap the project, "oblivious to the irony of censoring a monument to freedom" (Goldberger par. 3). As Fish observes, the gesture towards liberal tolerance under contemporary conditions all too often masks a deeper intolerance. The disembodied heads and decontextualized subjects of the multicultural community celebrated in *Artists Respond* may invoke the other, but their representational strategies reveal an other that one can all too easily assimilate. For Peter Brooker such strategies "reaffirm an assimilative American national imaginary" where liberal values work to homogenize difference in the name of tolerance and freedom (17). Another version of such an "imaginary" occurs in the one-page story by Pat Moriarty (*Artists Respond* 58), where a giant if somewhat beleaguered figure of Uncle Sam kneels and prays, asking "Dear God, Allah, Supreme Spaceman, Great Pumpkin, whoever you are—please stop the cycle of hatred," while behind him stand two opposing pro-and anti-U.S. groups holding placards. The manner in which the mythologized figure of Uncle Sam towers over the more (perhaps "too") human figures in the background is indicative of how a universalizing impulse, wrapped in national iconography, is derived at the expense of more worldly politics. Like Spider-Man, the iconic Uncle Sam is placed in the omniscient realm of the gods and outside of history with its transient squabbles and differences in opinion.

Behind nearly all of these graphic stories lies a disavowal of politics or history. The fable allows for one form of disavowal, the invocation of a universal-but-thin multiculturalism provides another. A third form, perhaps the most widespread within the two volume collection, involves the predominance of stories about children. Children form part of a more general trope of innocence. They are depicted as victims, witnessing but uncomprehending, even wielding model planes, unaware of their role in the mass destruction they are watching. In an image by Patrick Zircher, Derek Fridolfs, and Hi-Fi, two schoolgirls in a classroom hold hands as they witness the burning of the towers on a television screen. The innocence of their bond is all that is needed to protect them from the lessons of history (Quesada 12). Significantly their backs are turned to preclude the possibility of any individualized response as the focal point remains fixed on the televised event. Children are often shown in the absence of parents, who might invoke a more worldly connection to events. In a story by Robert Kirkman and Tony Moore, the only adult figure appears on television, as distant and as abstract as the burning towers that one child cannot help but witness (*Artists Respond* 164). In Figure 3.2, we see groups of children with their backs turned to the WTC playing games, unaware of the destruction behind them. The lone child who is witness, shares an awareness and spectator position with the reader. This identification allows a strategy of disavowal to come into play. Just as the question "why did this happen to us?" remained unanswerable after 9/11, so too the tension between knowledge and innocence is subsumed within this figure of the single child and our connection to her and her gaze. It allows the reader to

Figure 3.2 Published by Dark Horse Comics, Inc.

be both innocent *and* knowing at the same time by adopting the position of the lone child who witnesses as an adult. One can share an adult's horror at the degree of mass suffering, while retaining a child's innocence with respect to issues of causation and explanation.

The centrality of the child figure to many of these stories invokes a passive witness to suffering and as such resonates with the passivity of the civilian population at large, compelled to watch the events of 9/11 repeatedly on television. Here one might also recall President Bush's appeal to citizens to "shop, fly, and spend" at the outset of the "war on terror," a supplication that contrasts sharply with the more conventional rallying of the citizenry around a war effort, asking for civic support and individual sacrifice. Like the cultural response more generally, and in a similar way to *Amazing Spider-Man #36*, agency within these comics remains within the limited sphere of the new "heroes"—the fire fighters and rescue workers frozen within an idealized tableaux. For instance Rob Haynes, Tim Townsend, and David Self depict Captain America on his knees overcome by grief, and it is only a child wearing a t-shirt emblazoned with "I NY" that can restore him to purpose (Quesada 19). Agency outside of the heroic remains generally a taboo subject for 9/11; for example, one thinks of the search for the "falling man" a search where the very idea of suicide was rejected by the man's family as an inappropriate kind of agency (Singer). If these narratives are unable to register the complexities of 9/11, this is hardly a limitation of the genre. In appealing to multicultural difference that is both in its form and content predicated upon the refusal of difference, these little narratives reflect wider cultural pathologies. In their recourse to myth or allegory and the figure of the child/hero, such stories steadfastly refuse the political. In this sense they form precursors to the "gritty realist films" *United 93* and *WTC*, which emphasize a narrow field of action and heroism at the expense of any wider examination or contextualization of the events of 9/11.

CONCLUSION

This chapter has examined how mainstream comics mythologized events of 9/11 through a series of narrative and representative strategies. The creation of the superhero figure as transcendent witness and the invocation of a liberal imaginary worked to frame 9/11 in ways that precluded political and historically embedded interpretations. By standing outside of time and because of his already exceptional status, the superhero provides meta-commentary and heroic gestures that perform a kind of vicarious mourning and interpretation for a largely passive public. The superhero figure performs a conservative incorporation of 9/11, and in this sense can be compared to President Bush, whose own acts of witnessing and memorializing dominated the newscape immediately after 9/11. By contrast, the less epic stories in volumes such as

Artists Respond, focus on the public and "ordinary" citizens, and they invoke an ideal of pluralism and tolerance. However, in their use of myths, fables, children, and reified images of multiculturalism, such stories end up reducing the voices of the public to a largely singular perspective. Ultimately, the liberal collective and Spider-Man share an extremely limited form of articulation. Passivity and inaction applies to children and multiculturalism as much as it does to the world of heroes.

If politics is largely excluded from these comic book narratives, it is still possible to trace broad divisions between two forms of mythologizing. There is a difference between standing above history in the world of the gods, the certainty of conservatism often aligned with the American nation, and the idealized present of liberalism and the eternal good will. If the superhero as witness is transhistorical, the liberal ideal is always present as an imaginary that precedes the corruption of historical and religious intolerance. The liberal individual can never aspire to the godly and instead must find value in the innocence of the child or the unthreatening multicultural collective. We have seen that these comic books have had to respond to an anomalous situation, particularly in the relationship between serialization and the event, but rather than provide a critical response they have managed to domesticate the events of 9/11 within their own formal and mythological structures. It remains to be seen whether, with the passing of time and the increasing reflexivity of the genre, mainstream comic books will be able to go beyond these limited frameworks, perhaps adopting the formal innovativeness of works like Moore and Gebbie, which open up, rather than close off interpretative possibility.

NOTES

1. To take merely one example, just prior to invading Afghanistan, President Bush dismissed questions about the legality of the invasion with the remark, "I'll let others work out the legalities," thereby implying that the "law did not represent principles that ought to frame policy but was something to be gotten around or manipulated to suit a pre-established aim" (Brown par. 10).
2. A partial exception would be the patriotic Golden Age comic books produced during the Second World War. Their reactionary fervor and simplified moral universe is reproduced in some of the post-9/11 comics, for example *Freedom Three,* issue no 1. The cover shows a member of the Freedom Three punching Osama bin Laden in the face restaging an old *Captain America* cover where Captain America (dressed in red, white, and blue) punches Hitler in an identical fashion.
3. The division between mainstream and alternative comics is somewhat arbitrary but for the purposes of this chapter we state that mainstream comics are produced for an adolescent readership by large publishing houses such as Marvel and DC and are generally serialized superhero narratives. While the stories in the selected comic books stand alone as responses to 9/11, we would still categorize them as mainstream since the writers and artists are normally associated with superhero comics or other large print run comics produced by Marvel or DC.

4. We also make brief reference to *9–11 Emergency Relief*, which can be classified as non-mainstream due to its interest in non-fiction autobiographical narrative.

5. The major division in comic books is between speech balloons and captioned text with the latter most often placed in a square box close to the edge of the panel.

6. Øyvind Vågnes argues that in the wake of the attacks, there was a demand for exceptional images that could do justice to the "exceptionalism" of the event, of which the most noteworthy was Julien and Gedeon Naudet's documentary *9/11* (61–63).

7. In Dean Haspiel's *91101* the protagonist is watching the attacks on television and the subsequent panel shows him standing "unmediated" before the image of the planes hitting the towers (Mason 96). The lack of mediation is highlighted by the lack of panel borders suggesting that the image cannot be contained by the representational structure of the comic book.

8. Derrida talks of the need to understand the event and this involves various practices of "appropriation" that include "naming" and "recognition." The truly unforeseeable event will resist such appropriation (90). There is no model by which to interpret what is seen, and it is only through retrospective action that its meaning stabilizes. The question remains, however, at what *time* does the truly unimaginable become imaginable?

9. This is not say that the events are similar, only that some of the same tropes are invoked. Žižek states that the tendency to place the event of 9/11 in the same category as the Shoah is a mistake due to the fundamental difference in the structure and motivation underlying the event. In the Shoah, what was important was the application of bureaucratic procedures, the "banality of evil" spoken of by Hannah Arendt, and the wish to elude detection, to commit genocide without display unlike the contrived spectacle of the Twin Towers (136).

10. Although many of the features are derived from Holocaust representations, the act of bearing witness has had a significant role in U.S. culture, largely through the "Puritan immigrants" and their "evangelical metaphors of *vision* and *witness*" (Vågnes 63).

11. This division is often played out from the position of the comic book reader. In Danny Donovan's story, "Fiction is Better than Reality," the protagonist states that he supported his fictional heroes as they suffered many tragedies and crises but asks, "I was there. Why weren't they?" (Mason 20).

12. Another exception would be the image by Dave McKean in *Artists Respond* vol. 1 50–51, which, in its depiction of the Twin Towers as stone figures with hands clasped to their ears, is both highly evocative and open to a number of possible readings.

13. Space precludes a detailed reading of "This is Information," but it is worth noting that while the narrative constantly shifts interpretative perspectives and emotional register, this does not undermine its depiction of the horror and tragedy of 9/11.

WORKS CITED

Comic Books

9–11—Artists Respond. New York: Dark Horse, 2002.

Busiek, Kurt. "Astro City: 'Since the Fire.'" *9–11—The World's Finest Comic Book Writers & Artists Tell Stories to Remember*. Ed. Paul Levitz. Vol. 2. New York: DC Comics, 2002. 53–58.

Campbell, J Scott and Hi Fi. "Untitled." *Heroes.* Ed. Joe Quesada. New York: Marvel Comics, 2001. 23

Eisner, Will. "The Real Thing." *9–11—The World's Finest Comic Book Writers & Artists Tell Stories to Remember.* Ed. Paul Levitz. Vol. 2. New York: DC Comics, 2002. 17–18.

———. "Reality 9/11." *9'11 Emergency Relief.* Ed. Jeff Mason. Gainsville, Fl.: Alternative Comics 2002. 45.

Levitz, Paul. Ed. *9–11—The World's Finest Comic Book Writers & Artists Tell Stories to Remember.* Vol. 2. New York: DC Comics, 2002.

Mason, Jeff. Ed. *9–11: Emergency Relief.* Gainesville, Fl.: Alternative Comics, 2002.

McDonald, Brian and Brian O'Connell. "Untitled." *9–11—Artists Respond.* New York: Dark Horse, 2002. 99–100.

Moore, Alan and Melinda Gebbie. "This is Information." *9–11—Artists Respond.* New York: Dark Horse, 2002. 185–90.

Moriarity, Pat. "Untitled." *9–11—Artists Respond.* New York: Dark Horse, 2002. 58.

Quesada, Joe. Ed. *Heroes.* New York: Marvel Comics, 2001.

Raicht, Mike. Ed. *A Moment of Silence.* New York: Marvel Comics, 2001.

Seagle, Steven T. "Unreal." *9–11—The World's Finest Comic Book Writers & Artists Tell Stories to Remember.* Ed. Paul Levitz. Vol. 2. New York: DC Comics, 2002. 15–16.

Straczynski, J. Michael and John Romita Jr "Stand Tall." *Amazing Spider-Man.* 36, 14 Nov. 2001. New York: Marvel Comics.

Willems, Mo. "Walking the Williamsburg Bridge to Work." *9–11—The World's Finest Comic Book Writers & Artists Tell Stories to Remember.* Ed. Paul Levitz. Vol. 2. New York: DC Comics, 2002. 99–103.

Articles

9/11: The Falling Man. Dir. Henry Singer. Channel 4 UK, 2006.

Baetens, Jan. "Choses vues. Du regard en fantastique." *Image [&] Narrative* 2 (2001). 15 Aug. 2006 http://www.imageandnarrative.be/fantastiquebd/janbaetens.htm.

Bird, Jon. "The Mote in God's Eye: 9/11, Then and Now." *Journal of Visual Culture* 2.1 (2003): 83–97.

Brooker, Peter. "Terrorism and Counternarratives: Don DeLillo and the New York Imaginary." *New Formations* 57 (2005–6): 10–25.

Brown, Wendy. "Neo-liberalism and the End of Liberal Democracy." *Theory & Event* 7.1 (2003): 43 pars.

Derrida, Jacques. "Autoimmunity: Real and Symbolic Suicides—A Dialogue with Jacques Derrida." *Philosophy in a Time of Terror: Dialogues with Jürgen Habermas and Jacques Derrida.* Ed. Giovanna Borradori. Chicago: Univ. of Chicago Press, 2003. 85–136.

Eco, Umberto. "The Myth of Superman." Trans. Natalie Chilton. *The Role of the Reader: Explorations in the Semiotics of Texts.* Advances in Semiotics. Bloomington: Indiana University Press, 1979. 107–24.

Fish, Stanley. "Our Faith in Letting it all Hang Out." *New York Times* 12 Jan. 2006. 10 Mar. 2006 http://www.nytimes.com/2006/02/12/opinion/12fish.html.

Goldberger, Paul. "Zero Summary." *The New Yorker Online* 9 Nov. 2006.

Hustvedt, Siri. "New York: Big, Bad and Back to its Ballsy Best." *Observer* Sunday, Mar. 10, 2002. 15 May. 2006 http://observer.guardian.co.uk/waronterrorism/story/0,,665038,00.html.

Huyssen, Andreas. "Present Pasts: Media, Politics, Amnesia." *Present Pasts: Urban Palimpsests and the Politics of Memory*. Stanford: Stanford University Press, 2003. 11–29.

Jenkins, Simon. "Bin Laden is Laughing." *The Guardian Weekly* 15–21 Sep. 2006. 15.

Lovell, Jarret. "Step Aside, Superman . . . This is a Job [Captain] America! Comic Books and Superheroes Post September 11." *Media Representations of September 11*. Ed. Steven Chermak, Frankie Y. Bailey, and Michelle Brown. Westport and London: Praeger, 2003.161–73.

Murray David. "Unity and Difference: Poetry and Criticism." Ed. D. Murray. *Literary Theory and Poetry: Extending the Canon*. London: B.T. Batsford, 1989. 4–22.

Nyberg, Amy Kiste. "Of Heroes and Superheroes." *Media Representations of September 11*. Ed. Steven Chermak, Frankie Y. Bailey, and Michelle Brown. Westport and London: Praeger, 2003. 175–85.

Reynolds, Richard. *Superheroes: A Modern Mythology*. London: B. T. Batsford, 1992.

Ricoeur, Paul. *Memory, History, Forgetting*. Trans. Kathleen Blamey and David Pellauer. Chicago and London: Univ. of Chicago Press, 2004.

Vågnes, Øyvind. "'Chosen to be Witness': The Exceptionalism of 9/11." *The Selling of 9/11: How a National Tragedy Became a Commodity*. Ed. Dana Heller. New York: Palgrave Macmillan, 2005. 54–74.

Yarbrough, Beau. "Marvel to Take on World Trade Center Attack in 'Amazing Spider-Man.'" *Comic Book Resources*. September 24, 2001. Accessed March 10, 2006. http://www.comicbookresources.com/news/newsitem.cgi?id=461

Zelizer, Barbie. "Photography, Journalism, and Trauma." *Journalism after September 11*. Ed. Barbie Zelizer and Stuart Allan. Intro. Victor Navasky. London and New York: Routledge, 2003. 48–68.

Žižek, Slavoj. "A Plea for Leninist Intolerance." *Critical Inquiry* 28.2 (2002): 542–66.

———. *Welcome to the Desert of the Real!: Five Essays on September 11 and Related Dates*. London: Verso, 2002.

4 "Sometimes things disappear":
Absence and Mutability in Colson Whitehead's *The Colossus of New York*[1]

Stephanie Li

In *National Trauma and Collective Memory,* Arthur G. Neal argues that collective social identities emerge most prominently from moments of catastrophe. He writes: "Notions about 'who we are' and 'what we are to become' are shaped to a large degree from the shared identities that grow out of both extraordinary difficulties and extraordinary accomplishments in the social realm" (21). The events of September 11, 2001 certainly marked a national crisis as Americans, and New Yorkers in particular, struggled to understand the reasons for the attacks and the changes wrought upon their own sense of collective identity. In the aftermath of their destruction, the Twin Towers, already fraught icons of Americanness, became heightened symbols of capitalism, freedom, democracy, and other founding ideals. Although they were distinctive to New York, they easily laid claim to a broader symbolic imaginary, or as Sharon Zukin explains:

> Ugly, awkward, functional—like the city itself—the Twin Towers made their great impression by sheer arrogance. They took over the skyline, staking their claim not only as an iconic image of New York but as the iconic image of what a modern city should aspire to be: the biggest, the mightiest, the imperial center. (13)

Writing about the relationship between buildings and national identity, Neil Leach observes, "The nation, in effect, needs to read itself into objects in the environment in order to articulate that identity" (85). Ironically, through their absence the once inelegant, though imposing, Twin Towers became newly elevated symbols of national identity.

But how can absence function as a foundational source for a country's identity? According to Leach, "National identity is an essentially fantasy structure," and can only be "cathected onto objects" (84) in order to be perceived. However, in the case of 9/11, the objects, that is, the Twin Towers, achieved iconic status largely through their annihilation. Colson Whitehead responded to this paradox and to the crisis of identity caused by 9/11 in "Lost and Found," an essay published in the *New York Times*

Magazine two months after the attacks. The title of this piece suggests both the devastation caused by the destruction of the World Trade Center and the possibility of renewal: an absence paired with an emergent, if uncertain, presence. Despite Neal's claim that social identities are formed from national traumas, Whitehead takes the occasion of 9/11 to propose that loss has always been a constitutive aspect of the city and that the attacks have not fundamentally altered its relationship to individual inhabitants: "No matter how long you have been here, you are a New Yorker the first time you say, that used to be Munsey's, or That used to be the Tic Toc Lounge. . . . You are a New Yorker when what was there before is more real and solid than what is here now" (23). Though Whitehead begins this passage by describing personally specific locales, his final generalized reference to "what was there before" implies that there is a shared identity to be found in the awareness of absence. For a population still reeling from the events of 9/11, this allusion to the fallen Twin Towers reads as an affirmation of unity. The singular "you" who remembers Munsey's or the Tic Toc Lounge is transformed into the plural "you" for whom the Twin Towers are more real than the smoldering craters they have left behind.

Whitehead's conception of New Yorker identity implies that connection to the city is based not only upon familiarity with its geography, but more importantly, upon the experience of having endured change. Identification with New York requires longevity, the achievement of outliving physical markers, and the subsequent nostalgia produced by an awareness of absence. This approach to New Yorker identity, as premised upon lack and the experience of remaining despite major changes to the landscape of the city, has vital significance for a population overwhelmed by the destruction of the WTC. In the aftermath of this immense tragedy, Whitehead reminds New Yorkers that their sense of self is deeply entwined in the physical transformation of the city and its inherent instability. Reiterating E. B. White's 1949 description of New York as "both changeless and changing" (44), Whitehead presents the city as a place paradoxically rooted in its mutability.

Throughout "Lost and Found," Whitehead suggests that absence is both a consequence of the city's mutability—"This place multiplies when you're not looking"—and it is a condition that can be overcome by memory. What has been lost can be found anew because force of will makes it possible to see what once existed: "But look past the windows of the travel agency that replaced your pizza parlor. Beyond the desks and computers and promo posters for tropical adventures, you can still see Neapolitan slices cooling, the pizza cutter lying next to half a pie, the map of Sicily on the wall. It is all still there, I assure you" (24). Whitehead concludes this passage with the assertion, "The disappeared pizza parlor is still here because you are here," affirming a belief in the continuity of the past through memory. If we can simply imagine those meaningful places which, for whatever reason, have now disappeared, then they exist, they endure. A determined will is sufficient to conjure the past and make it real. This notion is wonderfully comforting and affirming, especially in the wake of 9/11, although, notably, there is no reference to the absent WTC.

By focusing on mundane locales, Whitehead reminds readers that the city's denizens have always experienced change as a condition of their environment. In this way, the events of 9/11 can be understood as part of its continuous evolution. While many commentators, like James Berger, declared that the attacks represented "some unbreachable rupture with the past" (56), Whitehead negates claims to its overwhelming significance. Suggesting that mutability is the foundation of New York's identity, he also debunks the notion that any physical icon or static image can represent its complexity. Though the missing Twin Towers became symbols of national identity, Whitehead proposes that their absence is better understood through the inevitability of the city's mutability; change is what defines New York, not buildings, absent or present, nor the meanings ascribed to them.

After affirming the power of memory to conjure past realities, Whitehead ends his essay with a direct reference to the missing WTC:

> The twin towers still stand because we saw them, moved in and out of their long shadows, were lucky enough to know them for a time. They are a part of the city we carry around. It is hard to imagine that something will take their place . . . after awhile the postcards of the new skyline will be available for purchase. Naturally we will cast a wary eye toward those new kids on the block, but let's be patient and not judge too quickly. We were new here, too, once. (26)

Though pizza slices may be harmlessly promised to "all still [be] there," it seems quite a different project to claim that the "towers still stand"; individual memories can be indulged as fantasies made real, but the WTC was a whole world's reality. Is Whitehead's statement delusional idealism or a clever symbol of imaginative power? And how is this assertion of stability to be read against his opening suggestion that New York is defined by flux and loss?

By suggesting that memory can counter the mutability of the city, Whitehead presents a provocative opposition between what he offers as the defining characteristic of the city and the need for its inhabitants to recapture past memories. If New Yorkers are made when "what was there before is more real and solid than what is here now," then Whitehead's claim that the "towers still stand" implies the prominence of a collective city identity (26). As before, while the pizza parlor belonged to a singular "you," the towers affirm a plural "you." Consequently, the towers exist because we have become New Yorkers through our shared awareness of their absence. If national identity can only be perceived through objects—flags, eagles, and apple pie—because, as Reneta Salecl writes, "the nation (in the sense of national identification) is the element that cannot be symbolized" (94), then absence is perhaps the only adequate sign of collective unity.[2] By describing absence and mutability as the hallmarks of New York's identity, White-head highlights the impermanence of physical structures and shifts atten-tion from structural landmarks to the city's embrace of transformation at both a spatial and individual level. An awareness of absence, as demon-strated through the text's unique narrative position and focus on fleeting encounters, becomes the unifying trope in Whitehead's New York, so that 9/11 loses distinction as a specific event to become emblematic of the city's continuous encounter with change.

NARRATING FROM ABSENCE:
THE COLOSSUS OF NEW YORK

"Lost and Found" represents only the beginning of Whitehead's explora-tion into the nature of the city and its denizens' identity in the aftermath of 9/11. Two years after the attacks, he published *The Colossus of New York* (2003), a portrait of the city told in thirteen vignettes. "Lost and Found" was reprinted as the book's first chapter though it was renamed "City Lim-its" and included two additional changes. Unlike the original title, which implies rediscovery amid absence, "City Limits" acknowledges the difficul-ties of such a project. This awareness of the city's imaginary limitations is emphasized in the paragraph added to the end of the opening chapter in which Whitehead describes the non-fiction book as "a guidebook" to "my city" which also "contains your neighborhoods. Or doesn't. We overlap. Or don't" (11). Despite the reach towards a shared city identity evident in "Lost and Found," as well as in *The Colossus of New York* as a whole, Whitehead is careful to delineate his own individual encounters from those of others. However, the possibility of overlap functions as one of the text's primary preoccupations. He begins "Lost Found" and "City Limits" with the observation: "I'm here because I was born here. . . . Maybe you're from here, too, and sooner or later it will come out that we used to live a block away from each other and didn't even know it" (3). Although Whitehead describes isolation as the most salient feature of urban life in *The Colossus of New York,* he continually highlights the commonality of this experience: the notion that every subway passenger and passing stranger is as alienated as every other. Though this is Whitehead's city, it is one in which all share a familiar experience of loneliness and longing.

The second change to "City Limits" was made to the longer passage previously quoted. Rather than name the Twin Towers, Whitehead writes: "Our old buildings still stand because we saw them" (10). *The Colossus of New York* makes no direct mention of 9/11, nor does it mention the physical void and psychological trauma produced by the attacks. Given Whitehead's striking claim that memory can recreate past structures, what does it mean that he does not directly memorialize the WTC in this text? He recalls pizza parlors and old hangouts, but not the Twin Towers. Is

Whitehead merely denying the overwhelming reality of 9/11, taking comfort in safe memories rather than confronting the void of Ground Zero? What implications does this approach have for how we understand and cope with the destructive consequences of the attacks?

In *Trauma Culture,* E. Ann Kaplan argues that art can function as a way of "'translating' trauma—that is, of finding ways to make meaning out of, and to communicate, catastrophes that happen to others as well as to oneself" (19). She explains that although there can be no return to a time before catastrophe, "Art that invites us to bear witness to injustice goes beyond moving us to identify with and help a specific individual, and prepares us to take responsibility for preventing future occurrence" (23). *The Colossus of New York* bears witness to mutability, but not to injustice, and therefore it avoids what Kaplan identifies as the "ethical response that will perhaps transform the way someone views the world, or thinks about injustice" (123). Whitehead is deeply concerned with describing absence as a constitutive aspect of New York, but he fails to present 9/11 as a politicized, deliberately organized act of violence. For him, the attacks signal the inevitable change that has always characterized the city, a perspective that naturalizes the resulting destruction. While critics and theorists have argued at great length about how best to memorialize and mourn for the loss produced by the attacks, Whitehead obviates such discussions by foregrounding absence to the exclusion of the changes that 9/11 as a wholly unique event wrought. If 9/11 is part of the natural cycle of mutability, there is no need to examine how and why this event occurred, and, more importantly, what changes need to be made to safeguard the future. Whitehead does not seek to commemorate the event at all, but rather to validate New York's mutability, a quality that predates the attacks.

In addition to the absence of any overt reference to 9/11, *The Colossus of New York* is notable for its rejection of a conventional narrative voice. In the chapters that follow "City Limits," Whitehead describes New York through the eyes of a shifting populace and only returns to a more stable second-person narrator in the final chapter, "JFK." The middle eleven sections are separated from the first and last chapters in the table of contents, suggesting that we are to read them in a manner distinct from the others. Each of these chapters examines one facet of the city—a familiar locale ("Central Park" and "Coney Island"), a time of day ("Morning" and "Rush Hour") or a common experience ("Subway" and "Rain")—through a range of anonymous, individual perspectives. While this narrative multiplicity attests to the diversity of New York's population, it also suggests a more over-arching authority that resonates with Michel de Certeau's encounter at the top of the WTC:

> To be lifted to the summit of the World Trade Center is to be lifted out of the city's grasp. One's body is no longer clasped by the streets that turn and return it according to an anonymous law; nor is it possessed,

whether as player or played, by the rumble of so many differences and by the nervousness of New York traffic. When one goes up there, he leaves behind the mass that carries off and mixes up in itself any identity of authors or spectators. . . . His elevation transfigures him into a voyeur. It puts him at a distance. It transforms the bewitching world by which one was "possessed" into a text that lies before one's eyes. It allows one to read it, to be a Solar eye, looking down like a god. (92)

Commenting on this passage, Barbara Gabriel describes "the World Trade Center buildings as offering the very type of the panoramic *view from nowhere*" (5). De Certeau presents a body independent of the city, a voyeur rather than a distinct individual, a being shed of individual differences and yet conscious of the masses below. This perspective is based upon an absence of self, yet one that can read the "text" of the city and the lives of its innumerable inhabitants. This is precisely the narrative strategy employed by Whitehead in his book's middle chapters, where there is no stable point of view. *The Colossus of New York* is narrated from a place of absence, which is to say directly from the heights of the missing Twin Towers.

From one sentence to the next, Whitehead shifts between first, second, and third person pronouns as he enters a diverse set of anonymous characters. The passage previously quoted helps to elucidate this unusual narrative strategy, which, I contend, is directly related to the text's refusal to reference 9/11. In considering the buildings that will take the place of the WTC (or in the second version of the passage, "Our old buildings"), Whitehead calls them "new kids on the block," and cautions readers to "not judge too quickly" because "[w]e were new here, too, once" (10). These lines personify the WTC or any "old buildings" as part of the mass of visitors who move through New York. Physical structures become people, become part of the citizenry that change the city with their own experiences and memories. Through this subtle personification, Whitehead implies that buildings are no more dependable than our own mutable selves.

The Colossus of New York presents readers with a series of discrete images—extremely specific yet remarkably diverse encounters with the city. From these individualized though anonymous moments, Whitehead constructs an identity built upon mutability. However, this is not a collective identity that has confronted the effects of 9/11. According to theorist Pierre Janet, memory unburdened by trauma involves "*the action of telling a story*" (663) or as Kathleen Brogan explains, "the resolution of trauma— the exorcism, we might say, of a possessing past—requires a movement into narrative" (80). The multiple, intersecting voices of *The Colossus of New York* do not tell stories; they narrate moments, not progressions. This lack of structured narrative prevents constructive confrontation with trauma, for as Patricia Yaeger notes: "Being able to move on from this threat to the self involves in part accepting the fact that what seemed impossible did actually happen by telling a narrative about it and feeling the appropriate affect for such an occurrence" (171). By limiting his description of New Yorkers to fleeting encounters, Whitehead further demonstrates an anxiety with confronting the consequences of 9/11. Though we may read his narrative strategy as a clever affirmation of the city's mutability and his representation of destruction as a promise of New York's continuous evolution, the text manipulates absence to avoid a confrontation with actual loss.

THE SELF AND THE CITY

Whitehead highlights the role of mutability in his conception of New York by linking the changing landscape of the city to the collective identity of its inhabitants, suggesting that physical transformations of the city are a mirror of our own shifting selves: "We see ourselves in this city every day when we walk down the sidewalk and catch our reflections in store windows, seek ourselves in this city each time we reminisce about what was there fifteen, ten, forty years ago, because all our old places are proof that we were here." Whitehead reads physical changes in the city as a reflection of our own human development, concluding, "When the buildings fall, we topple, too" (*Colossus* 9). This line is as close as Whitehead gets to a direct reference to the Twin Towers in *The Colossus of New York* and, perhaps most importantly, to the personal trauma that resulted for countless Americans. Yet if buildings are the keepers of our identities, what happens when they no longer exist?[3]

Whitehead follows this poignant if oblique reminder of 9/11 with an invocation of the longevity of the city, thus linking the identity of the city's inhabitants to this momentous tragedy:

> Maybe we become New Yorkers the day we realize that New York will go on without us. To put off the inevitable, we try to fix the city in place, remember it as it was, doing to the city what we would never allow done to ourselves. The kid on the uptown No. 1 train, the new arrival stepping out of Grand Central, the jerk at the intersection who doesn't know east from west: those people don't exist anymore, ceased to be a couple of apartments ago, and we wouldn't have it any other way. New York City does not hold our former selves against us. Perhaps we can extend the same courtesy. (9–10)

The city grants us the ability to change, to move past the people we once were and would prefer to forget, but most importantly, as we change, so does the city. Whitehead's personification suggests that it is a mistake to expect that the city is somehow immune to the same impulses that inspire us to become new people. Ultimately, New York is as mutable as we are, and we cannot assume that the stability of concrete and steel is any more lasting than our own turns of self. As the city has allowed us to change, so Whitehead contends, we must allow it to undergo its own evolution.

Despite this affirmative approach to change, Whitehead concedes that there are some difficult consequences to living without certainty in one's physical environment. He notes that the inherent mutability of the city means, "[w]e can never make proper good-byes" (7). It is impossible to know when the last time an encounter between the city and one of its inhabitants will occur: "I never got a chance to say good-bye to some of my old buildings. . . . And they never got a chance to say good-bye to me. I think they would have liked to—I refuse to believe in their indifference" (8). Whitehead insists upon a critical familiarity between himself and his "old buildings"; their "indifference" is unfathomable because "[t]he city knows you better than any living person because it has seen you when you are alone" (8).

Developing his use of personification, Whitehead proceeds to imagine what "all your old apartments would say if they got together to swap stories," and he details the various changes these places would have observed in us. He writes, "You tried on selves and got rid of them, and this makes your old rooms wistful: why must things change?" (9). The intimacy between the city and Whitehead's "you" is one built upon the mutability of the latter, the unstable "you" that adopts and discards selves like a restless teenager. We are guilty of the instability that Whitehead initially attributed to the city and, in fact, it is the apartment that is stable, wondering why change must occur at all. The city knows us for our true, variable selves; it knows that we cannot be trusted to be the same person everyday, to honor our commitments and stay true to our word, our habits, the people we love. It knows that our mutable selves are best reflected in Whitehead's unstable narrative voice, slippery, elusive and multiple, a voice absent of continuity. Consequently, the fact that the city's buildings and landscape are also subject to change seems like a type of betrayal; if we are so fickle, so unstable, then our world must and should be certain and reliable. The destruction of 9/11 proves that buildings and landmarks cannot be relied upon to act as guardians of our selves. In affirming that the loss of past identities and physical structures—here fused into a single entity—is foundational to the city's sense of self, Whitehead makes memory the agent of belonging; his defining colossus is not a physical structure, but rather it is absence that unites New York.

"HOPE AND WISH": WHITEHEAD'S TRANSIENT NEW YORKERS

The theme of absence is evident as well in the slippage between what Whitehead initially describes as "my city" and the anonymous individuals who become emblematic of the city's mutability. Although Whitehead is a native of New York, the book's second chapter, "The Port Authority," focuses on a series of disparate travelers who venture to the city by bus. Whitehead has surely been on countless buses bound for Port Authority, but he did not come to the city with the plans of relocation and naïve fantasies that characterize this collection of sojourners. The contrast between Whitehead and his anonymous travelers not only underscores the presence of another narrative authority at work in the text, one located in an absence of self, but it also demonstrates that for him New Yorker identity begins with a certain approach to the city, not upon familial roots or cultural history. New Yorkers are made through the twin elements of "[h]ope and wish" (20), which are described in this chapter as the impetus that inspires if not an actual journey to the city, then at least some engagement with self-reinvention. While New York welcomes diverse inhabitants of all social classes and categories, the motley group described in "The Port Authority" is marked by a shared flair for self-invention and individual pursuit, a characteristic further explored in later chapters of *The Colossus of New York*[4] The text's conception of New Yorker identity is fundamentally expansive, implying that it is constituted as much by a state of mind as by a mailing address.

Although native New Yorkers commonly call the bus station at 42nd Street "Port Authority," significantly, Whitehead entitles this chapter "The Port Authority." This is the name an outsider or a non-New Yorker might use to refer to the bus terminal, a category of people highlighted in this chapter: "Thousands of arrivals everyday, they won't stop coming. Different people but all the same. They try to sneak by with different faces but it is no use" (15). As he glosses over the individuality of these newcomers, Whitehead emphasizes their shared hope for a better life or at least a destination more impressive and exciting than the homes they have left behind. Already the city has inspired them to try to hide a part of themselves, to be someone different in a place that seems to demand transformation. While this chapter is peppered with acute personal details, readers are reminded that "on the bus they are all alike" because "[t]hey get on" (16).

By collapsing their individual differences and focusing instead on their general discomfort and their silent competitions for space and privacy, Whitehead contrasts their annoyance at one another with their eager anxiety to arrive in New York as changed, better people. In this way, he unites these future New Yorkers through their deliberate isolation and cultivated egoism. This juxtaposition suggests that New York is the ultimate site of individual fulfillment and self-invention, where "[s]he will be witty and stylish" (20), and "[n]o one will know the nickname that makes him mad" (21). Echoing Langston Hughes' description of New York as "truly the dream city" (qtd. in Butler 10), Whitehead tersely characterizes these reflections with the phrase: "Hope and wish" (20).

Despite their fantastic expectations and the small flourishes of specific dreams that Whitehead grants his nameless travelers, as they arrive at the Port Authority terminal, he again submerges their differences: "In effect, no matter what time of day it is, everyone arrives at the same time, in the same weather" (22). By erasing the specificity of his travelers, Whitehead shifts attention to what the city does to its visitors and possible inhabitants.

They are joined by a common dream of self-transformation and seduced by the possibility of a city that can change their meager fortunes. However, the dreams that inspired the bus riders in "The Port Authority" are tempered by their arrival to the city: "They wait for so long to see the famous skyline but wake at the arrival gate and with a final lurch are delivered into dinginess. This first disappointment will help acclimate" (22). The fact that the famous skyline is now gone underscores the inevitable collapse of dreams made of "[h]ope and wish." Mutability is the city's promise even as it implies eventual destruction.

DREAD AND LOSS

In contrast to the green pilgrims of "The Port Authority," subsequent chapters in *The Colossus of New York* describe people who are more settled into the fabric of city life. However, while these individuals are comfortable in New York's fast and crowded streets, they are also profoundly detached from others, suggesting an absence of connection and intimacy endemic to the city. For example, in "Morning," we read of people going to work, not what they do professionally; we eavesdrop on internal monologues, not on breakfast conversations or exchanges between loved ones. As Whitehead shifts from male to female pronouns and back to an insistent "you" in order to describe the routines of "Morning," each of these subjects encounters the day alone, impervious to surrounding events. Like the sojourners of "The Port Authority" and the commuters of "Morning," the visitors to Coney Island find: "Even out here still too close to neighbors. . . . Loathe neighbors and their loud boorish talk and unfortunate ditties" (93). Whitehead's New Yorkers treat one another as subtle, resentful antagonists who fail to recognize the mutuality of their disgust.

As other inhabitants are shunned, meaningful connections become an anomaly, produced only by spontaneous events such as the rain that forces strangers to seek shelter together—"Underneath the scaffolding the conversations among strangers range from grunts to bona fide connections. Quite serendipitous" (68)—or a group of dancers and musicians in Central Park:

> Brought together in this moment in a park on the first day of spring. A community. And fancy that in a city. Back to a time before zoning and rebar, one tribe, drums talking. Something that cannot be planned. Everybody knows they must remember this feeling because soon it is back to the usual debasement and they try to remember and then it stops. (45)

Whitehead's observation that communities are formed through spontaneous events has special significance given the renewed sense of unity witnessed in the city in the immediate aftermath of 9/11.[5] He seems to suggest here that the seeds of a collective unity are already in place, and the challenge lies in remembering such moments. Given this insight, it is especially ironic that Whitehead does not refer to 9/11, but, consistent with the text's emphasis on mutability, the crowd disperses aware that the impulse to remember will inevitably fade. Here and elsewhere in *The Colossus of New York* Whitehead makes vague allusions to 9/11 and its aftermath, but refrains from directly referencing the attacks. These insinuations serve to create a disturbing sense of dread. Whitehead coyly alludes to the possibility of sudden catastrophe, but always deflects such a possibility with reference to the mundane. There is no drastic event to jolt his detached New Yorkers into some collective awareness, only the insistent possibility of change.

The first of Whitehead's subtle references to impending catastrophe appears in "Morning." He writes of sleepy workers preparing for the day: "Listen to newscasters: while you were safe in here the world may have lost its way" (26). This sentence obliquely gestures toward the destruction of the WTC as radio reports first aired news of the tragedy in the morning hours, and the world never seemed to "lose its way" more than on 9/11. Whitehead's casual use of the word "may" suggests a time before 9/11 in which it was possible to believe that whatever happened in the world would not infringe upon one's well-being. This attitude toward the news and its consequences operates from an assumption of safety. The text recalls a time before threats of terrorism became a part of daily life. However, while Whitehead's New Yorkers do not wonder if some change in their routine foretells new destruction or if a conspicuous stranger conceals a bomb, they are still subject to moments of panic and fear.

In "Rain," a woman considers her anxiety boarding a bus: "She hides in the bus stand. She hasn't taken the bus in years and feels a secret terror" (64). In this age of terrorism, Whitehead's word choice is significant, and yet in his New York, fear comes from a bus ride, not from a plane trip or the speculated dangers of a subway attack. In this way, he normalizes current worries about travel and crowded spaces, suggesting that even without the attacks of 9/11, people naturally fear one another and anticipate unexpected disasters. Of a man on the subway, Whitehead writes: "His heart speeds up before his mind can process the fear: haven't they been between stations too long. Stationless for quite a while now and it is quite disconcerting. Suddenly realizing you've taken the express" (56). Similarly, in the section entitled "Central Park," he begins a new passage with: "So many people running. Is something chasing them. Yes, something different is chasing each of them and gaining slowly" (42). Although he proceeds to describe a pack of joggers, as with the frightened man in the subway, Whitehead invokes a sudden sense of panic before defusing the fear with a return to ordinary experiences. These sly allusions, which conclude in innocuous occurrences, point to a general sense of dread in the city. While the dangers prove harmless, they suggest that daily life in the city can be fraught with unknown peril.

In her study of personal experience narratives, Cornelia Cody observes that New Yorkers frequently relate stories of adversity in describing their encounters with the city. Even before 9/11, Eleanor Wachs demonstrated that New Yorkers tend to fixate on challenges they have confronted in their urban environment such as blackouts, petty crime or difficult encounters with city officials. Cody explains that these stories highlight "a dual sense of New York: on the one hand, New York is dangerous and violent; on the other, New York teaches one how to survive danger and violence" (232). The individuals that populate *The Colossus of New York* are all already survivors and not simply because they lived through 9/11. That event is not necessary to prove their fortitude because the city is overwhelming and frightening on its own terms. The moments of panic that Whitehead evokes in his text demonstrate the ubiquity of fear in urban life. 9/11 certainly produced a new level of danger in New York, but it did not create the suspicion and vigilance with which its inhabitants habitually approach the world.

In addition to the recurrent sense of dread in *The Colossus of New York,* the text also highlights an abiding awareness of loss. While Whitehead makes this most explicit in his opening discussion of missing landmarks, he returns to this theme in the section entitled "Rain."

> Forming an attachment to an umbrella is the shortest route to heartbreak in this town. Any true accounting would reveal that there are only twenty umbrellas in this city, in constant movement from palm to palm. Bunch of Lotharios. So do we learn loss from umbrellas. (62)

Although Whitehead's playful approach can be read as trivializing actual loss, this passage emphasizes his fundamental contention that loss is not a matter of permanent absence, but instead a type of endless exchange. Buildings fall only to rise anew just as umbrellas disappear only to be found again. For Whitehead, heartache is indeed derived from disappearance, but pain is offset by the recognition that another person enjoys the object of the original loss. This is a clever and fundamentally optimistic conception, especially as it is presented through such a trivial example. The light tone invoked here can be understood through Cody's observations on the personal narratives about negative experiences told by New Yorkers. She explains that a comic tone is necessary "to reconcile the dangers, threats, and inconveniences of the city with the fact that they have chosen to live here. Finding the humor in everyday travails also transforms narrators from victims to survivors" (220). There are certainly other types of loss more affecting and profound than that offered by the example of Whitehead's umbrellas. However, in using them to symbolize how loss produces the possibility of exchange, he reminds readers that loss is a condition of urban life which is ultimately experienced at all levels of existence.

Whitehead again takes up the theme of loss in the chapter entitled "Coney Island," which devotes special attention to the beach's sand, described as "an elementary with lessons" (91). Whitehead pointedly uses the term "cities" to characterize the castles children make and to reiterate his conception of mutability:

> What they shape are cities, no less so for being soft and miniature. Imposition of human order on nature. Sand slips through fingers but no one takes the hint. Our juvenile exercises. What they build cannot last. Fragile skylines are too easily destroyed. (91–92)

This oblique reference to the WTC parallels the city's skyscrapers to the sand castles of children. The use of the word "fragile," while apt for a sandcastle, implies a sense of dread in relation to massive physical structures like the WTC. The Twin Towers were hardly "fragile" constructions; their fragility only makes sense in the context of terrorism and fanatical hatred of the United States. Although Whitehead's comparison is valid in that both sand castles and buildings "cannot last," he elides discussion of the source of the WTC's collapse. This passage highlights the limitations of Whitehead's presentation of 9/11 and its aftermath. The Twin Towers did not fall because of the inevitable rising tide that destroys sand castles; they were not destroyed by a natural event, but by deliberate calculation.

In refusing to refer directly to the events of 9/11 in *The Colossus of New York*, Whitehead succeeds in demonstrating that mutability has always been a critical part of the city's identity and that the possibility of transformation has long been a goal of its inhabitants. He suggests that the fall of the WTC is best understood within a continuum of inevitable change. While this can be viewed as a broad, philosophical approach, which appreciates the inherent mutability of life and the ephemerality of human endeavor, it also makes a specific national catastrophe into a clever metaphor of New Yorker identity. For Whitehead, the events of 9/11 do not mark an irrevocable rupture with the past; instead, the absence of the WTC confirms the dynamic and transformative essence of the city. Accordingly, this spirit of change and its attendant courage to evolve are presented as qualities that make the city great, while also uniting its diverse inhabitants. Although this approach provides a reassuring interpretation of an overwhelming tragedy, it allows Whitehead to gloss over entirely the political complexities of a post-9/11 world.

This evasion is perhaps best exemplified in the title of his book, which naturally invokes an association with the *Colossus of Rhodes,* the giant statue of Helios built around 290 B.C.[6] Whitehead does not specify what his *Colossus of New York* refers to, but in a text marked by indirection, the WTC is a likely candidate, especially as both constructions were massive monuments that reflected the values and power of its builders. However, the pairing of the WTC with the Colossus of Rhodes is jarring because the latter was felled by an earthquake, while the events of 9/11 were not caused by an act of God, but were instead engineered by terrorists. Whitehead's soothing, seemingly broad-minded approach to the events of 9/11 falters in this gap between the natural and the political. While readers may take comfort in his notion that the tragedy of 9/11 inspires the key strength and defining quality of its inhabitants—the ability to endure beyond environmental transformations—*The Colossus of New York* ultimately forecloses discussion about the political consequences of the attacks.

In the text's final chapter, "JFK," Whitehead adopts the second person pronoun to describe someone about to embark on a plane as he writes: "Just a matter of time until you are home." The use of the word "home" implies that the city is not home; instead, it is part of a trip that may never be repeated because Whitehead writes, again with subtle dread, "Sometimes things disappear" (157). Whitehead suggests that the city's mutability defies simplistic conceptions of stability. And so like the Colossus of Rhodes, it too is destroyed: "Then the plane tilts in its escape and over the gray wing the city explodes into view with all its miles and spires and inscrutable hustle as you try to comprehend this sight you realize that you were never really there at all" (158). This sentence, with its slight allusion to 9/11 ("the city explodes"), suggests that the known, familiar city has already changed, and "you were never really there at all" because the "there" has since vanished into some new urban evolution. It is impossible then to capture the city, to make it into a home, because it thrives upon change. From this perspective, 9/11 is yet another permutation on the definitive New Yorker's sense of mutability. The city is in a constant state of flux; it perpetually "explodes," and thus it has already changed countless times since 9/11. What abides are not buildings, but the steady arrival of new inhabitants who make and remake the city with their dreams of "hope and wish."

"THE IMAGE" AND ITS AFTERMATH

Although *The Colossus of New York* is Whitehead's first book since 9/11, his first published piece after the attacks appeared in the *New York Times Magazine* on Sunday, September 23, 2001. His short meditation, "The Image," began a series of eight responses to 9/11 by writers such as Stephen King and Jennifer Egan, which were collectively entitled "Elements of Tragedy." Whitehead's contribution describes his experience on the morning of September 11. He and his wife were among a group of strangers looking out at the burning Twin Towers from Fort Greene Park in Brooklyn. As they stared across the water, Whitehead urged his wife to take a picture:

> Because it was a very nice shot, well composed. The three men in the foreground were obviously strangers, standing together, but not so close as to violate any rules about personal space. They were of different races; one had a dog that looked away from the scene at a bird or something, one had abandoned a bicycle on the ground. The bicycle

was a nice touch—couldn't have placed it better myself. In the sky before the men, the towers burned. The right part of the frame was unblemished blue sky, the left a great wash of brown and black smoke. The dynamic event, the small human figures. It was a nice shot. Call it "The Watchers" or "The Spectators." Frame it. Keep it away. (158)

Whitehead's description of the men framed against the towers demonstrates his keen eye for detail and his ability both to see and construct an artful, touching scene: the men of different races brought together by tragedy, the dog looks away as if overwhelmed, the fallen bicycle a symbol of a life forgotten and cast aside in the wake of inconceivable horror. Whitehead's suggested title for the picture indicates the limitations of human intervention in the face of catastrophe. The men are watchers or spectators, unable to participate in or change the horror before them. The picture captures their futility, but it does so in a pleasing, aesthetically balanced way, just as the title lends a poetic simplicity to the image.

However, Whitehead's picturesque image is suddenly destroyed when the wind shifts to reveal that one of the towers is gone, and moments later the second tower collapses. Confronted by the sheer violence of this transformation, Whitehead reconsiders his appreciation of the previous image: "It had been a nice shot. And certainly it had been easier to shape the horror into an aesthetic experience and deny the human reality. There was safety in that distance. A man picked up his bike and walked away. My wife and I went home. There had never been any safety at all" (21). In the wake of the fallen tower, Whitehead recognizes that his artful construction of the scene was a way of ignoring the devastation before him. He realizes that he is guilty of using art as an escape from reality rather than as a means of understanding or coping with its atrocities. As he correctly concludes, there is no safety in such easy, contained images or in the literary equivalent of manufactured clichés. Whitehead here evinces a sober recognition of the dangers of writing about tragedy. What had been an artful, even beautiful, image is shown to occlude a reality far more complex and painful than can be imagined or captured.

The title of Whitehead's essay, "The Image," is an apt way to understand the provocative, but ultimately limited, narrative strategy of *The Colossus of New York*. The text describes a series of disconnected images that fail to cohere into a sustained narrative of loss, grief, and healing. Readers must tease out oblique references to 9/11, and though there is meaning and insight to be found in such explorations, there is no sense of the specific loss produced by the destruction of the WTC. Whitehead does not allow his images to move forward into the subsequent fall precipitated by the attacks and into the place where there "had never been any safety at all." In his city, safety lies in an identity that has always borne the mutability of the city's landscape and which has long been sustained by its promise of transformation. It is a comforting, if ultimately inadequate, formulation.

While *The Colossus of New York* does not attempt to make an aesthetically pleasing picture from the destruction wrought by 9/11, its failure to address directly the consequences of the attacks suggests a degree of narrative subterfuge. Certainly the absence of the WTC is palpable in the text, but Whitehead keeps 9/11 in the background, at a safe distance from the life of the city's inhabitants. Although this approach does not entirely deny or erase 9/11, it normalizes the attacks so readers are led to believe that such tragedy is part of the inevitable rise and fall of life. Whitehead assures us that 9/11 didn't change anything—New Yorkers are as ambitious and individualistic as ever—and, in fact, the attacks simply made the city's inhabitants more of whom they have always been. This acceptance of tragedy and deliberate violence obviates the need to question both why 9/11 occurred and how we have changed as a result. By suggesting that the destruction of the WTC is no more than part of New York's natural inclination toward mutability, Whitehead permits his readers to avoid having to confront the specific changes wrought by 9/11. Mutability is the hallmark of his city, not the courage of deliberate transformation required in the aftermath of our national tragedy.

NOTES

1. The author would like to give special thanks to Dinah Holtzman for her insight into the development of this chapter.
2. As Leach explains, the notion that "[n]ational identity is an essentially fantasy structure" (84) borrows significantly from Lacanian theories in which identification is specular and involves a misrecognition of the self upon the other. Such a process is always an inadequate representation of the self, either individually or collectively.
3. Neil Leach applies a Lacanian model of identification to understand how buildings can become reflections of personal identity. He writes: "The environment must therefore serve as a kind of 'screen' onto which we would 'project' our own meaning, and into which we would 'read' ourselves" (79).
4. Numerous social theorists have observed that urban life produces multiple social roles for individuals to fulfill: "At any given time, any one of these parts of the whole personality may be experienced as the individual's proper self" (Smith 96). Georg Simmel in particular examined the consequences of this effect, noting that inner conflict may result from the incompatibility of these multiple roles; see in particular "The Metropolis and Mental Life" in *Simmel on Culture.*
5. Five years after the aftermath of 9/11, Frank Rich in an article entitled, "Whatever Happened to the America of 9/12?" reflected upon the unity that possessed the city following the attacks: "If you were in New York then, you saw it in the streets, and not just at Ground Zero, where countless thousands of good Samaritans joined the official responders and caregivers to help, at the cost of their own health. You saw it as New Yorkers of every kind gathered around the spontaneous shrines to the fallen and the missing at police and fire stations, at churches and in parks, to lend solace or a hand" (4,2).
6. The title of Whitehead's book may additionally refer to a rather obscure film by Eugène Lourié also entitled *The Colossus of New York* (1958). This

science fiction movie involves issues of absence and loss as it centers upon a father's attempt to reanimate his dead son by implanting the deceased's brain in a massive robot. Although the son was noted for his humanitarian efforts, the robot becomes destructive and is ultimately killed. The misguided attempt to resurrect the dead resonates with Whitehead's refusal to mention the WTC as if such a memorializing project, like that of the film's father figure, is doomed to failure.

WORKS CITED

Berger, James. "'There's No Backhand to This.'" *Trauma at Home: After 9/11*. Ed. Judith Greenberg. Lincoln: U of Nebraska P, 2003. 52–59.

Brogan, Kathleen. *Cultural Haunting: Ghosts and Ethnicity in Recent American Literature*. Charlottesville: UP of Virginia, 1998.

Butler, Robert and Yoshinobu Hakutani. "Introduction." *The City in African-American Literature*. Ed. Robert Butler and Yoshinobu Hakutani. Cranbury: Associated UP, 1995.

Cody, Cornelia. "'Only in New York': The New York City Personal Experience Narrative." *The Journal of Folklore Research* 42 (2005): 217–44.

de Certeau, Michel. *The Practice of Everyday Life*. Trans. Steven Rendall. Berkeley: U of California P, 1984.

Gabriel, Barbara. "'Writing Against the Ruins': Towards a Postmodern Ethics of Memory." *Post-Modernism and the Ethical Subject*. Ed. Barbara Gabriel and Suzan Ilcan. Montreal: McGill-Queen's UP, 2004. 3–24.

Janet, Pierre. *Psychologial Healing: A Historical and Clinical Study*. Trans. Eden Paul and Cedar Paul. 2 vols. New York: Macmillan, 1925. New York: Arno, 1976.

Kaplan, E. Ann. *Trauma Culture: The Politics of Terror and Loss in Media and Literature*. New Brunswick: Rutgers UP, 2005.

Leach, Neil. "9/11." *Diacritics* 33.3/4 (2003): 75–92.

Neal, Arthur G. *National Trauma and Collective Memory: Major Events in the American Century*. Armonk: M.E. Sharpe, 1998.

Rich, Frank. "Whatever Happened to the America of 9/12?" *New York Times*. 10 Sept. 2006, late ed.: 4, 2.

Salecl, Renata. "Ideology of the Mother Nation." *Envisioning Eastern Europe*. Ed. Michael Kennedy. Ann Arbor: U of Michigan P, 1995. 87–101.

Simmel, Georg. *Simmel on Culture*. Ed. David Frisby and Mike Featherstone. London: Sage, 1997.

Smith, Michael P. *The City and Social Theory*. New York: St. Martin's, 1979.

Wachs, Eleanor. *Crime-Victim Stories: New York City's Urban Folklore*. Bloomington: Indiana UP, 1988.

Whitehead, Colson. *The Colossus of New York: A City in Thirteen Parts*. New York: Doubleday, 2003.

———. "The Image." *New York Times Magazine* 23 Sept. 2001: 21.

———. "The Way We Live Now: 11–11–01; Lost and Found." *New York Times Magazine* 11 Nov. 2001: 23.

Yaeger, Patricia. "Rubble as Archive, or 9/11 as Dust, Debris, and Bodily Vanishing." *Trauma at Home: After 9/11*. Ed. Judith Greenberg. Lincoln: U of Nebraska P, 2003. 187–94.

Zukin, Sharon. "Our World Trade Center." *After the World Trade Center: Rethinking New York City*. Ed. Michael Sorkin and Sharon Zukin. New York: Routledge, 2002. 13–22.

5 Witnessing 9/11

Art Spiegelman and the Persistence of Trauma

Richard Glejzer

That's when time stands still at the moment of trauma . . . which strikes me as a totally reasonable response to current events!

Art Spiegelman, *In the Shadow of No Towers*, 2

The story of trauma, then, as the narrative of a belated experience, far from telling of an escape from reality—the escape from a death, or from its referential force—rather attests to its endless impact on a life.

Cathy Caruth, *Unclaimed Experience*, 7

As Art Spiegelman suggests, a "reasonable response" to the trauma of September 11, 2001, involves not attempts at constructing a knowledge or a history of the event, but rather a breaking of the temporal logic of such responses: time, he claims stands still in the face of the demand for history. It is this untimeliness of trauma that Cathy Caruth likewise emphasizes, a belatedness that continues to interrupt and undermine the simple telling of the story of an event. In *Unclaimed Experience,* Caruth argues that any act of historicizing trauma is doomed to miss its object; the emphasis on history in testimony ends up silencing trauma rather than recognizing traumatic events (18). Spiegelman, however, offers a more precise articulation of this relationship: trauma, he claims, resides in the very way an event disrupts the seemingly seamless boundary between when a witness sees and when she knows something about what she has seen. The structure of bearing witness thus involves not what history or memory can say about the traumatic occurrence or the act of seeing; rather, bearing witness involves the very breaking of this connection. This is ultimately Art Spiegelman's point in *In the Shadow of No Towers* when he defines trauma not as an external interruption that follows witness, but rather as something that resides in the temporality of the witness and more exactly in time's standing still.

Art Spiegelman's comix have consistently demonstrated a concern with this relationship between a memorable past and a present where such memory cannot bring the past to light.[1] Throughout his work, the past does not serve simply as a point of explanation, a cause of a future effect. Rather, Spiegelman uses the past and present as points of juxtaposition, markers of narrative's failure to bind events seamlessly together, which leave what Emmanuel Levinas would term a trace of the "saying in the said of the witness" (147). Levinas argues that the said itself is always a site of ethical failure since it inherently attempts to capture or thematize the subject's responsibility to the other. It is in the act of saying apart from the said, the moment that precedes such failure, that the subject as witness resides, a moment in which time must stand still. At the very beginning of *Maus,* for example, Spiegelman juxtaposes a shard from his own childhood relationship with his father with his father's experience during the Holocaust. Having fallen while skating, Artie approaches his father for comfort. When Artie tells his father that his friends have left him, Vladek stops his work, turns to his son, and says: "Friends? Your friends? If you lock them together in a room with no food for a week THEN you could see what it is, friends!" (6). This kernel of Artie's traumatic past with his father does more than inform his later relationship with him, which *Maus* later explores. Instead, the history of this relationship intrudes into the very recording of his father's Holocaust experiences: Vladek's story becomes an object of desire for Artie and a means of keeping his son close for Vladek. By framing the narrative of his father's Holocaust experience through the history of the father and son's complicated and difficult relationship, Spiegelman overtly disrupts the very project of testimony by keeping the focus on the act of speaking over what is spoken. By subjectifying his own role as a participant in his father's continued telling of his story, Artie makes his position as witness to the narrative a crucial part of the story, a trace of the saying that cannot be occluded by his father's story. There is more than the said here; something incomprehensible remains that even the opening fragment situating the boy Artie in terms of his father's past experience cannot explain.[2]

In the Shadow of No Towers continues this concern with the nature of trauma and bearing witness. But whereas *Maus* offered Spiegelman distance from the events he describes, *In the Shadow of No Towers* is about the failure to achieve such a distance. Though *Maus* fundamentally centers on his father's story even as it probes Artie's relationship with him, *In the Shadow of No Towers* has no such dialogue through which Spiegelman can elicit testimony. The presence of both Artie and Vladek in *Maus* offers the narrative both a physical locus for the traumatic retelling and another point of reference through which the event itself—the Holocaust—can be triangulated and made known. But *In the Shadow of No Towers* contains no such attempts to place Spiegelman's unmediated experience of 9/11 into a clarifying context or to get beyond his own raw images of that day. In this more recent work, Spiegelman wrestles with an event that lacks an historical buffer, an event that has yet to become an event in the historical sense of the term. This failure of context also affects the ways in which both texts rely on images to construe their testimony: like *Maus*'s use of mice and cats for people, Spiegelman's political commentary on 9/11 is cast in iconic images, this time drawn from historical comic figures and newspaper headlines from early in the last century. But whereas the use of mice and cats in *Maus* defines Spiegelman's central antagonism to his father's Holocaust narrative, the figures in *In the Shadow of No Towers* offer no similarly traumatic object, no other context that might offer coherence to the event. Finally, though there are clearly moments in which the narrative frame of *Maus* breaks, ultimately *Maus* is a text that attempts to mediate its trauma narratively, rather than undermining its narrative structure by confronting the temporal logic head on. *In the Shadow of No Towers* keeps its focus on the time before eventness takes hold; Spiegelman demonstrates the moment of witness before testimony, in which any movement toward understanding or knowing cannot bear the burden of the act of seeing, since the object of vision defies all previous contexts. In this sense, trauma is not simply an external event that refuses to be brought into a temporal or historical frame. Rather, what Spiegelman shows is that trauma persists in the temporal disruption itself, within the gap between seeing and knowing central to the act of saying that is not, following Levinas, ever rendered as said. For Spiegelman, the persistence of the trauma of 9/11 takes the form of the event's constant timeless present; even memory cannot place the event as past.

In the Shadow of No Towers focuses on Spiegelman's attempt to grapple with the traumatic events surrounding the collapse of the World Trade Center Towers on September 11, 2001. As a resident of Lower Manhattan, Spiegelman recounts the events of that morning, the sound of the planes, the furious search for his daughter whose school was near the towers, and his own horror as the towers fell. But equally important to Spiegelman's narrative is the persistence of the incomprehensibility of the experience, rather than of what may have given rise to the attacks or even of the loss suffered by families of the dead, though his text does point toward these concerns as well. It is the incomprehensibility of the place of the witness that is central to his text, the evisceration of any knowledge, memory, or relation that can secure his own position in light of what he saw. As in *Maus,* this moment of the saying resides in Spiegelman's demonstration of a disjunction between the past and present, a point where the viewer emerges from the viewed, where the act of saying maintains a grip on the said. However, whereas *Maus* explores a more distant past's intrusion on the present—a past that may never have receded into a distance for Vladek, or even Artie, but a past that has nonetheless become part of history—*In the Shadow of No Towers* concerns an event that has yet to recede for Spiegelman or for the public. Unlike the Holocaust, 9/11 persists as an event that still is unfolding and has yet to become history. As in *Maus,* Spiegelman's focus is on the becoming of history, but unlike in *Maus* he finds himself at odds with all attempts at historicizing the event. Time, he says again and again, stands still, and without movement the story cannot be told. There is only the witness who sees.

This is a very different reading of Spiegelman's work from those that focus on its coming to understanding. Karen Espiritu's article on Spiegelman's political engagement in *In the Shadow of No Towers* defines his comix form as one where the text attempts to "'master' or understand—though not completely—a particularly traumatic experience" (182). In her compelling reading of the central images of the text, especially Spiegelman's use of the image of the glowing tower prior to its fall, Espiritu argues that the text attempts to work through the trauma of 9/11: "For within its pages glow the unassimilable and irreconcilable remainders of Spiegelman's sense of loss that day, as well as the constantly thwarted attempts to work 'successfully' through its trauma-inducing memories" (188). Although Espiritu leaves the act of understanding incomplete and unsuccessful, her argument focuses on the coherence of Spiegelman's text rather than the ways it maintains fragmentation. This reading has much in common with critical responses to Spiegelman's *Maus*, a text that may better fit the model of "working through" to which Espiritu subscribes. Dominick LaCapra's discussion of the ways in which *Maus* functions as an act of "memory-work" follows this line of argument (179). However, even in *Maus*'s more conventional narrative (at least when compared to *In the Shadow of No Towers*), Spiegelman privileges the moment of witness as fundamentally disruptive to understanding and coherence: the first volume of *Maus* ends with the recognition that Artie's mother's story will never be known. *In the Shadow of No Towers* takes this disruption of coherence as its object. It is not a text that ultimately fails in its representation of grief or loss. Rather, it is a text fundamentally about the very failure of all representation to give substance to the act of bearing witness.

If Spiegelman's text focuses on the act of seeing, the image of the melting North Tower serves as his returning anamorphic disruption to any movement to understanding or knowledge, to coherence itself. Spiegelman insists that the image of the glowing North Tower about to collapse repeated throughout the collection is his own, one the media never captured:

> The pivotal image from my 9/11 morning—one that didn't get photographed or videotaped into public memory but still remains burned onto the inside of my eyelids several years later—was the image of the looming North Tower's glowing bones just before it vaporized. I repeatedly tried to paint this with humiliating results but eventually came close to capturing the vision of disintegration digitally on my computer. I managed to place some sequences of my most vivid memories around that central image but never got to draw others. (iv)

In every one of the volume's ten broadsheets this image is bound to the passage of time and to the difficulties of remembrance. Spiegelman uses the digitized image to demonstrate both the particularity of his own experience of

Figure 5.1 From *In the Shadow of No Towers* by Art Speigelman.

the event and also his inability to portray that experience. In the third of the full-page comix, for example, Spiegelman provides his reader with a synopsis running down the left side of the page, written over the background image of the glowing girders just before the North Tower's collapse (Figure 5.1).

> SYNOPSIS: / In our last / episode, as / you might / remember, / time stood / still. (And / maybe it's / just as well: / last week / the artist / began de- / scribing his / September / 11ᵗʰ morning / and only / got up to / about 9:15 . . . / Consider- / ing that it / takes him / at least a / month to / complete / each page / he should've / started this / "weekly" / series in / September / 1999 to get / it all told by / Judgment Day . . . (3)

The most significant temporal point in this passage is the claim that "time stood still," and that to tell it all in time requires that he begin two years before the event took place. Interestingly, Spiegelman comments earlier that he liked the "giant scale of newsprint pages," but his original notion of a weekly series had to be scrapped because each page took five weeks to complete: "The idea of working in single page units corresponded to my conviction that I might not live long enough to see them published" (iv). So even in his choice of medium there's a sense of temporal displacement. And this displacement is inscribed upon the skeletal image of the North Tower: this image only exists—only ever existed—in the eyes of Spiegelman as witness. Again, this is an image that was never recorded, that could not be recorded precisely because it is Spiegelman's own vision. This is not to suggest that he has made up the image or that he uses it simply as a metaphor for his experience. Rather, this image, and the timelessness it represents, mark the very moment of seeing that Spiegelman can't move beyond; it is the mark of the saying that remains apart from Spiegelman's recollections, the point of witness upon which an understanding of 9/11 continually stumbles.

The fourth page likewise uses the image of the glowing tower as a temporal link to the event and the earlier comix panels in the collection, again superimposing text on image (Figure 5.2). This time the entire left margin contains a close-up of the tower filling a full-page box. Beginning from top to bottom, the image of the tower pixilates, and by the bottom the glowing lines of the steel merge. Superimposed at three places is another link back to the previous pages:

> Our hero is trapped reliving the traumas of Sept. 11, 2001 . . . Unbeknownst to him brigands suffering from war fever have since hijacked those tragic events . . .

> His memories swirl and events fade, but he still sees that glowing tower when he closes his eyes.

Figure 5.2 From *In the Shadow of No Towers* by Art Spiegelman.

Meanwhile, an anniversary came and went . . . Many happy returns! (Amazing how time flies while it stands still).

Interestingly, in the second volume of *Maus,* Spiegelman makes a similar point about the passing of time while he is working on his book. The second chapter of *Maus II* is subtitled "Time Flies," and throughout the chapter Artie is plagued by flies as he attempts to draw his father's descriptions of Auschwitz: in one scene, he is surrounded by rotting corpses and flies buzzing around him and is unable to continue drawing (41). Here the association of time flying is similarly tied to the difficulties of connecting trauma and remembrance. Even as events fade, "the glowing tower persists"; even with the commemoration of an anniversary, the tower remains frozen in its falling. The image here isn't even considered a memory for Spiegelman: it persists even as "memories swirl." With all his attempts to move on from the experience, whether through public memory or political actions, the image of the tower remains, disrupting the very passing of time.

On the fifth broadsheet page Spiegelman likewise uses the glowing tower to define a temporal disruption of witnessing which begins with a series of panels throughout which the glowing skeleton of the tower similarly becomes more and more distorted (Figure 5.3). The first panel begins not with a synopsis, but with a rejection of the very testimony for which the deployment of a synopsis asks, "Leave me alone, Damn it! I'm just trying to

Figure 5.3 From *In the Shadow of No Towers* by Art Speigelman.

comfortably relive my September 11 trauma but you keep interrupting—"
And the second frame continues, "Like that mind-numbing 2002 'anniversary' event, when you tried to wrap a flag around my head and suffocate
me!" The third frame is, "You rob from the poor and give to your pals like
a parody of Robin Hood while distracting me with your damn oil war."
And the fourth, "Then the recent elections—OW! I've gotta shut my eyes
and concentrate to still see the glowing bones of those towers . . ." And then
the fifth begins: "Trauma piles upon trauma! . . ." These repeated images
of the glowing outline of the North Tower are bound to a disruptive temporal logic for Spiegelman. The image "interrupts" his narrative while also
marking the return of the event: "trauma piles upon trauma." As on the
previous page, even when "events fade" and "memory swirls," the glowing
tower remains. Similarly, the anniversary of 9/11 is invoked twice here, and
both references are linked to suffocation and annihilation. As in the previous pages, the image of the tower disrupts such acts of memory, and the
Bush administration's fabrication of memory during the anniversary of 9/11
attempts to create a uniform image of the event, an image that would require
Spiegelman to "forget" what he saw, something his own witnessing cannot
allow. Hence the glowing girders intrude more and more persistently. More
importantly, the logic of time moving while standing still, as in the previous
page, reflects the impossibility of identification and the horrors of an inadequate narrative to bear the weight of the subject's seeing. But there's also
the sense that Spiegelman's particular image of the collapsing tower frozen
in time will become wiped out by the constant barrage of media coverage
and expressions of nationalism: he must close his eyes and concentrate just
to envision this moment outside of time and memory.

In the week following 9/11, well before Spiegelman even considered the
broadsheet project that would become *In the Shadow of No Towers,* Spiegelman created one of the most memorable covers for the *New Yorker,* marking
the absence of the two towers by portraying them as shadows on a black
background. This image, which also appears on the cover to *In the Shadow of
No Towers,* posits an inability to give coherence to the very object of trauma:
all that remain are shadows. The comix form of *In the Shadow of No Towers*
continually subverts anything that might be placed in the position of casting
such a shadow. Spiegelman has said that he chose the collage style deliberately:
"I wanted to sort out the fragments of what I'd experienced from the media
images that threatened to engulf what I actually saw" (iv). One might suggest
that Spiegelman lets the repeated image of the glowing tower represent this
object whose shadow remains. But as Spiegelman himself admits, the image
of the dissolving tower offers no substance to stand in for what's lost; the towers themselves are mere shadows in this regard. Spiegelman's repeated use of
the glowing girders responds to the representation of the event's reality. In this
sense, these images and words show the subject's encounter with something
real: the recurring image of the glowing towers is real to Spiegelman but does
not match the reality ascribed by the media or other witnesses. The image

cannot render the event coherent, and images that offer coherence cannot do so without threatening to take the place of Spiegelman's image, which in turn would negate his position as witness. Spiegelman's deployment of the image points to the trouble with identifying reality with what's real, with confusing politics or other identificatory fictions with the moment of seeing and witness. To live in the shadow of no towers is to live without absolute referents, to bear witness without yet having construed a memory of the event.

Spiegelman's image of the glowing tower offers a contrast to Jean Baudrillard's claim that images of 9/11 become objects of consumption rather than means of bearing witness. In *The Spirit of Terrorism,* Baudrillard argues that

> The role of images is highly ambiguous. For, at the same time as they exalt the event, they also take it hostage. They serve to multiply it to infinity and, at the same time, they are a diversion and a neutralization . . . The image consumes the event, in the sense that it absorbs it and offers it for consumption. Admittedly, it gives it unprecedented impact, but impact as image-event. (27)

At one level, Spiegelman's text clearly supports Baudrillard's point regarding the media's packaging of the event such that all that remains is the package. However, his image of the glowing tower presents a radically particular image, an image that cannot be universally reproduced or experienced. In fact, this pixilated image offers an alternative to the infinitely reproduced image: it draws attention to the very mechanism of image reproduction, to how the image dissipates and fragments rather than offers the cohesive response that the media suggests. Likewise, Spiegelman subverts photographs, prototypical mass-produced images, identifying them as objects of propaganda. The central image in his text was, he says, never photographed. As points of juxtaposition, he does include some photographic images in his comix (or at least images that have a more precise photographic quality). Both are advertisements. The first is the picture of a large falling Doc Marten shoe framed as an advertisement for "Jihad Brand Footware," with the headline "Waiting for that Other Shoe to Drop" (1). The only other photograph in *In the Shadow of No Towers* is of a billboard advertising Arnold Schwarzenegger's film *Collateral Damage.* Spiegelman describes his encounter with this sign in the third person:

> He saw the burning towers as he and his wife ran to Canal Street toward the school . . . but his view was obstructed as he ran up the next block . . . He could only see smoke billowing behind a giant billboard . . . It was for some dopey new Schwarzenegger movie about terrorism. Oddly in the aftermath of September 11th, some pundits insisted that irony was dead. (2)

The irony here of course is that the image of a filmic terrorism occludes the actual event happening blocks away: the unreal photographic representation gets in the way of what is really occurring. Marianne Hirsch also comments on this moment in Spiegelman's text, offering a complementary reading of the film's title:

> But the giant poster obstructing the view of the burning towers itself exemplifies the movie's title, "collateral damage"—a euphemism for the destruction of people and property not directly targeted by the military. But in the context of 9/11 (and the wars that followed), "collateral damage" also describes both the cost of seeing the traumatic real and the costs of not being allowed to see. (1214)

Spiegelman also uses few photographs in *Maus* and as here they consistently indicate the fabrication of the narrative of the testimony; these images run the risk of obfuscating the real trauma. In *Maus II,* for example, he includes a photograph of his father posing in a prisoner uniform taken well after his release. Although Vladek's story is true, the photograph at one level is not: it was taken later as a souvenir. *In the Shadow of No Towers* also undermines the photographic image as a means of bearing witness, while offering the comix image as the only way Spiegelman can hold onto what he saw. It's the drawn image, the less *real* image, which is in fact more real. But even this "more real" comix image fails to represent the event as such. Instead it points toward the absence of such a real image.

Spiegelman makes a similar point when responding to the outrage and violence surrounding the publication of Danish comics using images of Mohammad. Spiegelman finds the uproar about the comics surprising considering that at the same time photographs were released depicting torture by American troops in Iraq:

> The most baffling aspect of this whole affair is why all the violent demonstrations focus on the dopey cartoons rather than on the truly horrifying torture photos seen regularly on Al Jazeera, on European television, everywhere but the mainstream media of the United States. Maybe it's because those photos of actual violation don't have the magical aura of things unseen, like the damn cartoons. ("Drawing Blood" 47)

Even here Spiegelman suggests that comics do not offer the possibility of representing that which defies imaging, for example Mohammad or the divine or the trauma of one man's experience of 9/11. Comics that attempt to do so are simply "dopey" and ultimately undermine their own aim: they and their readers simply confuse the "aura of the unseen" with the image of the unseen. And it is the power of this impossibility to represent that lures us, that makes images that are not realistic more real than the "real" thing.

In addressing these precise stakes of visual representation and trauma, Marianne Hirsch defines the inherently fragmented structure at work in Spiegelman's aesthetic. Her reading of *In the Shadow of No Towers* locates both its formal object and its epistemological challenges:

> Through its comics form, *In the Shadow of No Towers,* like its prede-
> cessor *Maus,* also performs an aesthetics of trauma: it is fragmentary,
> composed of small boxes that cannot contain the material which ex-
> ceeds their frames and the structure of the page. Architecturally mirror-
> ing the structure of the towers and thereby allowing us to keep them in
> view even as they collapse in front of our eyes, again and again, *In the
> Shadow of No Towers* operates on a number of levels at once. (1213)

Taking this slightly further, whereas photographs offer the illusion of full-
ness even while subjectifying the image as framed, Spiegelman's comix form
allows for the framing to be the subject; the glowing image of the tower before
it falls always dissolves before the frame can contain it. Hirsch continues:

> In the frames of Spiegelman's pages, words and images that in their
> media representation and repetition threaten to lose their wounding
> power reappear in newly alienated, and thus freshly powerful, form.
> In this work Spiegelman mobilizes comics and the acts of seeing and
> reading they demand in an attempt to see beyond the given-to-be-seen
> and to say what cannot otherwise be said. (1215)

Hirsch here maintains that Spiegelman's images offer something tangible
beyond the "given-to-be-seen" or, as in her comment about *Collateral
Damage,* that there is something visible behind the media advertisement.
However, Spiegelman's text suggests the contrary, that there is nothing he
can offer—that he can imagine—that could represent the towers falling
again and again. An object that did so would return to the logic of the
Danish cartoons. Rather, what Spiegelman does demonstrate is the problem of the towers having never completely fallen; for him, they and he are
stuck in the moment before the fall, before the action is complete. This
reading supports Levinas's claim that the ethics of representation begins in
this prioritizing of the saying in the said, the trace of the enunciation that
points outside a temporal order that cannot find its way into the said without tripping it up, without acknowledging the wound even as the wound is
made. And it is such a moment that marks the subject's act of witnessing,
what Jacques Lacan defines as the moment of seeing that is bound to the
moments of understanding and concluding. For Lacan, these are retroactive
moments where one can only speak of a moment of seeing within the context of concluding: the traumatic kernel itself only appears as a function of
representation. Spiegelman ultimately portrays this retroactive motion by
insisting on the glowing tower across his 9/11 narrative, a direct response
to the media images attempting to force his vision to a conclusion.

Another way Spiegelman defines the retroactive function of trauma and
image is by using old comic characters from early last century. One of Spiegelman's observations is that the reality of 9/11 as a space comes before the
event itself and the comic figures of a previous age prefigure the event of 9/11

not in their content or politics, but in their ephemeral existence. The comics, he says, like the towers, were not made to last. There are many other examples where previous images shape the production of 9/11 memory. Charles Hill and Marguerite Helmers, for example, discuss how the image of three fire fighters raising the American flag over the ruins of the World Trade Center is prefigured by the Marines' raising the flag over Iwo Jima, that the Iwo Jima photograph itself stages the 9/11 image (5–6). Like the repetition of this image, Spiegelman's deployment of earlier comic material marks a return of the event. However, unlike Hill and Helmer's example, Spiegelman's resurrected comics function as shadows to a previous age rather than as mechanisms for narrative emplotment. They prefigure the event of 9/11 through their own demise and subsequent return in Spiegelman's text. By invoking these ephemeral images, Spiegelman makes visible a kernel of something that depopulates the image as a receptacle for trauma that makes it impossible to hypothesize or fictionalize an event to take the place of its occurrence. By binding the insistent image of the glowing tower, an image outside of time (the tower always on the verge of falling but not falling), with a host of comic characters almost forgotten (only existing in archives), *In the Shadow of No Towers* demonstrates the temporal impossibility in the structure of bearing witness, a structure that rests on the anamorphic precession of the spoken and the seen, wherein, as Maurice Blanchot remarks, "every reality, safe and sound, sinks" (38).

Spiegelman's use of old comic figures in his comix offers an encounter between the past and present while also demonstrating a failure of such images to bear the weight of his vision, to move his act of witness into the realms of testimony and history. Spiegelman's comix form is filled with such persistent intertextuality to the point that the real brilliance of his work resides in the constant dialogue with past forms and figures. Spiegelman's tracings of comic history consistently find their way into his work, troubling the present with the past where memory intrudes. *Maus II*, for example, begins with a quote from a German newspaper article from the 1930s:

> Mickey Mouse is the most miserable ideal ever revealed . . . Healthy emotions tell every independent young man and every honorable youth that the dirty and filth-covered vermin, the greatest bacteria carrier in the animal kingdom, cannot be the ideal type of animal . . . Away with Jewish brutalization of the people! Down with Mickey Mouse! Wear the Swastika Cross! (3)

Spiegelman's portrayal of Jews as mice is itself an insertion of comic history into the present narrative of his father's retelling of his Holocaust experiences. And although such insertions help define the shape of the narrative, they are unable to bear the burden of witness explicitly.

In his commentary in the center pages of *In the Shadow of No Towers*, Spiegelman describes the intrusion of these comic figures from a now distant past into his own response to 9/11:

The only cultural artifacts that could get past my defense to flood my eyes and brain with something other than images of burning towers were old comic strips; vital, unpretentious ephemera from the optimistic dawn of the 20th Century. That they were made with so much skill and verve but never intended to last past the day they appeared in the newspaper gave them poignancy; they were just right for an end-of-the-world moment. (Center pages)

What links the towers themselves and the comics from early in the last century is their mortality: neither, says Spiegelman, were meant to last. Of course, the architects of the World Trade Center thought differently, but the comic figures that precede them contest that intent. Spiegelman addresses this idea explicitly on the top of the eighth broadsheet page.

With the title "In the Shadow of No Towers" across the top, Spiegelman draws a collection of old comic characters falling though space after being kicked by an Osama bin Laden-esque bearded goat wearing a turban (Figure 5.4). The caption reads: "The blast that disintegrated those Lower Manhattan towers also disinterred the ghosts of some Sunday supplement stars born on nearby Park Row about a century earlier. They came back to haunt one denizen of the neighborhood addled by all that's happened since" (8). This same image of falling cartoon characters also cuts across the front cover of *In the Shadow of No Towers,* slicing across the blackened image of the absent two towers marked only by their shadows. The fates of the two ephemera, the towers themselves and the archival comic figures, are bound for Spiegelman: the goat in the form of a media-generated image of Osama bin Laden functions both as the cause of the towers' collapse and of the comics' return. In both cases the central trauma lies in the inadequacy of any of these images to bear the weight of Spiegelman's witness.

Likewise, the most persistent use of these earlier comic characters is Spiegelman's representation of the two towers in the guise of Rudolph Dirk's Katzenjammer Kids, who appear on many of the broadsheets wearing a tower on top of each of their heads. However, these comic sketches, while offering critiques of American responses to 9/11, give no real coherence to what Spiegelman experienced. Similarly, there are several instances where Spiegelman places himself in the guise of Happy Hooligan. In one such example, in the tenth broadsheet, both Spiegelman and his wife are

Figure 5.4 From *In the Shadow of No Towers* by Art Speigelman

portrayed in Happy Hooligan attire, complete with tin cans on their heads, as they discuss an offer for Spiegelman to be interviewed by Tom Brokaw. Portraying his Happy Hooligan character on his way to the interview, Spiegelman includes the caption: "Note: Though Happy Hooligan is a *fictional* character borrowed from the first Sunday comics, the following interview is 100% nonfiction." At one level, surface similarities exist between these comic figures and the characters to which they refer. Portraying himself as Happy Hooligan answering questions posed by an NBC producer (his answers, he's told, will be spliced into Brokaw's subsequent asking of the questions) fits the disjointedness of Spiegelman's experience. When asked what "the place in America where I feel most American is . . . ," Spiegelman as Happy Hooligan replies, "Paris, France" (10). This return of the Happy Hooligan figure allows Spiegelman to speak pieces of his story askew, scripted as a character "clueless" about conventions. As Happy Hooligan, he offers a context for his own position outside media expectations: similarly when asked about his favorite American food, he responds "Shrimp Pad Thai." On the one hand, Spiegelman uses this comic figure to give the media responses to 9/11 coherence: both the Happy Hooligan and Katzjammer Kids references offer pointed commentary on the media's construction of 9/11 and Spiegelman's bewilderment at that construction. On the other hand, Spiegelman's deployment of these images fails to offer up a suitable response to 9/11 itself, fails to break through the timelessness that haunts his vision. As he says, because they were made not to last, these comic figures are just the thing "for an end-of-the-world moment," and it is for this reason that they "haunt" him.

Perhaps the immediacy of the event makes Spiegelman situate his comics within a very precise historical frame. Whereas Spiegelman's drawings make up the first ten pages of the text, the last six broadsheet pages contain a series of comics from early in the last century, many of which have explicit connections to New York City or to criticism of government policies of the time. But in all these cases, there's nothing really connected to the events of 9/11 except, as Spiegelman argues, their ephemeral nature. The images and his commentary on their history do provide a certain context for their reappearance in his own work. However, Spiegelman never offers anything that might localize that context into some insight into 9/11. There is no sense that history is recurring. Instead, these comics and the towers are only bound by a shared location (Lower Manhattan) and mortality. But this common mortality, their shared ephemeral nature, does not lead to coherence and memory but rather functions as a reminder of fragmentation and forgetfulness.

Spiegelman most directly critiques the inability of media representations of trauma to offer a point from which to bear witness on the inside front and back covers to *In the Shadow of No Towers*. Reproduced on both is the front page from the *New York World* from a different 9/11, September 11, 1901 (Figure 5.5).

Figure 5.5 From *In the Shadow of No Towers* by Art Speigelman.

The headline and stories describe the aftermath of the shooting of President McKinley, focusing specifically on the arrest of Emma Goldman as a potential co-conspirator of the self-confessed assassin Leon Czolgosz (McKinley was shot on the 6th and he would die on the 14th). On 9/11/1901, Emma Goldman had just been arrested and the *New York World* was feeding the frenzy of an "Anarchist Conspiracy." Written across this reproduction is Spiegelman's title along with the same image of the molten skeleton of the North Tower. The back cover reproduces

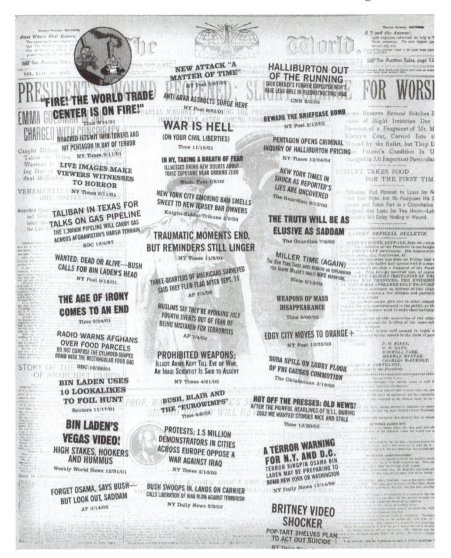

Figure 5.6 From *In the Shadow of No Towers* by Art Spiegelman.

the same front page from the *World,* but this time superimposes contemporary 9/11 headlines from papers and magazines (Figure 5.6). The headlines include the *New York Times*'s "Live Images Make Viewers Witness to Horror" (9/11/01), the *Weekly World News*'s "Bin Laden's Vegas Video! High Stakes, Hookers and Hummus" (12/3/01), and the *Oklahoman*'s "Soda Spill on Lobby Floor of FBI Causes Commotion" (12/30/02). Overtly, Spiegelman is playing with these two dates and their media responses, linking the yellow journalism charge to both 9/11 coverages. However, his point lies not in the causal overlap or even similarity between these two moments in history. Rather, in both reproductions of the *World* front page, Spiegelman points out the inability of any of the headlines to designate something real, the "eventness" of the event, to return to Blanchot. In fact, such headlines and articles simply articulate a position from which one might not see the object of inquiry, which is covered over by terms such as "assassination" and "terrorism." Likewise, on the inside back cover the recurring image of the North Tower's collapse is replaced with a repetition of Spiegelman's "Tower Twins," a return of the Katzenjammer Kids, Hans and Fritz. The image of the kids appears right above the headline from *Time:* "Fire! The World Trade Center Is on Fire!" By placing the molten image of the tower in the center of the *World* page in the front of his book, Spiegelman places his own memory, his own horror, at the center, an image with no words or description save the title "In the Shadow of No Towers." And by ending with the absence of that image, with ephemeral headlines and the redacted comics, Spiegelman recognizes what threatens the witness of such horror. Such headlines and redactions of 9/11 become acts of forgetting: "Nothing like commemorating an event to help you forget. September 11, 2001, was a *memento mori,* an end to civilization as we knew it. By 2003 genuine awe has been reduced to the mere 'shock and awe' of jingoistic strutting" (10). For Spiegelman, history becomes a means not of defining the present or even giving it context. Rather, Spiegelman's invocations of the past all speak to the inadequacies of scripting the present as a past, of constructing an adequate space from which to remember what one saw.

Spiegelman's use of varied images points to the fact that we have spent the past several years avoiding 9/11, actively forgetting it. Of course this avoidance takes form as a persistent preoccupation with the event. And it is precisely in this preoccupation that we find ways not to see *something.* Slavoj Žižek supports just such a conclusion in his reading of media coverage of 9/11:

> [T]he true choice apropos of historical traumas is not the one between remembering or forgetting them: traumas we are not ready or able to remember haunt us all the more forcefully. We should therefore accept the paradox that, in order really to forget an event, we must first summon up the strength to remember it properly. In order to account for this paradox, we should bear in mind that the opposite of existence is not nonexistence, but *insistence:* that which does not exist, continues to insist, striving towards existence. (22)

Spiegelman's text reveals this insistence by demonstrating the inadequacies of what is brought into existence to bear such a burden. By focusing on ironic turns and temporal displacement, *In the Shadow of No Towers* becomes less a text about political responses to a traumatic event than an exploration of how such an event persists amid such responses. The towers are gone, but their shadow remains, insisting without existing.

Most approaches to representations of trauma define a therapeutic value in such acts. Dominick LaCapra in his readings of Holocaust testimony, for example, suggests that such texts exhibit a "working through" of the material, where the representation itself serves as a necessary screen for and to the witness. Similarly, Michael Bernard-Donals and I have argued that representation offers a redemptive possibility. Though our argument acknowledges an inherent impossibility at the heart of such acts, we, like LaCapra, suggest that only acts of bearing witness make teaching and learning possible. Spiegelman's text, however, suggests that such resolution of trauma ultimately sacrifices something truthful in favor of a coherent history. Like Levinas, Spiegelman offers much less potential for any given said to get at the saying or any image to take the place of seeing. It is one thing to suggest that speaking about trauma involves an act of sublimation, a maintenance of the saying in the face of the said. It is quite another to suggest that through the act of saying the said becomes enough, that she who speaks about what she saw can put aside either the speaking or the seeing by offering up the spoken. When Levinas suggests that bearing witness is not simply the what-has-been-spoken but rather "other than that," other than the thematization that seamlessly leads to cause and effect, he offers us more than an ethics of reading that prioritizes a representation that remains unrepresented. Like Levinas, Spiegelman's *In the Shadow of No Towers* suggests that the witness as witness resides in the act of seeing and that this seeing remains in every act of witness, that the epistemology of witness is grounded on a moment that refuses to be incorporated into the movement of time. There is no redemption for the witness of trauma, no Benjaminian angel of history to make adequate meaning out of the traumatic event.

How, then, does one find one's way in the dark created by such a shadow without an object? How does one situate subjectivity when even Plato's allegory of shadow hides the absence of the objects from which shadow is cast? Even suggesting that testimony is in some way only a shadow of an event misses the mark since the event that could cast such a shadow never was. Put another way, testimony and remembrance are about reality; there is no privileging of the real in either remembrance or testimony just as there is no privileging of the real in reality. Quite the opposite. When Dori Laub suggests that there is something important in the testimony of a survivor who says she saw more than one crematorium exploding in flames during the uprising of the Sondercommando in Auschwitz when in fact there was only one, he is making a claim about the real of the woman's testimony over its mistaken factuality: in the seamlessness of factual reality, the anamorphic moment of the real is lost, occluded (59–62). It is this impossibility of the real that Spiegelman privileges in his text. Not the images of the towers as we all saw them that morning on television or even perhaps from our roof tops or car windows. It's the image of the glowing steel skeleton that persists in Spiegelman's vision, that doesn't go away, that never was, that is not occluded either by the narrative of his experience or the media/government memorials of the event or even the intrusion of disinterred comic characters.

Spiegelman's inclusion of the older comics and the newspaper page at the beginning and end gesture toward a prefiguring of the image that is not there even to cast a shadow; the disaster as such is in its anticipation (Blanchot); the object that comes into view is neither the anamorphic memento mori nor the mark of knowledge of the event. Rather, such images simply fill in the subjective space waiting for them; they may be reality, but they're not real. Spiegelman, on the other hand, places his claim not in an image that ever was, that can be reproduced, but in an image that can only be particularly construed. Spiegelman's image for 9/11 cannot take the place of the space that the loss of the towers opens. It is a shadow of no towers and thus confronts the very problem of not seeing what is demanded to be seen. Even his attempt at politicizing his response by couching some of his comix within an earlier comic strip tradition can't give substance to his own position as witness; unlike his use of mice and cats in *Maus,* these references do not lend coherence to his account nor do they offer a position from which to look back; even including the originals of the comics does not help. On the contrary, Spiegelman's text offers up a witness without such grounding, a witness who consciously does not know what he has seen, who only knows that he has seen.

NOTES

1. Spiegelman refers to his work as "comix," a term that suggests not only the overlapping of image and text, but also the blurring or mixing of genre and form. For discussions of Spiegelman's comix form in relation to his representation of trauma see James Young's "The Holocaust as Vicarious Past" and Dominick LaCapra's *History and Memory after Auschwitz,* especially chapter 5.
2. For a further discussion of Spiegelman's *Maus* and its focus on bearing witness, see my "Maus and the Epistemology of Witness."

WORKS CITED

Baudrillard, Jean. *The Spirit of Terrorism and Other Essays.* Trans. Chris Turner. London: Verso, 2002.

Bernard-Donals, Michael, and Richard Glejzer. *Between Witness and Testimony: the Holocaust and the Limits of Representation.* Albany: SUNY UP, 2001.

Blanchot, Maurice. *The Writing of the Disaster.* Trans. Ann Smock. Lincoln: U of Nebraska P, 1986.

Caruth, Cathy. *Unclaimed Experience: Trauma, Narrative, and History.* Baltimore; Johns Hopkins UP, 1996.

Espiritu, Karen. "'Putting Grief into Boxes': Trauma and the Crisis of Democracy in Art Spiegelman's *In the Shadow of No Towers*." *Review of Education, Pedagogy, and Cultural Studies* 28 (2006): 179–201.

Glejzer, Richard. "Maus and the Epistemology of Witness." *Witnessing the Disaster: Essays on Representations of the Holocaust*. Ed. Michael Bernard-Donals and Richard Glejzer. Madison: U of Wisconsin P, 2003. 125–40.

Hill, Charles and Marguerite Helmers. "Introduction." *Defining Visual Rhetorics*. Ed. Charles Hill and Marguerite Helmers. Matewah: Lawrence Erlbaum, 2004. 1–24.

Hirsch, Marianne. "Editor's Column: Collateral Damage." *PMLA* 119 (2004): 1209–15.

Lacan, Jacques. "Logical Time and the Assertion of Anticipated Certainty." *Ecrits: The First Complete English Translation*. Trans. Bruce Fink. New York: Norton, 2005. 161–75.

LaCapra, Dominick. *History and Memory after Auschwitz*. Ithaca: Cornell UP, 1998.

Laub, Dori. "Bearing Witness or the Vicissitudes of Listening." *Testimony: Crises of Witnessing in Literature, Psychoanalysis, and History*. Ed. Shoshana Felman and Dori Laub. New York: Routledge, 1992.

Levinas, Emmanuel. *Totality and Infinity*. Trans. Alphonso Lingis. Pittsburgh: Duquesne UP, 1969.

Spiegelman, Art. "Drawing Blood: Outrageous Cartoons and the Art of Outrage." *Harpers Magazine* June 2006: 43–52.

———. *In the Shadow of No Towers*. New York: Pantheon, 2004.

———. *Maus: A Survivors Tale*. New York: Pantheon, 1986.

Young, James. "The Holocaust as Vicarious Past." *Witnessing the Disaster: Essays on Representation and the Holocaust*. Ed. Michael Bernard-Donals and Richard Glejzer. Madison: U of Wisconsin P, 2003. 23–45.

Žižek, Slavoj. *Welcome to the Desert of the Real! Five Essays on September 11 and Related Dates*. London: Verso, 2002.

Part 2

9/11 Politics and Representation

6 Seeing Terror, Feeling Art
Public and Private in Post-9/11 Literature

Michael Rothberg

More than five years after the attacks of September 11, 2001, it is not yet clear what "literature after 9/11" will be. The question of whether September 11 represents a cultural rupture remains open. Indeed, there is much continuity to be found. While post-9/11 literary works replay many familiar themes and techniques of post-World War II American literature, numerous pre-9/11 works foreshadow contemporary concerns, sometimes in quite uncanny ways. Thus, I begin this chapter on literature after 9/11 with a pre-9/11 work that quite self-consciously addresses many of the questions that haunt writers working in the aftermath of the terrorist attacks. Don DeLillo's *Mao II* (1991), a novel written in proximity to the controversy surrounding Salman Rushdie's novel *The Satanic Verses*, suggests a critical framework that can help illuminate the political stakes of aesthetic acts in the wake of 9/11.

A reading of *Mao II* provides resources to formulate initial hypotheses about terrorism and literature. DeLillo's work suggests that we should not separate the discourse on terrorism after 9/11 from the discourse before 9/11; pre-9/11 discussion offers important insights into our world and suggests that we need to be careful about how we periodize the "before" and the "after."[1] In addition, DeLillo's pre-9/11 writings help us to reflect on the fact that terrorist acts today, and especially the attacks of September 11, are, among other things, a form of spectacle: they are intended for a global, mass audience of media consumers. Thus, we need to think about terrorism in relation to other aspects of mass-mediated society.[2] By virtue of being a mass-media spectacle, *Mao II* demonstrates, terrorist acts also create a short-circuit between the public realm of images and news and the private realm of the audience and its emotional responses.[3] Taking inspiration from these insights offered by DeLillo's pre-9/11 novel, I advance an argument about literature's potential social and political contribution in a post-9/11 age defined by a seemingly endless "war on terror."

My overarching claim is that literature and other forms of art are important sites of response to terrorism because, as my reading of *Mao II* will begin to demonstrate, they illustrate the interconnectedness of the public and the private and allow us to reconnect our faculties of seeing and feeling, two forms of connection that both terrorism and mass society threaten. These characteristics of literature suggest that the aesthetic has a particular role to play in responding both to acts of extreme violence and to the political processes in which they unfold and to which they give rise. The aesthetic is neither an apolitical zone closed off from violence nor a realm that can simply be subsumed under the seemingly more urgent activity of politics, even in a moment of perpetual emergency. Rather, the aesthetic constitutes a bridging realm that connects subjective experience to larger collectivities. In Kant's canonical understanding in the *Critique of the Power of Judgment,* aesthetic judgment provides a "transition" across the "incalculable gulf between the domain of the concept of nature, as the sensible, and the domain of the concept of freedom, as the supersensible" (63). In the works discussed in this chapter I find an attempt to bridge seeing, feeling, and understanding, on the one hand, and the subjective and the collective, on the other. This latter bridging is close to Kant's general definition of judgment as "the faculty for thinking of the particular as contained under the universal" (66). In the case of aesthetics, as Kant makes clear, the particular form of judgment is reflective, which is to say that the universal is not given in advance as it is in determinate judgment (67).[4] Aesthetic reflection consists of a groping after the universal from a particular, embodied position. Thus, although focused on the question of disinterested reception, Kantian aesthetic judgment does not presuppose a passive spectator but rather a spectator actively engaged with the world in both cognitive and affective registers. Within this context, the purely ideological concept of the "war on terror" reveals its moment of truth. By focusing on feeling ("terror") instead of a particular political tactic ("terrorism"), the phrase draws our attention to the affective level of politics and points us toward literature's potential counter-force—a reconstruction of relations between thinking and feeling that both acts of terrorism and the imperial war on terror attempt to sever.

In order to address these issues, I focus first on DeLillo's novel and then on two apparently "subjective" genres—the essay and the lyric—and argue that they all forge important moments of "transition" across the "incalculable gulf" described by Kant. After *Mao II,* I turn to DeLillo's initial response to the 9/11 attacks, "In the Ruins of the Future," an essay published in *Harper's Magazine,* and then to poems by three New York writers, Anne-Marie Levine ("Four November 9ths"), Suheir Hammad ("first writing since"), and D. Nurkse ("October Marriage"). I seek to demonstrate that literature has provided one of the most effective sites for reflection on the meanings of American life after 9/11. Even as they begin from the most intimate locations, the poems by Levine, Hammad, and Nurkse that I discuss here have, along with DeLillo's essay, begun the critical post-9/11 tasks of bridging the public and the private, the local and the global, and our faculties of seeing, feeling, and understanding. DeLillo, Levine, Hammad, and Nurkse offer aesthetic works that are also ethical and pedagogical acts; they seek to stimulate a movement out from writers' and readers' subjective experiences toward an encounter with global histories.

NOVELISTS AND TERRORISTS: BEFORE SEPTEMBER 11

Mao II tells the story of Bill Gray, a Salinger-esque (or perhaps DeLillo-esque!), secretive, and extremely private writer, who finds himself drawn into an uncertain world of conspiracy and terror. Near the beginning of the novel, Bill has taken the uncharacteristic step of agreeing to let himself be photographed by Brita, who is creating a documentary record of writers around the world. As Brita photographs Bill, they converse about the New York City skyline, including the World Trade Center, and Brita tells Bill about the fear associated with her project: "Yes, I travel. Which means there is no moment on certain days when I'm not thinking terror. They have us in their power. In boarding areas I never sit near windows in case of flying glass" (40–41). Brita's musings prompt Bill to expound one of his favorite pet theories:

> There's a curious knot that binds novelists and terrorists. In the West we become famous effigies as our books lose the power to shape and influence. Do you ask your writers how they feel about this? Years ago I used to think it was possible for a novelist to alter the inner life of the culture. Now bombmakers and gunmen have taken that territory. They make raids on human consciousness. What writers used to do before we were all incorporated. (41)

Later in the novel, Bill brings up a similar theme in a discussion with George Haddad, his link to a terrorist group in Beirut that is holding a Swiss writer hostage, a writer Bill is trying to help free: "For some time now," Bill tells George, "I've had the feeling that novelists and terrorists are playing a zero-sum game. . . . What terrorists gain, novelists lose. The degree to which they influence mass consciousness is the extent of our decline as shapers of sensibility and thought. The danger they represent equals our own failure to be dangerous" (156–57). In these passages, DeLillo creates the unlikely association of literature and terrorism in order to sketch a shift in the relation between public and private. Like a work of literature, terrorism is a public act that defines its success or failure by its ability to penetrate into the private sphere. Both literature and terrorism target "the inner life," "human consciousness," "sensibility," and "thought." As George Haddad responds to Bill Gray's "zero-sum" theory, "the more clearly we see terror, the less impact we feel from art" (157). It's important to take George's terms seriously: we *see* terror and thus do not *feel* art. Although written a decade before 9/11, DeLillo seems to forecast important aspects of our contemporary situation. For most of us, the terrorist attacks of 9/11 were experienced as something we saw—as a spectacle—and what we saw had an immediate impact on what we felt. The passage from seeing to feeling associated with terrorism in the age of instantaneous communications technology—and its effect on more traditional forms of media, such as literature—is an important point to hold on to in our discussion of 9/11.

There is another key aspect of Bill's discussion of the impact of terrorism—Bill is particularly concerned about the problem of how to affect "mass consciousness," not simply individual consciousness. Indeed, *Mao II*'s central concern beyond terrorism is with the way contemporary society is constituted by masses of people. As the novel prophecies, "The future belongs to crowds" (16). The famous opening scene of *Mao II* attempts to capture mass experience by describing the wedding of thousands of followers of Reverend Sun Myung Moon in Yankee Stadium, an event that, like terrorist acts, is frightening in the way it seems to crush the individual by substituting a spectacle for an intimate ritual. As the father of one of the brides describes the scene: "here is the drama of mechanical routine played out with living figures. It knocks him back in awe, the loss of scale and intimacy, the way love and sex are multiplied out, the numbers and shaped crowd. This really scares him, a mass of people turned into a sculptured object" (7). Crowds, like terrorism, threaten the individual, and thus might be seen as a threat to novelists as well, since novels would seem to require individual characters in order to succeed as works of literature, just as they require individual readers whose inner life and consciousness are open to the shaping power of art. With his prophecy, "[t]he future belongs to crowds," DeLillo suggests that the Moonie wedding does not represent an eccentric, far out anomaly, but rather a tendency within dominant society. For the "loss of scale and intimacy, the way love and sex are multiplied out," could be said to characterize our own spectacular media society as much as they do the behavior of one marginal cult. Indeed, this scene seems to illustrate perfectly one of Hannah Arendt's descriptions of mass society in *The Human Condition:* "people suddenly behave as though they were members of one family, each multiplying and prolonging the perspective of his neighbor" (qtd. in Warner 61). The fact that in *Mao II* that loss of scale and intimacy gives birth to a "sculptured object" reveals DeLillo's belief that mass consciousness is or has become a fundamentally aesthetic form, albeit an aesthetic that blocks cognition instead of providing a link between understanding and feeling (a point to which I return below).

DeLillo's apparent response to the dilemmas posed by the simultaneous, spectacular powers of mass society and terrorist violence is not, however, what one might suspect—and this will be true after 9/11 as well as in *Mao II*. Rather than fleeing from the crowd and all experiences of the masses, the novel addresses readers with a question: to which crowd will the future belong? The "crowd where everyone dresses alike," as in the mass wedding and, in another scene, the Chinese Army? Or the "motley crowd" represented by the protesters in Tiananmen Square and the homeless refugees speaking "multilingual English" in New York's Tompkins Square (177, 149)? The novel ends with a sort of repetition of the opening Moonie wedding, a scene that suggests an ambivalent triumph for the motley crowd. This time the wedding takes place in Beirut. By this point, Bill Gray has failed in his quest to save the kidnapped poet and has been left dead in a ship on its way to Lebanon. Brita, in the meantime, has stopped photographing writers and is now in Beirut to take pictures of the terrorist leader whose group had been behind the kidnapping (giving some credence to Bill's claim that terrorists have replaced novelists!). Late one night Brita is awakened by noise outside of her window. She walks out onto the balcony and sees the surprising scene that constitutes the novel's final statement on crowds and violence:

> She leans over the rail and sees a tank come chugging around the corner into her cratered street. Mounted cannon bobbing. . . . The tank moves up the street and she hears voices, sees people walking behind it. Civilians talking and laughing and well dressed, twenty adults and half as many children, mostly girls in pretty dresses and white knee-stockings and patent-leather shoes. And here is the stunning thing that takes her a moment to understand, that this is a wedding party going by. The bride and groom carry champagne glasses and some of the girls hold sparklers that send off showers of excited light. A guest in a pastel tuxedo smokes a long cigar and does a dance around a shell hole, delighting the kids. The bride's gown is beautiful, with lacy appliqué at the bodice, and she looks surprisingly alive, they all look transcendent, free of limits and unsurprised to be here. They make it seem only natural that a wedding might advance its resplendence with a freelance tank as escort. . . . The tank is passing right below [Brita], turret covered in crude drawings, and she hurries inside and pours another glass of melon liqueur and comes out to toast the newlyweds, calling down, "Bonne chance" and "Bonheur" and "Good luck" and "Salám" and "Skål," and the gun turret begins to rotate and the cannon eases slowly around like a smutty honeymoon joke and everyone is laughing. The bridegroom raises his glass to the half-dressed foreigner on the top-floor balcony and then they pass into the night, followed by a jeep with a recoilless rifle mounted at the rear. (239–40)

If the Moonie mass wedding that opens *Mao II* depicts the threat that a charismatic leader poses to the individuality and freedom of his followers, the wedding in Beirut reclaims a moment of beauty from the ruins of war and a motley band of revelers. What is particularly striking about this wedding is the way it combines the traditional components of the ritual of marriage—the wedding party, the gown, the champagne, the dance, the toast—with the most unlikely of elements: a graffiti-covered tank and its mounted cannon. Instead of rejecting entirely the experiences marked as threats in the novel—terrorist violence and mass experience—DeLillo brings us dangerously close to them. He depicts a scene of utopian possibility in which a crowd celebrates a new beginning in close proximity to mass destruction, and he sets this moment of possibility in a city scarred by decades of civil war and terrorism. If, as *Mao II* suggests, novelists are in competition with terrorists and cults for the power to shape consciousness, DeLillo indicates that the response of writers cannot be to retreat to a pure, private experience or to attempt to banish from view the forces that threaten the public role of the writer. Rather, the writer must become something of a photojournalist. He must occupy the space of danger and meet terrorism on its own terrain—a terrain in which public events and private emotions intersect, in which the writer, like Brita, must address the world in multiple languages from the vulnerable position of a "half-dressed foreigner."

GOD IS GREAT: A POST-SECULAR PUBLIC

DeLillo's pre-9/11 strategy of risk-taking and public exposure reappears in his first important post-9/11 work. Less than three months after the attacks on New York and Washington, DeLillo published an essay in *Harper's Magazine* titled "In the Ruins of the Future: Reflections on Terror and Loss in the Shadow of September." In an essay that often sounds uncannily like his fiction, DeLillo begins on a note that seems to echo Bill Gray's theory of terrorism:

> In the past decade the surge of capital markets has dominated discourse and shaped global consciousness. Multinational corporations have come to seem more vital and influential than governments. The dramatic climb of the Dow and the speed of the Internet summoned us all to live permanently in the future, in the utopian glow of cyber-capital, because there is no memory there and this is where markets are uncontrolled and investment potential has no limit.
>
> All this changed on September 11. Today, again, the world narrative belongs to terrorists. . . . Terror's response is a narrative that has been developing over years, only now becoming inescapable. It is our lives and minds that are occupied now. . . . Our world, parts of our world, have crumbled into theirs, which means we are living in a place of danger and rage. (33)

Like his character Bill Gray, DeLillo is concerned with the question of who and what shapes collective consciousness, although here "global consciousness" replaces "mass consciousness" as the area of interest. In the essay, DeLillo once again cites terrorism's ability to shape consciousness by providing a public narrative that penetrates into the private sphere and "crumbles" into "our" living space. There is also a kind of periodization involved here: DeLillo does not say 9/11 is unprecedented; he says it has changed the world of the last decade and has returned us to an earlier moment when terrorists also shaped the world narrative, apparently the moment he recounted a decade earlier in *Mao II*. As in the novel, DeLillo's discussion is here structured around a binary opposition—not writers and terrorists, this time, but us and them. Our world has crumbled into their world; we are now in their place of danger and rage. The rhetoric of "us and them" has been one of the dominant motifs of the post-9/11 period—a rhetoric frequently cited in the literary response to September 11 that has its origins in President Bush's famous declarations that "You are either with us or against us," "with us or with the terrorists."[5]

In his 9/11 essay, DeLillo repeats this rhetoric, but he also complicates it in several ways. First of all, he reveals the instability of "us and them" thinking. Not only does such thinking seem to be present on both sides of the apparent divide, thus throwing into question whether the two sides are as different from each other as they suppose. He also demonstrates that both sides share an ability to occupy the space of the other. DeLillo suggests that the terrorists' desire to crumble our world into *theirs* derives from the preexisting fact that their world has already been crumbled into *ours:* their "fury" is sparked in part by "the power of American culture to penetrate every wall, home, life, and mind" (33). Like terrorism, at least in this way, American culture crosses every boundary and moves from the public sphere to the most intimate zones of the private home and individual mind.

Besides showing the parallelism between the powers of American culture and of terrorism to penetrate "every wall, home, life, and mind," DeLillo also uses another strategy to complicate "us and them" thinking. Once again, DeLillo suggests that the proper response to the situation of global mass culture and terrorist violence is not a retreat into privacy or a defense of the home (or maybe even the homeland) from what is public and foreign, but exactly the opposite. Like *Mao II*, "In the Ruins of the Future" concludes by bringing us close to what is apparently dangerous in order to find a measure of hope. DeLillo closes his essay by recounting two walks he took on Manhattan's Canal Street before and after September 11. Describing the scene on Canal Street three days after 9/11, DeLillo remembers "[d]ump trucks, flatbeds, sanitation sweepers," all heading into the "cloud of sand and ash" at the site of the disaster. This brief evocation of the area around Ground Zero then gives way to a memory of a visit to the same place one month earlier. He mentions the "great crowds of people, the panethnic swarm of shoppers, merchants, residents and passersby, with a few tourists and the man at the curbstone doing acupoint massage, and the dreadlocked kid riding his bike on the sidewalk. This was the spirit of Canal Street, the old jostle and stir unchanged for many decades" (40). After describing this incarnation of the motley crowd, DeLillo comes across a scene that he turns into a symbol and with which he ends his essay: "Then," he writes,

I saw the woman on the prayer rug. I'd just turned the corner, heading south to meet some friends, and there she was, young and slender, in a silk headscarf. It was time for sunset prayer, and she was kneeling, upper body pitched toward the edge of the rug. . . . Some prayer rugs include a *mihrab* in their design, an arched element representing the prayer niche in a mosque that indicates the direction of Mecca. The only locational guide the young woman needed was the Manhattan grid.

I looked at her in prayer and it was clearer to me than ever, the daily sweeping taken-for-granted greatness of New York. The city will accommodate every language, ritual, belief, and opinion. In the rolls of the dead of September 11, all these vital differences were surrendered to the impact and flash. The bodies themselves are missing in large numbers. For the survivors, more grief. But the dead are their own nation and race, one identity, young or old, devout or unbelieving—a union of souls. During the *hadj*, the annual pilgrimage to Mecca, the faithful must eliminate every sign of status, income, and nationality, the men wearing identical strips of seamless white cloth, the women with covered heads, all recalling in prayer their fellowship with the dead.

Allahu akbar. God is great. (40)

In this final section of DeLillo's essay, Manhattan becomes analogous to Beirut at the end of *Mao II*. It is at once the site of extreme violence and death and also of the cosmopolitan possibilities that come with the coexistence of multiple languages and cultures. What is most striking about the passage is DeLillo's staging of these possibilities through a Muslim in prayer, who occupies public space to perform a private ritual. We've come a long way since the fall of 2001, but perhaps not so far that we cannot remember the atmosphere of those days; it was a time when to be visible as Muslim was a dangerous proposition and to speak with sympathy of a Muslim in prayer was to risk an association with the terrorists who acted in allegiance to a perverted interpretation of Islam. In our post-9/11, retrospective view of the young woman, we recognize her vulnerability, a slender, kneeling body in the middle of a bustling city. Perhaps in seeing her through DeLillo's eyes, we as readers also come to feel our own vulnerability to the "impact and flash" of violence. There is no way to find sympathy for terrorism in DeLillo's essay. Rather, we have something different: an understanding that our well-being—whoever "we" are—is intertwined with that which *seems* most "foreign," most dangerous, just as the young woman's prayer is intertwined with the "Manhattan grid." Instead of retreating into an us/them logic based on a secular/religious or reason/fanaticism divide, as many liberals have in the wake of September 11, DeLillo offers what might be considered a post-secular alternative: a vision that integrates private devotion into public space; a rooted cosmopolitanism that establishes a universalist "fellowship with the dead" at the same time that it finds a place for "half-dressed foreigners" and headscarf-clad citizens.

The two texts by DeLillo that I have discussed so far have a series of implications for our attempts to understand literature and terrorism before and after September 11. While I don't think we can assert based on two documents that *nothing* has changed since September 11, I do think that DeLillo helps us see that *not everything* has changed. *Mao II* reveals a fact that should be obvious but that is easy to forget or overlook in the immediacy of our current concerns: a discourse on terrorism (as well as the political tactic of terrorism) long preexisted 9/11 and continues to play a role in how we think about terror today. Since that lesson can be found in a multitude of places, what interests me most in DeLillo is how he negotiates the relationship between the public and the private and addresses the emotional politics of terror. I see his most important insights echoed not only in "In the Ruins of the Future," but also in some of the works that are emerging as a literature of 9/11: that terrorism and mass culture both involve a transformation of the relationship between the public sphere and the intimate realms of the personal; and that if we want to respond adequately to the very different threats that terrorism and mass society represent, we cannot simply reassert a separation of public and private spheres or attempt to wash our hands of the violence that spawns terrorism and that terrorism propagates.

Literature and other forms of art are especially important after 9/11 because they allow us to imagine alternative responses to the violence of terrorism and the spectacles of mass-mediated culture. Literature and art can become sites for exploring the intersections between the public and the private and for understanding the feelings that terrorism draws on and produces. Remember what George Haddad said to Bill Gray in *Mao II:* "the more clearly we *see* terror, the less impact we *feel* from art" (157; emphasis added). DeLillo's texts, I believe, help us to reimagine the possibility of seeing and feeling *at the same time* in order to foster an embodied form of understanding. This simultaneous seeing and feeling is close to what eighteenth-century philosophers like Kant meant when they talked about aesthetics. Combining Kant's terminology with DeLillo's, we can suggest that aesthetic acts (in other words, works of art) allow us to see and to feel simultaneously in a way that is different both from terrorism and from the mass media through which we inevitably experience terrorist acts.

Of many possible works, I want to focus on three poems published soon after the events of 9/11 by New York-based poets. Anne-Marie Levine's "Four November 9ths" and D. Nurkse's "October Marriage" both appeared in *Poetry after 9/11,* one of the first collective literary responses to the attacks, while Suheir Hammad's "first writing since" circulated widely on the Internet before appearing in various collections, including *Trauma at Home: After 9/11.* All three works link public and private experience in provocative ways, thus demonstrating an ongoing engagement with opportunities for bridging and transition that aesthetic experience makes possible according to the Kantian tradition: Levine bridges individual and collective histories while "provincializing" national memory; Hammad returns us to the questions of religion and difference in the public sphere; and Nurkse draws particular attention to sensory experience in an age of media and terrorism.

THE NUMEROLOGY OF DISASTER: WHAT HISTORY TEACHES

Anne-Marie Levine's poem "Four November 9ths" links world history and the individual lifespan through the figure of coincidence. Levine, a New York-based writer and artist born in Belgium and raised in Southern California, meditates on the curious accident of her birthday, November 9, 1938. The date, she writes:

> was evidently not a thing
> to be remembered or told,
> because I was not made aware of the coincidence
> of my birthday until several months before my 50th birthday,
> which coincided with, and was commemorated and announced as
> the 50th anniversary of Kristallnacht. (53)

And not only that, as the poet will later discover. Soon a friend informs her that November 9th "is a very big day in the history of Germany," a day that commemorates four of the most significant events of the twentieth century: not only the 1938 pogrom against German Jews, but also the abdication of the Kaiser in 1918; Hitler's first attempt to seize power (the failed "Beer Hall Putsch"); and, finally, the fall of the Berlin Wall. Between familial silence and excessive public commemoration, the date has become an ambiguous portent: "So there I was, and even more than that here I am, / quite surprised, not to mention still unprepared / and quite unable to avoid thinking about both at once" (53). For what is she unprepared? For the juxtaposition that links her own life with that of the twentieth century; for the fortune that marks her as a survivor at the same time that it links her to the crimes of Kristallnacht—crimes that would soon escalate into genocide and from which her own family would only narrowly escape.[6] What is the lesson of these coincidences, these "visible traces of invisible principles"? She concludes: "all of this to say what Gertrude Stein has already said, / what can I teach you about history—history teaches. / It is not a simple matter, the birthday, or the telling" (53). Levine's prose-like poetry captures the everyday, matter-of-fact way in which citizens of the modern world are taken up by national and global histories that seem not to be their own, but in which they are caught nevertheless.

"Four November 9ths" is not simply a meditation on what links an immigrant American life to the history of old Europe, however. It is also a poem that slyly evokes the numerology of American disaster. Published in one of the first poetry anthologies to address the attacks on the World Trade Center and Pentagon, Levine's poem subtly reminds us that for most of the world, 9/11 is not shorthand for September 11; but it is, of course, precisely how you abbreviate November 9. Once this implicit reference to 9/11 emerges, one rereads the iconography of the events described: the Wall that comes down; the governments that fall; the buildings that are destroyed. Through this virtual layering of events, the relationship between the different histories of 9/11 and 11/9 comes to possess a double resonance: twenty-first-century disaster finds itself encoded in and heightened by reference to the well-known events of the twentieth century, but it is also relativized and resituated in a more encompassing, global framework. Such a recognition gives new meaning to the poet's inability "to avoid thinking about both at once," for now "both" refers not merely to the coincidence that unites individual and collective history, but also to the shadows that two collective histories (German and American) cast on the poet's life. "It is not a simple matter" to tell this story about what "history teaches," because history's pedagogy is open-ended: there is always another event to add to the series, always another seemingly far-away place or time to incorporate into one's sense of one's location (53, 54).

Levine's poem joins DeLillo's pre- and post-9/11 writings in being both a nuanced reflection on how individual lives intersect with powerful and destructive historical forces beyond their control and a subtle rebuke to a certain narrow-mindedness that has afflicted many citizens of the United States in the aftermath of September 11 (and, of course, long before that, too). The world outside the United States has a history, and it is a history that it encodes in its own way—sometimes even in the *opposite* way. So 9/11 becomes 11/9, and 11/9 becomes 9/11. But the point cannot be simply that we are *not* the world, although this is true. Because, as "In the Ruins of the Future" reminds us, we (Americans) also occupy the world in ways that we have trouble imagining. As embodied and local as we are (as everyone is), we also have an asymmetrical virtual and real presence in the world that derives from the globalization of our culture and our economic, political, and military power. What can literature say or do about this? Levine's poem is by no means as explicit a reflection on this question as is DeLillo's essay, but it does begin the necessary task of provincializing American meanings and inviting Americans to understand themselves in relation to non-American histories. What looks like coincidence from one angle, can also be a "constant and grim" reminder (Levine 53) that we are not the sole inhabitants of the globe—and *that* is indeed "not a simple matter" to tell.

As a reflection on the meaning of dates, Levine's poem also raises questions about periodization, that is, about how we divide up and parcel out historical time around privileged moments of rupture, revolution, catastrophe, or other forms of significant social transformation. Levine approaches periodization ironically, emphasizing its sometimes accidental and contingent qualities. And yet, for all that, the seemingly arbitrary repetitions she high-lights begin to take on a more necessary logic of their own in so far as a par-ticular national community recognizes them as meaningful. Thus, November 9 does become "a very big day in the history of Germany," and it does so in part because it can become the subject of a "book written . . . called *The Four November 9ths*" (53). In channeling her oblique response to September 11 through reflection on the categories and processes of national commemora-tion, Levine draws attention to the role writing (including her own) plays in the construction of collective memory. Her poem thus addresses three of the overlapping issues crucial to my discussion of "literature after 9/11": the ques-tion of periodization, the relationship between the public and the private, and the politics of remembering and representing terrorism. The particular strat-egy Levine uses in addressing these issues is dominated especially by a certain reserve. It is precisely what she doesn't say that prompts what Kant would call reflective judgment: an attempt to grasp the particularities of her life and the contingencies of world-historical dating within a cognitive framework that is not given in advance. The answer—if there is one—to what "history teaches" is not in the poem but in the cognitive processes that the experience of the poem produces in the reader.

DOUBLE TROUBLE: EMPATHIC UNSETTLEMENT

Levine writes implicitly as a double survivor—as one who evaded the disas-ter in Europe and avoided the carnage of Lower Manhattan. Although intimately connected to the histories she recounts, her recounting in "Four November 9ths" is nonetheless characterized by a certain distance, a distance that results from the mediated quality of her experience of Ger-man history and her reserve about events in New York. In "first writing since," Suheir Hammad writes from a very different subject position—one immersed in the aftermath of the events of 9/11. Hammad no more offers unmediated access to those events than does Levine, but her work is gripped with a different and more overtly political urgency than found in "Four November 9ths." Furthermore, Hammad's poem not only stages the intersection of public and private, as does Levine's; the poem itself became something of a public artifact.

In considering Hammad's poem, it is also worth revisiting the final, post-secular image of DeLillo's essay: a Muslim woman in prayer. In DeLillo's essay, the woman occupies a central place, but she remains silent. Even the last line, "*Allahu akbar*. God is great," which comes from a prayer, is not represented as issuing directly from the woman; it is DeLillo's own addition to the scene, although how it is meant remains mysterious. But what if the woman could speak? Would her response to the attacks of September 11 dif-fer from DeLillo's? Of course, access to her perspective is not forthcoming; as an anonymous figure in an essay, her voice is obviously unrecoverable.

"first writing since," a work by a Palestinian-American writer from Brooklyn, does not provide that missing voice either, of course, but it may help us locate some of the parameters of the absent perspective. Written just weeks after September 11, Hammad's poem, which is both emotionally powerful and politically astute, clearly struck a chord with many people. Within a few months, references to the poem and often its full text could be found on more than 150 websites, including MSNBC.com and Middle East Report; it also circulated across the globe via e-mail, and Hammad read it on college campuses (including my own) and even on HBO. In the way it has circulated and in its content, "first writing since" crosses back and forth between public and private, representing both how public events shape private lives and how private emotions entered the public realm after 9/11.

"first writing since" consists of seven sections, each of which is made up of two or more stanzas of prose-like poetry.[7] Written in lower case with minimal punctuation, the poem reads like a series of diary entries that record the impact of the World Trade Center attack on the speaker, her family, and the anonymous people she meets in the streets of the city. The poem begins by locating itself in a tradition that questions art's ability to respond adequately to historical trauma:

> there have been no words.
> i have not written one word.
> no poetry in the ashes south of canal street.
> no prose in the refrigerated trucks driving debris and dna.
> not one word. (139)

Like DeLillo on Canal Street, Hammad locates herself close to the scene of the crime and yet distanced from its effects. The paradox of the poem's opening (she *writes,* "i have not written one word") emphasizes both the gap between language and bodily remains (ashes, DNA) and the attempt to saturate language with materiality—because there is "no poetry in the ashes," she attempts to bring ashes to poetry.[8] The poet's temporary wordlessness attests to a traumatic shock—a period of silence that quickly gives way to a flow of discourse. The tone of this outpouring is varied and ranges from stricken to searching to accusatory and even to comic—as in section 2, in which we find a chorus of "thank yous" by people who narrowly avoided being at the site of the tragedy: "thank you for my lazy procrastinating ass. . . . thank you, my attitude, you had me fired the week before" (140). This comic and slightly blasphemous litany attests to the poem's commitment to working on multiple levels and mobilizing conflicting emotional responses.

Crucial to the poem, as the "thank yous" also demonstrate, is its choral structure. While mostly spoken in an autobiographical first person, the poem attempts to document something of the collective dimension of the trauma and the heterogeneity of the city. Like DeLillo, Hammad is interested in mass experience and the importance of the media. She alludes to one of the most visible emblems of collective mourning that emerged spontaneously after the attacks, the posters and flyers featuring the names and images of the missing:

> the dead are called lost and their families hold up shaky printouts in front of us through screens smoked up.
> we are looking for iris, mother of three. please call with any infor-mation. we are searching for priti, last seen on the 103rd floor. she was talking to her husband on the phone and the line went. please help us find george. also known as adel. his family is waiting for him with his fa-vorite meal. i am looking for my son, who was delivering coffee. (140)

These lines, which follow immediately after the comic section 2, shift the tone dramatically and catch the reader by surprise, thus providing a kind of analogy to the shock of the events themselves. The victims are semi-anony-mous and yet rendered in their particularity, identified in relation to family, personal taste, and work. However, they are not offered up for our unmedi-ated consumption; we are at a remove from them, witnessing only through smoky television screens and shaky printouts. While Hammad refuses to let her readers confuse themselves with the position of the victims, she does bring us closer to their loss by temporarily inhabiting the voices of the rela-tives. This negotiation between proximity and distance is itself an ethical act, and produces in the reader what the theorist Dominick LaCapra names "empathic unsettlement": "a kind of virtual experience through which one puts oneself in the other's position while recognizing the difference of that position and not taking the other's place" (78).

While Hammad elicits empathic unsettlement in relation to the victims of the World Trade Center attack, she employs other forms of unsettle-ment to address the wider context of the events and the contemporary political scene. Just as she refuses to speak in the voice of the victims, Hammad also does not attempt to provide direct access to the perspective of the perpetrators:

> i do not know how bad a life has to break in order to kill.
> i have never been so hungry that i willed hunger
> i have never been so angry as to want to control a gun over a pen.
> not really.
> even as a woman, as a palestinian, as a broken human being.
> never this broken. (139)

There is no attempt at "exoneration" here, although the poem also does not allow us to distance ourselves from the conditions that may lead to vio-lence (without excusing it). In the place of "exoneration" or even simplistic attempts at explanation, Hammad stages skepticism:

today it is ten days. last night bush waged war on a man once
openly funded by the
cia. i do not know who is responsible. read too many books, know
too many people to believe what i am told. i don't give a fuck about
    bin laden. his vision of the world does not include me or those i
    love. . . . shit is complicated,
and i don't know what to think. (141)

Knowledge of the world—even, or especially, unsettled knowledge based
on doubt—emerges as the counterpoint to terror: the pen, not the gun.

"first writing since" is unsettling: it unsettles us through empathic
address by families of victims, and it unsettles us by refusing to provide
easy explanations or exoneration for the violence of September 11, by
refusing to take sides in the kind of "us and them" logic DeLillo stages and
undoes. Furthermore, it troubles our settled assumptions about what constitutes home and what constitutes foreignness. The poet describes receiving comfort from a woman on the street: "'my brother's in the navy,' i
said. 'and we're arabs.' 'wow, you got double trouble,'" the woman replies.
"Word," confirms the poet to us in her hip-hop voice (141). Referring again
later in the poem to her brother, Hammad also anticipates DeLillo by using
an invocation of prayer to put the boundaries of the domestic and foreign
into question. Her brother's "double trouble" is further exacerbated by his
religious practice:

my baby brother is a man now, and on alert, and praying five times a
day that orders he will take in a few days time are righteous and
will not weigh his soul down from the afterlife he deserves.

both my brothers—. . . both
palestinian, practicing muslim, gentle men. both born in brooklyn
and their faces are of the archetypal arab man [. . .]

what will their lives be like now?

over there is over here. (142)

As DeLillo's young woman's act of prayer is integrated into the streets
of Manhattan, so is Hammad's brother's religious practice integrated
into the U.S. military. Defying stereotypes of Arabs, her Brooklyn-born
brothers also defy the "us and them" logic that has defined so much of
public discourse in post-9/11 America. With the attacks on New York
and Washington, worlds have crumbled into each other, as DeLillo
would say—or, rather, as Hammad might respond, we have been forced
to recognize that "over there" has always been "over here," that global
tensions have long had local effects and vice versa.[9] Hammad's unsettled

and unsettling aesthetic mobilizes affect and subjective experience to open up received forms of knowledge and gesture toward new ways of knowing a heterogeneous and increasingly integrated globe.

THE RED GLOW: A TRANSMISSION OF AFFECT

DeLillo, Levine, and Hammad all situate the events of September 11 in a global framework and question the relationship between the public and the private, the domestic and the foreign; in "October Marriage," D. Nurkse continues this project. Like DeLillo in *Mao II,* Nurkse uses marriage to raise questions about art and terror in an age of media spectacle. In three short and fragmentary sections, "October Marriage" appears to tell the tale of a New York couple married soon after September 11.[10] Nurkse's portrait of the couple turns, as DeLillo's George Haddad might have predicted, on questions of seeing and feeling. In Nurkse's poem, as in Bill Gray's account of novelists and terrorists, violence is a visual spectacle with the power to penetrate intimate spaces and affects. Here poetry emerges as a counterforce that attempts to shift the conditions of vision in order to produce new affects commensurate with an age of permanent anxiety and war.

"October Marriage" emphasizes the conflicting affective impact of September 11 and its aftermath. Initially, terrorism and counterterrorism seem to dull or "nullify" feeling, like the bottled water the couple collects in case of emergency:

> We stockpile Poland Spring
> under our bed
> and feel that bulk
> nullify the give
> when we make love. (87)

As the somewhat ominous reference to "Poland Spring" indicates, the poem's first section employs brand names and other proper nouns as fetishes, commodified substitutes through which the couple attempts desperately to ward off loss and fear in the wake of the attacks:

> We dial a recording
> and order Vitamin K,
> Cipro, twin masks. [. . .]
> We borrow a Glock and wrap it
> in a Chamois cloth and lock
> the bullets in a separate drawer—
> where to hang the key? (87)

Later, the poem goes on to reveal the compulsion behind the stockpiling of objects and goods as the product of another compulsion: the repeated act of watching terror. This latter compulsion, a common one in the aftermath of 9/11 when image loops of the Twin Towers flooded television screens, bears witness to the intensified affect transmitted by televised violence. The final section of the poem reveals the traumatic moment as a function of vision:

> We saw it
> and can't stop watching:
> as if the plane entered the eye
> and it was the mind
> that began burning
> with such a stubborn flame. (88)

Like the fear that nullifies love when translated into the fetish of security (the stockpiled Poland Spring, the Glock), terrorism doesn't so much eliminate as *readjust* affect. In contrast to fear, however, this traumatic readjustment increases instead of decreasing the emotional current. The repeated watching of terror doesn't dull the act of love, but rather overwhelms human capacities, "burning" the brain and cutting through its defenses—a metaphor close to Freud's account of trauma in *Beyond the Pleasure Principle.*

If the act of terrorism monopolizes the eye—"occupying" it, as DeLillo might say—the official response to terrorism follows the same logic, "crumbling" our world into theirs (DeLillo again) and further eroding the bridge between seeing and feeling. The one stanza middle section of the poem links the couple's October wedding to the United States' October war in Afghanistan:

> Huddled before the news,
> we touch the screen—
> our bombs rain on Kandahar—
> we can't feel them:
> just a thrum, the pulse,
> a film of dust, a red glow
> shining through our nails. (87–88)

Here media functions as a different kind of fetish; it seems to eliminate the gap between New York and Kandahar, but its mode of presence is illusory. The television draws the couple in, yet it simultaneously blocks access to what it portrays and "nullifies" their affective connection to the events ("we can't feel them").

Yet, at the very point where feeling seems not just to readjust itself but to risk disappearing into the simulacrum of war's mass-mediated spectacle, Nurkse's poem attempts to offer a counternarrative. The balance he seeks is a delicate one, as it is in DeLillo, Levine, and Hammad: how to register both Americans' distance from the rest of the world and their (willed or involuntary) presence there. The media, here represented by the television news, attempt a false solution to this dilemma, offering hyper-real images and blocking affective connection with the "foreign." The poem, on the other hand, puts forth a more tenuous and uncertain language: the poet finds vocabulary for this in the "thrum, the pulse, [the] red glow" that the television gives off. In place of recognizable feelings or images, Nurkse highlights a minimal, but still significant sensory experience. In front of the television, a transmission of affect takes place, but it is not that of the spectacle, deployed equally by terrorism and the war machine.[11] Instead, we have the image of "a red glow / shining through our nails." This image highlights the vulnerability and permeability of human subjects, the thin layer that simultaneously protects us and opens us to experience of the outside, the far away, the foreign. There is no utopian solution here to the problems of violence, globalization, and media saturation, yet nevertheless: Nurkse's couple attempts to reappropriate the media, to take it in through touch instead of remaining beholden to the spectacle. The attempt to touch Kandahar fails, but in the attempt a pulse and a glow are produced, a minimal disturbance of the media's anesthetizing spectacle, a slender bridge between intimacy and the wider world.

FOR A GLOBAL AESTHETIC EDUCATION

"October Marriage" does not offer a political solution to the manifold problems of the twenty-first century, but like all the works I've considered here it strives to create an ethic for an age of terrorism, counterterrorism, and globalization. This ethic is also an aesthetic, an attempt to reconnect the senses and to realign them with cognition in order to confront a world where distance has not been erased but where worlds crumble into each other nonetheless. Seeking to recalibrate distance and proximity to match a world of asymmetrical power and experience, these works do not remove themselves from the dangers that surround them. Rather, like Nurkse's couple, DeLillo's young woman, Hammad's brothers, and Levine's autobiographical narrator, they seek to approach and integrate themselves into the world, by whatever means. If the effort doesn't always succeed, it nevertheless offers an ethical stance and a pedagogical moment—an opportunity to consider what "history teaches," as Levine might say. Has the majority of literature after 9/11 followed this path and taken advantage of the possibilities for a pedagogy that would be simultaneously global and local and would be able to recognize the losses in New York and in Kandahar? Probably not. But enough works already exist to make it worth attending to the construction of an aesthetic that faces up to the manifold forms of violence on a world scale. In its preconditions, in its mass media unfolding, and in its deadly repercussions, September 11 was a global event. It demands a literature that takes risks, speaks in multiple tongues, and dares to move beyond near-sightedness.

NOTES

I am grateful to Ann Keniston and Jeanne Follansbee Quinn for their comments on an earlier draft of this chapter.

1. As this chapter went to press, DeLillo published his first novel-length response to 9/11, *Falling Man*. It should also be noted that *Mao II* is not by any means the first or only DeLillo novel to address terrorism or even the World Trade Center!
2. My thinking about the necessity of taking account of spectacle in relation to 9/11 and the subsequent wars parallels that of Retort's *Afflicted Powers*.
3. For a nuanced discussion of the multiform relation between public and private, see Michael Warner's essential *Publics and Counterpublics*. Deborah Nelson provides a rich account of discourses of privacy in a pre-9/11 American context that remains relevant.
4. The Guyer and Matthews translation renders reflective and determinate judgment as "reflecting" and "determining," respectively.
5. Various literary texts have critically explored this rhetoric, including poems by Suheir Hammad and Ishmael Reed, and Lynn Sharon Schwartz's novel *The Writing on the Wall*.
6. Levine's poem "Ghosts," published in her 1994 collection *Euphorbia*, tells some of this story as does the biography on her website: www.annemarielevine.com.
7. These next four paragraphs draw on and revise my earlier discussion of Hammad in the context of trauma theory. See Michael Rothberg, "'There Is No Poetry In This.'" Parenthetical references refer to the seven sections of the poem. The poem's seven sections seem to correspond to the poem's moment of enunciation: "today is a week, and seven is of heavens, gods, science" (1).
8. Perhaps the most famous instance of this kind of "thinking against itself" in relation to the aesthetics of trauma comes in Theodor Adorno's dictum that "to write poetry after Auschwitz is barbaric." On Adorno, see my *Traumatic Realism,* chapter 1.
9. See Pieterse for a rich description of this fact.
10. Nurkse's poem has since been published in his collection *Burnt Island*. In that context, "October Marriage" is renamed "October Rendezvous" and included in a series titled "The Reunification Center," which includes some other poems that address September 11. Despite the title change, marriage remains a central concern of *Burnt Island* as a whole. Other poems in this volume include "The Marriage in Canaan," "Space Marriage," and "Marriage in a Rented House."
11. My reference here is to Teresa Brennan's fascinating book *The Transmission of Affect*. In some ways, Nurkse's poem confirms Brennan's desire to shift the focus of transmission from a visual domain to that of other senses (especially olfactory). While I don't follow Brennan in downplaying the importance of the visual in the transmission of affect, I find her book compelling and suggestive for the project sketched here.

WORKS CITED

Arendt, Hannah. *The Human Condition*. Garden City: Doubleday Anchor, 1959.

Brennan, Teresa. *The Transmission of Affect*. Ithaca: Cornell UP, 2004.

DeLillo, Don. "In the Ruins of the Future." *Harper's Magazine* (December 2001): 33–40.

———. *Mao II*. New York: Penguin, 1991.

Hammad, Suheir. "first writing since." *Trauma at Home: After 9/11*. Ed. Judith Greenberg. Lincoln: U of Nebraska P, 2003. 139–43.

———. *Zaatar Diva*. New York: Rattapallax, 2006.

Kant, Immanuel. *Critique of the Power of Judgment*. Ed. Paul Guyer. Trans. Paul Guyer and Eric Matthews. New York: Cambridge, 2000.

LaCapra, Dominick. *Writing History, Writing Trauma*. Baltimore: Johns Hopkins UP, 2001.

Levine, Anne-Marie. *Euphorbia*. Provincetown: Provincetown Arts, 1994.

———. "Four November 9ths." *Poetry After 9/11: An Anthology of New York Poets*. Ed. Dennis Loy Johnson and Valerie Merians. New York: Melville House, 2002. 53–54.

Nelson, Deborah. *Pursuing Privacy in Cold War America*. New York: Columbia UP, 2002.

Nurkse, D. *Burnt Island*. New York: Knopf, 2005.

———. "October Marriage." *Poetry After 9/11: An Anthology of New York Poets*. Ed. Dennis Loy Johnson and Valerie Merians. New York: Melville House, 2002. 87–88.

Pieterse, Jan Nederveen. *Ethnicities and Global Multiculture: Pants for an Octopus*. Boulder: Rowman and Littlefield, 2007.

Reed, Ishmael. *New and Collected Poems, 1964–2006*. New York: Carroll & Graf, 2006.

Retort Collective. *Afflicted Powers: Capital and Spectacle in a New Age of War*. New York: Verso, 2005.

Rothberg, Michael. "'There Is No Poetry In This': Writing, Trauma, and Home." *Trauma at Home: After 9/11*. Ed. Judith Greenberg. Lincoln: U of Nebraska P, 2003.

———. *Traumatic Realism: The Demands of Holocaust Representation*. Minneapolis: U of Minnesota P, 2000.

Schwartz, Lynne Sharon. *The Writing on the Wall*. New York: Counterpoint, 2006.

Warner, Michael. *Publics and Counterpublics*. New York: Zone, 2002.

7 "We're Not a Friggin' Girl Band"

September 11, Masculinity, and the British-American Relationship in David Hare's *Stuff Happens* and Ian McEwan's *Saturday*

Rebecca Carpenter

Post-September 11, 2001 developments have exacerbated British anxieties about its place in the world and particularly about its relationship with the United States. These anxieties are far from new: former U.S. Secretary of State Dean Acheson's barb, "Great Britain has lost an Empire and has not yet found a role," still has the power to nettle. Given this history, Tony Blair's unequivocal backing of the Iraq War has touched a nerve in British public opinion, not only because many British citizens, like many continental Europeans, question the morality of this war, but also because Blair's unequivocal fidelity to U.S. foreign policy has been widely perceived as transforming the "special relationship" from one of partners—albeit senior and junior partners—to one of superpower and satellite. That some British journalists have employed terms as provocative as "adjunct," "51st state," and "client state" to describe the current relationship between the United States and Great Britain shows how dramatically they feel the ground has shifted.[1] Even harsher language has been employed to describe Blair himself, including the nearly ubiquitous "poodle" and "lapdog." Novelist John LeCarre has even gone so far as to describe him as "a minstrel for the American cause" (qtd. in Naughtie 116). Many Blair critics believe that British prestige in the world has perhaps been irreparably harmed by Blair's dogged loyalty to Bush's foreign policy. While Blair's late February 2007 announcement that Great Britain would withdraw some troops from Iraq suggests that Blair is willing to compromise between his commitment to the "coalition of the willing" and the demands of the British public, most domestic British commentators agree that the damage has already been done; Blair has already lent credibility to the United States' war effort.

Blair's fealty to Bush's foreign policy has been constructed in markedly gendered terms. Blair has been accused not only of failing to act in his nation's best interest, but also of acting so obsequiously that he has in effect compromised British sovereignty. Metaphorically, he has been repeatedly depicted as either feminine or castrated. The widespread representations of Blair as Bush's poodle or lapdog not only depict him as a dog, but as a fluffy, cosseted, drooling, obedient, feminine one, who wants nothing more than to be stroked by its owner. This incarnation of Blair/Britain stands in stark contrast to iconic personifications of Great Britain as the female but martial figure of Britannia, equipped with helmet, spear or standard, and shield, which has functioned as a metonym for the state since the Renaissance. The figure of Britannia simultaneously connotes a beloved motherland in need of protection and an imperial force to be reckoned with. This dual identity of Britannia is personified in the lyrics of "Rule Britannia!": "Blest isle! With matchless beauty crowned/And manly hearts to guard the fair." Despite her female form, there is no implication of feminine submissiveness in Britannia.

The U.S.-British "special relationship" has most frequently been construed as a relationship between two friends, one more powerful and the other acting as a judicious advisor and check on that power. In the post-9/11 world, however, the "special relationship" has far more frequently been represented in gendered terms, both because of the United States' increasingly hyper-masculine and bellicose posturing on the world stage and because of the growing perception on both sides of the Atlantic that Great Britain has become a submissive, feminized partner acquiescing to the will of an assertive, masculine one.[2] Political power and subservience are often described metaphorically in primal, animalistic, and gendered terms. The intersection (and, sometimes, the conflation) of power on the world stage with conceptions of masculinity manifests itself both in obvious ways (e.g., Ronald Reagan's assertion that Gorbachev blinked first, making them sound like two male animals challenging each other for dominance) and more subtle ones. Masculinity in this context is loosely equated with dominance, that is, with the ability to assert one's will successfully and to triumph over any who might challenge one's right to do so. In the post-9/11 world, the United States has been particularly invested in a rhetoric of masculinity and power, labeling both perceived enemies—and, interestingly, even weaker allies—as either feminine or deviant in their masculinity.

On September 11, the United States was faced with a script that threatened to position the United States as weak, indolent, oblivious to threats, and possibly even symbolically feminized (by the penetration of the towers) or castrated (by the collapse of the towers). Julie Drew argues that public discourse in the wake of September 11 (such as newspaper coverage) even positioned the people fleeing the WTC and the Pentagon as feminine, weak, passive, and vulnerable (Drew 71–72).[3] The U.S. government countered with a script that firmly re-established the United States as active and masculine. As Laura Shepherd points out, not only were traditional gender roles reaccentuated and reaffirmed in the wake of September 11, but the Bush administration drew on the oppression of Afghani women as an additional reason for bombing Afghanistan: the United States, as masculine Figure of Authority, would police and punish the barbaric and deviant masculinity of Afghani men who abused women by "making" them wear the burqa, beating them, etc (Shepherd 25–27).[4] Meghana Nayak argues that, symbolically, protecting Afghani women undoes previous U.S. humiliation:

> The paternalistic mission, wherein only a real man can save suffering women under the shadow of the gun, is crucial for alleviating the anxiety that the USA has experienced since 9/11. Because states feminize boundaries, the invasion of such translates into imagery of an impotent, emasculated man unable to protect his possessions from being violated and destroyed. (50)

Positioning the U.S. as delivering Afghani women from oppression "allows the redemption of the emasculated citizen and state that could not fight off 9/11" (Nayak 50). Susannah Radstone similarly argues that September 11 was an event that assailed the United States' sense of itself, disturbing what she refers to as a fantasy of "impregnability and invincibility," a masculine narcissistic fantasy that projects vulnerability onto women. Radstone suggests that the United States projected its own violence as justified and rational as opposed to the "perverse, evil, excessive" violence of the terrorist Other (120–21). The construction of true masculinity as the sole property of the United States not only surfaces in the rhetoric of the United States government, but thoroughly saturated American popular culture, as Bill Maher learned the hard way when his assertion that the 9/11 terrorists were courageous (and thus masculine) rather than cowardly (and thus feminine) got him fired.

The United States' need to view the British as feminine might seem less obvious. As the United States' only major ally in the Iraq War, the United States on some level would seem to be best served by rhetorical constructions of the British as significant and powerful. Yet this need is tempered by the need of the United States to be seen as the sole dominant force in the "war against terror" (possibly explaining reports that the United States military hesitated when British forces asked for permission to try to capture Osama bin Laden). Furthermore, Blair's position, with its greater emphasis on humanitarian concerns rather than morally policing the world, helped the United States define itself by contrast: the British position was constructed as soft, naïve, idealistic, and utopian as compared to the clear-sighted, hard-headed, rational, truly masculine position of the United States, a nation which understood the need for overwhelming force and the value of shock and awe.[5] Ultimately, though, it is the British public as much as the United States which has increasingly come to cast the special relationship in gendered terms. The widespread belief that Blair has failed to assert British sovereignty and has transformed the "special relationship" into one of assertive superpower and submissive devotee has frequently been depicted as a feminization of the nation.

This metaphor of femininity is crassly illustrated in George Michael's 2002 animated music video entitled "Shoot the Dog." Michael depicts

George W. Bush dancing the tango with Tony Blair, with Tony Blair as the female partner in a flowing gown. Later in this same video, Cherie Blair is represented in bed with George Michael who is propositioning her. For Cherie Blair to be so lacking in male companionship that she might entertain the suggestions of an openly homosexual pop singer is obviously meant to suggest that things have reached truly dire straits on Downing Street. A bit later, Tony Blair is literally depicted in bed with Bush. Despite the patent absurdity of the video, its popularity suggests it tapped into something vital in the British zeitgeist.

Blair's representation as a castrated man finds one of its most virulent incarnations in Steve Bell's cartoon of January 21, 2004, in which he depicts the Iraq War team as characters in "The Wizard of Oz" traveling up the Yellow Brick Road. While Dick Cheney is the Scarecrow with No Brain and Donald Rumsfeld the Tin Woodsman with No Heart, Blair is Toto, Dorothy's (Bush's) dog with "No Nuts" (Bell 27). The gendered insult of this cartoon is particularly emphatic, as traditional "Wizard of Oz" iconography would have had Blair as the Cowardly Lion with "No Courage" rather than a neutered dog. While this would have effectively made the same criticism Bell is making, "No Nuts" is a more pointed insult.

Recent British literature has also reconceived the "special relationship" in notably gendered terms. David Hare's 2004 play *Stuff Happens* and Ian McEwan's 2005 novel *Saturday* both center around the issue of British prestige and strength in the post-9/11 world, for which British masculinity serves as a metaphor. *Stuff Happens* represents Tony Blair as politically emasculated by the Bush White House. Hare's version of recent events suggests that the contemplative rationality of British leaders is little more than road kill in the way of the American juggernaut as it powers on to war, fueled by the machismo of the American president and supported by the idiocy of the American people. Ian McEwan's *Saturday,* by contrast, constructs a more masculine image for England, one which decisively rejects hotheaded American cowboy-ism in favor of a bold, but more rational and level-headed version of masculinity, rooted in tradition, culture, and expertise. Set against the background of the February 15, 2003 protests against the incipient war in Iraq, *Saturday* tells the story of a microcosmic terrorist incident: the attack of an upper-middle-class British family by a gang of thugs, a story that rather miraculously ends with the restoration of peace and patriarchal order when the father of the family capably and competently dispatches the threat against his family and then, in an act of remarkable benevolence, doing what he can to repair the body of the man who had been his tormentor. Looking at *Stuff Happens* and *Saturday* in tandem suggests that the decision to go to war in Iraq has been definitional for Great Britain, forcing its leaders and citizens to articulate precisely what its role in the world is after the decline of Empire.[6]

Both of these works reflect the tension inherent in the Anglo-American relationship. The history of this tension goes back at least as far as the Suez

Crisis of 1956. Great Britain felt humiliated when it was forced to withdraw from its joint military assault on Egypt with the French and the Israelis because of pressures brought to bear by the United States. Ever since Suez, Great Britain has longed to repair its national pride and establish itself on a more equal footing with the United States. While recognizing that the United States has a military arsenal far surpassing that of Great Britain, the British hope has always been that the United States would fully recognize the value of the expertise and know-how it can provide.

The post-September 11 world initially seemed to offer such an opportunity, with Tony Blair appearing as a courageous and steadfast voice in the face of a crisis that everyone recognized would affect more than just the United States. On January 1, 2002, Jack Straw optimistically commented in an interview with the *Times,* "It has taken the foreign policy of the Prime Minister finally to lay the ghost of Suez" (Riddell 141). The weeks that followed would prove the polar opposite to be true. In fact, in some sense, the war in Iraq has proved to be even more humiliating and emasculating than the Suez Crisis. During the Suez Crisis, the British were forced to retreat from their initial aggressive, imperialistic posture because of pressure brought by the United States, including a U.S.-triggered devaluation of the pound, which sent the British economy spiraling, and a U.N. resolution condemning their actions. This crisis was a defining moment in which Great Britain came to understand its reduced position in the world and that its "special relationship" with the United States did not preclude the United States exercising its superpower position to rein in British power.[7]

If that moment was humiliating, however, it at least tacitly acknowledged Great Britain as a meaningful military power that needed to be reined in. By contrast, on March 11, 2003, Donald Rumsfeld implied that British participation was non-essential to the Iraq War effort and that, while Great Britain's participation would be highly welcome, what it actually had to offer militarily was negligible from a United States perspective. Rumsfeld verbally relegated Great Britain to a similar category as Poland, Albania, and Lithuania—countries which are part of the "Coalition of the Willing," but that contribute a negligible number of troops. This was far more emasculating than anything that happened during Suez.

Stuff Happens dramatizes this recent history. Tony Blair is represented in the script as a reasonable, rational, but occasionally dithering presence, whose nuanced views do not always fare well when faced with the anvil of American certainties and the Machiavellian manipulations of neo-cons like Dick Cheney, Donald Rumsfeld, and Paul Wolfowitz. Hare initially represents Blair as moral and principled, but also as politically and psychologically savvy enough to recognize the importance of publicly declaring his loyalty to the United States. Ultimately, though, this strategy backfires on Blair as the British view his loyalty as subservience and the neo-cons take his loyalty for granted when they realize it is too late for him to change positions. This painful reality becomes abundantly apparent in one of the most significant scenes in this play, an imaginative reconstruction of Bush's war cabinet debate on whether to get a second U.N. resolution, something that Blair absolutely needs politically. The neocons ridicule Blair in decidedly gendered terms, highlighting what they see as his impractical, naïve, and spineless nature:

> CHENEY. I don't trust him. New Labour. What the hell does that mean? We don't call ourselves the New Republicans.
> RUMSFELD. We're not a friggin' girl band. (103)

Cheney implies that referring to one's party as "New Labour" is a cheap and unworthy marketing ploy and that any party with any serious sense of gravitas would not stoop to such tactics. Rumsfeld takes this insult one step further, however, when he suggests that the name is reminiscent of a "girl band," thus implying that "New Labour" is a frothy, lightweight, ineffectual political entity, worthy of about the same amount of serious consideration as The Spice Girls. Rumsfeld makes the comparison all the more provocative by comparing New Labour to a female pop group, rather than a male one. The initial implication is that New Labour is not just lacking in seriousness, but in masculinity, power, and hard-nosed reality. The further implication is less that Blair is castrated than that he was never a man in the first place, but a prepubescent girl with all the connotations of naiveté that role conjures. Cheney and Rumsfeld's Blair is an idealist with his head in the clouds, dreamily yearning for a happy world of peace where everyone follows the rules, leaving "real men" to make timely decisions before the situation on the ground deteriorates further.

The neo-cons in Hare's play view Blair's principles as the sissified concerns of an altruist, whose first concerns are international philanthropy and the creation of a utopian international community, not international security. As the scene continues, Blair's principles are cast as fantastical and out of touch with the "legitimate security concerns" that guide the decisions of real men:

> CHENEY. He wants the right to go into any country anywhere and bring relief from suffering and pain wherever he finds it. And I don't. What I want is to follow this country's legitimate security concerns. (II, 20)

Blair's impractical idealism stands in stark contrast to the neocons' hard-nosed *realpolitik* and crass, bottom-line assessments. The scene ends with Bush making a political calculation and deciding that he can't risk Blair's government falling, but it also implies that Bush has no fundamental respect for Blair.

A couple scenes later, Hare incorporates the infamous Rumsfeld press briefing in which he, in essence, implied that British participation in the war was optional.

RUMSFELD. To the extent that they're able to participate, that would be welcome. To the extent they're not, there are workarounds and they would not be involved, at least in that phase of it. (104)

Blair is furious, perceiving these comments as absolutely emasculating. Hare depicts him calling up Bush and angrily reminding him that he has "risked everything" to support the war. Bush is apologetic, but in a decidedly understated way, and, in fact, exchanges a deadpan look with Cheney and Rumsfeld during his phone conversation with Blair. Blair's emotional reaction and personal neediness further feminize him.

Scene twenty-three opens with the United States' embarrassingly premature declaration of victory in Iraq. This is a scene that all but satirizes itself. Hare focuses on the absurd machismo of the American president and of American foreign policy with its apparently compulsive need to impress the globe with its phallic power:

AN ACTOR. Thanks to an artful arrangement of jump-suit groin-straps, George W. Bush, 43rd President of the United States, shows his balls to the world. (110)

The landing is followed by a passage in which Bush speaks with messianic certainty about the good that has been done, the crisis that has been averted, and the freedom that the previously oppressed are sure to feel now that western forces have done their job.

Yet Hare is hardly less sparing of Blair, whose last appearance on the stage suggests a man who is rudderless and ineffectual. Blair's final action in the play is to accede to Bush's support of Israel's unilateral peace plan, which does not include any plan to negotiate with the Palestinians. Earlier in the play, Blair is firmly committed to helping the Israelis and the Palestinians jointly negotiate peace. When the White House retrenches on what it seemed to have promised Blair earlier, however, An Actor laconically remarks, "Tony Blair refuses to dissent from the new policy." Tony Blair then speaks directly to the audience:

BLAIR. After the war, I did consider apologising. But I wasn't sure what I'd be apologising for. And besides, the moment has gone.
Blair looks at us a moment, then goes. (115)

Blair's final speech depicts him as a man who has fundamentally lost his bearings. His attempts to gain influence with Bush are an abject failure; in the end, he is castrated, voiceless, and rudderless, allowing the British ship of state to founder in ways he should have been able to foresee.[8]

Stuff Happens ends with the sense that Great Britain is quietly shambling off the world stage, ceding the field to the more powerful, virile, testicle-displaying Americans. In Hare's dramatic universe, America swaggers and asserts, while Great Britain obsequiously backs down, acceding to the will of the United States. Hare represents the "special relationship" as no longer one of two partners, one with greater military power and the other with history and expertise that merit respect. Instead of gaining power on the world stage because of his alliance with the United States, Tony Blair is trapped by it, unable to dissent from the Bush administration policy without fundamentally undermining himself.[9]

McEwan's *Saturday,* in contrast, presents a more empowering image of British masculinity. *Saturday* sets up two opposing models of masculinity: a hotheaded, unreflective, lower-class brand of masculinity whose primary tools are strength, self-assurance, and swagger, and a cool-headed, intelligent, upper-class masculinity whose primary tools are knowledge and reasoning. Even though both the violent thug Baxter and the physician Perowne are British, within the metaphoric universe of this novel, Baxter is the representation of terrorism (in a perhaps too easy displacement of the otherness of a particular incarnation of Islam with the otherness of the lower class), and Perowne the representation of civilization, rationality, and paternal authority. His ultimate ability to classify and diagnose Baxter's problem and protect his family principally through his intellect, and with a minimal amount of violence, represents the restoration of patriarchal order, but also importantly proposes an alternative to the American model of masculinity, in which force must be countered with greater force, and in which any emotions which might make one qualify the amount of shock and awe one is willing to dole out—including any degree of sympathy with one's enemies or reservations about the justice of punitive measures—is badly misplaced. *Saturday* endorses a vision of masculinity whose magnanimous, paternalistic grandeur is more in keeping with the imperialist ethos of Arnold's Victorian era when Great Britain reigned supreme than with the contemporary world. Perowne subdues the threat to civilized order, and (with help from his son) protects his vulnerable wife and pregnant daughter from harm, but also paternalistically adopts a feeling of responsibility toward the erstwhile insurgent. Authority and order are restored, but importantly, it is the tools of western civilization and the medical expertise of the patriarchal figure which allow him to triumph, not brute force.[10] While Perowne is highly ambivalent about the rightness of the War in Iraq, the text associates the use of overwhelming force with thugs and terrorists, and suggests that force often covers over massive insecurities. The novel proposes that the most effective form of patriarchal authority is that which governs principally by moral force and expertise, rather than by the violent assertion of one's will.

The protagonist Henry Perowne's experiences on February 15, 2003 mirror what the United States experienced on September 11, 2001, on a microcosmic level: what starts out as a peaceful day is unexpectedly disrupted by a brutal attack by men whose primary goal is to strike terror in the heart of his family. This home invasion is indisputably positioned as a terrorist event. Its purpose is not to rob the Perowne family or even principally to satisfy violent urges, but to gain retribution by terrorizing Perowne's family and making Perowne feel vulnerable and helpless. Perowne survives a potentially humiliating and unmanning crisis and saves his family using both his brains and his brawn, then goes back to the work of saving the world by using his skills as a brain surgeon to save his assailant, an almost superhuman act of compassion. Within the contemporary rhetorical context in which this novel was released, the privileging and reifying of Perowne's civilized, rational masculinity of expertise over Baxter's macho bravado suggests that the ability to outwit one's opponent is far more central to masculinity than the ability to dole out physical punishment, an assessment which sets this particular version of professional British masculinity not only over lower-class thuggish masculinity, as embodied in Baxter, but also over the Al Qaeda terrorists' masculinity and hawkish American masculinity, all of which valorize physical self-assertion. There are other, uneasier implications as well: given that Baxter is clearly on some level a stand-in for the terrorists, his sudden abandonment of his contempt for Perowne and all he represents suggests that the terrorists' reasons for hating those whom they terrorize are also not deeply rooted and rational, but stem from an irrational desire to humiliate those who make them aware of their relative lack of power and privilege. The fantasy that contact with the proper masculine spirit can restore in would-be terrorists a respect for an imperial, patriarchal order threatens to reinscribe some of the neocon logic that *Saturday* otherwise seems to reject.

Saturday is pervaded by references to and echoes of September 11, 2001. Perowne's day starts when he believes he is on the verge of witnessing a literal reenactment of September 11: he sees what looks like a plane on fire streaking across the London sky and wonders if this is an accident, or another terrorist attack. (His fears prove to be unfounded.) The book takes place on Saturday, February 15, 2003, a day of massive protests against the War in Iraq across Europe, including an estimated 750,000 to two million protesters in London, whose presence plays a minor role in the plot. The morality of the impending war is also a recurrent subject: Perowne rehearses his American friend Jay Strauss's pro-war argument in his head in the car (101–02), watches the news and thinks about his own ambivalence about the war (153–54, 185), and engages in a lengthy argument with his anti-war daughter (190–98). The reality of the post-9/11 world is an unavoidable frame of reference against which Perowne will measure his own actions and inactions on this day, his own certainties and uncertainties.

In the inaugural chapters of *Saturday,* however, the idea that terrorism might touch him personally and intimately seems improbable. Perowne's life is almost annoyingly perfect. He embodies masculine success in every realm. A highly skilled, professionally respected brain surgeon living a life of urban luxury, he enjoys an active sex life with his gorgeous wife (who is herself a highly successful lawyer), and has two wildly successful, articulate, and artistic children who love him: a talented poet whose first book is just coming out and a gifted blues musician who has already had the opportunity to study with some of the best in his field thanks to his precocity and charm. Perowne still makes time for squash and is in excellent physical shape for a man of his age. With the exception of a mother with Alzheimer's, his life seems blessed in every respect.[11] Then, on that fateful Saturday, all this bliss is jeopardized when Perowne twice crosses paths with a violent young man, Baxter.

The first encounter occurs when Perowne's trip to his squash game in his silver Mercedes S 500 is unexpectedly interrupted. Perowne has just been meditating on life in the modern world: "The world probably has changed fundamentally and the matter is being clumsily handled, particularly by the Americans. There are people around the planet, well-connected and organized, who would like to kill him and his family and friends to make a point. The scale of death contemplated is no longer at issue; there'll be more deaths on a similar scale, probably in this city" (80). Just a minute or two later, these thoughts seem almost prescient, although the people Perowne encounters are neither well-connected nor organized, but street thugs harboring huge class resentments. Perowne gets into a minor car accident with Baxter and Baxter's friends Nigel and Nark. The gang's first instinct is to try to intimidate Perowne and shake him down; upon his refusal to comply with their financial demands, their second instinct is to threaten to inflict severe physical damage.

Perowne's initial response to Baxter is one of bluster and bravado; not only does he refuse to give in to Baxter and his friends' demand for cash, he uses his medical expertise to humiliate Baxter in front of his friends, threatening to expose his secret shame: that he has a degenerative disorder. Perowne later recognizes this response as a misstep. Although it allowed him to escape from danger at the time and even to get to his squash game, humiliating another man in front of his followers was not a smart move. Furthermore, he worries that on some level, as the man with the superior class position and knowledge base, he has abused his position and behaved arrogantly and presumptuously.

Perowne's American friend Jay Strauss, an anesthesiologist, is seemingly incapable of such ambivalence. In the extended Saturday-morning squash game scene at the center of this novel, Perowne's incarnation of upper-class British masculinity squares off directly against this somewhat formulaic picture of American masculinity. Strauss is confident and affectionate, and his matter-of-fact, upbeat manner reassures patients that everything will be all right. He is also brash, direct, bellicose, and alienates many hospital colleagues. He is pro-war, viewing the conflict in Manichean terms. Perowne thinks of him as

> a man of untroubled certainties, impatient of talk of diplomacy, weapons of mass destruction, inspections teams, proofs of links with Al-Qaeda and so on. Iraq is a rotten state, a natural ally of terrorists,

bound to cause mischief at some point and may as well be taken out now while the U.S. military is feeling perky after Afghanistan. And by taken out, he insists he means liberated and democratized. The U.S.A. has to atone for its previous disastrous policies—at the very least it owes this to the Iraqi people. Whenever he talks to Jay, Henry finds himself tending towards the anti-war camp. (101–02)

Strauss's black-and-white morality is reminiscent of those of the American leadership, and his interplay with Perowne suggests some of the fundamental tensions in the British-American relationship.

Both Perowne and Strauss are highly invested in the squash game, their masculine pride tied up in the outcome. Notably, however, for Strauss winning is everything. The game finally comes down to a match point that Perowne wins, colliding with Strauss seconds later, only to have Strauss claim that he won the point, on the grounds that he could have returned the ball if he hadn't been knocked down. The implications in the icy exchange that follows are that Strauss is so determined to win that he is willing to ratchet up the stakes, falsify evidence, and instigate a potentially friendship-ending argument in order to get Perowne to replay the point: "'You didn't see the ball come off the back wall. I did because I was going towards it. So the question is this. Are you calling me a liar?'" (118). Strauss goes on to win the game, but the implication is that he cheated in order to do so.

McEwan positions Perowne and Strauss's behavior as in some ways emblematic of their nationalities. As the two colleagues prepare to leave, Strauss stops to buy a Coke, and Perowne reflects that "You have to be an American to want, as an adult, anything quite so sweet" (118). The petulant and self-indulgent Strauss does seem like a child compared to Perowne. What is in some sense a brash, masculine challenge to Perowne—to name him a liar to his face—is also in some sense the most petulant and manipulative of behaviors, more characteristic of grade school playground behavior than of adult masculinity. It is Perowne's more mature British masculine sensibility that ultimately comes to seem necessary in a world always on the verge of erupting into violence. It is when Perowne fleetingly abandons this rational, deliberative version of masculinity in his confrontation with Baxter and behaves with American bravado and impulsivity that he initiates the chain of events that puts his family in danger. Normally, however, he resists the cowboy mentality that *Saturday* classifies as immature and boyish.

McEwan not only draws a distinction between British and American versions of masculinity, but also implies that it is only a small sub-set of British men who are true exemplars of this judicious incarnation of masculinity. Tony Blair is notably excluded from this select grouping. In Blair's one cameo appearance in *Saturday,* McEwan positions him as betraying an obsession with his image thought to be more typical of American politicians, building on widespread criticisms of Blair in the British press as "phony Tony." Perowne remembers meeting Blair at an opening at the Tate Modern. Blair misidentifies him as a painter, and when Perowne tries to correct him, Blair has "a moment of fleeting self-doubt," before making the "rapid calculation" to stick to his guns rather than risk "a derisive press tomorrow" (146). This model of masculinity, for all its outward self-assurance, cannot allow for doubt or even self-correction; certainty in one's actions and judgments is at the very heart of the model. Perowne possesses these qualities, which McEwan implies Blair possesses in insufficient measure.

In the early evening of February 15, 2003, Baxter and Nigel intrude into Perowne's domestic space and hold the family hostage at knifepoint. Rather than trying to use physical force and be heroic—a strategy which would be unlikely to succeed given Baxter and Nigel's much more extensive experience doling out physical punishment—Perowne balances coolness, assertiveness, and empathy in his response to the men who are terrorizing his family, projecting a judicious masculinity that ultimately saves the day. This is not to say that Perowne easily dismisses the possibility of physical heroism. His mind, desperately searching for a way out, repeatedly conjures up heroic schemes: "'rushing' Baxter with Theo, . . . pepper sprays, clubs, cleavers" (217); "Perhaps he should act alone, wrestle Baxter to the floor and trust the others will pile in" (221). He recognizes, however, that these are hopeless fantasies. He is utterly helpless as Baxter compounds his terror and humiliation: breaking Perowne's father-in-law's nose in response to a defiant comment, holding a knife to his wife's throat, and forcing his daughter to strip in front of the whole family, with the understanding that he is planning to rape her. The fear affects Perowne physically, alternately making him nauseous, leaving him "rocking on his feet in fear and indecision," and making him feel "a strong urge to urinate" (220). McEwan's representation of Perowne makes him seem almost utterly unmanned: powerless to defend his loved ones, irresolute, and having to concentrate on not losing control over his bodily functions. The man who revealed the secret of how Baxter will eventually lose control of his body is now faced with a possible parallel humiliation.

Perowne attempts to steal a trick from James Bond, who always manages to get his nemeses talking while he stalls for time and plots a way out of his difficulties. He tries to persuade Baxter that he has information about an American drug trial he can get him in on, but when Baxter accuses him of lying and threatens to cut Perowne's wife's throat if he doesn't shut up, he backs off. Evidently, verbal heroics aren't going to save the day either. Instead, he bides his time, hoping that Baxter's mental condition will cause him to make a mistake that he can exploit. Perowne's ability to keep his cool at a time of great stress is in fact both wise and implicitly highly masculine.

The denouement of this climactic scene is so strikingly improbable that it stretches the limits of credulity, as several critics have remarked.[12] Metaphorically, however, it could not be more fitting for McEwan's project: British tradition (as embodied by Matthew Arnold's poem "Dover Beach") saves the day, and thuggish terrorism is put down by the keepers of the British spirit of fair play. The terrorists have been threatening Daisy with sexual violence when they discover the manuscript of her poetry book *My Saucy Bark* and force her to read one of what they anticipate will be the salacious poems found inside. This moment temporarily suggests that it will be female intelligence that will determine the fate of the family, as Daisy becomes the center of attention, her words having the power to shape the course of events. Yet the feminist possibilities of such a scene are multiply undercut. First, Daisy is the center of attention principally because of the abject humiliation represented by the possibility of raping or sexually humiliating the daughter in front of her father and male relatives. Second, and perhaps even more pivotally, it ultimately is not Daisy's words that save the day, but the much anthologized words of one of the great white men of the British literary canon, Matthew Arnold. It is not even Daisy's idea to invoke his words rather than her own; her brilliant poet grandfather conceives the plan of pretending to read one of her poems but in fact reciting "Dover Beach," and Daisy is largely reduced to the role of a brave actress in a drama scripted for her by others. "Dover Beach," of course, suggests the futility of violent confrontation between "ignorant armies" and within this context functions as another reference to the impending Iraq War. Hearing this beautiful poem sends Baxter into a manic state, suddenly rendering him receptive to the idea that Perowne's drug trial is real. He demands to see the materials on it, and the expedition upstairs gives Perowne and his son the opportunity to engage in physically heroic action at last: they jump Baxter and toss him down the stairs.

Perowne, however, is no cowboy, and his goal is not justice. He is compassionate and believes in fair play, even for his enemies. Rather than seeking further revenge on his victim, when he gets called into the hospital by someone not knowing that Baxter had victimized his family, Perowne goes in and applies his surgical expertise to saving his life. Credulity is stretched near to the breaking point for a second time: could one really operate calmly on a man who held a knife to one's wife's throat, broke one's father-in-law's nose, and threatened to sexually assault one's daughter? Yet McEwan suggests that this commitment to the Etonian spirit of fair play is fundamental to British masculinity and British character. You do not kick your enemy when he is down or exploit his relative powerlessness. Instead of seeking retribution, Perowne empathetically enters into the world of the man who victimized him, recognizes his own partial culpability in provoking the events of the evening, and does his best to make things right. *Saturday*, then, implicitly comes to a reasonably sanguine stance about British masculinity and Great Britain's place in the world. McEwan's text suggests that British composure and rationality in the face of crises are indispensable traits in a world that is increasingly violent, extremist, and irrational, and that Britain has an important role to play in the postimperial world as the rational counterpoint to the bellicose United States.

Many other writers, however, are not so sanguine. Dean Acheson's comment is in some respects right on target: Great Britain clearly feels it has a role to play on the world stage beyond that which its economy, military power, or size might dictate, but precisely what that role might be is hard to define, and the tensions between Atlanticism and Europeanism make that role all the harder to delineate. Great Britain's fear of political and cultural obsolescence has manifested itself repeatedly. Since 2002, these fears have increasingly coalesced around Tony Blair and the vexed issue of the relationship between Great Britain and the United States. Blair's masculinity—and, more broadly, the British nation's masculinity—has come to stand in metaphorically for national sovereignty and self-assertion. David Hare's recent work takes a pessimistic view; *Stuff Happens* concludes that Tony Blair simply does not have the spine to stand up to George W. Bush and that it is Bush alone who gets to "show his balls" to the world. Ian McEwan, on the other hand, takes a more positive view, and posits that the more coolheaded, unflappable masculinity of the British, a masculinity tempered by judiciousness, rationality, and empathy, is absolutely necessary in a post-9/11 world. Though they reach different conclusions, both Hare's and McEwan's work probe the anxious territory of Great Britain's role in the contemporary world, examining whether Great Britain can still function as a meaningful independent voice in the face of the American juggernaut, with its increasingly unilateralist leanings, or whether its reduced geopolitical and military positions leave it in the position of being able to do no more than ruefully shake its head in the face of United States hegemony.

NOTES

1. For example, Peter Riddell of the *Times* feels a need to declare that "Britain is a European power with global interests, not an adjunct of the U.S." He also writes that "Britain's future is primarily as part of Europe, rather than as a 51st state" (viii). James Naughtie of the BBC Radio 4's *Today Show* claims that "Blair became an adjunct of his [Bush's] presidency" (xiv). One of the harshest assessments comes from David Leigh and Richard Norton-Taylor of the *Guardian,* who claim that "Britain has by now lost its sovereignty and has become a client state." After outlining seven ways in which British national sovereignty has been undermined, they opine that "If we really were the 51st state, as anti-Americans imply, we would probably have more protection against Washington than we do today" (par 1).

2. Indeed, two post-9/11 articles about the "special relationship" written from diametrically opposed political perspectives both chose the title "The End of the Affair," a phrase with obvious romantic and sexual connotations, to describe a break with the United States (which Marquand wishes for and Holmes and Gardiner do not). And while Marquand's use of the title seems to refer both to the special relationship and to the Labour Party's relationship to Blair, both articles imply that Great Britain has been emotionally involved with the United States. See Marquand, "The End of the Affair," and Holmes and Gardiner, "The End of the Affair?"

3. Drew's thesis is an intriguing one: "What is particularly interesting about post-9/11 public discourse is not that it argues that the U.S. is masculine,

but that the U.S. is far too feminine, and thus must work to become more masculine in order to be safer" (71).

4. See Shepherd. My use of sanitary quotes is not meant to imply that Afghani men never force women to wear the burqa or that there is not a substantial problem with violence against women in Afghanistan, but rather, as Shepherd and others have suggested, that first-world feminists need to resist reducing the burqa to a symbol of oppression and recognize that Muslim women are not universally voiceless victims, but have agency. Some may even elect to wear the burqa for religious, cultural, or familial reasons, and we should not discount that. Shepherd urges us to resist reducing Afghani women to the prototype of the Helpless Victim of Afghanistan, as much as Bush administration rhetoric does.

5. Shepherd argues that the dominant construction of masculinity, the Figure of Authority, needs to construct alternative masculinities in binary opposition. She refers to one alternative as the Irrational Dreamer and notes that this figure tends to get constructed as irresponsible, childlike, dangerously idealistic, and subordinate relative to the Figure of Authority. Although Shepherd's analysis centers on the domestic context, and even though Blair is hardly a pacifist, the same kind of binary thinking seems to apply here.

6. That writers as dissimilar as David Hare and Ian McEwan both felt drawn to this subject matter itself suggests an increasingly widespread belief that 9/11 and the War in Iraq mark an essential shift in the Anglo-American relationship. While Hare is known as a political writer, McEwan's literary corpus is only occasionally punctuated by contemporary politics, yet after 9/11, he abandoned his plans to write "a little novella about a tabloid journalist" and write this book instead because "we're now living in horribly interesting times. There are great grinding sounds of shifting axes of power and interest and alignment and politics and alliances and differences between nations" (Miller). Those grinding shifts of axes of power involve not just the industrialized west and the Arab World, or the United States and its erstwhile continental European allies, but also the United States and Great Britain.

7. As Donald Neff remarks, "The Suez crisis marked the end of Britain and France as world powers. The two countries entered the affair as colonial giants and emerged from it as faintly disrespectable second raters" (25).

8. What makes this representation of Blair even more striking is that David Hare was initially pretty enthusiastic about Tony Blair (although, perhaps presciently, even in 1995 he longed for Blair to find direction). In a 1995 interview in the *Sunday Telegraph,* Hare wrote,

> My own hope . . . is that when Tony Blair finally stops fiddling with his rear-view mirror and tells us what direction he proposes to drive in, then he will offer a Labour programme for which all intelligent men and women will be able to vote. But meanwhile, for the first time since I became an adult, I am ruled by a man who appears to be fundamentally decent and honest. Having a prime minister I am not ashamed of is a feeling I like. (qtd. in Boon 134–35)

In a 2002 interview, when Blair was already clearly aligned with Bush, Hare distinguishes his position from his sometimes collaborator Howard Brenton and identifies Blair with the British nation:

> I don't find Tony Blair contemptible. He does a whole lot of things that I disagree with and don't like, but I don't find him ridiculous. I find the mess that he's now in our mess. It's a mess that I identify with. His confusion is not so different from my own. . . . He's us, Blair. We may not like it, but that's what he is. (qtd. in Boon 173–74)

9. This is not because the British have no worthwhile advice to impart. In Hare's follow-up play *The Vertical Hour*, an anti-war British character reminds a pro-war American character that Great Britain has been in the United States' position before: "In the United States, you're building an empire. Remember, we've dismantled one" (Hare, *The Vertical Hour* I, 3). From the neocons's perspective, however, this devolution of power and Blair's philanthropic (and therefore implicitly feminine) concern with morality are precisely the reasons why Great Britain does not need to be taken seriously.

10. Jago Morrison suggests a somewhat similar use of medical information in order to restore patriarchal order in McEwan's earlier novel, *Enduring Love*. Morrison points out that Joe Rose's masculinity is "embattled," but restored when Parry's problem is identified as de Clerambault's syndrome. Morrison points out that the text even includes "case notes and a full reproduced and referenced journal article on de Clerambault's syndrome, the condition with which the 'fanatic' Parry is ultimately identified," and suggests that "Within the legitimizing discourse of science, both the standard of a 'normal' masculinity and narrativity as a privileged mode of its articulation have been secured." Morrison goes on to argue that "On another level, however, the text specifically invites our incredulity toward this grand narrative of male affirmation" (255). By making Baxter's condition neurological rather than psychological and by elevating the protagonist's authority to brain surgeon, the restoration of masculine normality and authority in *Saturday* does not share this ambivalence.

11. Some critics argue rather persuasively that the excessive perfection of Perowne's life takes away from our ability to engage with the family and the crisis at the center of the text. As Sophie Harrison rather wittily remarks, "Hearing about them is like reading one of those Christmas round robins in which you learn that Charlotte got five A*s in her A-levels and is now studying Cantonese in her time off from the orphanage" (48).

12. Elaine Hadley asks, "Are other readers as taken aback as I am by this use of 'Dover Beach' in a post-9/11 novel? Does it seem to others that McEwan, the Homeland Security Chief of the Novel, has offered up duct tape and plastic sheeting as a response to the unknown agents and unpredictable consequences of the new world order?" (97). David Orr concurs with this sentiment: "In this book's climactic set piece . . . the main character's daughter . . . is about to be raped by a group of thugs, when one of them mockingly demands that she 'read out your best poem.' Instead, she pretends to read from her own collection while actually reciting Matthew Arnold's classic 'Dover Beach.' The thug in chief is amazed ('It's beautiful'), the threat of rape is dispelled, and the nine Muses swap high-fives with the better angels of our nature. Woot!" (15). After describing the incident in some detail, Zoe Heller concludes, "This, it is safe to say, is a faintly preposterous episode. Apart from the credibility-defying spectacle of the fiendish underclass tamed, even momentarily, by verse, there is the garish literalism with which the novel's constituent ideas are made manifest. Here is civilized joy threatened by Caliban-like hordes. Here are the twin feelings of culpability and helplessness foreshadowed at the beginning of the book. Here is the conflict between hatred and sympathy for one's enemy. Here, too, of course, is the transformative capacity of art" (1). Similarly, Jennifer Szalai evaluates this scene as "the grand opera of McEwan's ending, which rivals Enduring Love for whatever prize might be given for histrionic silliness with a home-invasion scene" (89). Andrew Crumey tartly remarks "Perowne's earlier getaway was improbable; his later one is frankly ludicrous. His daughter, having been made to strip naked in a scene so well written as to be almost unbearable, recites a poem.

Baxter likes it so much he decides to leave her alone. If there is any kind of moral message, it appears to be that crazy knife-wielding people can be tamed by the beauties of Western literature. I wonder if anybody tried that approach on 9/11. Certainly, plenty of school teachers have tried it, and have found that Matthew Arnold won't even stop a pea-shooter, never mind a knife" (8). A few critics are more receptive to what McEwan is seemingly aiming for in this scene. Paul J. Griffiths appreciatively writes, "there is a seduction and transformation by beauty. McEwan is horribly explicit in his description of the long-term prospects of those suffering from Huntington's, and he is careful to depict Baxter as a man who knows exactly what is in store for him. Baxter, a sociopath whose brain has begun its irreversible decay, is temporarily transformed, remade, exalted, and inspired by the beauty of Arnold's poetry on the lips of a naked woman under threat of rape. Beauty, in McEwan's view, does have the power to make people remember who and what they are and to act accordingly" (42).

WORKS CITED

Bell, Steve. *Apes of Wrath*. London: Methuen, 2004.

Boon, Richard. *About Hare: The Playwright and the Work*. London: Faber, 2003.

Crumey, Andrew. "Perils of Seizing the Day." *Scotland on Sunday* 6 February 2005: 8.

Drew, Julie. "Identity Crisis: Gender, Public Discourse, and 9/11." *Women and Language* 27 (Fall 2004): 71–77.

Griffiths, Paul J. "Nor Certitude, Nor Peace." *First Things* (August/September 2005): 40–44.

Hadley, Elaine. "On a Darkling Plain: Victorian Liberalism and the Fantasy of Agency." *Victorian Studies* 48 (2005): 92–102.

Hare, David. *Stuff Happens*. London: Faber, 2004.

———. *The Vertical Hour*. New York: Faber, 2006.

Harrison, Sophie. "Happy families." *New Statesman* 24 January 2005: 48–49.

Heller, Zoe. "One Day in the Life." *New York Times* 20 March 2005: sec. 7: 1.

Holmes, Kim R. and Nile Gardiner. "The End of the Affair?" *Wall Street Journal* 28 February 2007: A15.

Leigh, David and Richard Norton-Taylor. "We Are Now a Client State: Britain Has Lost Its Sovereignty to the United States." *The Guardian* 17 July 2003 http://www.guardian.co.uk/politics/2003/jul/17/usa.world

Marquand, David. "The End of the Affair." *New Statesman* 24 November 2003: 18–20.

McEwan, Ian. *Enduring Love*. New York: Nan A. Talese, 1997.

———. *Saturday*. New York: Nan A. Talese, 2005.

Miller, Laura. "The Salon Interview: Ian McEwan." *Salon* 9 April 2005 http://dir.salon.com/story/books/int/2005/04/09/mcewan/index.html.

Morrison, Jago. "Narration and Unease in Ian McEwan's Later Fiction." *Critique* 42 (2001): 253–68.

Naughtie, James. *The Accidental American: Tony Blair and the Presidency*. New York: Public Affairs, 2004.

Nayak, Meghana. "Orientalism and 'Saving' U.S. State Identity after 9/11." *International Feminist Journal of Politics* 8 (2006): 42–61.

Neff, Donald. *Warriors at Suez: Eisenhower Takes America into the Middle East*. New York: Simon & Schuster, 1981.

Orr, David. "Who Needs Mace? Whip Out That Sonnet." *New York Times* 26 June 2005, sec. 7: 15.

Radstone, Susannah. "The War of the Fathers: Trauma, Fantasy, and September 11." *Trauma at Home: After 9/11*. Ed. Judith Greenberg. Lincoln: U of Nebraska P, 2003. 117–23.

Riddell, Peter. *Hug Them Close: Blair, Clinton, Bush and the "Special Relationship."* Rev. ed. London: Politico's, 2004.

Shepherd, Laura. "Veiled References: Constructions of Gender in the Bush Administration Discourse on the Attacks of Afghanistan Post-9/11." *International Feminist Journal of Politics* 8 (2006): 19–41.

Shoot the Dog. 2DTV Production Team. Perf. George Michael. Universal-Island, 2002.

Szalai, Jennifer. "DAY-TRIPPER: The mundane raptures of Ian McEwan." *Harper's Magazine* 310 (May 2005): 87–92.

8 "We're the Culture That Cried Wolf"
Discourse and Terrorism in Chuck Palahniuk's *Lullaby*

Lance Rubin

While promoting his fifth novel *Lullaby* in 2002, Chuck Palahniuk was asked if the attacks of September 11 changed the way he wrote, a particularly relevant question given that his *Fight Club* (1996) opens with a domestic terrorist group about to destroy the world's tallest building, while *Survivor* (1999) opens with the narrator telling his life story into the black box of a hijacked jumbo jet he plans to crash. Palahniuk answered by claiming that since 9/11, "You can't really do what used to be called 'transgressive' fiction. . . People just don't have the tolerance. They won't laugh at things—even like *Thelma & Louise* sort of things—they won't laugh at acts of rebellion. . . . [It] all gets lumped together as terrorism" (qtd. in Ellis). More disconcerting for Palahniuk is that publishers and authors themselves seem willing to suppress any writing that has the slightest chance of being interpreted as endorsing or minimizing "terrorism." Subversive novels are being avoided, he claims, suggesting "a backhanded tendency [after 9/11] to censor fiction, and I have to wonder where it's coming from, if it's just happening or is somebody generating this?" (qtd. in Russo).

If one considers the cultural climate after 9/11, the institutional fear of the transgressive novelist is understandable. After being repeatedly warned by government officials that "you are with us or against us," Palahniuk's dystopic vision of America in pre-9/11 satires like *Fight Club, Invisible Monsters, Survivor,* and *Choke*—with home-grown terrorism, hijacked planes, highway shootings, even comical dissent like feeding LSD to monkeys—is going to seem less attractive to publishers trying to sell books to a nation on the verge of a nervous breakdown. Rather than stop writing subversively after 9/11, Palahniuk claims that the collective unease toward rebellion confirmed his admiration for "genre" fiction as a means for presenting cultural critiques. Explaining his decision to use the forms of "popular" fiction in *Lullaby,* Palahniuk claims that "writers like Orwell found ways to get their message out cloaked in genre, whether it was horror or science fiction or fantasy. . . . Going through a period of repression, or at least not public acceptance of overt social criticism . . .

forces us to be a little more clever and seductive in the ways we present ideas" (qtd. in Stein).

Indeed, Stephen King notes how horror fiction's monsters "are often political, economic, and psychological rather than supernatural," functioning as allegories for current anxieties and suspicions (5). Typically, though, genre fiction tends to be more conservative and "convention-bound" than "literary" fiction (Geldar 43). Horror fiction, as Valdine Clemens notes, attracts more readers during "crisis periods, when the public mood becomes uneasy and pessimistic" (5). That is, interest in horror can be seen as reflecting the need to confirm traditional values, for while the genre provides "a temporary release from civilized constructions," it "neither challenges nor alters the essential nature of those constructions" (Clemens 11). King confirms that beneath the blood and violence, horror's primary purpose "is to reaffirm the virtues of the norm" (395). Likewise, Linda Holland-Toll claims that horror readers are encouraged to worry more about the destruction of the "ordered environment" of a monster's victims than the monster itself, suggesting that, politically, the genre's concern is "the preservation of the community and its accepted values" (20).

However, there is a branch of horror that, rather than reinforcing the traditional mores of the community threatened by a "monster," works as a critique of those conventions and customs. These subversive horror texts practice what Terry Heller refers to as "anti-closure," denying narrative resolution so as to keep the terror raised active after readers close the book (98). Holland-Toll calls this "disaffirmative horror fiction" for its ability to "actively produce feelings of extreme dis/ease and cultural dread" (10). These works thwart readers' attempts to retain confidence in their value systems; rather, they expose their hollowness, "lay them bare as the agenda-ridden social constructs they undoubtedly are." This smaller, transgressive strain of horror "tends to point up the gaps, discontinuities, and deliberate exclusions which must take place to allow people to accept the values in the first place"; they force us to examine our cultural assumptions that position the monstrous threats as Other and to expose our "tacit agreement to gloss over the monstrous" in ourselves and our social practices (10–11).

Lullaby represents horror's more dissident form, employing what Christina Milletti labels a "terrorist aesthetic," the ability to defy the "normative discourses [that] constrain subjectivity" (352–53). The transgressive writer may not have killing as a goal, but like the terrorist, s/he seeks to challenge the universality or legitimacy of the predominant forms of discursive power. *Lullaby*'s "terrorist aesthetic" subverts horror's conventions and expectations in a number of ways. There are witches, haunted houses, and spells, but these traditional elements are accompanied by other "monsters" like necrophiliacs and terrorists. Also, readers cannot find "safe" identification in the novel, since "good" characters perform questionable actions, while the "bad" characters articulate unnervingly convincing cultural critiques. In addition, the novel employs Palahniuk's signature non-linear, fragmented structure and minimalist style which, rather than imposing a dominant narrative, forces readers to take an active role in the creation of meaning, to resist the singularity of any dominant narrative, a primary goal of the terrorist, as explained below. Finally, *Lullaby* does not have a monstrous threat which readers can dismiss as a fantastic Other. In seeking to reinvent the horror novel and update its metaphors, which he feels have become "stuck" in the twenty-first century, Palahniuk employs a "monster" from which we cannot disassociate ourselves: language itself.

Lullaby centers on reporter Carl Streator, living in isolation since his wife and daughter died mysteriously after he read them a lullaby out of *Poems and Rhymes from Around the World.* Years later, writing an article on Sudden Infant Death Syndrome, Streator notices a copy of the book at every home in which a child has died, opened to the same lullaby he read to his family. The lullaby turns out to be an African "culling poem" that kills whoever it is read to; in Africa, it is used in times of famine, overpopulation, or incurable sickness. Initially, after rediscovering the poem, Streator inadvertently (at first) kills people when the poem runs through his head, often in uncontrollable flashes of anger. Considering whether or not to share his discovery with anyone, Streator realizes that a collective fear of language would profitably put an end to the mindless distractions of the mass media, allowing people to create their own identities without the help of a culture industry that reinforces a collective distraction. However, he also knows that the poem could kill millions if made public, and he recognizes the inevitable government policing of language that would follow, complete with book burnings and censorship of all "unapproved" ideas. Streator therefore contacts Helen Hoover Boyle, a real estate agent whose husband and child died in the same manner. They embark on a cross-country quest to find and to destroy all remaining copies of the lullaby, accompanied by Helen's Wiccan secretary Mona and Mona's boyfriend Oyster, a fanatical environmentalist and would-be ecoterrorist. Helen, though, has an ulterior motive: to find the original *grimoire,* or book of spells, from which the poem was taken in the hopes of reversing its power and reanimating her child, whom she has had cryogenically frozen. Mona and Oyster also desire the *grimoire,* believing its words can help them implement their environmental ideals and reverse what they see as the inevitable self-destruction of the planet. The second half of the novel details their travels and the conflicting power play among the four over control of the language and symbols in the book of spells.

Read in aftermath of 9/11, Palahniuk's combination of lethal words, government control of language, an infantilizing mass media, and linguistic power struggles invites analysis as an allegorical exploration of the power of language and the battle to shape the discursive framework of the so-called "war on terror." Of course, official attempts to frame cultural discourse and to police speech are not unique to post-9/11 America. *Lullaby,* however, provides an opportunity to consider how language and cultural narratives are contested and fought over. The responses to the lullaby, like the responses to 9/11 (including the invasion of Iraq), make visible the omnipresent struggle to control the systems of meaning and language in the culture. *Lullaby*'s allegory of semantic power also implicates our all-too-eager willingness to shy away from the subversive fiction and other forms of counter-discourse that made us uncomfortable after 9/11, ultimately arguing for the dissident artist's necessity in polemical political times. To put this all another way, the lullaby in *Lullaby* can be read as a Derridian *pharmakon* of both poison and cure. It serves as an allegory *for* the 9/11 and anthrax attacks, revealing a continuum between discursive practices and the physical destruction wrought by terrorism. At the same time, the lullaby is also positioned as a *form of resistance* to the imposition of *any* absolutist discourse. That is, the poem is imagined as the solution to the fearful self-censorship and imperialist ideology that characterized post-9/11 discourse, with the words-as-weapon metaphor making a plea for the power of language and the possibility of alternate narratives not sanctioned by those who would wield absolute discursive control, whether from the terrorist or the state.

* * *

Lullaby immediately establishes the issue of framing and controlling discourse with Streator questioning the authority of all narratives: "The problem with every story is you tell it after the fact. . . . Another problem is the teller. The who, what, where, when and why of the reporter. The media bias. How the messenger shapes the fact. What journalists call The Gatekeeper" (7). In a novel concerned with discursive power, Streator immediately introduces the idea that our understanding of events is inevitably mediated by subjective language and images. Discourse is never objective. Because we only apprehend the authenticity of any incident through words, images, and analysis, language itself is as tangible as the events that it portends to be objectively capturing, an instrument of control—a weapon that shapes and persuades readers into understanding events in a certain way.

Streator makes these points so as to introduce the novel's primary focus, the notion that language is more of a tool to wield power than a vehicle through which to communicate or to articulate objective perceptions. Here, Streator is not only referring to news, but to all media. Sitting in his apartment listening to the "siege of noise" (17) invading his senses, Streator echoes Richard Terdiman's notion of how "in a world saturated by discourse, language itself becomes contested terrain" (43). Unable to escape the heavy beats of music or the laugh tracks from a blaring television, Streator realizes that we are all engaged in an "arms race of sound," fighting a discursive war: "This isn't about quality. It's about volume. This isn't about music. It's about winning. . . . You dominate. This is really about power" (17).

The metaphor of discourse-as-weapon becomes literal for Streator after recognizing that the lullaby is responsible for the death of his wife and daughter. Streator sees how easily the lullaby could be a weapon of mass destruction if it is "read over the radio to thousands of people" or how a "million people might watch a television show, then be dead the next morning because of an advertising jingle" (40–41). He realizes the "question isn't, *Would the poem leak out? The question is, How soon would the human race be extinct?*" (40). After 9/11 and the anthrax attacks that followed, it is impossible to read Streator's apocalyptic speculations without connecting the poem to terrorism. The anxiety Americans felt among color-coded terror alerts and breaking news warning that schools, bridges, and malls were terror targets mirrors Streator's horrific awareness that mass casualties could happen anywhere, at any time: "The new death, this plague, can come from everywhere. A song. An overhead announcement. A news bulletin. A sermon. A street musician. You can catch death from a telemarketer. A teacher. An Internet file" (41). The ultimate horror of this anxiety is that the poem is "available to anyone. To everyone," making it a "plague unique to the Information Age" (40–41). With the knowledge of bomb-making, lethal viruses, and nuclear weaponry readily available on the Internet—combined with the vitriolic rhetoric from all sides of the "war on terror"—Palahniuk's lullaby raises the ominous specter of terrorism. Indeed, Helen reinforces Streator's positioning of the lullaby-as-weapon by suggesting that she has used it on the publisher of the book of poems: "if I had just killed my husband, after killing my son, wouldn't I be a little angry that some plagiarizing, lazy, irresponsible greedy fool had planted the bomb that would destroy everyone I love?" (86).

At the core of *Lullaby*'s framework, then, Palahniuk implies the linguistic performance of violence and "terror," a term that has been reduced to images of the smoking Twin Towers and Al Qaeda videotapes since 9/11. The idea of language-as-weapon-of-mass-destruction, however, broadens the concept of "terror" by suggesting that its roots are discursive. To be sure, speech and action—the discourse of violence and the violence itself—are not the same things, and one must be cautious in making terrorism's carnage too academic. *Lullaby* suggests, though, a formal and ideological link between discourse and terrorism. In considering Palahniuk's allegory, it is worth noting Jean-Francois Lyotard's claim that discursive control is at the core of all acts of terror; the violent terrorist act, ultimately, is "the efficacy gained by eliminating, or threatening to eliminate, a player from the language game one shares with him" (63). For Lyotard, terrorism is part of the battle for discursive supremacy. Whether coming from the marginalized cell or the official nation-state, totalizing metanarratives, he argues, are terroristic by their very nature. The official state's fundamental goal is a domination that imposes a hegemonic authority on the heterogeneity of contrasting events and possible meanings. Likewise, terrorists attempt to subvert or disrupt those discursive and symbolic orders that suppress differences or alternative visions. Reacting against the perceived rigidity of global or cultural metanarratives, the terrorist is not so much seeking plurality as to impose its own authoritative metanarrative onto a stunned and frightened populace.

As Joseba Zulaika and William Douglass have argued, "Whatever else it might be, 'terrorism' is printed text" (31). From the printed pamphlet or militant website to the implementation of violence and the death of innocents, terrorism works by putting words and symbols into deadly action. David Apter calls this relationship between terrorist rhetoric and action "linguistic alchemy," a process in which violence is merged into the discourses of certain marginalized groups, eventually becoming central to their self-sustaining narratives. When those narratives rely on violent acts to sustain their meaning, "events become metaphors," demonstrating the rationality of the terrorists' positions (17). However, *that* narrative also allows the victim of terrorism to enact his *own* counter-narratives in response. As Margaret Scanlan notes, nations like the United States "respond to terrorism—which seeks to disturb our metanarratives—with our own narratives that are already in circulation" (109–110). Once this cycle begins, though, separating the language of violence from the acts of violence and their terrible aftermath becomes increasingly difficult. "Violence begets discourse," Apter claims, "and discourse begets violence" (18).

Lullaby's dramatization of the cyclical, intertwined nature of discourse and violence is sharpened when Streator wrestles with the decision of whether or not to share his revelation with government authorities, foreseeing their inevitable reaction. He anticipates the strict policing of language, including book-burnings, that would be implemented if the truth about the poem were known: "The kind of security they now have at airports, imagine that kind of crackdown at all libraries, schools, theaters, bookstores, after the culling song leaks out. Anywhere information might be disseminated, you'll find armed guards" (43). Everything would be taken off the airwaves save "a few government broadcasts" and "well-scrubbed news and music." All new writing and art "will be tested on lab animals or volunteer convicts," and people would begin paying "for a supply of 'pure' news, a source for 'safe' information and entertainment. . . . Certified. Approved for consumption." Streator anticipates that people "will be happy to give up most of their culture for the assurance that the tiny bit that comes through is safe and clean" (43). Envisioning how language would be controlled by the government in the same manner as a weapon of mass destruction—as well as how much people would give up to feel safe—he presciently foresees a policing of discourse in a manner that came to fruition after 9/11.

Indeed, one cannot read Streator's musings without recognizing how counter-discourse concerning the sanctioned narratives of 9/11 was managed, including the feverish rhetorical run-up to the 2003 Iraq invasion. Streator's forecast that language would be hunted down with the same urgency as weapons of mass destruction presciently anticipates how only discourse that fits within a traditional, conservative framework would be authoritatively reinforced as acceptable, with any dissenting ideas or solutions silenced:

> Imagine the books burning. . . . Imagine people chanting prayers, singing hymns to drown out any sound that might bring death. Their hands clamped over their ears. . . . Any new word. Anything they don't already understand will be suspect, dangerous. Avoided. A quarantine against communication. (42)

Reinforcing an understanding of language's role in the cycle of terroristic violence, Streator deftly forecasts the strategies to gain discursive power immediately after the 9/11 attacks—to control the flow and direction of the narratives that would explain the motives and lay the groundwork for policy decisions and responses. Streator imagines people reacting to the killer lullaby by "chanting prayers" and "singing hymns," as well as "the soothing constant protection of safe music" (43) to shield them from unfamiliar ideas. America responded to 9/11 in similar fashion: Church attendance increased by 25% to 90% after the attacks, "depending on which pastor, which rabbi, which culture warrior you asked" (Sharlet).[1] And as Stuart Croft outlines, the White House quickly scripted soothing, intertwined narratives to interpret the events of September 11 and the nation's response to them: "the construction of an enemy image; the avoidance of blame on any other than the enemy; a definition of core values that were at risk; and a claim . . . that these values were global as well as American, and that the world accepted American leadership in protecting them" (69). The "Gatekeepers" in the American media dutifully repeated this discourse, never questioning whether this narrative was being constructed with subjective political purposes. According to Stefan Halper and Jonathan Clarke, what was only a set of ideological assumptions and wishes for groups like Progress For a New American Century—including a millennial belief that the world was divided between Good and Evil and a desire for America to use its military to influence foreign policy—was immediately "championed as the logical solution as a new world order where the United States would lead other nations toward the ultimate ideal of freedom and security," a discourse which excluded "other more moderate responses" (207).

These metanarratives also deflected dissent and important questions of perspective, labeling those who carried out the destruction of 9/11 "evil-doers." Those who deviated from the discourse of patriotism, American exceptionalism and "Islamo-Fascist" evil were labeled as the "Hate America Crowd." The fervent reaction against them became analogous to Streator's belief that angry, fearful mobs "will attack microwave stations. People with axes will chop every fiber-optic cable" to avoid hearing anything that does not already fit into their preconceived notions of reality (42). One of the first causalities of this discursive battle was Bill Maher, host of ABC's *Politically Incorrect*. Questioning one of the official narratives—that the

9/11 attacks were carried out by "cowards"—Maher claimed, "we have been the cowards lobbing cruise missiles from 2,000 miles away. That's cowardly" (qtd. in Jurkowitz 11–12). As skittish sponsors abandoned the program, White House spokesman Ari Fleischer responded by warning, "There are reminders to all Americans that they need to watch what they say, watch what they do, and that this is not a time for remarks like that. It never is" (qtd. in Jurkowitz 11–12). ABC soon cancelled the show amid public pressure.

Maher was but the first real-life enactment of Palahniuk's allegory of a "world where people are afraid to listen, afraid they'll hear something" (42). After 9/11 and the Maher incident, it was "intellectually difficult and even politically dangerous" to raise questions or "to assess the meaning of a conflict that phase-shifts with every news cycle, from 'Terror Attack' to 'America Fights Back'" (Der Derian). Those who subverted the narrative of American exceptionalism and Islamist evil, having been warned by Fleischer, were vilified, including musicians The Dixie Chicks and Steve Earle, cartoonists Aaron McGruder and Art Spiegelman, and journalists Peter Jennings and Dan Rather.[2] Academic discourse was also policed, with Lynne Cheney's Association of College Alumni and Trustees condemning higher education for refusing to repeat the Administration's line. Claiming that "the American public had no difficulty calling evil by its rightful name," they ask, "Why is it so hard for many faculty to do the same?" (Martin and Neal 4). Their report juxtaposes quotes from President Bush and Rudy Giuliani ("We're right and they're wrong. It's as simple as that") with those by "radical professors" and "radicalized" students ("We don't feel military action will stop terrorism, but it will lead to racism and hate") to argue how "moral relativism" infects academia. "Rarely did professors publicly mention heroism," they decry, or "discuss the difference between good and evil . . . Indeed, the message . . . was clear: BLAME AMERICA FIRST" (3).[3]

Perhaps the most open display of the fear of language as a virus is demonstrated in official attempts to control the Al Qaeda tapes released periodically after 9/11. News networks submitted to the White House's "suggestion" to "abridge any future videotaped statements from Osama Bin Laden or his followers to remove language the government considers inflammatory" (Carter and Berringer A1). Concerned that the tapes would incite violence against Americans or contain codes to terrorist cells in the United States, the networks "voluntarily" agreed to the White House's recommendation of self-censorship, thereby denying Americans the opportunity to hear directly any counter-discourse, any potential reasons for the attacks by those who supposedly planned them. These few examples of the concerted effort to limit debate on 9/11 can be seen as Palahniuk's parable in action: "No one talks because no one dares to listen" (43).

But if the lullaby serves as an allegory for the 9/11 attacks in one reading of the novel, with Streator's anticipated reactions from the government and media analogous to the national response, it can also be seen as a *solution* to the fearful self-censorship that characterized post-9/11 discourse and the imposition of any dominant, binaristic metanarrative. As Streator decides what to do with his knowledge of the poem, he considers how a fear of language might actually be beneficial. In an apparent nod to William S. Burroughs's notion of the word virus,[5] Palahniuk suggests that being forced into comparative silence, we "noise-aholics" and "quiet-ophobics" would be left to our own mental devices without the discursive guideposts and cultural cues of political parties, big business, religious organizations, and mass media constructing models of reality for us: "The upside is maybe our minds would become our own" (59–60). Thinking that "it would be nice to see words come back into power," Streator suggests that our "cluttered world of language" is designed to keep us confused and preoccupied, discouraged from thinking too hard about *how* that language is used (60, 246). The pervasive, inescapable din of the culture industry guarantees that "no one's mind is their own. . . . You can't think. There's always some noise worming in. Singers shouting. Actors crying" (19). Suggesting Orwell's fears in *1984* were misplaced, Streator realizes,

> Big Brother isn't watching. He's singing and dancing. He's pulling rabbits out of a hat. Big Brother's busy holding your attention the very moment you're awake. He's making sure you're always distracted. . . . He's making sure your imagination withers. Until it's as useful as your appendix. He's making sure your attention is always filled. . . . With the world always filling you, no one has to worry what's in your mind. With everyone's imagination atrophied, no one will ever be a threat. (18–19)

Streator's idea of Big Brother echoes Michel Foucault's notion that while the state cannot "occupy the whole field of power relations," its discourse is inevitably linked to all networks of power: the law, politics, economics and, ultimately, mass communication (122). Distracted with the sheer glut of discourse, we are rendered politically and intellectually ineffective, unable to challenge the status quo or to imagine why we would want to do so. Perceiving that we are kept entertained and intellectually lazy, Streator sees how effectively our news media, entertainment industries, political parties, and religious organizations have scripted our lives: "I don't know the difference between what I want and what I'm trained to want" (228). The lullaby, then, is not only the lethal poem, but the culture industry putting us to sleep, which Streator finds equally toxic: "There are worse things than finding your wife and child dead. You can watch the world do it. You can watch your wife get old and bored. You can watch kids discover everything in the world you've tried to save them from. Drugs, divorce, conformity, disease. All the nice clean books, music, television. Distraction" (19). While the culling poem may kill immediately, the cultural lullaby is just as deadly, though slower acting, to our intellectual and creative lives.

By specifically calling out the "clean books" that wither one's imagination, Palahniuk clearly considers his own role in the culture industry, for metonymically, the killer poem and the transgressive writer occupy the same position in the culture. Both disrupt or subvert the discourse of the dominant culture by demanding our attention and calling our values into question. As Anthony Kubiak notes, "the ability of narrative . . . to construct a world that is fearful, uncertain and dangerous is its link to terror" (298). Palahniuk's lullaby and *Lullaby,* like the terrorist act, attempt to destabilize the discourse of the dominant culture, "urging the reader to consider an alternate perspective, hoping to free up some space in the real world for another interpretation of the patriotic myth, the official version, the sacred text" (Scanlan 21). Both transgressive art and terror attempt to weaken the power of all-encompassing narratives that impose a seemingly "naturalized" hegemonic ideology.

At the same time, Palahniuk figures our addictive consumption of violence as having paved the way for the metanarratives that reify the 9/11 attacks and ignore (or distract us from considering) alternative rhetorical and symbolic models through which to think about *why* others would want to fly airplanes into buildings or send toxins through the mail. Imagining the potential benefits of the killer lullaby, Streator suggests that disastrous spectacles like 9/11 simply brought to life the images we had been consuming steadily in the name of entertainment:

> Through the walls comes horses screaming and cannon fire. . . . Down through the ceiling comes a fire siren and people screaming that we're supposed to ignore. The gunshots and tires squealing, sounds we have to pretend are okay. They don't mean anything. It's just television. An explosion vibrates down from the upstairs. A woman begs someone not to rape her. It's not real. It's just a movie. *We're the culture that cried wolf.* (94, emphasis mine)

In contrast to one of the plot points of the official narrative after 9/11, *Lullaby* suggests that Americans ought *not* to be shocked by or convince ourselves that 9/11 was unimaginable. Streator's idea that we constantly distract ourselves with spectacular images of violence and destruction anticipates Slavoj Žižek's claim that 9/11 was "the stuff of popular fantasies long before they ever took place" (17). The attacks uncannily realized our desire to see "King Kong and Godzilla pulverize Fifth Avenue [and] extraterrestrials broil Soho in brimstone and pitch" (Davis 36). Streator's insights also coincide with Baudrillard's claim that while "it was *they* who perpetrated the attack . . . it was *we* who wished it" (150).

Streator's observation that we are a docile, intellectually atrophied "culture that cried wolf" also deftly anticipates how the entertainment produced before and after 9/11 implicitly reinforces American hegemony and the "war on terror," part of a larger apparatus designed to keep us simultaneously politically distracted and obedient. Streator sees how "[t]he music and [canned TV] laughter eat away at your thoughts. The noise blots them out. All the sound detracts" (19). Any understanding of history gets lost in a blur of television images: "On television, someone is showing how to poach a salmon. Someone is showing why the *Bismarck* sank" (216). Likewise, as Scanlan notes, the glossy paperback thrillers we consumed before 9/11 tended to represent the terrorist as a pathological Other that the West, with its higher moral code, inexorably defeats (161). As Christopher Lockett has perceptively noted, in pre-9/11 films "the Islamist fanatic tends to be the enemy of choice when the blockbuster logic of the action film demands sheer villainy" (291). The Middle Eastern "terrorist represents the capital-O Other—an individual whose actions proceed from inscrutable and motiveless malice" (291). After the attacks, this reification continued. As Croft notes, "some in the news media, and in the think tanks, were involved in acts of co-production with the administration" (264). Streator's consideration of the lullaby's potential benefits, then, anticipates how the "war on terror" would become entertainment.

Indeed, shows like *24, Alias, Threat Matrix, Profiles From the Front Line,* and *Over There*—as well as films like *United 93* and *World Trade Center*—decontextualize the events they dramatize and implicitly support the dominant discourse of the "war on terror." Seeing the threats of mass destruction becoming "force-multiplied by media technologies of mass distraction," Der Derien correctly foresaw how images of "virtuous war" would become "our daily bread and nightly circus." The culture industry's acceptance of official metanarratives after 9/11 tacitly confirmed the superiority of American ideologies and the official military and rhetorical responses to the attacks. Less comfortable, however, is the idea that Americans habitually fantasize in the same ways about the same sort of destruction to their national symbols as any terrorist group, that the reactions to 9/11 were a collective cry of wolf. As Baudrillard contends, "Without our profound complicity, the event would not have reverberated so forcefully" (151). The spectacle of 9/11, in other words, revealed as much about American identity as the terrorists'.

Lullaby explores this idea of complicity—and the cyclical nature of discourse and violence—as Streator, Helen, Mona and Oyster travel the country in search of books containing the lullaby. On the road, they find themselves causing as much death and destruction as the poem itself. This begins with Palahniuk's darkly satiric commentary on talk radio, the medium through which official metanarratives of post-9/11 patriotism and morality were staunchly reinforced. Listening to Dr. Sara Lowenstein (an obvious stand-in for Dr. Laura Schlesinger), Streator unwittingly kills her on the air as she calls a young female caller a "slut" and a "stupid whore" who "spread her legs without even getting paid" (74). Thinking "[h]ere's Big Brother, singing and dancing, force-feeding you so your mind never gets hungry enough to think," the poem flashes through his mind, silencing

Dr. Sara, followed by other radio hosts who eulogize her as "a noble and hard-line moralist who refused to accept anything but steadfast righteous conduct" (131) and "the flaming sword of God sent to route the misdeeds and evildoers" (132). Mona, knowing what Streator is doing, castigates him unironically, arguing that a "radio personality is just as important as a cow or a pig" (132).

Later, though, Palahniuk treats their actions less satirically. Helen, unable to find three copies of the anthology in The Book Barn, kills the security guards with the lullaby and burns the store to the ground. Forecasting the Orwellian irony of America's invasion of Iraq, Streator asks, "We're killing people to save lives? We're burning books to save books? I ask, what is this trip turning into?" (160). Shortly thereafter, Streator and Helen contact a man whose child was killed by the poem. His wife has accused him of murder, and he is awaiting trial. Streator, knowing he can save this man, also imagines the dangers of doing so: "Maybe this guy and his wife would reunite, but then the poem would be out. Millions would die. The rest would live in that world of silence, hearing only what they think is safe" (173). Rephrasing the military term "collateral damage," Streator sees his silence and complicity in this man's inevitable imprisonment as "constructive destruction" (172). In another act of "constructive destruction," Streator recites the poem to a police detective who wants to question him about the death of his wife and some fashion models (who, in another example of discursive power, are the victims of a paramedic named Nash who is using the lullaby to fulfill fantasies of necrophilia). As Streator anguishes that he is becoming what he is trying to eliminate, the novel reveals the symbiotic relationship between "good" and "evil." Killing in order to save, imprisoning in order to keep free, and creating distinctions on exclusive terms between "us" and "them," all reinforce the idea that discursive paradigms are never neutral.

The inability of binary discourses to frame rhetorically the righteousness of the quest for the poem also seems to comment on our actions before and after 9/11. *Lullaby* explores these boundaries through the conflict between Streator and Oyster, an environmental fanatic who is on this journey to find the book of spells. He wants access to the words and symbols that will give him the power to remake the world according to his rigid environmental narrative. Like the terrorist, he considers himself "a fucking patriot" who is selflessly subjecting himself and others to a higher cause, reversing man's abuse of the environment. Reinforcing the link between terrorism and discourse, Oyster envisions using the language in the book of spells to end "the big lie about how we can continue to be fruitful and multiply" by "wiping the slate clean, of books and people, and starting over" (160–161). Though his plans involve killing innocents, even, Streator observes, children, vegans, and those who earnestly "live green and recycle," Oyster, voicing a fundamentalist righteousness, claims, "'This isn't about guilt or innocence. . . . The dinosaurs weren't morally good or bad, but they're all dead. . . . I want to be what killed the dinosaurs'" (161).

Once he seizes the *grimoire* after trying to kill Helen, Oyster heals animals while simultaneously killing people through certain spells. He brings his ideologies to life by destroying Seattle and its citizens with indestructible, fast-growing ivy: "the residents of the Park Senior Living Center found their lobby doors sealed with ivy. That same day, the south wall of the Fremont Theatre, brick and concrete, three feet thick, it buckled onto a sellout crowd. That same day, part of the underground bus mall caved in" (166). With the effects of the spells heralding "the end of civilization in slow motion," Oyster, like Tyler Durden from *Fight Club,* crosses the line between subversion and fanaticism, from giving voice to a cultural critique silenced by the dominant discourse to enacting a rigid fundamentalism that dismisses death in the cause of a utopian ideology. While Tyler and Oyster help others to deviate from the corporate scripts that have become naturalized, they ultimately replace the dominant metanarrative with one even more unyielding. As Tyler becomes an authoritarian leader of a paramilitary terrorist group that mirrors the corporate world it would destroy, Oyster reveals a misanthropic willingness to sacrifice others to enact his ideals, demonstrating the inevitability with which fundamentalist, binary thinking breaks down and the ease with which we can become the Other we vilify.

Tellingly, Oyster's subversion is initially no different than that of the transgressive writer. He too writes for a living, fake ads for class-action lawsuits against corporate America. "'Attention Owners of Dorsett Fine China. . . . If you feel nauseated or lose bowel control after eating, please call the following number,'" or "'Attention Patrons of the Apparel-Design Chain of Clothing Stores. . . . If you've contacted genital herpes while trying on clothing, please call the following number,'" are representative of the dozens he creates (100, 141). Inevitably, the company calls Oyster and pays him to cancel the ad. Mona's explanation of Oyster's tactics provides a clear connection between him and a transgressive author: "Other people fill in the blanks . . . he's just planting the seed of doubt in their mind" (152). Claiming its legitimacy against corporate advertising which falsely promises "something to make you happy," Mona's rationale for Oyster echoes the goal of the subversive artist: "to undermine the illusion of comfort and safety in people's minds" (152). This is also the primary purpose of the terrorist, and given the opportunity Oyster immediately shifts from discursive subversion to physical destruction, from getting people to rethink their way of life through writing to destroying them with other language. Palahniuk and other transgressive artists do the same, minus the killing, by employing a "terrorist aesthetic," upsetting "the system's gears" by rhetorically dismantling traditional systems of discursive power (Milletti 352–53). But by exposing Oyster's motives, Palahniuk explores the transgressive artist's role in wresting discursive authority from both the fundamentalism of the terrorist *or* the state that rigidly upholds norms and values by only publishing "safe" books "approved for consumption."

Lullaby resists the all-encompassing discursive tactics of both, which is illustrated in the different strategies Streator and Helen employ to deal with trauma, strategies which surfaced in the cultural debates over the appropriate responses to the 9/11 attacks and the decision to invade Iraq. Rather than face his trauma, Streator blocks his anger and grief through distraction, obsessively building models of miniature towns and cities to exercise a sense of control over his life: "cobble things together. Make order out of chaos. . . . Organize every detail. It isn't what the therapist will tell you to do, but it works" (20). Avoiding thoughts of his dead family by focusing on re-building the world, Streator meticulously puts the tiny pieces together, and from "far away it looks perfect. Perfect and safe and happy. . . . As if everything's just fine" (21–22). Longing for a structured, coherent world, Streator imposes order via the models. But once finished building the safe houses and idyllic towns, Streator smashes them to pieces with his bare feet: "Stomp and keep stomping. No matter how much it hurts, the brittle broken plastic and wood and glass, keep stomping" (22). He cannot imagine a reaction other than rage, the cycle of building and destroying. The shards of the model, the "broken homes and trashed institutions" of Western civilization, lodge deep in his feet causing him to limp with the pain of the past (154). The cyclical pattern is literally what holds him up; he feels it with every step he takes.

Streator's use of a prefabricated model as a means to distraction and temporary amnesia is important here, for despite the illusion of creativity, the outcome of a store-bought model is prearranged. There is literally no thinking outside the box. Rather than building something new or original, the end result is predetermined. Limited, the model-builder is simply going through the motions, assembling prearranged pieces. This is a fitting metaphor for America's reaction after 9/11. Enraged, mournful, frightened, our exceptionalism and professed "innocence" shattered by a faceless enemy, America stood at a crossroads. One option was to validate pre-emptive wars against a growing list of current and future "evil" enemies, a coping mechanism analogous to Streator's reaction to the death of his family. Like his unwillingness to look at the big picture and inability to imagine a reaction other than destruction to assuage his anger, the novel suggests that a policy of endless, "defensive" war does not allow for imaginative, creative responses to dealing with the tragic complexities of 9/11 or its aftermath. What it reveals is the tendency for America to act in "'irrational' fits of destructive rage" as a way of compensating for "an awareness of missed opportunities" to consider positive, perhaps radical alternatives to alter personal and political problems (Žižek 24). Reacting aggressively, as Streator says, "isn't what the therapist will tell you to do"; likewise, as Fredric Jameson notes, "All Americans are now receiving therapy, and it is called war" (57). Streator's self-therapy is similar: it is a lashing out that temporarily satisfies sorrow and fury, but ultimately results in further pain as the shards of what he destroys lodge in and infect his feet, making it difficult for him to walk without a reminder of the ruins of his models, which, in turn, points to his failure to confront and to comprehend fully his family's death and his own response.

Similarly, America can be the global policeman, can bomb civilians to save them from tyranny, and can torture in the name of freedom, but in doing so we will not stand with the same moral authority we claim to be enacting. Instead, we stand like Streator, with our destruction infecting us, unable to think outside the box. Mona's advice to Streator can also be seen as a warning against our inevitable response to 9/11: "To justify any crime you have to make the victim your enemy. After long enough, everyone in the world will become your enemy. . . . More and more, you imagine the whole world is against you" (134). That Mona could also be talking about those who attacked on 9/11, America's response to those attacks, Oyster, or Streator is perhaps the point. The binary lines threaten to blur the more we resort to predictable models of violence and killing to stop violence and killing. *Lullaby* suggests that 9/11 gave the nation an opportunity it did not take.

Lullaby presents alternative solutions for reacting to the events of 9/11 through Helen's coping strategies. She does not share Streator's desire for "containing this disaster, [d]oing damage control," or "learning a way to forget" the poem or its aftermath (85). Rather, she wants to remember so as actively to alter the future. While she and Streator discuss their possible alliance in an antique warehouse, they get lost in the maze of armoires and other old furniture crammed in the huge building. Suggesting the power of history to imprison one's future, Helen refers to the furniture as relics of the past, as "parasite[s] surviving the host . . . big fat predator[s] looking for [their] next meal" (52). Asking Streator if he feels somehow "buried in history," Helen drags her keys and diamond rings across the historic pieces, scarring them forever. She does this to symbolically assert herself against the entrapping maze of history, literally brushing against its grain *à la* Walter Benjamin, refusing to be ruled by it. She tells Streator she loves the antique she ruins, but "I'll only have it on my own terms" (53). Helen's gesture is a powerful contrast to Streator's cycle of building and destroying. Carving the arrows in order to find her way out of the maze of antiques serves as a metaphorical image for trying to find a way out the past that haunts her. As she walks and scars the pieces, she proposes that they not destroy the *grimoire,* thinking of the other possible spells that could change the world: "Maybe you could bring about world peace. . . . Maybe you could turn sand into bread. . . . Maybe you could cure the sick. . . . maybe you could give people rich full happy lives" (86–87). In other words, language can *destroy,* but it can also *heal.* Helen offers Streator a chance to use his losses constructively, but to do so he must resist the automatic urge to lash out in vengeance. Not content to remain passively lost among the models of the past, she warns Streator—who wants only to destroy the poem—that "maybe you don't go to hell for the things you do. Maybe you go to hell for the things you don't do" (87). Streator does not want this kind of power or responsibility to affect history, to accept the past or alter the future, and purposely walks the opposite way from the way that Helen's arrows are pointing, "limping along" into the maze with the pain and weight of the world in his feet (87).

Only later in the novel does Streator realize that "the easiest way to avoid living is to just watch. . . . Don't participate. Let Big Brother do the singing and dancing for you" (216). Looking over his stagnant existence—his infected feet full of a destroyed past limiting his movement—he sees the need to abandon the models. If he is going to stop the endless cycle of building and destroying, he realizes that "the only way to find freedom is by doing the things I don't want to do . . . I need to do what I most fear" (232). Streator commits himself to re-engaging with the world again, to stop running away from his responsibilities and obligations to act, to help, and to connect with others. He calls his father, with whom he had not spoken since he ran away and changed his name after his family's death. He confronts Nash, who is using the lullaby to kill and then sleep with fashion models, but who also knows that the police are looking for Streator.

Ultimately, Streator's epiphany is what *Lullaby* implies as the appropriate response to the events of 9/11—to do what seems most difficult or unimaginable for us in order to break the spells that occupy us. Whether those words come through the white noise of popular culture or political sloganeering, their message is the same: "Big Brother is singing and dancing, and we're left to watch. . . . To just pay attention and wait for the next disaster" (246). Palahniuk's allegory of language and power calls for readers to break the invisible, self-inflicted censorship that creates a culture of passive acceptance in which imagination and perspective have been withered away by a simplified, ideological discourse that fills an aching void left by 9/11. Any sort of self-examination on the personal or collective level is rendered unnecessary because the discourses of tradition, entertainment industries, religious organizations, and political parties provide us with explanatory models that exude authority, comfort, and easy answers; they are attractive because they require very little action or commitment for most of us. Like Streator, the novel suggests, we have to have the strength to face our fears and complicity in the status quo squarely, free from Big Brother's singing and dancing that keeps us from being a threat by all-but forcing us to internalize the ideological discourse, the culling poems of politics and marketing, that destroy our autonomy.

Yet the novel ends with the sense that Streator and Helen are going to be forever chasing Oyster and Mona, only able to trace them through the damage their spells leave behind. The novel suggests that there is no way to slay this discursive monster. The horror of *Lullaby*—our language itself—is not contained as the novel closes. In fact, Streator reminds us that we are constantly being infected with it at every moment of our lives: "We're all of us haunting and haunted. Something foreign is always living itself through you. . . . A theory. A marketing campaign. A political strategy. A religious doctrine" (258). While readers might wish for closure to the monster Palahniuk has loosened, the novel, enacting Heller's notion of "anti-closure," continues to haunt us as readers once we have finished the last word, forcing us to look at language in a new, more critical way, and ultimately questioning our ability to imagine alternative realities that are not structured by Big Brother. On one level, then, *Lullaby* questions its own efficacy in weaning us off of and ultimately subverting the word-virus. But finally, the open-ended conclusion shows Streator and Helen's unwavering determination to catch Oyster and Mona, suggesting Palahniuk's own refusal to submit to authoritarian politics or fundamentalist absolutism. While 9/11 revealed the uneasy connection between the goals of terrorists and subversive writers, *Lullaby* ultimately affirms the need for the transgressive artist lest we tacitly authorize political forces and social groups—from official states or terrorists—to impose discursive models which allow no room for self examination or dissenting expression.

NOTES

1. As Sharlet notes, however, nearly all surveys showed that this was a short-lived surge, with attendance reverting to the normative 40+% within a month after 9/11.
2. See Rich, Kellner, Heard, and Scherer for details of these and other examples of how straying from the official discourse was treated after 9/11 and in the run-up to the Iraq invasion.
3. The condemnation of higher education reached its crescendo with the outcry against University of Colorado professor Ward Churchill's essay exploring how U.S. foreign and domestic policies helped to create 9/11 ("The Justice"). Colorado was also the site of another nationally-recognized incident when Overland High School geography teacher Jay Bennish noted comparisons between Bush's 2005 State of the Union address and Adolph Hitler's speeches (Vaughn and Doligosa). In response, Governor Bill Owens initiated a so-called "Academic Bill of Rights" which sought to increase "intellectual diversity" by hiring more "conservative" faculty (Gerstein).
4. Burroughs postulates that language spawns the vast majority of global crises. Rather than allowing us to communicate, words have instead been used as weapons of submission and control by the daily press and by corporate media. Breaking the need to compulsively verbalize would, Burroughs suggests, be the first step in re-imagining our assumptions about religious doctrine, the reasons we go to war, nationalism and patriotism, economic and foreign policy (see Odier 59). That Palahniuk is paying tribute to Burroughs is implied in the novel's opening chapter, in which Helen tells Mona, "get me Bill or Emily Burrows on the phone," and ends with Helen asking, "Bill Borrows?" into the receiver (5–6).

WORKS CITED

Apter, David. "Political Violence in Analytical Perspective." *The Legitimization of Violence*. Ed. David Apter. London: Macmillan, 1997. 1–32.

Baudrillard, Jean. "L'Esprit du Terrorisme." *Dissent From the Homeland: Essays After September 11*. Ed. Stanley Hauerwas and Frank Lentricchia. Durham: Duke UP, 2003: 149–62.

Carter, Bill and Felicity Barringer. "Networks Agree to U.S. Request to Edit Future Bin Laden Tapes." *New York Times* 11 Oct. 2001: A1.

Clemens, Valdine. *The Return of the Repressed: Gothic Horror from* The Castle of Otranto *to* Alien. Albany: SUNY P, 1999.

Croft, Stuart. *Culture, Crisis, and America's War on Terror*. Cambridge: Cambridge UP, 2006.

Davis, Mike. "The Flames of New York." *New Left Review* 12 (2001): 34–50.

Der Derian, James. "9/11: Before, After, and In Between." *Social Science Research Council Online* 16 Nov. 2006 www.ssrc.org/sept11/essays/der_derian.htm.

Ellis, Joshua. "Pugilistic Prose: *Fight Club* Author Chuck Palahniuk's New Short Story Hits People So Hard They Puke." 11 Feb. 2004. *Las Vegas CityLife Online*. 13 December 2006 http://lasvegascitylife.com/articles/2004/02/11/ae_cover/ae.prt.

Gelder, Ken. *Popular Fiction: The Logic and Practices of a Literary Field*. London: Routledge, 2004.

Gerstein, Josh. "Push is on for Academic Bill of Rights to Protect Against 'Political Pollution.'" 9 Feb. 2005. New York Sun Online. 15 Dec. 2006 http://www.nysun.com/article/8936.

Halper, Stefan and Jonathan Clarke. *America Alone: Neo-Conservatives and the Global Order*. Cambridge: Cambridge UP, 2004.

Heard, Chris. "Protest Singer Earle Blasts War." 17 Aug. 2001. BBC Online. 18 Dec. 2006 http://news.bbc.co.uk/1/hi/entertainment/music/3569926.stm.

Heller, Terry. *The Delights of Terror: An Aesthetics of the Tale of Terror*. Urbana: U of Illinois P, 1985.

Holland-Toll, Linda J. *As American as Mom, Baseball, and Apple Pie: Constructing Community in Contemporary American Horror Fiction*. Bowling Green: Bowling Green State U Popular Press, 2001.

Jameson, Frederic. "The Dialectics of Disaster." *Dissent From the Homeland: Essays After September 11*. Ed. Stanley Hauerwas and Frank Lentricchia. Durham: Duke UP, 2003. 55–62.

Jurkowitz, Mark. "The Big Chill." Boston Globe Magazine, 27 Jan. 2002: 11–12.

"The Justice of Roosting Chickens: Ward Churchill Speaks." 18 Feb. 2005. Democracy Now! Online. 15 Dec. 2006. http://www.democracynow.org/article.pl?sid=05/02/18/157211

Kellner, Douglas. *From 9/11 to Terror War: The Dangers of the Bush Legacy*. Lanham: Rowan and Littlefield, 2003.

King, Stephen. *Danse Macabre*. New York: Berkeley, 1981.

Kubiak, Anthony. "Spelling It Out: Narrative Typologies of Terror." *Studies in the Novel* 36 (2004): 294–301.

Lockett, Christopher. "Terror and Rebirth: Cathleen ni Houlihan, from Yeats to *The Crying Game*." *Literature/Film Quarterly* 33 (2005): 290–305.

Lyotard, Jean-Francois. *The Postmodern Condition: A Report on Knowledge*. Trans. Geoff Bennington and Brian Massumi. Minneapolis: U of Minnesota P, 1984.

Martin, Jerry L., and Anne T. Neal. "Defending Civilization: How Our Universities Are Failing America and What Can Be Done About It." Feb. 2002. American Council of Trustees and Alumni Website. 15 Dec. 2006 http://www.goacta.org/publications/Reports/defciv.pdf.

Milletti, Christina. "Violent Acts, Volatile Words: Kathy Acker's Terrorist Aesthetic." *Studies in the Novel* 36 (2004): 352–73.

Odier, Daniel. *The Job: Interviews with William S. Burroughs*. New York: Penguin, 1989.

Palahniuk, Chuck. *Lullaby*. New York: Anchor, 2003.

Rich, Frank. *The Greatest Story Ever Sold: The Decline and Fall of Truth From 9/11 to Katrina*. New York: Penguin, 2006.

Russo, Charles. "The Lit Interview: Chuck Palahniuk." 30 Oct. 2002. *San Francisco Bay Guardian Online*. 9 June 2006 http://www.sfbg.com/lit/oct02/int.html.

Scanlan, Margaret. *Plotting Terror: Novelists and Terrorists in Contemporary Fiction*. Charlottesville: UP of Virginia, 2001.

Scherer, Michael. "Framing the Flag." March/April 2002. *Columbia Journalism Review Online*. 12 December 2006 http://www.cjr.org/issues/2002/2/flag-scherer.asp.

Sharlet, Jeff. "The Capitalist Spirit." 24 Jan. 2005. *New York Online*. 17 May 2006 http://nymag.com/nymetro/news/bizfinance/biz/features/10894.

Spiegelman, Art. *In The Shadow of No Towers*. New York: Pantheon, 2004.

Stein, Martin. "The Author of *Fight Club*, *Choke* and the New *Diary* Brings His Perverse Prose to Las Vegas." 12 Feb. 2004. *Las Vegas Weekly*. 18 Dec. 2006 http://www.lasvegasweekly.com/2004/02/12/feature.html.

Switzer, Chris. "From Destruction to Creation: Chuck Palahniuk Discusses *Choke* and His Writing." 1 Dec. 2003. *Turtleneck.net*. 29 July 2005 http://turtleneck.net/summer01/leat . . . l/palahniuk.htm.

Terdiman, Richard. *Discourse/Counter-Discourse: The Theory and Practice of Symbolic Resistance in Nineteenth-Century France*. Ithica: Cornell UP, 1985.

"Transcript of Rice's 9/11 Commission Statement." 19 May 2004. *CNN.com*. 1 Dec. 2006 http://www.cnn.com/2004/ALLPOLITICS/04/08/rice.transcript.

Vaughan, Kevin and Felix Doligosa. "High school in turmoil over teacher's remarks about Bush." 2 March 2006. Rocky Mountain *News* Online. 18 Dec. 2006. http://www.rockymountainnews.com/drmn/local/article/0,1299,DRMN_15_4508688,00.html.

Walker, Joseph S. "A Kink in the System: Terrorism and the Comic Mystery Novel." *Studies in the Novel*. 36 (2004): 336–51.

Žižek, Slavoj. *Welcome to the Desert of the Real: Five Essays on September 11 and Related Dates*. London: Verso, 2002.

Zulaika, Joseba, and William A. Douglass. *Terror and Taboo: The Follies, Fables and Faces of Terrorism*. New York: Routledge, 1996.

9 Still Life
9/11's Falling Bodies

Laura Frost

Wisława Szymborska's poem "Photograph from September 11" ("Fotografia z 11 Wrzesnia") begins with one of the least poetic images from that day: "They jumped from the burning stories, down /—one, two, a few more / higher, lower" (69). The fate of the people who leapt from the World Trade Center is a particularly terrible subset of the events in New York on September 11, 2001.[1] Two weeks afterward, Anthony Lane wrote in the *New Yorker* that "The most important, if distressing, images to emerge from those hours are not of the raging towers, or of the vacuum where they once stood; it is the shots of people falling from the ledges." The people falling from the WTC were the most visible victims of the disaster in New York City on 9/11, and their very public deaths registered as especially dreadful. Psychological studies after 9/11 singled out witnessing falling people—live or on TV—as a major predictor of post-traumatic stress disorder (PTSD): this, of the many upsetting images from the day, had a lasting traumatic effect on some viewers.[2]

Taking up these charged figures, Szymborska's poem seems to trace a complete journey in its three opening lines; the sentence's single verb, "jumped," implies the moment before the leap, the plunge itself, and the aftermath. Yet instead of representing all three parts of the narrative, Szymborska shows only one, arresting the bodies in their downward movement by referencing a still image: "A photograph captured them while they were alive and now preserves them / above ground, toward the ground. / Each still whole" (69). Following the camera in freezing the bodies in the air, the poem yearns for the photograph's capacity to preserve life. If, as Susan Sontag suggests, "Photographs are a way of imprisoning reality, understood as recalcitrant, inaccessible; of making it stand still" (*On Photography* 163), Szymborska's poem is especially powerful. The first half of the poem unfolds in the past tense ("They jumped"), and the second half is set in a continuous present that resists the narrative progression from a jump to a fall:

> There is still time
> for their hair to be tossed,
> and for keys and small change
> to fall from their pockets. They are still in the realm of the air. (69)

In the English translation from Szymborska's Polish, the repetition of "still" applies the idea of a static photographic print to the bodies themselves. They are "still" in that they are motionless, and also in the adverbial sense of continuing, but Szymborska adds to this present tense a future frame ("There is still time") through imagining the humanizing, banal gestures of these anonymous plunging figures.

The poem continues to resist the implied mortality of the people right to its concluding lines: "There are only two things I can do for them /—to describe this flight / and not to add a final word" (69). The jump has now become a "flight," suggesting purposefulness and agency that attribute to the people the superhuman power of birds or planes. Szymborska implies that following the "flight" through to its end, acknowledging mortality or adding some idea of what these figures "mean," would be disrespectful. The poem's tribute to these people involves a temporal sleight of hand that preserves the camera's present tense—discontinuous time—while alluding to a hypothetical future ("There is still time") that disavows the real narrative end of these figures. The punctuating "final word" is also specifically *not* a final word; it is at the same time a presence and an absence: a suspension. The story has no end and no beginning, but only a perpetual middle. These haunting figures remain forever falling but never having fallen.[3]

In the spring of 2006, "Photograph from September 11" was one among many poems that conceptual artist Jenny Holzer selected for her memorial in the newly rebuilt 7 World Trade Center. Elaborating on her trademark aphoristic text sculptures, Holzer designed a light sculpture of scrolling poetry in which Langston Hughes's "I Dream a World," Claude McKay's "The City's Love," Walt Whitman's "Crossing Brooklyn Ferry," and other paeans to New York City progressed like ticker tape at what Holzer called "a processional pace" across a lobby wall (Collins). As the plans for the building moved forward, developer Larry Silverstein said that he was worried about the memorial: "Sometimes the message of artists is a downer.... Down here, after 9/11, we need positive stuff. Good stuff, as opposed to the miseries of 9/11" (Collins). His comments reflected the almost uniformly heroic mode in which 9/11 has been, to date, narrated and memorialized. Silverstein put his wife on the task of vetting the poetry Holzer had selected. The *Times* reported that

> Mrs. Silverstein reviewed Ms. Holzer's poetry selections and felt that several "were too graphic; I felt that they would bring back images that people might want to forget," she said. . . . Among the rejected works was a poem, "Photographs of Sept. 11th" [*sic*] by the 1996 Nobel Laureate, Wisława Szymborska; it focused on those who jumped from the World Trade Center. (Collins)

Silverstein read the poem's ekphrastic gesture literally, suggesting that its "graphic nature" would re-traumatize the reader, even as the tone of Szymborska's poem is one of wistful consolation. The poems that survived

Silverstein's cut were uplifting and celebratory; there was not a "downer" among them. This public act of literary criticism is typical of debates about the memorialization of traumatic events: "Should a memorial remind viewers of the terribleness of the catastrophe? Should it deliberately reevoke the horror, emphasizing aspects of human nature that cannot be denied?" (Kaplan 139). Or should a memorial soothe viewers, help them mourn their loss and "work through" the trauma of the event? In the case of 7 WTC, these concerns resulted in a memorial emphasizing "positive stuff" and excising "the miseries of 9/11." But what is the price of representing 9/11 in a strictly "positive" mode? Silverstein's injunction to avoid images "that people might want to forget" suggests that the institutional management of 9/11 is at odds with what individuals—Szymborksa and many others—need to remember and what they are still trying to sort out about that day.

Disturbing as they are, images of 9/11's falling bodies have emerged as a significant concern in art and literature, fiction and nonfiction, from poetry to prose and from documentary film to sculpture. One of the first major works of public art about 9/11, Eric Fischl's bronze sculpture *Tumbling Woman*, depicted one of these figures to great controversy; the piece was removed from its scheduled display in Rockefeller Center when people complained that it was offensive.

Figure 9.1 Tumbling Woman, 38" x 72" x 48," bronze, 2001–2002, Eric Fischl.

Another artist, Sharon Paz, displayed silhouettes of falling people on the windows of the Jamaica Center for Arts and Learning; these were also removed because of viewers' objections. The first major film to directly address September 11, *11'09"01*, a collection of short films—each 11 minutes, nine seconds, and one frame long—by directors from different countries, includes a contribution by Alejandro Gonzalez Iñárritu that is constructed around video footage of people tumbling from the WTC. Five years after 9/11, one of the Whitney Biennial's most praised works was Paul Chan's *1st Light*, a digital animated floor projection showing shadows of random objects drifting downward while shadows of bodies float upward. The falling people have been the subject of two documentary films.[4]

In literature, too, the falling bodies have appeared in both the earliest and the most recent responses to 9/11, including Szymborska's poem as well as one by Diane Seuss, Frederic Beigbeder's *Windows on the World*, one of the first novels to explicitly treat 9/11, Hugh Nissenson's *Days of Awe*, Stephen King's novella "The Things They Left Behind," Deborah Eisenberg's *Twilight of the Superheroes* and, midway between art and literature, Art Spiegelman's graphic memoir *In The Shadow of No Towers*, in which the author remarks that three months after 9/11, "He is haunted now by the images he didn't witness . . . images of people tumbling to the streets below," and "especially one man [according to a neighbor] who executed a graceful Olympic dive as his last living act" (5–6). Spiegelman draws himself plummeting down the side of two pages, head over heels, alongside the burning tower. There appears to be no end to this literary haunting. Don DeLillo's most recent novel, *Falling Man*, describes a landscape of New York City after 9/11 that includes a controversial performance artist known as "Falling Man" who makes unannounced appearances around the city suspending himself in a falling position to simulate the bodies dropping from the World Trade Center.

Despite Silverstein's advice to artists to move on to "positive stuff," the continuing appearance of these figures in art and literature suggests that they still disturb or raise questions that have not yet been answered. The falling people represent the national trauma of 9/11 in ways that are particularly difficult to understand, mourn, and assimilate, and are still more difficult to "memorialize." And yet, these representations are ultimately just as invested in preserving a "positive" or heroic narrative of 9/11 as is Silverstein himself.

This chapter will explore how the falling people are central to 9/11 storytelling in literary narrative. While there are strong commonalities among artistic and literary representations of 9/11's falling bodies, literature both responds to visual culture and, I will argue, often offers a critique of the common idea that visual culture is the medium best suited to representing 9/11.[5] Such is the case with Jonathan Safran Foer's *Extremely Loud & Incredibly Close*, one of the most remarked-upon novels about 9/11. Foer's work explicitly takes up visual representation of 9/11 but also asserts

Figure 9.2 World Trade Center Jumper © 2001, Lyle Owerko.

its failings. *Extremely Loud & Incredibly Close* is illustrative of literary responses to 9/11 at this moment in its treatment of visual culture, particularly in relation to the falling people and in its method of representing the trauma evoked by those figures.

Foer is less concerned with exploring the direct events of 9/11 than with tracing the repercussions of that day for a nine-year-old boy, Oskar Schell, whose father died on 9/11 when he was having breakfast at Windows on the World. The novel is set a year after 9/11, but the falling people are a fundamental part of Oskar's quest to determine how his father died—and specifically to find out if he was among them. Part magic realism, borrowing from Günter Grass's willfully stunted boy hero in *The Tin Drum,* part postmodern gamesmanship, *Extremely Loud & Incredibly Close* is by turns precious and poignant. Oskar collects photographs and documents in a notebook he calls "Stuff That Happened to Me," and this visual material is key to his understanding of 9/11. Among images of fingerprints, astronauts, Sir Laurence Olivier playing the graveyard scene in *Hamlet,* tortoises mating, and a CNN screen showing a Staten Island ferry accident, one image appears many times: a black and white photograph of a man falling from the WTC. This picture becomes the centerpiece of the novel's striking conclusion.

Foer's novel attempts to memorialize the people who jumped from the WTC, but it also steers away from the very problems that these people present. I will examine *Extremely Loud* in light of the recent discussion of photography as a tool for the resolution of trauma. Like Symborska, Foer expresses longing for the "still time" of the photograph as a form of memorialization; however, his novel also radically questions photography's efficacy to resolve the trauma of the falling people. These figures are the crux of a struggle between visual evidence and narrative evidence, between discontinuous time and narrative time, between knowledge and uncertainty, and between traumatic repetition and narrative resolution. The recurrence of 9/11's falling bodies emblematizes the lingering uncertainty about the meaning of 9/11 and a resistance to assimilating all the events of that day.

"WOULD I JUMP OR WOULD I BURN . . . ?"

For most people, September 11 was, above all, a visual event. CBS's archival book about 9/11, for example, is called *What We Saw.* The planes crashing, the buildings collapsing, the blanket of gray ash that cast the city into darkness, and the smoking wreckage afterward were the dominant images through which the event was witnessed. Yet the parts of 9/11 that could not be seen—could not be witnessed—are arguably equally important and possibly more disturbing. Even as we mourn the loss of human life during 9/11, there is almost no visual record of those deaths. Victims at the WTC were rarely shown in the media; those who died on the planes were invisible. The falling bodies, therefore, have deep symbolic resonance, although the record of their history has been obfuscated in central ways. Live video footage and photographs appeared briefly on TV and in newspapers, but then the images were taken out of circulation and continued to be carefully edited from retrospective coverage of 9/11 in America.[6]

In his prize-winning *Esquire* essay on "The Falling Man," Tom Junod discusses how the images of 9/11's falling bodies were driven from mainstream American news sources into more obscure channels such as Internet sites that traffic in sensational and pornographic material: "In a nation of voyeurs, the desire to face the most disturbing aspects of our most disturbing day was somehow ascribed to voyeurism, as though the jumpers' experience, instead of being central to the horror, was tangential to it, a sideshow best forgotten" (180). While Junod's observation rings true, the situation was more complicated: after the days in which the falling people were televised, most stations shifted to showing footage of bystanders reacting to the falling people. As the images themselves were held back and in their place was put the image of wondering, speculating witnesses, questions about the interpretation of what was being seen came to the forefront.

Visual imagery plays a constant if evasive role in *Extremely Loud & Incredibly Close*. Oskar has great difficulty talking and thinking about 9/11. He refers to it as "the worst day" (11, 68) "because of what happened" (14), and only indirectly admits some of the details of the experience. Oskar's grandmother insists that he not see the live images of the New York drama on television. Indeed, Foer does not give much direct description of the events of 9/11;[7] instead, historical violence is registered through a witness's account of the Hiroshima bombing (187) and a letter from Oskar's grandfather describing the Dresden bombings (210–16). 9/11 is the allusively rendered trauma around which the narrative is structured. In the absence of linguistic representation of 9/11's dramatic visual spectacles, the photographs from Oskar's notebook take on heightened significance. He includes photographs that are tangential to or irrelevant to the plot (e.g., stuffed early humanoids at the Museum of Natural History and a box full of gems), those that elliptically allude to the drama of 9/11 (a cat falling, birds flying, a Staten Island ferry crashing), and others that represent puzzles that must be solved: a keyhole that needs to be unlocked, a person he interviews, a notepad with his father's name scrawled on it, and photographs of a falling man. While some photographs directly refer to narrative events, others have a more elusive significance. Just as the title of the notebook, "Stuff That Happened to Me," is misleading, the anonymous falling man did not "happen" to Oskar, but the picture registers the impact of the event for him and alludes to details behind it that the novel does not admit.

In the absence of television, Oskar searches the digital highway for information about his father's death: "I found a bunch of videos on the Internet of bodies falling. They were on a Portuguese site, where there was all sorts of stuff they weren't showing here, even though it happened here. . . . Whenever I want to try to learn about how Dad died, I have to go to a translator program" (256). As he Googles "people jumping from burning buildings" in different languages, Oskar remarks that "It makes me incredibly angry that people all over the world can know things that I can't, because it happened *here,* and happened to *me,* so shouldn't it be *mine?*" (256). Oskar's search through public sources for information about his private loss is exacerbated by the impediments to this quest that were established in America as a service to the families of the dead. But while families of victims working on the floors of the WTC where the planes struck could be fairly sure of how their loved ones died, the fate of people on other floors was more difficult to determine. The fact that many families never recovered a body or recovered only fragments of a body leaves the exact history of these people unknowable. Oskar's father was buried in an empty coffin.

The first words of *Extremely Loud* are Oskar imagining inventing a teakettle that could "whistle pretty melodies, or do Shakespeare, or just crack up with me[.] I could invent a teakettle that reads in Dad's voice, so that I could fall asleep" (1). Over the course of the novel, he invents a detective game for himself in which he tries to solve the "mystery" of a vase he finds in his father's closet containing a piece of paper scrawled with the word "Black." Convinced that Black is the last name of a person his father contacted, Oskar spends eight months traveling around all the boroughs of New York City asking "Blacks" in the phone book if they knew his father. All of Oskar's imaginative antics in *Extremely Loud* are attempts to restore his father or discover the circumstances of his death: "I need to know how he died so I can stop inventing how he died. I'm always inventing" (255).

Literary treatments of 9/11's falling bodies constantly circle around such failures of knowledge. The tension between knowing the general contours of the drama and having to invent the details is a routine problem of fictionalizing history that becomes exacerbated in the case of the falling people. There is both a wealth of information about what happened in the towers on 9/11 and very little information about the people jumping.

It is, however, erroneous to suggest that if only there were a fuller visual record of the falling bodies, Oskar would have the answers he needs. He scours the Internet for contraband videos, but they lead him nowhere. As he looks at the images of falling people, he thinks

> If I could know how [his father] died, exactly how he died, I wouldn't have to invent him dying inside an elevator that was stuck between floors . . . and I wouldn't have to imagine him trying to crawl down the outside of the building, which I saw a video of a person doing on a Polish site, or trying to use a tablecloth as a parachute, like some of the people who were in Windows on the World actually did. There were so many different ways to die, and I just need to know which was his. (256)

Even as Oskar considers other kinds of death for his father (e.g., dying in an elevator), the only visual images of death he has are the falling people, and it is clear that these do not satisfy him. Oskar's *how* hints at one of the persistent questions about these figures. When Oskar meets the family of a woman who was a waitress at Windows on the World, he wonders if she might have met his father on that day. "The real question was *how* they died together, like whether they were on different ends of the restaurant, or next to each other, or something else. Maybe they had gone up to the roof together. You saw in some of the pictures that people jumped together and held hands. So maybe they did that" (196). The images that Oskar mentions are particularly upsetting because they imply consciousness or some degree of agency ("crawling," "trying," "using"). Oskar struggles with what the act of jumping or falling meant and with the context that is not depicted in the photograph.

More than any other genre of fiction, *Extremely Loud* resembles a detective novel—but it is a detective novel that resists its own findings. Oskar turns to the only evidence he has: visual evidence that cannot produce the knowledge he purports to seek. During an affecting visit to the Empire State Building, Oskar imagines what it was like to be in the WTC: "the building would sway, almost like it was going to fall over, which I know is what it felt like from descriptions I've read on the Internet, although I wish I hadn't read them. . . . Would I jump or would I burn . . . ?" (245). This awful question whose answer may seem irrelevant persists in many literary representations of the falling figures.[8]

The New York medical examiner's office called these people "homicides," refusing to use the terms "jumpers" or suicides. A spokeswoman stated that "A 'jumper' is somebody who goes to the office in the morning knowing that they will commit suicide. . . . These people were forced out by the smoke and flames or blown out" (Cauchon). Calling the people "suicides" not only suggests that they willed their death, but it also casts them in the company of the other suicides of that day, the hijackers. Yet the comparison is almost inevitable; one fire fighter recalled, "Somebody yelled something was falling. . . . We didn't know if it was desks coming out. It turned out it was people coming out, and they started coming out one after the other. I felt like I was intruding on a sacrament. . . . They were choosing to die and I was watching them and shouldn't have been" (CBS "9/11 Tapes"). The contrast between this Masada-like reading of these people as a noble suicide, a "sacrament," and the reading of them as victims of homicide illustrates the powerful investments involved in imagining their motivations. Both accounts involve an imposition of an explanatory narrative upon the falling people: "These people were forced out" or "They were choosing to die." Unlike the deaths of passengers on United 93, which sources such as *The 9/11 Commission Report,* A&E's drama *Flight 93,* and the film *United 93* narrated as a proactive deed of heroism, the falling people present a catch-22. If they were victims of horrendous circumstances, driven to act out of blind instinct, then their story is one of pure loss, nightmare, passivity, victimhood. If they had some degree of agency, then there is the possibility of heroism, but also an excruciating choice to jump or to burn.[9] Given the memorial's primary function to remind its viewer of an historical event, in the case of the falling bodies it is unclear what, precisely, we are to be reminded of, or the exact nature of the act being memorialized. The real dreadfulness of the "jumpers" is not captured by the still frame. It is what comes before and after: the drama of the compelled choice or suicide. The falling bodies have been seen, but they have not been understood; and their representation, by news sources and artistic forms alike, suggests a general desire that they remain beyond the reaches of understanding.

THE FAILURE OF PHOTOGRAPHY

Oskar's turn to photography and video to help him understand his father's death is at first glance consonant with current critical consensus on the role of photography in managing trauma. Sontag remarks that "Nonstop imagery (television, streaming video, movies) is our surround, but when it comes to remembering, the photograph has the deeper bite. Memory freeze-frames: its basic unit is the single image" (*Regarding* 22). This idea has become a critical truism in the case of 9/11. Months after 9/11, Marianne Hirsch wrote that "still photography has emerged as the most responsive medium in our attempts to deal with the aftermath of September 11" ("I Took Pictures" 71) and that "the snapshot . . . has become the genre of the moment" ("Day"). Hirsch, Barbie Zelizer, Ulrich Baer, Nancy K. Miller, and others have explored the ways in which the photographic gesture of arresting time allows the viewer to process and contemplate otherwise traumatic events. Against the bombardment of video images of the WTC attack, Hirsch proposes that,

> still photography, not film, is the visual genre that best captures the trauma and loss associated with September 2001– the sense of monumental, irrevocable change that we, as a culture, feel we have experienced. This is related to the photograph's temporality. Photography interrupts time. It is inherently elegiac. ("Day")

Critics have long asserted photography's relationship to death, whether as an indexical "tracing" of reality, as Sontag proposes, as a "witness," as Max Kozloff suggests, or as a melancholic foretelling of mortality, as in Barthes's mediations in *Camera Lucida*. These theories become chillingly literalized in the case of the falling bodies, showing, as they do, what Barbie Zelizer has called an "about-to-die moment" ("The Voice"). Szymborska and Foer both ground their representations of falling people in photographs not only because this was the form in which most people experienced the falling people, but also because photography allows a mournful meditation on its subjects. Photography makes possible the split-second appearance of the falling people to be lengthened indefinitely. Extending the findings of trauma theory to visual culture, Zelizer proposes that photography

> is well-suited to take individuals and collectives on the journey to a post-traumatic space. The frozen images of the still photographic vi-sual record are a helpful way of mobilizing a collective's post-traumatic response. They help dislodge people from the initial shock of trauma and coax them into a post-traumatic space, offering a vehicle by which they can see and continue to see until the shock and trauma associated with disbelieving can be worked through. ("Photography" 49)

Defined by psychoanalysis as a failure to experience an event in the moment, leading to a delayed response, trauma is understood as a disorder of time. In PTSD, Cathy Caruth writes, "The pathology consists . . . solely in the *structure of its experience* or reception: the event is not assimilated or expe-rienced fully at the time, but only belatedly, in its repeated possession of the one who experiences it. To be traumatized is precisely to be possessed by an image or event" (*Trauma* 4; emphasis Caruth's). The temporality of photog-raphy coincides with the time of trauma: discontinuous and unintegrated into narrative flow. Both Hirsch and Zelizer see a therapeutic function in photography. For them, photography is a bedrock of reality that can, by holding its ground temporally, give the viewer time to assimilate shocking circumstances. It is the temporality of the photograph—discontinuous time, "still life"—that renders it powerful enough to represent "authenticity" in historical circumstances that were surreal or unbelievable.

Photography was undoubtedly effective in capturing some parts of 9/11. Repeated viewing of images of the crumbling towers, first one, then the other, was probably the only way to absorb that mind-boggling spectacle. However, Foer suggests that photographs did *not* function this way in the case of the falling people; Oskar's repeated returns to the picture of the falling man do not help him to comprehend what happened to his father. The phenomenon of the "disappearing" falling bodies—shockingly pres-ent one day and suppressed the next—and the ensuing confusion about their meaning echoes the structure of trauma. Acts of witnessing were undermined and thrown into question by the consensus that attempted to make the pictures go away. Moreover, the frozen quality of the pho-tographs—the way in which they capture discontinuous time—prevents access to information outside that time frame, beyond "still life." Oskar's and Symborska's photographs, then, are not so much elegies, which suggest a degree of acceptance and resolution of an event, but rather an ambiva-lent—and ultimately thwarted—attempt to work through the meaning of the event captured in the frame.

This is dramatically illustrated by Tom Junod's essay "The Falling Man," which focuses on one remarkable photograph by Richard Drew ("A Person Falls Headfirst from the North Tower of the New York World Trade Center, Sept. 11, 2001") that appeared on the front page of several newspapers on September 12, 2001 (http://en.wikipedia.org/wiki/Image:The_Falling_Man. jpg). The picture shows a man, apparently a businessman, falling upside down in what seems uncannily like a pose of normalcy. The photograph's composition is highly symmetrical; the man's body is perfectly parallel to the vertical girders on the WTC, and his legs are lifted as if marching to work. The photograph's caption did not identify the man. After many readers protested to newspapers for violating the privacy of this man's family, a reporter was dispatched to identify the man and contact his family. The reporter had the photograph enlarged, revealing what seemed to be a kitchen worker, and he interviewed several people who were convinced that the falling man was or was not their relative/friend/co-worker. Catholic families in particular insisted that the falling man—a suicide—could not be their relative. At the end of the article, Junod gives up on the search for the man's identity: "all we know of him becomes a measure of what we know of ourselves. The picture is his cenotaph, and like the monuments dedicated to the memory of unknown soldiers everywhere, it asks that we look at it, and make one simple acknowledgment. That we have known who the Falling Man is all along" (199).

The need to locate a particular death in this field of visual information underscores the fact that the falling people are individuals and also that they are an anonymous group: "the jumpers." The photographs produce the awful intimacy of witnessing a public death that is also anonymous. But the process of focusing on one photograph drives Junod to abdicate the investigative mission which began as a search for the particular identity of the man, and it turns the focus away from the image itself to the viewer ("we have known who the Falling Man is all along" [199]). "The Falling Man" ends up as a generalized memorial to anonymity, a cenotaph or "empty tomb," while the spectator's reaction becomes particularized. As monuments to epistemological failure, Richard Drew's and similar photographs allow the spectator to witness the same moment endlessly, but they cannot put that moment to rest, either in the sense of Junod's quest for information and meaning or in the sense of Oskar's "how."

Oskar also repeats Junod's effort to understand the falling man through visual enlargement. The repeated images of the falling man in Oskar's notebook include a close-up version. Despite its size, the photo is still fuzzy and reveals little more about the man's identity than the lower-resolution photos. The man resembles an action figure, feet flexed and elbows bowed out symmetrically from overdeveloped shoulders; his facial features remain obscured. "I printed out the frames from the Portuguese video and examined them extremely closely," Oskar remarks. "There's one body that could be him. It's dressed like he was, and when I magnify it until the pixels are so big that it stops looking like a person, sometimes I can see glasses. Or I

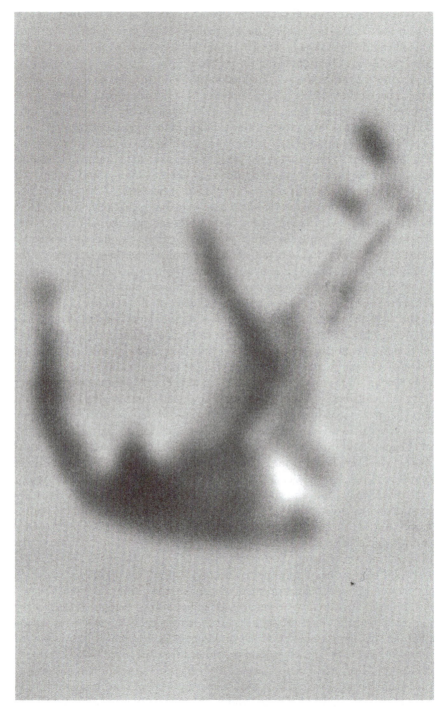

Figure 9.3 Detail, *World Trade Center Jumper* © 2001, Lyle Owerko.

think I can. But I know I probably can't. It's just me wanting it to be him" (257). The image resonates with others interspersed in the novel—birds flying, a cat leaping through the air—but it makes a mockery of the forensic "open sesame" of the photographic blow-up as the key to the mystery: "I started thinking about the pixels in the image of the falling body, and how the closer you looked, the less you could see" (293).

Photography's therapeutic function seems to fail in the case of the falling people in that it does not move its viewer out of the stunned present of traumatic time. Sontag concedes that photographs are powerful, "But they are not much help if the task is to understand. Narratives can make us understand. Photographs do something else: they haunt us" (*Regarding* 89). In the case of the falling people, the "still life" of photography represents disavowal or a repetition compulsion that cannot reach its goal. The stories of people falling from the buildings are impossible to reconstruct unless done through narrative.[10]

Foer's novel makes this transition from discontinuous still time to narrative time in its dramatic conclusion. At the end of his fruitless searches for information about his father's death, Oskar turns back to the images of the falling man in the final pages of the novel.

> Finally, I found the pictures of the falling body.
> Was it Dad?
> Maybe.
> Whoever it was, it was somebody.
> I ripped the pages out of the book.
> I reversed the order, so the last one was first, and the first was last.
> When I flipped through them, it looked like the man was floating up
>   through the sky. (325)

Oskar thinks that if he "had more pictures," his father would have "flown through a window, back into the building," the plane would have retreated, backward through the sequence of September 11, concluding with his father returning home. "We would have been safe" (326). Fifteen images of the falling man follow, each showing the figure moving progressively upward until he has disappeared from the final page of the novel. As the reader flips through the pages, the man appears to float "up" into the sky.

The novel ends not in words, but in images, and not with a solution to the novel's tension, but with another "invention" of Oskar's. Critics were divided over the sequence. In a slate.com exchange on "Jonathan Safran Foer's Unusual Talent," Ruth Franklin contends that "*Extremely Loud* ends with an elaborate and, I thought, puerile fantasy of turning back time. Critics have been oohing over the novel's final visual sequence, a 'flip book' that reverses the order of a series of photographs showing a body falling from the World Trade Center so that it appears instead to be rising. I found this the book's most egregious example of inappropriate whimsy." Megan

O'Rourke responds, "I *do* find the final 'flip book' sequence curiously mov-ing—and justifiable. Images were a crucial part of 9/11, and are crucial to Oskar's experience of the day." The novel's conclusion gives way to those images entirely, suggesting that for all the linguistic arabesques around the question of his father's death, Oskar's emotional understanding of the mat-ter ultimately rests not in words but in images and is unresolved.

The novel concludes with an act of wish fulfillment that is so strong that it defies gravity and temporality. The flip-book creates a narrative out of the arrested, unrelenting presentness of the snapshot.[11] It attempts to break the frame of photographic stillness by inventing a new ending (which is, by inversion, its beginning) for the falling man. This kind of inversion appears in a number of imaginative treatments of 9/11's fall-ing bodies: in Frederic Beigbeder's novel *Windows on the World,* peo-ple jumping from the WTC imagine themselves as "flying" upward like "superheroes," Paul Chan's digital human silhouettes in *1st Light* "fall" upward, and Symborska's poetic "flight" implies an upward movement. However, if one closely examines the photographs that comprise Oskar's "flip-book"—supposedly stills from a video sequence on the Internet—they seem to have been doctored in another way. The man is in exactly the same pose at every point in his ascent. It appears that this is not a true narrative in the place of a photograph, but rather a rearrangement of the same still photograph. The result is repetition compulsion rather than narrative development. Like Szymborska's "final word" that both is and is not an ending, Oskar's flip-book substitutes a photograph for nar-rative explanation, a fantasy of wish fulfillment for coming to terms with the falling people. This act of "invention" is a fiction-making that not only ultimately steers around the trauma at its center but also reinstates the trauma in the novel's conclusion. If Foer gives visual imagery the last word, the effect is to return, unresolved, once again, to the trauma of still life embodied by the photograph.

"THERE IS STILL TIME . . ."

The significance of the photograph is its temporality. But it is deceptive: can one visual moment unlock a whole narrative? Memorials serve a simi-lar function, as a way of managing time, and specifically the relationship between memory and history.[12] Memorials are sites for individual memory to become collective and for events to be shaped for transmission through history. A traditional memorial is static, discontinuous—like the time of photography—but it settles on a moment that can stand as a representation of the event and will be accessible to viewers of different perspectives and experiences. Time has figured prominently in the discussion around 9/11 memorials ("Is it too soon?"). The annual memorial ceremony at Ground Zero is structured around four bells tolling in real time to mark each plane striking the towers and each tower falling. Journalistic accounts regularly feature timelines—often rendered graphically—tracing how the events unfolded.[13] While this observation of time is not unusual for the treatment of such a disaster, a swiftly moving series of interlocking events that unfolded in a highly concentrated amount of time, the preoccupation with temporality—and specifically, the simultaneous observation and distortion of it—is magnified in storytelling about 9/11, and all the more so around the falling people. Judith Greenberg remarks that,

> Time became crucially important on 9/11. For people in the Twin Towers, where they were located and what time they tried to leave were facts of life and death . . . As we construct narratives, we can look at how delays not only give us time to mourn but also complicate the very notion of 9/11 as a fixed "event." "Memory is, after all, a process and is everlasting only when it remains a process and not a finished result," James Young reminds us. (qtd. in Greenberg xvi)

Nearly all narratives of 9/11, nonfiction and fiction, focus on the question of time, and many emphasize the confluence of the temporalities of trauma and photography. In *Extremely Loud,* time is a key to Oskar's attempt to discover how his father died, but it is, significantly, linked not to a visual moment but to aural evidence. One of Oskar's secrets is that he was home as his father frantically phoned from Windows on the World, leaving six messages on the family's answering machine. Message one arrives at 8:52 ("Is anybody there?" [14]), message two at 9:12, message three at 9:31, message four at 9:45, message five at 10:04, and the final phone call at 10:22:27. Oskar finds the first five messages on the machine when he comes home from school on September 11, and he listens as the final one comes in "live," but he is too paralyzed to pick up the phone:

> I just couldn't pick up. I just couldn't. *Are you there?* He asked eleven times. I know, because I've counted. It's one more time than I can count on my fingers. Why did he keep asking? . . . Sometimes I think he knew I was there. Maybe he kept saying it to give me time to get brave enough to pick up. Also, there was so much space between the times he asked. There are fifteen seconds between the third and the fourth, which is the longest space. You can hear people in the background screaming and crying. And you can hear glass breaking, which is part of what makes me wonder if people were jumping. (301)

Without reference to visual evidence, the tapes are a rare window into an otherwise invisible terror: what happened inside the buildings. Given the care with which he documents the time of the calls, according to his own account, Oskar does have a strong idea of how his father died. Thomas Schell made his final call home at 10:22; Oskar times it at "one minute and twenty-seven seconds. Which means it ended at 10:24. Which was when the building came down. So maybe that's how he died" (302). This would seem to suggest that his father did not, therefore, jump, but was in the building when it collapsed. Yet the question seems unanswered to Oskar.

Oskar's focus on the chronology of the messages, the moments elapsed between them, and the time of the final message heightens the fact that his calculations are *wrong*. That morning's 102-minute sequence, widely and precisely chronicled in numerous newspaper, magazine, and Internet time-lines, shows that the North Tower collapsed not at 10:24 but at 10:28 a.m.

A four minute difference. To a boy who claims to desperately want to know how his father died, for whom a one-word note in a vase leads to an eight-month door-to-door search through the boroughs of New York, this four-minute difference is important. These four minutes mark the difference between a building that is standing and a building that collapses. A living father and a dead one.

The four minutes in which Oskar's father died—arguably, the most important minutes of the novel—are rendered lost time. This four-minute void serves to suspend Oskar's knowledge about how his father died. Does he really want to know? This erasure of time is something like Szymborska's decision "not to add a final word." Excising four minutes allows the photographic still of the intact jumper to persist, forever suspended in his "flight"; it also keeps the before and after, as well as the "how," absolutely unknowable.[14] Oskar's evasion shows how closely an inability to know is related to a refusal to know. If literary treatments of 9/11 insist that the story of the falling people can only be expanded through a narrative act, they also—like Oskar—refuse to perform that imaginative work. The result is a dynamic of disavowal.

To delve fully into narrative time, the time beyond the frame of the still image, would be to engage fully the implications of the falling bodies: something few authors are willing to do in their fiction even as they constantly circle around it.[15] While striving to move beyond photographic time into narrative time, Foer creates loopholes through which to reinscribe voids, aporias, and evasions. His novel is constructed around the figure of a "jumper," only to retreat from the task he has set out for himself through a touching but ultimately avoidant fiction, a boy's wish of a fiction as simple and as impossible as turning back the clock. The point is not that the gruesome details of the deaths should be graphically depicted, but that by repeatedly returning to the suspended fall and rendering the falling figure not only surviving but supernaturally triumphing, the narrative is unable to assess the larger symbolic and political meanings of these bodies.

"A KIND OF HOLOCAUST SUBJECT"

Five years after 9/11, the cover of the *New Yorker's* September 11, 2006, issue shows a tightrope walker suspended in a blank white background; he seems to tread the air. When the reader turns the page, the figure appears again, but this time superimposed upon a background: he is precariously poised high above the "footprints" of the WTC. The man walks purposefully and is holding a balance bar, but the drop beneath him is dizzying.

Figure 9.4 Soaring Spirit, John Mavroudis and Owen Smith.

Figure 9.5 Soaring Spirit, John Mavroudis and Owen Smith.

This cover strongly alludes to Philippe Petit's 1974 dance on a wire strung between the North and South Towers, an act that was said to "humanize" buildings that had been thought until then to be architectural monstrosities, and also to the people jumping from the WTC. While the man's supernatural suspension in the air resembles Oskar's wishful fantasies of a man flying upward, the balance beam suggests that he is staying up through his own human effort, a concentrated attempt to keep his equilibrium. The walk is still in progress.

Soaring Spirit plays on the same fluctuations—here, not here—as Szymborska's and Foer's work. Its flip-book style creates an oscillation between presence and absence that also calls to mind "Tribute in Light," the annual projection of two massive beams of light from the footprints of the WTC, a photograph of which appears, unreferenced, in Oskar's scrapbook, "Stuff That Happened to Me." However, while "Tribute in Light" has great formal control of its negative or reverse imagery, its pull and push of absence and presence, Foer is more erratically evasive. We see in his novel a repetition compulsion, a morbid return to the "how" of death, but also the substitution of an avoidant fantasy for a reckoning with loss or a narrative resolution. Like Junod and Szymborska, Foer's falling bodies remain unknowable, rather than a trauma that can be cauterized or cathartically expressed through the historicized assertion of a memorial. The bodies are rendered similarly in Don DeLillo's *Falling Man*. Near the end of the novel, a character who has witnessed one of the so-called Falling Man's public performances—suspending himself upside down from a train track—comes across an obituary announcing his sudden death. She continues to look online for more information about him. While "she could believe she knew" the other people among whom she watched the man dangle from the tracks that day, she could not believe that she knew "the man who'd stood above her, detailed and looming." "The man eluded her. All she knew was what she'd seen and felt that day" (224). Both the falling people and the performance artist who styles himself after them are enigmas marking the limits of what can be known and understood about 9/11.

Writing in 2006, Joyce Carol Oates made a provocative observation:

> Though a glut of material has appeared on the subject of September 11, much of it the recorded testimony of survivors and eyewitnesses, very few writers of fiction have taken up the challenge and still fewer have dared to venture close to the actual event; September 11 has become a kind of Holocaust subject, hallowed ground to be approached with awe, trepidation, and utmost caution. The reader's natural instinct is to recoil from a purely fictitious treatment of so profound and communal a subject, for the task of fiction is to create a self-defined, self-absorbed, and highly charged text out of language, and the appropriation of a communal trauma for such purposes would seem to be exploitative.

In calling 9/11 "a kind of Holocaust subject," Oates joins a startling number of critics who propose such an analogy.[16] Writing about New York artists responding to 9/11, Arthur Danto asserted that September 11 was "symbolically, I suppose, our Holocaust, it being caused by a parallel order of evil." Dori Laub, Art Spiegelman, and many others have pursued this analogy;[17] in *Windows on the World,* Beigbeder remarks that "Claude Lanzmann says that the Shoah is a mystery. September 11 is too" (263). If analogy is a device for clarification and explanation, the 9/11-Holocaust analogy is paradoxically based on the supposedly inscrutable, "unfathomable," and "unimaginable" nature of the events.[18] The analogy bears not only on the acts of terrorist violence but also on the voids and evasions at the heart of 9/11 narratives.

Oates's point, however, is not that 9/11 bears an historical resemblance to the Holocaust, but rather that at this point, 9/11 is considered, figuratively, hallowed ground and requires sanctimonious treatment. What's immediately noticeable about most 9/11 fiction to date is its unerring emphasis on redemption, courage, noble sacrifice, dignified human connection and, above all, heroism.[19] Even Oliver Stone, conspiracy theorist *par excellence,* cannot get beyond heroic clichés in *World Trade Center.* Nor do these works treat their subject truly *imaginatively.* As Oates suggests, the act of fictionalization itself—"the appropriation of a communal trauma" for artistic purposes—is perceived as "exploitative." In treating 9/11 imagery gingerly, these artists and authors leave in place the myth of American invulnerability that the falling bodies call into question.

There is good reason to question why the heroic mode remains dominant. Marita Sturken proposes that "Narratives of redemption tend to be politically regressive in that they are attempts to mediate loss through finding the good—a newfound patriotism, feelings of community—that has come from pain" (382). Memorials participate in that redemption; many critics have recently suggested that memorial-monuments "may not remember events so much as bury them altogether beneath layers of national myth and explanations" and "displace" rather than embody or represent memory (Young, *Texture*, 5). Larry Silverstein's editorial mandate for Jenny Holzer's memorial created an "upbeat" monument to American values and the democratic, optimistic pluck of New York City (translating, for a real estate developer, into a willingness to invest in his new buildings), and many of the memorial projects of 9/11 have had similar political underpinnings. David Simpson contends that the "culture of commemoration" around 9/11 is constantly shaping the country's current political imbroglios; he suggests that the *New York Times* obituary series, "Portraits of Grief," for example, with its unrelentingly smiling faces, masks the missing pictures of the dead abroad. In this light, because they are intransigent to a redemptive reading, the falling people may be the best figure for an interpretation of 9/11 that resists simplistic resolution through national myths.

Even as memories and memorials of 9/11 remain primarily visual, endlessly recirculating the same images such as the towers and brave firemen, the falling bodies undermine the adage that seeing is believing. They continue to remind us that what we saw is not the whole story, and that the focus on sanctified images may keep us from facing what lies beyond the frame. What the falling bodies do make visible is the continued difficulty of seeing the events of 9/11 as a national wound that was in some ways enabled by the nation's political role leading up to 9/11 and of taking full measure of the vast systematic failures of internal measures that were supposed to protect the nation. As much as our understanding of the falling people will always be limited, the way in which these figures appear in art and literature shows how difficult it is to imagine a national narrative of vulnerability and dignity as well as complicity. On a deeper level, the arrested, suspended bodies reflect a tendency to think of 9/11 as a moment frozen in time, as a city's and a nation's's disaster, rather than as part of a political process that is still unfolding.

NOTES

In many ways, this chapter grew out of a seminar I taught at Yale on "Literature and 9/11." I want to thank my students, whose insightful discussions were a productive springboard to my work on the subject, as well as a way of getting some intellectual distance from my own experience of that day, living on Maiden Lane, two blocks away from Ground Zero. I also want to thank Chris Bregler, Karen Gehres, Nancy K. Miller, Teri Reynolds, Victoria Rosner, Martha Sanders, and Chris Wiggins for their conversations about 9/11. I am especially grateful to Dr. Randall Marshall at Columbia, who discussed his work on 9/11 and PTSD with me in 2005.

1. See Flynn, and Junod on the effort to estimate the number of people who fell from the WTC. The figures vary from figures in double digits to around two hundred.
2. See Galea et al.
3. Diane Seuss's poem "Falling Man," like Szymborska's, emphasizes time through verb tenses: "he has not fallen: he is falling."
4. *9/11: The Falling Man* (2006), directed by Henry Singer, and a short film, *The Falling Man*, by Kevin Ackerman, which was screened at the 2006 Tribeca Film Festival.
5. See, for example, Joyce Carol Oates's remark that "the greatest art form to deal with this might be film, because it can capture the hallucinatory nature of the long hours of that siege" (Wyatt 1).
6. See Junod, Brottman, Rutenberg, and Zelizer's "The Voice of the Visual in Memory." Jules and Gedeon Naudet's *9/11: A Documentary,* for example, did not show footage of people falling but did include the sound of the bodies hitting the pavement, but even this was edited to suggest that there were fewer "jumpers" than there actually were.
7. Oskar's grandmother gives an account of 9/11 as she watches television from Oskar's family's guest room: "A ball of fire rolled out of the building and up . . . One million pieces of paper filled the sky. They stayed there, like a ring around the building" (225). She recounts,
   Planes going into buildings.
   Bodies falling.
   Planes going into buildings.
   Buildings falling.
   Planes going into buildings.

Planes going into buildings.
Planes going into buildings. (231)

8. In *Windows on the World,* Frederic Beigbeder's protagonist, a man trapped on the 107th floor of the North Tower—the same place as Oskar's father—has a debate with the "author" about how human beings react under such circumstances. Beigbeder makes high claims for people's agency:

> "Jumpers" are not depressed, they're rational people. They've weighed the pros and the cons and prefer the dizzying freefall to being burned alive. They choose the swan dive, the vertical farewell. They have no illusions, even if some try to use a jacket as a makeshift parachute. They take their chances. They escape. They are human because they decide to choose how they will die rather than allow themselves to be burned. One last manifestation of dignity: they will have chosen their end rather than waiting resignedly. (148)

The character immediately retorts,

> Bullshit, my dear Beigbeder. If somewhere between 37 and 50 people threw themselves from the top of the North Tower, it was simply because everything else was impossible, suffocation, pain, the instinct to survive, because jumping couldn't be worse than staying in this suffocating furnace . . . You don't jump to preserve your humanity, you jump because the fire has reduced you to a brute beast. The void is not a rational choice. (149)

9. Diane Seuss's "Falling Man" opens with this conflict:

> The man falls. I'm told
> he jumped: he had no choice,
> or two bad choices. Burn
> or fall. He chose
> falling. . . . (350)

10. Hugh Nissenson imagines an improbable account of such a conversation in his novel *The Days of Awe,* in which one character calmly counsels her lover to jump from the 102nd floor of the North Tower. Their conversation is not especially believable—he has the presence of mind to tell her that "a woman in a floral dress just fell past my window" (150); he hangs up after she's endorsed his decision to jump: "Then jump, darling. Jump into my arms, where I'll hold you close for good" (151).

11. This tension between the photograph and narrative—between discontinuous and continuous time, and between traumatic time and linear time—is illustrated by Alejandro Gonzalez Iñárritu's contribution to *11'09"01.* The first minutes show an ink-black screen accompanied by some voices chanting in Arabic and others speaking in numerous languages, evoking the Tower of Babel, to which the WTC has been compared more than once. The purely aural effect dislocates the audience from the visual sense that one expects to be dominant in a video, and especially from how most people experienced September 11. These minutes that confront the viewer with a black screen demonstrate how difficult it is to imagine 9/11 apart from its visual manifestations. (Michael Moore uses the same strategy in *Fahrenheit 911.*) Suddenly, an image of a falling man flashes onto the screen for a split-second and then disappears into the blackness. Other images of falling bodies follow in momentary bursts of light followed by an ominous thud. Iñárritu crops these frames to suggest photographic stills, but the eye detects in these split-second glimpses that the figures are moving, tumbling through the air. The result is an image somewhere between photographic stillness and film, pushing forward but also arresting the flow of time. The editing calls attention to the edges of the frame and the parts of the story that are excluded. It makes the

inaccessible parts of the falling people (the parts we can't see, can't know, can't understand—like the unintelligible voices that speak with such conviction) seem more urgent than ever as we strain to see them in the dark voids between the images.

12. Following Pierre Nora, James Young writes of the play between memory and history, "time may be the crucible for this interaction" (*Texture* 48).

13 Each chapter of Frederic Beigbeder's *Windows on the World* represents (and is titled) a minute from 8:30 to 10:29, a minute after the World Trade Center's North Tower collapsed. "Hell lasts an hour and three quarters. As does this book" (6), Beigbeder writes, pointing out that the time of the attacks corresponded to the average length of a Hollywood film. The inexorable march of the clock drives the book's sense of suspense, even as its end is predetermined. Some chapters—some minutes—are brief, a handful of words, and others are elongated. 9:15 presents violence in blank verse:

> For half an hour now we've had a plane under our feet
> Still no evacuation
> We are metal shrieking
> People hanging out the windows
> People falling from the windows . . .
> Hands in tatters
> skin hanging from arms
> like an Issey Miyake dress
> A rain of bodies over the WTC Plaza. (145–47)

Some minutes are agonizing. At 8:44, a minute before American Airlines 11 struck the North Tower, Beigbeder writes "Welcome to the minute before. The point at which everything is still possible" (50), and, like Szymborska's longing for "still time," the reader longs for that moment to last.

14. This distorted treatment of time is addressed by Stephen King's novella *The Things They Left Behind*. The story is narrated by a loner, Scott, who worked for an insurance company in the WTC and was one of two survivors of 9/11 because he skipped work that day. His fellow survivor, Warren, claims to have seen a photo in a newspaper that showed one of their coworkers, Sonja, who "jumped from the one hundred and tenth floor of the stricken building" (463). Scott remarks that "The description [of the falling woman] made me think of 'Falling,' the poem James Dickey wrote" (463). In "Falling," an airline stewardess is sucked out of a plane and slowly tumbles—or rather, floats—to her death in a Kansas cornfield, her clothes unfurling from her body like a slow striptease or like an exalted goddess and her form undergoing a number of protean shifts, flying and tumbling. Time balloons and distorts as the woman meditates on her life, her body, and death. Dickey remarked of the poem that, "I was interested in using the kind of time-telescoping effect that Bergson talks about in discussing the difference between clock time and lived time" (175). For Dickey, temporality is largely a formal question; for Foer, Szymborska, and others, it is a matter of tremendous urgency. Their falling bodies are captured like little pockets of present tense, lengthening the last moments of life. Clock time is observed time, camera time, and also traumatic time: the images of people jumping holding hands, with makeshift parachutes, and doing swan dives. Lived time, with which Dickey has such fun is, in the case of 9/11's falling bodies, unbearable.

15. Exceptions include Hugh Nissenson's aforementioned *Days of Awe*, which harrowingly describes one man's plunge from the WTC (152), and Beigbeder's *Windows on the World*, which references a widely circulated photograph of people jumping from the WTC with tablecloths for parachutes and

proceeds to describe one such person's fall, quite shockingly and harshly, in narrative, linear time (201–02).

16. The different receptions of Eric Fischl's *Tumbling Woman* and Paul Chan's *1st Light* would seem to demonstrate Oates's point. Fischl's semi-realistic bronze showing a woman's fall was too stark for public consumption and received hostilely, while critics were much more hospitable to Chan's dreamy narrative elements that cast the falling bodies in a gravity-defying narrative similar to Foer's.

17. In an article written six months after 9/11, Dori Laub, whose theories of trauma draw from work with Holocaust survivors, remarked that "Perhaps ... there is a resemblance between the attacks of September 11 and something equally unimaginable that happened in the Holocaust. ... [9/11] was about something unfathomable, at the roots of which there may be evil for which no ways of explaining or understanding yet exist" (Greenberg 207). Art Spiegelman invokes the Holocaust comparison at several points of *In The Shadow of No Towers,* suggesting that the feelings of victimhood he experienced on 9/11 are comparable to those experienced by Jews in Europe on the eve of the Holocaust.

18. Lanzmann's statement to which Beigbeder alludes goes on to insist that trying to understand the motivations of the Nazis and the "logic" of the Holocaust entails an "obscenity of understanding."

19. On the first anniversary of 9/11, salon.com invited its readers to send in "forbidden thoughts" about 9/11 that departed from the heroic themes.

> Many of us didn't just feel sad or angry or proud in the face of the day's horrors. ... We also felt indifferent, confused, selfish, annoyed and, in some cases, even happy or excited. All these forbidden thoughts are sometimes painful or mortifying to hear. Many could be accurately described as disgraceful. But they emerged from our mental ether, and they deserve to be part of the record of that day and its aftermath. ... They keep us from creating a distorted, overly sentimental picture of our national reaction to disaster. (Cave)

Many sheepish readers shared their "disgraceful" thoughts.

There have been some, but not many, fictions that articulate these "forbidden" impulses, including Neil LaBute's play *The Mercy Seat* and a curious group of novels that imagines conquering terrorism through domesticating it: Helen Fielding's *Olivia Joules and the Overactive Imagination,* Claire Tristram's *After,* and Chris Cleave's *Incendiary.* All of these novels elicited some scathing reviews cast on explicitly moral grounds. The expectation of 9/11 fiction is that the author engage seriously, with mimetic faithfulness and reverence toward the event. That said, more recent publications such as Jess Walter's *The Zero* and Ken Kalfus's *A Disorder Peculiar to the Country* suggest that more nonheroic fictions are on the way.

WORKS CITED

Baer, Ulrich. *110 Stories: New York Writes After September 11.* New York: New York UP, 2002.

———. *Spectral Evidence: The Photography of Trauma.* Cambridge: MIT, 2002.

Barthes, Roland. *Camera Lucida: Reflections on Photography.* New York: Hill & Wang, 1981.

Baudrillard, Jean. *The Spirit of Terrorism.* Trans. Chris Turner. New York: Verso, 2002.

Beigbeder, Frederic. *Windows on the World: A Novel*. Trans. Frank Wynne. New York: Miramax, 2004.

Brottman, Mikita. "The Fascination of the Abomination: the Censored Images of 9/11." *Film and Television After 9/11*. Ed. Wheeler Winston Dixon. Carbondale: Southern Illinois UP, 2004. 163–77.

Caruth, Cathy. *Trauma: Explorations in Memory*. Baltimore: Johns Hopkins UP, 1995.

Cauchon, Dennis, and Martha T. Moore. "Desperation Forced a Horrific Decision." *USA Today* 3 Sept. 2002: 5A.

Cave, Damien. "Forbidden Thoughts About 9/11." Salon.com 7 Sept. 2002 http://dir.salon.com/story/mwt/feature/2002/09/07/forbidden/index.html.

CBS/AP. "9/11 Tapes Evoke Horror and Chaos." 12 Aug. 2005 http://www.cbsnews.com/stories/2005/08/12/terror/main773198.shtml.

CBS. *What We Saw*. New York: Simon & Schuster, 2002.

Cleave, Chris. *Incendiary*. New York: Knopf, 2005.

Collins, Glenn. "At Ground Zero, Accord Brings a Work of Art." *New York Times* 6 Mar. 2006: A1.

Danto, Arthur. "9/11 Art as a Gloss on Wittgenstein." http://www.apexart.org/exhibitions/danto.htm.

DeLillo, Don. "In the Ruins of the Future" *Harper's Magazine* 303 (Dec. 2001): 33–40.

———. *Falling Man*. New York: Scribners, 2007.

Dickey, James. *Poems 1957–1967*. New York: MacMillan, 1968.

———. *Self-Interviews*. New York: Dell, 1970. Baton Rouge: Louisiana State UP, 1984.

Edkins, Jenny. *Trauma and the Memory of Politics*. Cambridge: Cambridge UP, 2003.

Eisenberg, Deborah. *Twilight of the Superheroes*. New York: Farrar, Straus and Giroux, 2006.

Fielding, Helen. *Olivia Joules and the Overactive Imagination*. New York: Viking, 2004.

Flynn, Kevin, and Jim Dwer. "Three Years Later: Victims, Falling Bodies: A 9/11 Image Etched in Pain." *New York Times* 10 Sept. 2004: A1.

Foer, Jonathan Safran. *Extremely Loud & Incredibly Close*. New York: Houghton Mifflin, 2005.

Franklin, Ruth. "The Missing." *The New Republic*. 10 Sept. 2004 https://ssl.tnr.com/p/docsub.mhtml?i=sources&s=franklin091004.

Franklin, Ruth, and Megan O'Rourke. "Jonathan Safran Foer's Unusual Talent." *Slate* 31 Mar. 2005 http://www.slate.com/id/2115207/entry/0/.

Galea, Sandro, Heidi Resnick, Jennifer Ahern, Joel Gold, Michael Bucuvalas, Dean Kilpatrick, Jennifer Stuber, and David Vlahov. "Posttraumatic Stress Disorder in Manhattan, New York City, After the September 11th Terrorist Attacks." *Journal of Urban Health* 79 (2002): 340–53.

Goldberger, Paul. *Up From Zero: Politics, Architecture and the Rebuilding of New York*. New York: Random House, 2004.

Greenberg, Judith. *Trauma at Home: After 9/11*. U of Nebraska P, 2003.

Hirsch, Marianne. "I Took Pictures: September 2001 and Beyond" *Trauma at Home*. Ed. Judith Greenberg 69–86.

———. "The Day Time Stopped." *Chronicle of Higher Education* 48 (25 Jan. 2002): B11–B13.

Junod, Tom. "The Falling Man." *Esquire* 140 (Sept. 2003): 176–99.

Kalfus, Ken. *A Disorder Peculiar to the Country*. New York: HarperCollins, 2006.

Kaplan, Ann E. *Trauma Culture: The Politics of Terror and Loss in Media and Literature*. New Brunswick: Rutgers UP, 2005.

King, Stephen. "The Things They Left Behind." *Transgressions*. Ed. Ed McBaine. New York: Forge Books, 2005.

Kozloff, Max. *Photography & Fascination*. Danbury: Addison House, 1979.

LaBute, Neil. *The Mercy Seat*. New York: Faber, 2003.

Lane, Anthony. "This is Not A Movie." *New Yorker* 24 Sept. 2001: 79.

Lanzmann, Claude. "The Obscenity of Understanding: An Evening with Claude Lanzmann." *Trauma: Explorations in Memory*. Ed. Cathy Caruth. Baltimore: Johns Hopkins UP, 1995. 200–20.

Linenthal, Edward T. The Unfinished Bombing: Oklahoma City in American Memory. New York: Oxford UP, 2001.

Mendelsohn, Daniel. "September 11 at the Movies." *New York Review of Books* 21 Sept. 2006: 43–46.

Miller, Nancy K. "Portraits of Grief: Telling Details and the Testimony of Trauma." *Differences: A Journal of Feminist Cultural Studies* 14.3 (2003): 112–35.

National Commission on Terrorist Attacks upon the United States. *The 9/11 Commission Report*. New York: Norton, 2004.

Nissenson, Hugh. *The Days of Awe*. Naperville, Illinois: Sourcebooks, 2005.

Oates, Joyce Carol. "Dimming the Lights." *New York Review of Books*. 6 April 2006: 33–36.

———. "The Mutants." *I Am No One You Know: Stories*. New York: Ecco, 2004. 281–88.

Rutenberg, J., and F. Barringer. "The Ethics: News Media Try to Sort Out Policy on Graphic Images." *New York Times* 13 Sept. 2001: A20, A24.

Sontag, Susan. *On Photography*. New York: Farrar, Straus & Giroux, 1973.

———. *Regarding the Pain of Others*. New York: Farrar, Straus & Giroux, 2003.

Spiegelman, Art. *In The Shadow of No Towers*. New York: Pantheon, 2004.

Seuss, Diane. "Falling Man." *September 11, 2001: American Writers Respond*. Ed. William Heyen. Silver Springs, MD: Etruscan, 2002. 350–51.

Sturken, Marita. "Memorializing Absence." *Understanding September 11*. Ed. Craig Calhoun, Paul Price, and Ashley Timmer. New York: New Press, 2002. 374–84.

Szymborska, Wisława . *Monologue of a Dog*. Trans. Clare Cavanagh and Stanislaw Baranczak. New York: Harcourt, 2005.

Tristram, Claire. *After*. New York: Picador, 2004.

Walter, Jess. *The Zero*. New York: Regan Books, 2006.

Weingarten, Gene, and David Von Drehle. "A Death Better Than Fate's." *Washington Post* 13 Sept. 2001: C1.

Wyatt, Edward. "After a Long Wait, Literary Fiction Begins to Address 9/11." *New York Times* 7 March 2005: E1.

Young, James A. *At Memory's Edge: After-Images of the Holocaust in Contemporary Art and Architecture*. New Haven: Yale UP, 2000.

———. *The Texture of Memory: Holocaust Memorials and Meaning*. New Haven: Yale UP, 1993.

Zelizer, Barbie. "Photography, Journalism, and Trauma." *Journalism After September 11*. Ed. Barbie Zelizer and Stuart Allan. New York: Routledge, 2002. 48–68.

———. "The Voice of the Visual in Memory" *Framing Public Memory*. Ed. Kendall Phillips. U of Alabama P, 2003. http://www.sas.upenn.edu/folklore/center/ConferenceArchive/voiceover/voice_of_the_visual.html#twentynineback.

Part 3

9/11 and the Literary Tradition

10 Telling It Like It Isn't

David Simpson

Iain Pears's extraordinary novel *The Dream of Scipio* begins with an appropriately extraordinary risk: it describes in meticulous scientific detail the sequence of events by which a man dies in a burning building. After eight minutes he is unconscious from the smoke; three minutes later his clothes start to smoke and his skin begins to "bubble." But it takes twenty-three minutes in all before "his heart gave out, his breath stopped" (3). Assuming Pears has done his research, that makes fifteen minutes of life beyond the end of consciousness, fifteen minutes in which we, who are conscious while reading, imagine sensations that the dying man is, we hope, not having. Or we may find ourselves wondering whether the end of consciousness really means the end of pain: a medical question whose answer seems self-evident but—since we are still conscious—creates an uncomfortable uncertainty, at least it does for me. I imagine the pain that I hope Julien Barneuve is not experiencing; I hope that if I were him I would not be feeling it.

But this is the start of the novel. And if it seems odd that the hero is already dead, then this opening scene is made somewhat more bearable because we have not yet formed a bond with any one, not yet entered empathically into (or perhaps learned to despise—for that cannot yet be clear) the life that is being so implacably extinguished, and because we know that there is a book before us that will bring him back to life in order for there to be a story to tell. The novel will thicken and complicate its bond with fire in many ways in different times and places, so that we will be encouraged to constitute an intellectual framework for assimilating the experiences of its characters, a pattern of images and affinities that may (though it need not) help hold off any full immersion in the physical sufferings of dying people, of whom there will be many. Fiction will do its work, and its work will enchant and fascinate even as it reports on a series of experiences of physical pain and death we might otherwise or might still pronounce unbearable.

The Dream of Scipio is a novel, though it tells of events that could well have happened as real history and which certainly had many parallels in real history: it touches, for example, on the histories of the Holocaust and the Black Death. Novels that draw upon what is consensually accepted as real history are held to a different and more demanding standard, especially when that history is recent and unresolved. W.G. Sebald, in a series of lectures delivered in Zurich in 1999, called to attention what he saw as the inability of German writers to confront the horrors of the air war against Germany during World War II, a situation for which he offers a number of possible explanations: the sense of national humiliation that came with losing the war; the sense of having deserved punishment; the unwillingness of the new Germany to look back to its own foundations in heaps of rubble; the sheer horror of what happened, which meant that "we are always looking and looking away at the same time" (ix). His claim that "no German writer, with the sole exception of Nossack, was ready or able to put any concrete facts down on paper" (30) generated a debate not only about the extent of his research (he forgot Gert Ledig, whom he acknowledged in a later postscript) but also about whether any writer ever puts down the concrete facts and nothing more, especially if the writer is a novelist. What is or was the "real state of affairs" that the writer is supposed to reflect or "cast some light on" (9)? Is it what happened as recounted in the scientific manner assayed by Iain Pears, and involving numbers of bombs, lists of the dead, and minute descriptions of the kinds of deaths? Or is it the states of mind of those who suffered through the bombings, producing "an extraordinary faculty for self-anesthesia" (11) that has more to do with how one copes with experiences "exceeding what is tolerable" (79) than with any politically sponsored effort at strategic communal repression?

Sebald acknowledges the well-known limits of eye-witness testimony in such situations, their "curious vacuity" and their "tendency to follow a set routine and go over and over the same material" (80), their predilection for anecdotes of familiar routine preserved in the face of extinction—"how Granny still works all hours in house and garden" (83). But he still regrets and queries why it is that "we have not yet succeeded in bringing the horrors of the air war to public attention through historical or literary accounts" (93), and he still holds up a standard of documentary realism that he thinks should aspire to free itself from all literary or philosophical glossing:

> The ideal of truth inherent in its entirely unpretentious objectivity, at least over long passages, proves itself the only legitimate reason for continuing to produce literature in the face of total destruction. Conversely, the construction of aesthetic or pseudo-aesthetic effects from the ruins of an annihilated world is a process depriving literature of its right to exist. (53)

This is a tall order, if understandably so from a writer who has struggled with the German national past as a source of pornographic fascination both in its own excesses and in the forms of revenge handed to it during the air war, and who is certainly aware of the investment of Nazi mythmakers in the image of the "final battle" of Germany's doomed heroes.

The writer's job in these limited situations is then, for Sebald, to try to record what he "actually" sees "as plainly as possible" (51). This Sebald tries to do himself by drawing upon Nossack's example in describing the "bluish little phosphorus flames" flickering around the corpses which have been "roasted brown or purple and reduced to a third of their normal size ... doubled up in pools of their own melted fat, which had sometimes already congealed" (28). This kind of writing does pass, horribly, as realism, although it was not real to Sebald, who takes up these details by trusting those who did actually witness them. He reproduces some photographs in their support—photographs now no longer "brought out from under the counter of a Hamburg secondhand bookshop, to be fingered and examined in a way usually reserved for pornography" (98). We can see them also, now, in the English translation of Jörg Friedrich's book *The Fire,* which shows us, for instance, pictures of the piles of bodies in Dresden and the horribly charred and shriveled bodies, in Hamburg, of what must have been a woman and child, dumped in a metal washtub (379, 383). Before September 11, 2001, there was 7/27/1943, and other all-too-countable and yet ultimately unaccountable horrors perpetrated both by and upon Germany and Japan; nor need we limit ourselves in compiling these dismal chronicles to the events of 1939–45 alone.

What then does the writer do, and what should be done? Günter Grass, in publishing a novel about the sinking of the *Wilhelm Gustloff* by a Russian submarine in the closing months of the war—an event that took over nine thousand lives, many or most of them civilians and children—decided not to try to describe the minute details of the stampedes for the exits and the drownings, whether out of a wish to avoid pornographic stimulation or a reluctance to play more fully than he already does into the tragification of the Nazi years and the sudden willingness among Germans at last to confront the horrors unleashed upon them as well as the ones they themselves administered.[1] So Grass's narrator claims that "what took place inside the ship cannot be described in words ... I won't even try to imagine those terrible sights ... no matter how my employer is pressuring me to present a series of individual fates, to convey the entire situation with sweeping narrative equanimity and the utmost empathy and thus, with words of horror, do justice to the full extent of the catastrophe" (144–45).

Timing is indeed of the essence. *Crabwalk* was published in 2002 in both German and English. It must have been well under way before September 11, 2001, and its interests are consonant with the preoccupations of much of Grass's fiction, especially his recent books. It would have been widely read without the events of 9/11 alerting the Anglophone world to issues surrounding the representation of extreme horror, and it draws upon debates in Germany that Sebald and Friedrich had already taken up. Nossack's book however, according to its translator, had aroused no interest among American publishers: others among his translated novels had reached few readers and "aside from that, I was told, Americans just weren't prepared to sympathize with a German description of the suffering of Germans in World War Two" (xi). Especially not, one assumes, when the British and the Americans were those dropping the firebombs and doing so, as is now well known, according to a scientifically calculated and experimentally developed (by way of over a hundred German cities) technology for causing the maximum possible amount of material destruction and loss of human life by sequencing the various kinds of bombs—high explosives, blockbusters, and incendiaries—in tightly condensed patterns aimed at increasing the chances of the firestorm that would transform quantity into quality. Was it 9/11 that generated a publisher's interest in Nossack's account of the destruction of Hamburg in 1943? Did the fall of the Twin Towers and the unimaginable suffering of those trapped inside them contribute to a change of heart about the sales prospects for a book first published in 1948 in another language and another place? Did Nossack's documentary prose, certainly not fiction if not quite the merely factual record that Sebald desired, promise to play a role in allowing the reading citizens of the United States to take their place in a global community of suffering from which they had been for so many years blissfully exempted?

9/11 must surely have been a factor in the decision to publish Nossack in English, although there should have been enough of a case already thanks to the international awareness of Sebald's Zurich lecture (itself only published in English after 9/11) and Friedrich's best-selling historical account. Nossack took five years to publish his book; Gert Ledig's *Payback (Vergeltung)* appeared ten years after the end of the war, but it is narrated as if part of an arrested and very recent experience. Literature, we know and expect, takes time. Politicians and their accomplices in the mass media are in a hurry, anxious to get on with acts of retribution, with invading foreign countries, with whipping up the national imaginary to a point where all sorts of liberties can be taken and pushed aside, and above all with justifying their own short term perspicacity and indispensability.[2] 9/11 gave rise to lots of rushed judgments and reflex responses, but literature was generally recalcitrant, in the spirit of Jacques Derrida's remark that the telegraphic condensation of the very phrase 9/11—which caught on so fast and so thoroughly—indicates that "we do not yet know how to qualify, that we do not know what we are talking about" (ed. Borradori, 86). It takes time to write a novel or craft a poem, even for the most opportunistically facile writers. And a deliberate delay in the face of pressures to offer immediate findings is received as a mark of literary quality in a culture of mass communication and instant replay.

So our novelists and their publishers have waited awhile, though not as long as Gert Ledig waited (or had to wait), and it is a safe bet that, given the currency of 9/11 as a global event and the general prestige and marketability of American culture, they will not have to wait very long for translations to appear. But as time passes and the massive implications of such radically dishonest responses as the invasion of Iraq by a U.S.-led "coalition of the willing" become more and more apparent to more and more people, the expectations placed upon the slower literary response may tend to become greater and more and more intimidating, as if we who are elite, specialized readers are supposed to confirm our own patience and caution by discovering in the novel something we cannot find in politics or television, something we can think of as a truth. Günter Grass invoked the film of the sinking of the *Gustloff* as the sort of response he was not attempting, wherein the enormity of death is embodied in a few shots of rising waters, drowning people and "children holding dangling dolls" (*Crabwalk* 145), and it is indeed the language of the movie that slow reading and high literature both commonly conceive as that which they must work hardest to unseat. How true must that be of *this* movie, the endlessly replayed fifteen-second epic of impacting planes and falling towers that has produced a narrative sound-bite (or sight-bite) open to world-wide distribution and iconic adaptation without straining anyone's attention span and above all without (after the falling bodies were disappeared, as they soon were) asking anyone to come face to face with the deaths of people and the destruction of frail human bodies. The very currency of this movie (which is not a movie though, as everyone remarked, it was as if they had seen it already) as it repeats itself over and over without further clarification or analysis has by now become the motif of a deliberate opacity, a piece of history before the history has even been properly projected or deciphered. Now more than ever, one might say, is the time for taking time, the time of the novel.[3]

It is then with some impatience that one looks to the fruits of patience, the first novels about 9/11 to arrive in the bookstores. So far no one in the books I have read has taken up the mode of Iain Pears's opening page, the meticulous account of how people probably died. Even the non-fictional *102 Minutes,* an effort by journalists Jim Dwyer and Kevin Flynn to reconstruct the sequence of events in and around the towers as they occurred in real time, is more about the struggle to survive than the mechanics of death itself.[4] Lamentably few of those who stared death in the face returned to tell of it. But there has been a visible taboo cast over the real or imagined representation of dead and dying people, one that is not fully explained by appealing to the feelings of the survivors or of the families and friends of the victims. The rhetorical colonization, within hours of the event, of Lower Manhattan as "sacred ground" and the reiterated description of the dead as "heroes" by the politicians seeking to make something of their deaths has effectively imposed a scrim of pious exceptionalism that has made it almost impossible to face the materialist implications of death by high explosive, by fire or smoke, by falling thirteen hundred feet to the sidewalk. I have written elsewhere of the huge and ideologically transparent tidying-up job performed by the *New York Times'* obituary series "Portraits of Grief," which I believe to have played directly into the hands of those who were committed to killing a lot more people (and innocent people) in revenge for the deaths in New York, Washington, and Shanksville.[5] The image of a happy and fulfilled American mainstream embodied in those biographies enshrined every victim as beyond and above disappointment and firmly unconcerned with death. Their stories were sanitized just as flagrantly as they had been by the rapid removal from mass media circulation of all pictures of falling bodies.

Jonathan Safran Foer, in his inventive and impressive 9/11 novel, makes his protagonist raise exactly this question about why we are at once bidden to know and forbidden to know what happened, why we are being constrained to know only what is deemed—by someone—appropriate:

> I found a bunch of videos on the Internet of bodies falling. They were on a Portuguese site, where there was all sorts of stuff they weren't showing here, even though it happened here. Whenever I want to try to learn about how Dad died, I have to go to a translator program and find out how to say things in different languages . . . like . . ."people jumping from burning buildings," which is *"Menschen, die aus brennenden Gebäuden springen."* Then I Google those words. It makes me incredibly angry that people all over the world can know things that I can't, because it happened *here,* and happened to *me,* so shouldn't it be *mine?* (256)

Indeed. Is this the therapeutic state at work, protecting us from what it knows we cannot bear, or something more sinister, a purposive repression of the physicality of death in order that a culture of undying energy can maintain itself and continue to avoid facing up to the deaths of those in other parts of the world, and in its own enclaves (the inner cities, the prisons, and elsewhere), the deaths which its own mighty resources might work to avoid rather than continue to perpetrate? Spend a few days in Mexico, pick up a newspaper, and you will probably find within it a "police" section full of photographs of dead bodies, the bodies of those who have died violently in car crashes, gunfights, or murders.

Here we think ourselves more tasteful and respectful. We ought nonetheless to wonder if we are missing something and whether someone else is exploiting our missing it for reasons we have not understood. The arresting value of any sight or reproduction of human bodies being destroyed may at best not last long. The call to attention that the publication of the first round of Abu Ghraib photos brought about when they appeared in the spring of 2004 seemed a positive event, a challenge to the entire culture of bureaucratically encouraged torture and brutality that was shown to be as pronounced in "the west" as it was in any so-called primitive society. For a while the unhinged and uncontrollable circulation of those famous images leveled a playing field and placed "terrorists" and their victims in much closer proximity than coalition propaganda had been willing to imagine. Their power may still be operating or latent in relation to understandings yet to develop. But when a second round of photos was finally published in the Australian magazine *Salon* in 2006 and circulated on the Internet, there was hardly a ripple of response, popular or official, in the headquarters of the coalition of the willing. The relative silence was all the more remarkable in that this batch of photos included those deemed by our governing powers to be too distressing to allow to be published in the first batch: they included, for example, an image of the man sodomized with the chemical light. The point is that even the most shocking and challenging evidence has only one shot at making news, and Abu Ghraib had already had its moment. Perhaps the reiterative image of the falling towers—one falling after the other, just like the other—which inscribed in its very originality the principle of indefinite, depth-free repetition, is a better sign of the times, and of the global event as not much more than a tick and a tock. Abu Ghraib the second time around suggests at least that there are going to be few opportunities for shaking up the sleep of patriotic sentiment with even the most graphic of images.

What is a novelist, a practitioner of slow writing and a prophet of slow reading, to do? To seek to represent the material details of dismembering and dying bodies and minds is one way to go but, as Rousseau and Wordsworth among others well knew, there is no guarantee that literary representations of the sufferings of others will produce active sympathy in the world; they can equally well serve as inoculations against further responsiveness. The attempt might still be worth making, and Abu Ghraib gave evidence that it can work at least for a time.[6] The hegemonic assembly of corporate media and governing elites that produces the news and tries to limit how it will be received is certainly frightened of this, enough so to do what it can to keep the sordid realities of death as far away as possible and to blame those alternative sources (like the now-infamous *Al Jazeera*) for doing things differently. The *New York Times* from time to time gives out images of dead Iraqis and Palestinians, but (with the honorable exception of some columnists) more for variety than out of any apparent commitment to what Sebald called reality. It is much too early to suggest that the contemporary novel is going in some clearly visible directions rather than others, but it is the case that neither of the writers I will discuss in what remains of this chapter, Claire Messud and John Updike, chooses to take on the task of describing death up close and in detail. In so choosing they share certain instincts about what can and should be said of our response to 9/11, a response that they (or their books) suggest is, after all, distinctly local and arguably even parochial, and by no means as far from the ideological mainstream as we or they might like.

John Updike's *Terrorist* and Claire Messud's *The Emperor's Children* were both published in New York by Alfred A. Knopf in 2006, and both are prefaced by the standard disclaimer that they are works of fiction and not about real people. The disclaimer introducing *The Emperor's Children* is the more elaborate of the two, as perhaps befits a Manhattan "society" novel that will remind knowing readers of various people they know or think they know about. Updike dwells instead with the anonymous blue collar citizens of New Jersey and with characters no one would imagine him knowing. Messud's is a countdown narrative, moving us from March to November in a single year which is obviously 2001; Updike's book is a post-9/11 novel and as such surely the harbinger of a genre destined to flourish under that name. 9/11 subsists in *Terrorist* as the prototype of a second event which in the end does not happen, although something like it happened in London on 7/7/05; in *The Emperor's Children* the fall of the towers is a spectacle seen through a window and at the same time on television and an opportunity for some not very admirable people to invent new lives and refurbish old ones. (To them Manhattan is all that matters—there is no mention of Washington or of Shanksville, PA.).

The two novels share a common intuition—that nothing has changed, that life goes on, and that life is not very interesting or satisfying. In this they show themselves suspicious of the rhetoric of 9/11 as a world-changing event and not at all confident that the lives of these fictional Americans have been transformed by the tragedy or even by the spectacle. The question they raise is whether this response (or lack of it) is a tribute to the resilience of ordinary life or a more damning indictment of the sheer indifference and self-centeredness of the homeland mainstream. Messud inclines to the second emphasis, while Updike is not readily decipherable, partly because his mainstream is more various and includes a young Arab-American as one of its two main characters. But the ethos of both books is—despite their relation to a world-historical "tragedy"—closer to the comedic, where mishap and mayhem are risked but finally (mostly) avoided and the really bad things happen offstage and to others.

In this way both authors seem to refute or refuse the logic of terrorism itself as specified by Jean Baudrillard as that which "restores an irreducible singularity to the heart of a system of generalized exchange" (9). And yet neither is sure that it is a good thing that normal service is restored. In Messud's novel one minor character from among the working poor, mentioned but never introduced as a character, dies in the towers; one of the more central characters who is thought to have died and whose family puts on a service of remembrance turns out to have used the chaos in Lower Manhattan as an opportunity to skip town with an advance on his paycheck and start a new life in Florida. Frederick Tubb (known as "Bootie") would thus have been a false entry in the columns of the "Portraits of Grief" which were so widely received across the country as moving evocations of lives well spent and tragically cut off. The vaporization or total disappearance of so many bodies that has caused such grief among the mourners because there are no bodies to bury or bid farewell to—only occasional body parts if anything—is for Bootie transformed into a career opportunity and a way to escape the opprobrium of those past misdemeanors told about in the novel. Marina Thwaite, not the least amiable of the various airheads who populate this book, is convinced that her crazy cousin is going to spoil her wedding day by trying to kill the family (323), and when faced with the event of 9/11 itself is able only to manage a massive bathos: "Do you realize, when I put this Kleenex in my pocket, the world was a completely different place?" (386). Updike does report the death of a character for whom the book has developed a certain qualified affection: Charlie Chehab is an "asset" planted by homeland security to ferret out the members of an Al Qaeda-style terrorist cell in northern New Jersey. His cover is exposed, and he is beheaded; we hear about his body being found in the Meadowlands.

This is as close as either book gets to a confrontation with violent death. Messud intimates the experience of terror in having Bootie stuck in a subway car for 23 minutes with the lights out and only minimal information coming over the intercom, his body sweating and his heart pounding: "For Bootie, it was a mind-altering experience: he wasn't at once sure exactly how he had been changed by it, sure merely that he would always be different" (244–45). Here is an ordinary and not uncommon drama, which this narcissistically deranged young man wants to make into a decisive and transformative event, a Baudrillardian "irreducible singularity" that changes his world. His anxiety is entirely reasonable, but his conclusions are to say the least questionable, and they are studiously held up for comparison to the experiences of those who will soon die in the Twin Towers, whose terror the book does not describe but which we cannot fail at this point to summon up.

This is as much reality, Messud implies, as Bootie and those like him can bear; this is what a life-changing experience looks like to them. The odious Ludovic, an Australian magazine editor on the make who is the novel's only foreign protagonist and by now Marina's husband, reacts violently to the posters of the missing as a fantasy spun out by those living in "the fucking land of lies" who want a "happy ending," but his outrage is received by others on the street as the distress of a grieving relative; he is moreover principally concerned with the now-inevitable failure of his new magazine: "It's over. We're fucked" (376–77). Murray Thwaite, the famous father, inadvertently gains a new life to his career by offering restrained liberal commentary on 9/11 and its consequences, but his private life reflects an instinctive return to a normality he never had: he abandons his new mistress and runs home to his long-suffering wife. The mistress, who may be the novel's most likeable figure, in turn calls her mother and the two head off for a vacation in Florida. All around, the response to 9/11 within this precious (albeit often jobless) enclave of smart and relatively privileged people is a return to middle-American rituals and routines. Ludo's ambition of fomenting a kind of "revolution" was always more Napoleonic than Jacobin (his magazine was to be called *The Monitor*); these are people who compare themselves to the characters in *War and Peace* but don't actually read very much or very deeply. *The Monitor* is indeed financially supported by a right-wing Australian media mogul whose ventures are made up of "everything in English and all to the right" (10).

What can we make of Messud's recourse to social satire as the mode of a "9/11 novel"? It might be taken as a fitting acknowledgment of the limits of fiction in the face of an appalling and indescribable event, rather as those who did not experience the Holocaust are sometimes told that they should not purport to tell about it. Or it might be read as a cry of quiet rage against the capacity of these people not to be radically moved or changed by an event whose enormous importance they can neither understand intellectually nor sense upon their private pulses. An interior monologue most plausibly attributable to Ludo may carry some authorial weight here. After the millionaire mogul cuts off the financing for the magazine and Ludo decides to move to England to "call in" his "UK connections" we read as follows: "So much for revolution. The revolution belonged to other people now, far away from them, and it was real" (403). Messud is too deft or too undecided a writer either to claim or deny this statement as her own, but it does sum up a sense that the fictional characters whose lives and loves we have been following for four hundred pages (and who are probably passionate voters in the world's most powerful country) are trivial and inadequate to the challenges of responding to the global situation. From this perspective one might read the novel as an epitaph to itself, or to the society novel of modern manners and its accumulations of petty ambitions, silly happenings and routine infidelities. Or, if one is so-minded and has happened to identify with anyone in the book, it might appear as a salutary homage to the ability of most people to keep going, like those Germans whom Sebald reported as relentlessly focusing on normality: "Granny still works all hours on house and garden" (83).

Petty ambitions and routine infidelities have of course constituted the backbone of John Updike's prolific career, and they indeed appear as familiar compound ghosts in his post-9/11 novel *Terrorist*. But here the mode is not quite satiric nor is the tone as carefully measured and controlled. Updike gives us two characters who share more or less equal space as prime movers and thinkers, and they evoke the conventions of two different genres. Ahmad Mulloy is an Arab-American teenager and, as such, the sponsor of a coming-of-age narrative, while sixty-three-year-old Jack Levy is the flag-bearer for a midlife crisis narrative. (If sixty-three seems late for this, we should not miss the moment where he is able, given the right woman, to manage a second orgasm in fairly short order). Updike's writing is anything but measured, and he uses the freedoms of indirect free style to wander in and out of the minds and mouths of his protagonists with little apparent concern or control. The distaste for the culture of blue-collar America is shared by Ahmad, who is trying to be an Islamic fundamentalist, and by Jack, who is an unobservant Jew, as well as by other characters: they are both vehicles for Updike's dislike of a squalid life world where, in Jack's words, "this whole neighborhood could do with a good bomb" (32). It can only be Updike who describes a furniture showroom as full of the "massed equipment for living the mortal aura . . . of organic humanity, its pathetic six or so positions and needs repeated in a desperate variety of styles and textures" (151) or who reports a perception of the post-9/11 security staffing of airports as evidence that "a dusky underclass has been given tyrannical power" (46). The misogyny that has Jack's wife Beth "giving off too much heat through her blubber" (20), or describes her sister Hermione's "sallow spinster skin" (48) or, bizarrely, imagines Theresa Mulloy's pubic hair above the panty-line as "like the head on an impatiently poured beer" (162) smacks not so much of dramatic narration as dyspeptic authorial obsession.

Much of this is unappealing: the male figures, even when they are sex-obsessed or radical ascetics, are treated more kindly than the women. Jack is biding his time before death after a fairly long life, and alternately struggling against and wishing for it. Ahmad foresees death as a martyrdom and a means of cleansing a corrupted world. Jack is perfectly at ease with the loose sexual mores of his culture and even discovers a good time with Ahmad's mother (some 20 years his junior, she of the beer-like pubes), while Ahmad disapproves doctrinally of unmarried and irreligious sex but is both fond of and attracted to a young black woman with whom he went to high school. Ahmad is at the point of pressing the button and blowing up the Lincoln Tunnel, but doesn't do it. Jack, in the seat beside him, reveals neither a fully-fledged death-wish nor a heroic altruism that risks itself to save the world. Nor does his big speech (303–04) seem designed to change the young man's mind. What triggers the change seems to be a serendipitous connection between something Jack says about wanting to die and a memory of the "fifty-sixth sura" of the *Qur'an* where God refuses to approve of enabling someone else to die (306). What saves the Lincoln Tunnel is a moment of literary-critical skepticism of the sort that Ahmad has indeed shown before and which his teacher Shaik Rashid has himself modeled for Ahmad despite his apparent intention to train him as a suicide bomber.

Ahmad, in this final moment, is unable to construe the truth of the holy book as unambiguously endorsing blowing up Jack Levy, even as he had previously resolved to blow up several hundred others who were not looking to die. There are contributory circumstances—allusions to the insects whom Ahmad has pitied and assisted, his fondness for Joryleen, his technician's pride in his truck and in his own driving skills—that mark Ahmad out as something more than a suicide case. He is after all American, and he has "a native trace of the American lope" in his walk though the early morning streets on what was to be his last day on earth (281). And there is enough here to make sure that Jack is not to be received as a hero. This is where Updike's novel gets interesting. His desire to put himself into the mind of a young would-be jihadist (although the title word is terrorist) seems to be enabled by a strong authorial identification with the critique of a modern America without meaningful faith or moral conviction—a critique to which Jack also gives voice on more than one occasion. So what is "saved" at the end is not declared unambiguously as worth saving. Christianity appears only in narratively debased forms: Beth's and Hermione's residual but inactive Lutheranism, the self-serving bigotry of the "born-again right-wing stooge" (20) who is Secretary for Homeland Security, the theater of the black church service which, Ahmad thinks, implies that

"God is an entertainer" (50). There are no grounds for active patriotism and little, if any, described sympathy for the victims of the disaster that occurred just across the river a mere twelve months before the time of the novel. Ahmad's martyrdom is not upheld as a proper course of conduct, but neither is it thoroughly negated, and Updike has gone to some trouble in transliterating Arabic into English script in order to communicate at least the sound of otherness in the Islamic holy book.

But the culture that persuades Ahmad that he might want to be a martyr is not defended or justified with any strong conviction. The fairy tale happenstance whereby Beth's sister works for the Secretary of Homeland Security seems to be what saves the tunnel, because only her brother-in-law can track down Ahmad on the day of decision. The homeland security forces mishandle the raid, and Charlie is killed because, apparently, he had "seen too many movies" and waited too long (292). There is more than a minimum of narrative conviction to Ahmad's lament that America has taken away his god. What turns the plot, finally, what makes it possible for Jack to stand on the street and flag down Ahmad's truck, is the minimal professionalism and human decency (he is a school careers counselor) that has made him pay attention to the boy in the first place as a hopeful case among a crowd of losers. It isn't much to crow about, nor is it necessarily or uniquely American, and Updike's conclusion is accordingly muted. Modern America does not encourage religious faith or devout living; even Shaik Rashid sees his *Qur'an* class reduced to a single student. But living without faith does not produce happiness, as Updike reminds us again and again. He cannot bring himself to celebrate the impurity of ideals that characterizes modern secular life, although such a view is suggested by one of his epigraphs.

The two novels I have been discussing do then have a good deal in common. They are not comedies in the fullest sense because they do not have happy endings. They avoid the pornography of death by not describing death, but in so doing they raise questions about whether this decision is the result of a moral-aesthetic decorum or a critical testimony to the utter self-centeredness of the people in their books. The self-centeredness is echoed in the list of protagonists, which, in Messud's case, almost entirely excludes the foreign (just three Australians, only one figuring significantly); Updike does include and develop a Yemeni Imam and three Lebanese-American furniture dealers, along with the less defined figures of the bomb makers. He transcribes some Arabic. But in neither novel is there mention of Iraq, adumbrated in Ian McEwan's 2005 novel *Saturday,* but there too rendered marginal, as issues of life and death are experienced as highly localized in one fashionable square and a few streets in London. Compared to, for example, Foer's *Extremely Loud & Incredibly Close* or Beigbeder's *Windows on the World,* the two novels I have been discussing are both formally and thematically conservative in a manner that seems deliberate and self-imposed. Foer summons up a whole litany of suffering and violent death, including Dresden and Hiroshima. He purposively does not play up the Holocaust (one of the topics of his first novel), bravely using his fiction to remind us that 9/11 was not only not the first such event, but that it was also by no means the major one and that some of the others were performed by the civilized west upon its enemies. Love and death, including violent death, are writ large in Foer's work; there is nothing of the society novel about his book, whose magical realist touches speak their own conventionality but to a very different end.

It is hard to say what is most fitting, what fictional manner and matter are most useful to the range of tasks that fiction has been asked to perform: imagining a better life, encouraging an acceptable distribution of international justice, or merely depicting how things are in our bit of the world. We cannot expect *War and Peace,* the book that Messud's characters keep citing but have not deeply received. And it may be that some fiction's modestly satirical inclination to keep us talking about ourselves and our visible limitations is a productive counterpoint to the increasingly overreaching and visibly fragile rhetoric of triumphalist imperial politics. Many of those coming home from Iraq might find a personal truth in Jack Levy's remark that "once you run out of steam, America doesn't give you much" (*Terrorist* 304). Many others who will never set foot in Iraq or anywhere like it might register the notable preoccupation in both Updike and Messud with the question of fat. In *Terrorist* Beth Levy has far too much of it, being "a whale of a woman" with too much "blubber" (20), causing her a pointless and unproductive anxiety about dieting that will never of itself, Jack says, make either of them young again (303). In *The Emperor's Children,* a novel about a world in which thinness is all, Bootie Tub's fatness is the object of both Murray Thwaite's and Julius Clarke's contempt (303, 362), Marina's thinness is a major acknowledged source of the beauty which helps attract the "long, feline slope" of Ludo (4) away from the more voluptuous Danielle, and Julius's lover David reaches the low point of his degradation when he is observed "moving like a fat man" (283). The only asceticism respected in this subculture is that of the exercise routine and the low-fat diet. The firestorm as Sebald reported or imagined it offered a more radical cure for obesity, as bodies were "reduced to a third of their natural size" and discovered lying in "pools of their own melted fat" (*Natural History* 28). Two kinds of fiction, two kinds of facts. It is not possible to be sure that one rather than the other projects an inevitable moral and aesthetic urgency in all times and places; but it is clear that, in these early years of the post-9/11 novel, few of us in the west want to read or write about the material nature of violent death, about the fate of the body when it no longer offers tenure to a recognizable social subject. That is not our only problem, by any means, but it is a problem. If we cannot think about how *we* die, there is no place to start to think seriously about the deaths of those faraway others we seem willing enough to both bring about and to supervise.

NOTES

1. In relation to the pornographic appeal, Hans Erich Nossack asks himself: "why record all of this? . . . what if they read it only to enjoy something strange and uncanny and to make themselves feel more alive?" (36–37).
2. Friedrich remarks rather wryly that after the assiduous clean ups and compensations extended by the Nazi party to the victims of the bombings, "surveys showed that fifty-eight percent were satisfied with the care they received" (390). The other end of the carrot was the high incidence of state executions carried out among those accused of looting (396).
3. The images of falling towers that were so ubiquitous in the days following 9/11 are, notably, not included in Paul Greengrass's impressive movie *United 93*, which also generally withholds and marginalizes scenes of graphic, proto-pornographic violence or subdues them by the use of montage. Oliver Stone's *World Trade Center* employs a much more conventional plot and cinematography but also avoids these images, representing the passage of the second plane only as a shadow and having most of the important information circulate by cell phone or on TV rather than as epic cinema.
4. See Dwyer and Flynn. Beigbeder's *Windows on the World* (2003), a bestseller in France, also adopts a moment-by-moment narrative. It has been critiqued for various reasons, among them its dense self-inscriptions, but its metafictional dimension achieves a critical extension of both complicity and involvement, and the details of the last hour of life inside the North Tower are powerfully imagined by way of a conviction that "books must go where television does not" (295). Beigbeder is intensely critical of the "patriotic" media suppression of physical suffering (e.g., on pp. 261–2). Don DeLillo's *Falling Man* (2007) also sets out to confront the physicality of death, albeit by way of a survivor narrative. Both writers focus on the "forbidden" topic of the jumpers.
5. See David Simpson, *9/11*.
6. See David Simpson, "The Mourning Paper"; and David Simpson, *9/11* (103–19).

WORKS CITED

Baudrillard, Jean. *In the Spirit of Terrorism and Requiem for the Twin Towers.* Trans. Chris Turner. London: Verso, 2002.

Beigbeder, Frédéric. *Windows on the World.* Trans. Frank Wayne. New York: Hyperion, 2004.

Borradori, Giovanna. *Philosophy in a Time of Terror: Dialogues with Jürgen Habermas and Jacques Derrida.* Chicago: U of Chicago P, 2003.

DeLillo, Don. *Falling Man.* New York: Scribners, 2007.

Dwyer, Jim and Kevin Flynn. *102 Minutes: The Untold Story of the Fight to Survive Inside the Twin Towers.* New York: Henry Holt, 2005.

Foer, Jonathan Safran. *Extremely Loud & Incredibly Close.* Boston: Houghton, 2005.

Telling It Like It Isn't 223

Friedrich, Jörg. *The Fire: The Bombing of Germany, 1940–45.* Trans. Alison Brown. New York: Columbia UP, 2006.

Grass, Günter. *Crabwalk.* Trans. Krishna Winston. Orlando: Harcourt, 2002.

Nossack, Hans Erich. *The End: Hamburg, 1943.* Trans. Joel Agee. Chicago: U of Chicago P, 2004.

Pears, Iain. *The Dream of Scipio.* New York: Riverhead, 2002.

Sebald, W. G. *On the Natural History of Destruction.* Trans. Anthea Bell. New York: Random House, 2003.

Simpson, David. "The Mourning Paper." *London Review of Books* 20 May 2004: 3–5.

———. *9/11: The Culture of Commemoration.* Chicago: U of Chicago P, 2006.

11 Portraits 9/11/01
The *New York Times* and the Pornography of Grief[1]

Simon Stow

"We will read their names. We will linger over them, and learn their stories, and many Americans will weep."

—President George W. Bush, 9/14/01

Modernity has been marked by a triumph of private grief over public mourning; in memorialization, pornography is now the dominant mode. Nowhere, perhaps, is this more evident than in the *New York Times* series "Portraits of Grief"—the newspaper's publication of individual biographies of the New York City victims of the September 11, 2001, terrorist attacks. For, although the series was conceived of, and praised as, a form of "democratic" mourning—transcending race, gender, sexuality, and economic status by assigning equality to the deceased—placing the series in its historical context suggests that such individuation would have long been considered decidedly *anti*-democratic—permitting private grief to intrude upon the anonymous public mourning considered essential to the well-being of the city. Turning to the Greeks for critical leverage on our current practices, this chapter traces the long-standing connection between pornography and death, and it identifies both the prurience at the heart of our contemporary modes of mourning and remembrance and its potentially negative consequences for the American democratic process.

To suggest that America's dominant mode of public mourning is pornographic is, however, to be forced to engage with some of the frenzied emotion that it necessarily engenders, that which, it will be argued, robs its victims of the balanced perspective that the Greeks believed was essential to democratic discourse. It is therefore necessary to distinguish what is being argued here from some of the more hyperbolic or problematic claims with which it might otherwise be grouped, such as that of Ward Churchill, the University of Colorado professor who, in 2005, became the *bête noire* of the conservative media when his essay questioning the "innocence" of the World Trade Center attack victims was widely circulated in the Internet. Drawing on the work of Hannah Arendt, Churchill suggested that the dead—who, he said, "formed a technocratic corps at the very heart of

America's global financial empire"—were guilty of the type of unthinking-ness and evasion of moral responsibility that Arendt ascribed to the Nazi war criminal Adolf Eichmann—claims about the *victims* of the attacks. Likewise, William Langewiesche's discussion of possible looting by New York City fire fighters as the towers fell—which produced a similar outcry—was a claim about the *dead*. While it is clear that the uncritical depiction of the fallen—a tradition which, as Socrates's criticism in the *Menexenus* suggests, stretches back to the Ancients—is part of the problem, the claims being made here are claims about us, the *living*—*about* the producers and consumers of what is being termed the "pornography of grief." As such, the subject matter is our contemporary practices of American public mourn-ing, not the worth, or otherwise, of the fallen.

"PORTRAITS OF GRIEF" AND CONTEMPORARY MOURNING

On September 17, 2001, the *New York Times* began to publish a series of brief essays on the men and women believed killed six days earlier in the terrorist attack on the city's World Trade Center. Based on discussions with the families of the lost and offering what one of its writers called "a snapshot of each victim's personality, of a life lived" (Scott), under head-ings such as "Host of Patio Parties," "Daffy Downhill Skiing," "Too Busy to Retire," and "Striving for the Best," the paper titled the series "Portraits of Grief." When it officially ended fifty-one weeks later—on the eve of the first anniversary of the attacks—the *Times* had offered 1,910 sketches of lives lived and lost,[2] sketches that were collected together in 2002 and published as a book entitled *Portraits of Grief 9/11/01*. A second edition of the book, published in 2003, offered a total of 2,310 obituaries, providing the additional details of the lives of those whose families chose to cooperate with the project once the initial series was over and, in at least one case, removing from the official record an individual whose existence and victim status could no longer be verified (*Times* "Editors"). Although some fami-lies declined to have their relatives or loved-ones included in the series, the *Times* offered portraits of the great majority of the World Trade Center vic-tims, and while one writer noted that a "small number of family members complained, saying certain profiles had failed to capture the people they knew" (Scott), the response was overwhelmingly positive.

The 2002 Pulitzer Prize awarded to the *Times* for "Public Service" spe-cifically mentioned the "Portraits of Grief" profiles. *The Boston Herald* asserted that the series was "a memorable way to engrave the costs of terror-ism on American hearts for the rest of our days" and called it "[o]ne of the most remarkable accomplishments in American journalism" ("Victims"). The series was featured on *Nightline,* its writers feted and photographed in *Vanity Fair,* and one of its editors interviewed on *The Today Show.* Letters from readers testified to the popularity, impact, and perceived appropriateness of the "Portraits," and even one of the few dissenting voices—the novelist Thomas Mallon—admitted in an essay that was otherwise critical of the series: "These Portraits were, it is not an exaggeration to say, the talk of the city . . . a conversation staple . . . a matter of pride" (6). Nor was the praise for the series confined to New York City. *The Oregonian* started publishing the profiles in mid-September 2001. In October, the paper's Ombudsman Dan Hortsch raised the question of when *The Oregonian* would stop publishing the series. According to the *Times'* own reporting of the story, "When he checked his voice mail that afternoon, he found 68 messages. Hundreds followed. The gist, he said, was: Don't stop" (Scott).

Attempting both to explain the popularity of the series and to add their own voices to the chorus of praise for it, a diverse group of academics and intellectuals offered assessments. "Every day, for several months," wrote Howard Zinn, "the *Times* has been doing what should always be done when a tragedy is summed up in a statistic: it has painted miniature portraits of the human beings who died in the attacks" (33). Similarly, novelist Paul Auster observed, "One felt, looking at those pages every day, that real lives were jumping out at you. We weren't mourning an anonymous mass of people, we were mourning thousands of individuals. And the more we knew about them, the more we could wrestle with our own grief" (Scott). Indeed, the individuation of the dead drew the most effusive praise. The suggestion that, by offering these "snapshots" the writers allowed their readers to understand the enormity of the event, was made repeatedly. "The peculiar genius of it," noted Kenneth T. Jackson, professor of history at Columbia University and director of the New York Historical Society, "was to put a human face on numbers that are unimaginable to most of us. . . . As you read those individual portraits about love affairs or kissing children goodbye or coaching soccer and buying a dream home . . . it's obvious that every one of them was a person who deserved to live a full and successful happy life. You see what was lost" (Scott).

Scholars of memorialization might note, however, that such individuation of the deceased was by no means original to the "Portraits of Grief" series. Throughout the twentieth century, identifying the dead by name has become something of a commonplace in memorialization of war and tragedy. Maya Lin's Vietnam Veterans' Memorial with its approximately 58,000 names is, perhaps, the most famous example of the phenomenon, but the memorial to the victims of the Oklahoma City Bombing is similarly specific: it consists in part of 168 bronze chairs, each marked with the name of a victim, including nineteen half-sized chairs to memorialize the children killed in the Alfred P. Murrah Building's day-care center. Similarly, the great majority of the panels on the Aids Quilt commemorate an individual who died of the disease, and a reading of the names of the deceased is a tradition that accompanies nearly every public display of the artwork (Names). Indeed, first among the requirements for the design of the World

Trade Center memorial was that it "[r]ecognize each individual who was a victim of the attacks" (Lower Manhattan 19). The proposed memorial for the 184 people killed at the Pentagon on September 11, 2001, is similarly rich in individual detail. Each victim is to be memorialized by an individual marker: 59 of them will point toward the Pentagon, commemorating those killed in the building, and 125 will face outward, commemorating those killed on American Airlines Flight 77. The markers themselves are to be arranged according to the age of the victims, with the western edge of the site to be defined by an "age wall" that grows an inch in height relative to the age represented by the memorial markers (Pentagon).

In its detailing of the individual lives of the fallen, "Portraits of Grief" was then very much a manifestation of a contemporary trend in memorialization, one that seeks to assign some notion of equality to the dead. In this, "Portraits" was widely regarded as a democratic form of mourning. Howell Raines, the Executive Editor of the *Times* observed: "'Portraits of Grief' reminds us of the democracy of death, an event that lies in the future of every person on the planet" (New York Times, *Portraits* vii). Furthermore, he suggested, democracy was not only reflected in the product, but also in the process of production. "Among the reporters," he declared, "another kind of democracy—the democracy of craftsmanship—came into play." It was, he says, "an emblem of pride to join in the largely anonymous labor of creating these pieces; some of our most senior correspondents insisted on participating" (New York Times, *Portraits* vii). Similarly, in her introduction to the collected volume, Janny Scott called the pieces "utterly democratic" (ix). Elsewhere she explained, "[E]xecutive vice presidents and battalion chiefs appeared alongside food handlers and janitors. Each profile was roughly 200 words" (Scott). That the *Times* could stretch the concept of democracy to explain not only the *identification of individuals* and the details of their lives—as in the case of the fallen—but also as *anonymity*—as in the case of the series' writers—suggests, however, a certain degree of tension in their claims about the democratic value of the "Portraits of Grief" series. Indeed, the history of democratic mourning—both ancient *and* modern—would seem to suggest that such individuation would have long been regarded as *anti*-democratic.

ANONYMITY AND THE DEMOCRATIC DEAD

On November 19, 1863, Abraham Lincoln delivered the most famous eulogy in U.S. history: the Gettysburg Address. The speech was notable for—among much else—its deliberate refusal to name the dead, to identify the details of their death, or, indeed, to offer any kind of detail at all. In stark contrast to our contemporary practices, Lincoln referred only to "a great battlefield," "the brave men," "these honored dead," and "this nation." Indeed, such is the difference between the mourning practices of the nineteenth and twenty-first centuries that when the Gettysburg Address was chosen as a eulogy for the September 11 dead in New York City on the first anniversary of the attacks, a list of the 2,801 people then believed to have been killed in the attacks was also read out by way of compensation for the speech's unfashionable lack of specificity (Stow). In its lack of specificity and its refusal to name names, the Address reflected its origins in the Greek funeral oration tradition—most obviously in that of Pericles's famous address in Thucydides' *History of the Peloponnesian War* (Wills, Goodman)—a tradition in which the anonymity accorded to the dead was directly linked to the promotion of Athenian democracy and democratic values.

So integral was the public eulogy to Greek democracy that Nicole Loraux argues that the funeral oration invented Athens as much as Athens invented the oration (*Invention*). It provided an opportunity for the city to tell stories about itself that were essential to the creation of what Benedict Anderson calls the "imagined community" of the nation, in the Greek instance, for the creation of a democratic public. The role ascribed by Garry Wills, among others, to the Gettysburg Address in the founding of a second American republic dedicated to the proposition that "all men are created equal," and that speech's reliance upon the tropes and traditions of the Ancients suggests that the importance of the public eulogy to democratic life continues to resonate in modernity. Indeed, the history of the funeral oration suggests that the mode of mourning that cities and nations adopt and the stories they tell about their dead have important implications for the kinds of policies they adopt in response to mass death. In Athens, Pericles adopted an unquestioning mode of mourning that simply furthered Athens' tragic decline by reinforcing her partial perspective. At Gettysburg, Lincoln offered a more balanced mode of mourning that offered an implicit critique of the nation, thereby paving the way for the emergence of quite a different polity (Stow). Although the ultimate failure of Pericles's speech suggests that, by itself, the anonymity accorded to the democratic dead was insufficient to achieve the kind of balance the Greeks believed was essential to balanced democratic thought and practice; it was nevertheless a mainstay of their efforts to achieve such a perspective.

Although the Greeks did offer casualty lists known as *stēlai,* the lists were notable for their lack of detail. The names were given and grouped according to tribal division, without patronymic or demotic—the standard indicators of a person's position in Greek society. Beyond the *stēlai,* the Greeks provided no other individual details in their funeral ceremonies: nothing about the ages of the fallen, their social status, or even their military rank, and certainly nothing about their interests, hobbies, or personal relationships in the manner of the "Portraits of Grief." Such details were deliberately omitted in favor of praise of the city. The oration was, writes Loraux, "an institution of speech in which the symbolic encroached on the functional, since in each oration the codified praise of the dead spilled over into generalized praise of Athens" (*Invention* 2). As such, it deliberately drew attention away from the details of the fallen. "Some of them" says Pericles of the dead, "no doubt had their faults; but what we ought to remember is their gallant conduct against the enemy in defence of their native land. They have blotted out evil with good, and done more service to the commonwealth than they ever did harm in their private lives" (Thucydides 148). All that was to be remembered was the manner of their deaths, the glory of which was to be ascribed not to the fallen, but to the city alone. Although such anonymity for the dead stands in stark contrast to the modern—allegedly "democratic"—traditions of remembrance, for the Greeks the conventions, tropes, and rituals of the funeral oration and the procession served an essential democratic function: they placed limits on public mourning. In so doing, they sought to protect the polity from the necessarily distorting *álaston pénthos,* the mourning that could never end.

TEARS OF GRIEF, TEARS OF RAGE

At the end of his funeral oration, Pericles dismisses the crowd: "And now, when you have mourned for your dear ones, you must depart" (Thucydides 151). The implication is clear: the period of mourning is over and citizens should return to their ordinary lives. In stark contrast to the contemporary assertion—ubiquitous after 9/11—that "We will never forget," the Greeks sought, after an appropriate ceremony of mourning, to do precisely that in order that they might go about the business of the city. Indeed, in *Mothers in Mourning* Loraux notes that in addition to strictly regulating the funeral procession certain Greek cities made "prohibitions against wailing at the cemetery over the ones already long dead and against lamenting on specific anniversary dates" (21*fn*34). Such emotion was inextricably associated with women, and their role in the rituals of mourning was strictly regulated. In his funeral oration, for example, Pericles relegates women to the role of childbirth and to being "least talked about by men" (Thucydides 148, 150–51). Similarly, the city of Ceos, believing that the women who laid-out and prepared the body were contaminated, kept them separate from those attending the ceremonies for the dead. Those women who did attend left the graveside before the men lest their unbridled emotion disturb the male mourners and allow female laments to have the last word (Loraux, *Mothers* 21–22). Thus, *oikeîon pénthos*—the intimate mourning of the household—was subordinated to the public mourning of the procession. "This," argues Loraux, was "the civic way of assigning limits to the loss of self, limits that for women are the familiar walls of the *oîkos.* The reasoning is that the *oikeîon pénthos* must not contaminate the city, just as more generally, funeral rites should not intrude on the political institutions' operations" (Loraux, *Mothers* 26).

In June 2006, conservative columnist Ann Coulter caused a furor when she attacked the four 9/11 widows known as "The Jersey Girls" whose political activism was instrumental in the formation of the 9/11 Commission. Most (in)famously Coulter declared: "These broads are millionaires lionized on TV and in articles about them, reveling in their status as celebrities and stalked by grief-arazzis. I've never seen people enjoying their husbands' deaths so much" (103). Beneath the calculated hyperbole of Coulter's attack was, however, a claim that would have resonated with the Greeks. Coulter asserted that the Democratic Party had adopted "an ingenious strategy." "They would choose," she wrote, "only messengers whom we're not allowed to reply to [*sic*]. That's why all Democratic spokesmen these days are sobbing, hysterical women. You can't respond to them because that would be questioning the authenticity of their suffering" (101). Coulter's—very Greek—suggestion was that such tears and public displays of grief distorted the democratic process. While Coulter is perhaps mistaken about *who* sought to subvert the democratic process by waving the bloody shirt of 9/11—the Bush administration, who vastly extended executive power and overrode the Constitution, or a group of women who used the institutions of government to argue for a formal commission into the causes of their husbands' deaths—her comments nevertheless suggest the dangers to democratic deliberation and discussion of such public manifestations of private grief. For the Greeks, the danger of such grief was "the affinity that exists between grief and anger. The emotions of grief, which are the wellsprings of lament, spill over into emotions of anger, even rage" (*Mothers* xi). When mourning cannot end, when it becomes anger that can never be erased from the mind, Loraux argues, "we see the ultimate justification for revenge, for the spirit of vendetta, for all the horrors of retaliation against earlier horrors" (xii). It becomes, she writes, the grief-wrath of *mênis,* the "worst enemy of politics" (98), that which clouds good judgment, eroding all considerations of justice, reciprocity, and even self-interest in favor of its own singular perspective. It is a mode of mourning inextricably associated with tragedy and, as such, not one to be emulated in a democracy lest it, too, befall similarly tragic fates. As the grief-wrath of Achilles over the death of Patroclus demonstrates, it is a mode of mourning which, while most obviously associated with women in Greek thought, is not confined to the feminine, but can infect the polity as a whole (Muellner), threatening to undermine democratic deliberation and good judgment.

It should, of course, be noted, that it was not grief *per se* that was the problem for the Greeks, but rather the *excess*—the grief without limits, the mourning without end. For the Greeks, any excess was a form of *hubris,* the quality most often associated with the protagonists of Athenian tragedy. Indeed, the philosopher Walter Kaufmann argues that *hubris* is best translated by contrasting it with "established usage, order, and right" and "moderation, temperance, [and] (self-) control" (64). In engaging in, or in failing to limit, such grief, the Greeks risked emulating the characters in Athenian tragedy. Indeed, Herodotus recounts how, after the performance of Phrynichus' play the *Capture of Miletus* reduced the audience—and thus, the city—to tears by reminding them of their defeat at the hands of the Persians, the Athenian Assembly fined the playwright and passed a law banning future use of the play. Thereafter Athenian tragedy would never again depict events that had affected its audience so directly—setting its stories in Ancient lands and the far-off past—in order to avoid the risk of drowning the democratic city in the tears of its citizens. It is here, perhaps, that the contrast between the literature of mourning—Ancient and contemporary—is most starkly drawn.

In his *Letters to a Young Journalist*, Samuel G. Freedman addressed the issue of "journalistic temperament" by recounting the visit of Mirta Ojito— one of the authors of the "Portraits of Grief" series—to his journalism class. "She told [them]," wrote Freedman, "about how she had cried over the phone as she spoke with the father of two daughters killed in the Twin Towers. She recalled going into the women's bathroom at the *Times* and finding a colleague there sobbing from the strain. Mirta understood that tears didn't undermine her as a journalist" (31). Similarly, Janny Scott described the process of writing the "Portraits" as "heartbreaking work." It was not only the producers of the series who were so affected. Numerous consumers also testified that they found the "Portraits" "heart-wrenching to read" (Friedman 255); that the "short profiles had touched the hearts of readers across the country" (Nacos 196); or that they had been "deeply moved" (Zinn 34). Indeed, describing how affected one had been by the series became a way of paying tribute to it. Most obviously this was demonstrated by the production of tears. "Never before in my forty-plus years as a reader," wrote Jack Bogdanski in a letter quoted in the "Introduction" to the collected "Portraits," "have I been moved to close my eyes, place my palm on the page of a newspaper, shed a tear, and say a prayer" (ix). Even Susan Sontag, who had earlier deplored the way in which "the politics of a democracy" had been "replaced by psychotherapy" (Sontag), felt obliged to share her reaction to the series. "I read the 'Portraits of Grief,' every last word, every single day," she wrote. "I was tremendously moved. I had tears in my eyes every morning" (Scott). The "Portraits," argued Thomas Mallon, "impelled their readers, time and again, to express their extravagant admiration" (7). In so doing, the tears and the testaments became themselves somewhat frenzied, an example of what Loraux—in the Greek context—calls "the pleasure of tears" (*Mothers* 10). Such frenzied pleasure was as evident in Sontag's luxuriating in "every last word, every single day," as it was in the near desperate demand—"Don't stop"—of *Oregonian* readers about to be deprived of the source of their perverse joy. It was in provoking, and indeed, seeking to provoke this reaction, that the series took on a pornographic form.

PORNOGRAPHY AND DEATH

Although the claims being made here about pornography and memorialization might simply seem to be a replication of the mode of calculated hyperbole previously ascribed to Ann Coulter, it is clear that pornography and death have been connected since Ancient times. As Walter Kendrick points out in his seminal work *The Secret Museum,* pornography was effectively invented in the nineteenth century during the attempts to catalogue the erotic artifacts discovered during the excavation of the Roman city of Pompeii. Placing the objects in a "secret museum" that was hidden from the general public—lest said public be corrupted by the images and artifacts—the guardians of public decency gave the items the name "pornography," a word which first appeared in print in English in the translation of German art historian C.O. Müller's *Handbuch de Archäologie der Kunst* (Kendrick 11). Although the Ancient Greeks— with their shockingly explicit comedic traditions—would, as Kendrick points out, "have had no idea what 'pornography' was supposed to mean" (x), the nineteenth-century neologism drew upon a Greek source—the word *pornographoi,* meaning "whore painter" (11). It is an etymology that immediately introduces the complex economy of prostitution in the Ancient world, one that is, perhaps, instructive when considering the problems of the pornographic mode of much of contemporary American public mourning.

There were at least two major categories of prostitutes in Ancient Athens: the "common whores" known as *pornai,* who openly advertised their wares and willingness to perform certain acts in written price lists; and the far more ambiguous *hetaerae,* for whom gifts were given in the hope—though not necessarily expectation—of companionship and sexual favors (Davidson). Both were linked with death. In the case of the *pornai,* the connection was geographical. The road out of Athens was lined—in an area known as the Ceramicus—with the monumental tombs of its notable fallen. In addition to being the location of Pericles's famous funeral oration, the Ceramicus was also the city's "red-light district." It had, says James Davidson, a reputation as an area "for quick and surreptitious sexual transactions" so much so that it was commonly identified as "a place in Athens where prostitutes (*pornai*) stood" (80). So closely linked were the extra-mural activities of mourning and whoring that the connection became something of a trope in Attic comedy: in Aristophanes' *The Acharnians,* the playwright reduces the causes of the Peloponnesian War to a dispute over prostitutes. A subgroup of the *pornai* known as the *aulētrides* were also linked with death and mourning through the *aulos,* a double-reeded flute that they used to draw attention to themselves and to entertain at the symposia. These *aulētrides* or "flute girls" were among the cheapest and most despised of all Greek prostitutes, despite, or perhaps because, their music was said to be inordinately beguiling. The intimate connection between the beguiling power of the flute and the equally—if not more—beguiling power of grief lies in the etymology of the word "elegy." Arising from the Greek *elogoi,* the couplets traditionally accompanied by the *aulos,* the earliest meaning of "elegy" was "flute song of grief" (Gilbert 120). The *hetaerae* were, of course, most famously connected to death via *Aspasia,* Pericles's mistress, to whom Plato ascribes the funeral oration in the *Menexenus.* The danger of such women—and indeed, of such grief—to the democratic process was, for the Greeks, the incitement to excess.

Inscribed at Delphi was a statement that has been translated as both "Remember your mortality" and "Nothing in excess" (Euben 17). The close connection between these two concepts suggests the way in which, for the Greeks, excess was associated with death. In the case of tragedy, death was itself often the product of the *mênis* generated by excessive grief, itself a form of *hubris*. Davidson further suggests that *hubris* was also intimately associated with sex, more specifically with *bought* sex, indeed, the etymology of *pornai* arises from the verb *pernēme,* which means "to buy." "For the Greeks," he writes, "sex becomes *hubris* when it is reduced to an impersonal activity, a mere commodity, sex that means nothing, rather than sex which reflects mutual attachment" (117). As such, the *pornai* met Aristotle's definition of sexual incontinence—involving the wrong people, the wrong time, and the wrong places (Davidson 167). Those who engaged with the *pornai* were themselves likely to become like the man described by Socrates in the *Gorgias,* one who spends his life "itching and scratching." "Is it possible to live life happily constantly scratching an itch?" asks Socrates, knowing full well, as ever, the answer (Plato 281). Such a man is, says Davidson, a *kinaidos,* a sexual incontinent, who leads "the life of endless pleasure, the leaky vessel, the supreme example of appetite unbridled" (173). For, although such a man pursues pleasure endlessly, he is, as Socrates notes, destined never to achieve happiness: his quest becomes endless, his desire always prolonged, but never ultimately satiated, no matter how many his sexual encounters. In this the *pornai*—and the flute girls in particular—become symbols of an insatiable and destructive obsession, one that mirrors the destructive and endless grief-wrath of *mênis*. Indeed, the two intersect most obviously when Xenophon describes Athens' defeat— itself a product of a certain *hubris, mênis,* and lack of judgment—in the Peloponnesian War. He recounts how the city's walls were pulled down to the musical accompaniment of the flute girls: the polity laid low by the kind of indulgence that Socrates ascribes to the eternally scratching man. It is an example that vividly suggests the dangers to democracy of a pornographic mode of mourning that destroys its capacity for balanced deliberation.

PORNOGRAPHY AND GRIEF

It was, as has been observed, something of a trope among those writing about, and falling over themselves to praise, the "Portraits of Grief" series to note their own tears. In this, it might be argued, the series was something of a "melodrama." Certainly in their depiction of the innocence of the 9/11 victims, Ward Churchill notwithstanding, the "Portraits of Grief" series shares much with the melodramatic mode that has, as Elisabeth Anker points out, shaped much of the public response to September 11. The connection between melodrama and pornography is, however, a close one. Building on the work of Carol Glover, Linda Williams has called pornography, melodrama, and horror, "body genres," arguing, "the success of these genres seems a self-evident matter of measuring bodily response." Indeed, in the case of pornography, Williams notes the "peter meter" capsules in *Hustler* magazine which measure the power of a porn film in degrees of erection of little cartoon penises, and in melodrama, the long-standing tradition of measuring the success of "women's films" in terms of one-, two-, or three handkerchief movies ("Bodies" 730). The success of the "Portraits of Grief" series—among both producers and consumers alike—seems to have been measured in tears, the bodily fluid more commonly associated with melodrama than pornography. Nevertheless, what seems to distinguish the response generated by the "Portraits of Grief" series from melodrama is that the latter must, by necessity, have an end in order that the righteous get their reward and the evil doers get punished; the "Portraits in Grief" series, in both style, and intent, seems, however, to be committed to the endless mourning of *álaston pénthos,* to the claim that "We will never forget."

Central to the endlessness of the mourning engendered by the "Portraits of Grief" series is its fundamental *repetitiveness*. Although Wendell Jameson, a series editor, observed that the individual portraits "all had to be different. If they all started off the same way readers wouldn't read them" (Warner 77), it is clear that many of them demonstrate a fundamental similarity, not least, as David Warner points out, because of the similar demographics of the victims. "The challenge," observed Tina Kelley, a *Times* staff writer, "is to make your 12th employee of the same company or agency stand out . . . doing research I found two fire fighters from West Islip. In a city like this you're going to get a lot of diehard Yankees and Mets fans" (Warner 79). The universally positive depiction of the dead—in which "anyone depressed over his weight became a 'gentle giant' and every binge drinker was the life of the party" (Mallon 7)—added to the sameness of the portraits, with any possible differences smoothed away by the need to reflect positively upon the deceased. Echoing Socrates's similar critique in the *Menexenus,* Thomas Mallon observed of the "Portraits": "these squibs were, in the end, less about their ostensible subjects than about the people reading them. But insofar as they had to do with grief, it was a feel-good, aren't-I-sensitive grief: manageably poignant, and no doubt useful in reaching 'closure,' as we like to say in America" (6). Although Mallon would seem to be correct about the "pleasure of tears" implicit in the "Portraits," and, indeed, about the suggestion that they are more about the readers than the subjects—as Walter Kendrick observes, the term "whore painter" from which "pornographer" is drawn is ambiguous about on which end of the brush the whore is to be found (13)—he is, nevertheless, mistaken about the "closure" allegedly offered by the series. The ubiquity of the term "closure" in the discourse of American mourning should, however, perhaps indicate the ironic and endless repetition of the term in our broader public discourse, something which itself suggests the pleasure that emerges from the repetition and endless deferral of the satiation it claims to identify. It is a pleasure that, as Zabet Patterson points out, is intimately associated with the pornographic. Building on Williams's claims about pornography as a "body genre," Patterson extends the claim of the pornographic to encompass the pleasure that emerges from "the deferral of satisfaction itself" (109). In this sense, it is—in part at least—the endless repetition and deferral of satisfaction that may generate much of the pleasure in the pornographic even—as Ara Osterweil points out—to the point of boredom. The user, writes Patterson, "constantly shifts on to new images . . . in an endless slippage of desire in which part of the pleasure derives from habitual repetition and habitual deferral" (110).

The editorial decisions that shaped the "Portraits of Grief" series further served to accentuate its pornographic qualities. "I'm convinced," wrote editor Howell Raines in his "Foreword" to the collection, "that the core of the portraits' appeal lies in our metropolitan desk's decision to cast these stories as snapshots of lives interrupted as they were actively being lived, rather than in the traditional obituary form" (vii). In identifying the "appeal" of the "Portraits," Raines echoes his colleagues Wendell Jameson and Tina Kelley, suggesting a clear desire among the series' authors to make the individual portraits attractive to the reader—to engage the reader as a means of generating tears. Another of the writers—Jan Hoffman—observed that writing the portraits was "an experience of falling in love and then having your heart broken every single time" (Mallon 7). It was not enough simply to catalogue the dead, as in previous individual memorializations; the dead had to be made attractive to the living in a kind of emotional necrophilia. In this, the writers deliberately sought to engender the kind of emotional response that Greek democrats so feared.

Like pornography then, the "Portraits" offer a multitude of possibilities for the physical expression of stimulation that they seek to generate—in this case tears—and one in which there is a deferral of satisfaction for the insatiable reader, be she Susan Sontag or the readers of *The Oregonian*. Like the leaky vessel in Plato's *Gorgias,* they offer the life of the man who is always scratching but is never satiated, a parallel that invokes the etymology of the word "prurient," whose earliest use, the Oxford English Dictionary reminds us, is of scratching an itch. Lest this claim seem too excessive—too *hubristic* itself—we might also note the quasi-sexual language with which the reaction of some of the readers of the series was described. Certainly it does not take too much of a leer to regard Janny Scott's account of the rituals of reading the series as being rife with masturbational connotations. Noting that for many the series became a ritual—perhaps even a compulsion—that was observed in a variety of locations including "before computer screens late at night," Scott notes that one woman told the *Times* that without reading them "she found she could not drop off to sleep at night" (ix). The series also appeared to provide comfort to Charles Zachary Bornstein, a symphony orchestra conductor who "lives in Fairfield, Connecticut, and performs around the world," who e-mailed the *Times* demanding that they collect the series as a book. "It would be one that I would always travel with for the rest of my life," wrote Bornstein, "as there is something consoling to know these people, each out of the mass" (x). The suggestion that such a collection might provide consolation for the lonely professional traveler in hotel rooms around the world would, perhaps, be enough to raise eyebrows, even without the further connotation of his desire "to know" these people more intimately. In this, perhaps, the strangely pornographic qualities of the "Portraits of Grief" find their most troubling expression.

THE AMERICAN OB/ON/SCENE

The claim that America's dominant mode of representation in mourning is pornographic would be more *genuinely* shocking—as opposed to the faux cries of outrage that such a mode generates at the first sign of criticism, faux cries that, perhaps, unconsciously echo the exaggerated and faux cries of passion implicit in the pornographic—if pornography were not already a dominant mode of representation in American life. In this, perhaps, the pornography of grief is itself simply a disturbing subset of a much more pervasive turn to pornography in American culture. In May 2001, during the period of alleged "American innocence" prior to 9/11, *New York Times* columnist Frank Rich pointed out that Americans spent some $4.2 *billion* a year on pornographic video sales and rentals. His figures were for the year 1998, when Internet porn contributed only one-fifth of all porn revenues; nearly ten years later the figures are likely to be considerably higher. As Rich pointed out, this 1998 figure did not take into consideration the between $10 and $14 billion dollars spent on pay-per-view movies in hotels, on cable, and via satellite, or the dollars spent on phone-sex, sex toys, and magazines. Even at the low-end of the estimate, Rich notes, "pornography is a bigger business than professional football, basketball and baseball put together." In this, suggests Rich, pornography in the United States in no longer a sideshow: it is the mainstream. Nevertheless, Rich observes, "So few Americans fess up when asked if they are watching adult product. . . . Porn is the one show that nobody watches but that, miraculously, never closes."

The point here is not to join Dinesh D'Souza, Jerry Falwell, or Pat Robertson in identifying those who preach tolerance and sexual frankness as the real cause of 9/11 (D'Souza, CNN), but rather to identify the peculiar tension in American life concerning the pornographic, a tension that also extends to the pornography of grief. Tracing the tangled history of pornography in the United States, Walter Kendrick notes, "It is ironic . . . that the land of the free should have occupied itself so obsessively with the menace of individual freedom" (124). Noting that the word "obscene" means "off-stage, or that which should be kept "out of public view," Linda Williams has coined the phrase "on/scenity" which she defines as "the gesture by which a culture brings on to its public arena the very organs, acts, bodies, and pleasures that have here-tofore been designated ob/scene and kept literally off scene" (*Porn Studies* 3). In so doing she recalls Foucault's "repressive hypothesis." "What is peculiar to modern societies," writes Foucault, "is not that they consigned sex to a shadow existence, but that they dedicated themselves to speaking of it *ad infinitum,* while exploiting it as *the* secret" (35). The tension, that is to say, between the shame and secrecy associated with the pornographic, shame and secrecy that fuels the "polymorphous incitement to discourse" (34), makes the pornographic a central part of our American public discourse, even as we pretend that it is hidden from public view.

In 1955, Geoffrey Gorer famously identified "The Pornography of Death." In the twentieth century, he noted, "whereas copulation has become more and more 'mentionable,' particularly in the Anglo-Saxon societies, death has become more and more 'unmentionable'" (195). Compared to the nineteenth century, death has become something to be hidden away, even as violent representations of death have "played an ever growing part in the fantasies offered to mass audiences—detective stories. Thrillers, Westerns, war stories, spy stories, science fiction, and eventually horror comics" (197). Identifying a similar dynamic to that identified in sex by Foucault, Gorer notes the pecu-liarity of this increasingly excessive exploitation of the secret of death. In the American context, argues Peter Euben, there is "a prototypical American way of dealing with death," that is "not dealing with it all" (111). Nevertheless, as the work of both Gorer and Foucault suggests, the act of not dealing with death, or its by-product, grief, may play itself out in an excessive and deeply conflicted fascination with the subject in the public sphere. In this sense, the pornography of grief embodied in the *New York Times*'s "Portraits of Grief" is a part of the broader pornography of death that has framed the depiction of the events of 9/11. That the images of 9/11, so widely disseminated during and in the days and weeks after 9/11, are now effectively hidden from us—with the major networks agreeing not to show their footage of the attacks except in specific, highly regulated circumstances—returns the attacks to the realm of the "secret museum" and the association between pornography and death with which the genre began. That the footage, and much else about 9/11, is, nevertheless, still available—like most other fetishes—via a quick Internet search, suggests that it is an American on/scene by Williams's defini-tion. Much the same might be said about the pornography of death implicit in *Portraits 9/11/01.*

THE PORNOGRAPHY OF GRIEF: LESSONS FROM THE PAST

Critics of the preceding claims might regard them as somewhat anachro-nistic, arising from the application of the categories drawn from an Ancient democracy to the institutions and practices of a post-Enlightenment republic.

The aim here is not, however, to hold up our current practices to those of the Ancients and to find them wanting, but rather to use these Greek traditions as a way of thinking through our current modes of memorialization. As Loraux observes in her *Divided City:* "it is . . . possible . . . that the far-off history of the Athenian democracy constitutes a valuable experimental terrain for helping us to think this present full of uncertainties" (245). Certainly the work of, among others, Hannah Arendt and Peter Euben suggests the value of this kind of theoretical exercise, not least because of the apparent reluctance of contemporary liberal-democratic theory to address the centrality of human mortality to the political (Seery). Certainly, the Greeks seem to have much to tell us about the value of certain memorialization practices to democratic government, most obviously about the value of placing limits upon public expressions of private grief, for it is clear that let loose upon the public sphere they can become insatiable and destructive. Pericles's failure was a failure to limit the desire for revenge among the Athenian citizenry, for revenge as opposed to justice is necessarily unbalanced and self-destructive. As with the man addicted to scratching in Plato's *Gorgias,* or the person addicted to pornography, the polity addicted to the pornography of grief can only demand more and more explicit material—that which is likely to distort the democratic process by making *mênis,* not careful deliberation our dominant mode. What began as a tradition of naming the individual dead as a way of bringing home the enormity of national tragedy—in the manner of Maya Lin's Vietnam Veterans' Memorial—has devolved into a self-defeating focus on the individual, both victim and viewer, that ultimately serves to erase the very thing it was supposed to remember, with the political now obscured by the personal.

In the years since 9/11, America has become involved in, at the time of writing, two wars, only one of which—the war in Afghanistan—can be plausibly linked to the terrorist attacks on America. That the Bush administration was able to exploit the individual and collective grief of the American people to elide the differences between Iraq and Afghanistan and to connect the former to the increasingly amorphous "war on terror," is, perhaps, evidence of the power of the grief-wrath of *mênis* to corrupt the careful and deliberate thought that democratic politics requires. With critical patriotism all but eclipsed by an empty nationalism, it is, perhaps, not too great a leap to suggest that the fetish of our remembrance embodied in the "Portraits of Grief" series has helped to fuel and promote this empty nationalism. Indeed, Despina Kakoudaki has traced an intimate connection between pornography and American militarism, one that encompasses both the World War II "pinup" to the explicitly pornographic (and often anti-Arab) "nose art" on U.S. aircraft during Operation Desert Storm. Indeed, she recounts the possibly apocryphal tale that a pinup of Rita Hayworth was attached to the nuclear bomb dropped on Hiroshima (343, 336n4). By way of parallel, Eugene Jarecki's 2005 documentary *Why We Fight* included the story of Wilton Sekzer, a retired New York City police officer who successfully lobbied the Pentagon to allow the name of his son—killed in the World Trade Center—to be written on a bomb dropped on Iraq. The unfortunate connection between an uncritical nationalism destructive of democracy, American militarism, and the pornography of grief finds, perhaps, its most poignant link in the "Portraits of Grief" series which includes the portrait of a Jason Sekzer, a 31-year-old, married employee of Cantor Fitzgerald, the son of a New York City Police officer (549), and in Wilton Sekzer's own second thoughts about his actions following President Bush's retraction of the long-asserted connection between Iraq and 9/11 (Jarecki).

In adding his voice to the chorus of praise for the "Portraits of Grief" series, David Warner congratulated the editors of the *New York Times*. "Whoever winds up creating a memorial on the site of the World Trade Center could do worse," he wrote, "than to take a page from their book" (85). Paradoxically, perhaps, the *New York Times* seems to disagree. In December 2006, the long debate about how to group the names on the 9/11 memorial in New York City seemed to have finally been resolved. In January of 2007, however, a small group of victims' families mounted a campaign against the compromise decision, demanding that the memorial list the age, corporate affiliation, and floor upon which each person worked. They would, they said, discourage contributions to the already considerably delayed memorial until their demands had been met. In a January 29, 2007, editorial, the *New York Times* came out against the families, arguing:

> [G]round zero cannot be turned into a private memorial. If Cantor Fitzgerald, for example, feels it is important to create its own separate memorial to its terrible loss on that day, it should certainly do so. But a public memorial must be more expansive than that. There is a stark beauty and essential simplicity to the proposed listing of names as it now stands. It honors the nature of public memory. . . . As painful as the private loss of this small group of mourners is, it must be accommodated as part of the larger public loss (*Times* "Public Memorial").

Having played a significant role in promoting this pornography of grief, the *New York Times* now seems concerned to stop it. That pornography is now a dominant perspective—literary, cultural, and political—in the representation of 9/11, and that its consumers are apparently insatiable, suggests that they will be unsuccessful. As with Athens, perhaps, the beguiling flute songs of grief threaten to distract us from the careful deliberation that democracy requires, and our misleading laments now bode ill for the polity.

NOTES

1. The author is grateful to the editors of this volume for their helpful comments upon earlier drafts; to Ara Osterweil and Libby Anker for their invaluable discussions of pornography and melodrama respectively; to Tim Delaune

for his insightful comments on the AIDS Quilt and memorialization; and especially to Cheryl Hall for her helpful criticism of a paper whose central argument she rejects. Finally, he wishes to thank the students in the spring 2007 seminar "The Politics of Death and Mourning" at the College of William and Mary for their illuminating discussions of these and other topics. The views expressed here, along with any mistakes, are, of course, his own.

2. There were subsequent sets of profiles published on December 8, 2002, and March 9, 2003.

WORKS CITED

"A Public Memorial." Editorial. *New York Times* 29 Jan, 2007.

Anderson, Benedict. *Imagined Communities.* New York: Verso, 1991.

Anker, Elisabeth. "Villains, Victims and Heroes: Melodrama, Media, and September 11." *Journal of Communication* 55 (2005): 22–37.

Arendt, Hannah. *Eichmann in Jerusalem: A Report on the Banality of Evil.* New York: Penguin, 2006.

Bush, George, W. "President's Remarks at National Day of Prayer and Remembrance September 14, 2001." 12/15/2006 http://www.whitehouse.gov/news/releases/2001/09/20010914–2.html.

Churchill, Ward. "Some People Push Back: On the Justice of Roosting Chickens." 12/15/2006 http://www.kersplebedeb.com/mystuff/s11/churchill.html.

CNN. "Falwell Apologizes to gays, feminists, lesbians." CNN.com 14 Sept. 2001. 15 Jan. 2007 http://archives.cnn.com/2001/US/09/14/Falwell.apology/.

Coulter, Ann. *Godless. The Church of Liberalism.* New York: Crown Forum, 2006.

Davidson, James. *Courtesans & Fishcakes: The Consuming Patterns of Classical Athens.* New York: Harper Perennial, 1997.

D'Souza, Dinesh. *The Enemy at Home: The Cultural Left and Its Responsibility for 9/11.* New York: Doubleday, 2007.

"Editors' Note." *New York Times* 5 Oct. 2002.

Euben, J. Peter. *Platonic Noise.* Princeton: Princeton UP, 2003.

Foucault, Michel. *The History of Sexuality.* Vol. 1. Trans. Robert Hurley. New York: Vintage, 1990.

Freedman, Samuel F. *Letters to a Young Journalist.* New York: Basic, 2006.

Friedman, Sonya, and C.B. de Swaan. *Take it From Her: Growing Up, Getting Real, And Moving On.* New York: Kensington, 2004.

Gilbert, Sandra M. *Death's Door: Modern Dying and the Ways We Grieve.* New York: Norton, 2006.

Goodman, Florence Jeanne. "Pericles at Gettysburg." *The Midwest Quarterly* 6 (1965): 311–36.

Gorer, Geoffrey. *Death, Grief, and Mourning in Contemporary Britain.* New York: Doubleday, 1965.

Herodotus. *The Histories.* London: Penguin, 2003.

Jarecki, Eugene, dir. *Why We Fight.* Sony Classics, 2005.

Kakoudaki, Despina. "Pinup: The American Secret Weapon in World War II." *Porn Studies.* Ed. Linda Williams. Durham: Duke UP, 2004. 335–69.

Kaufmann, Walter. *Tragedy and Philosophy.* Princeton: Princeton UP, 1968.

Kendrick, Walter. *The Secret Museum: Pornography in Modern Culture.* 2nd ed. Berkeley: U of California P, 1996.

Langewiesche, William. *American Ground: Unbuilding the World Trade Center.* New York: Farrar, Straus and Giroux, 2002.

Lincoln, Abraham. "The Gettysburg Address." *Speeches and Writings 1859–1865*. New York: Library of America, 1989.

Loraux, Nicole. *The Divided City: On Memory and Forgetting in Ancient Athens*. Trans. Corrine Pache with Jeff Fort. New York: Zone, 2002.

———. *The Invention of Athens: The Funeral Oration in the Classical City*. Trans. Alan Sheridan. Cambridge: Harvard UP, 1986.

———. *Mothers in Mourning*. Trans. Corrine Pache. Ithaca: Cornell UP, 1998.

Lower Manhattan Development Corporation. *World Trade Center Memorial Competition Guidelines*. New York: Lower Manhattan Development Corporation, 2003.

Mallon, Thomas. "The Mourning Paper." *The American Scholar* 7.2 (2002): 5–8.

Mueller, Leonard. *The Anger of Achilles: Mênis in Greek Epic*. Ithaca: Cornell UP, 1996.

Nacos, Brigitte Lebens. *Mass Mediated Terrorism: The Central Role of the Media in Terrorism and Counter Terrorism*. Lanham: Rowman & Littlefield, 2002.

Names Project. *The Aids Memorial Quilt*. 12/31/06 http://www.aidsquilt.org/index.htm.

New York Times. *Portraits: 9/11/01. The Collected "Portraits of Grief" from the New York Times*. New York: Times Books, 2002.

New York Times. *Portraits: 9/11/01. The Collected "Portraits of Grief" from the New York Times*. 2nd ed. New York: Times Books, 2003.

Osterweil, Ara. "Andy Warhol's *Blow Job:* Toward the Recognition of the Pornographic Avant-garde." *Porn Studies*. Ed. Linda Williams. Durham: Duke UP, 2004. 431–60.

Paterson, Zabet. "Going On-line: Consuming Pornography in the Digital Era." *Porn Studies*. Ed. Linda Williams. Durham: Duke UP, 2004. 104–23.

Pentagon Memorial Project. *Pentagon Memorial*. 12/31/06 http://memorial.pentagon.mil/default.htm.

Plato. *Euthyphro, Apology, Crito, Meno, Gorgias, Menexenus: Dialogues of Plato, Vol. 1*. Trans. R.E. Allen. New Haven: Yale UP, 1989.

Rich, Frank. "Naked Capitalists." *New York Times Magazine* 20 May, 2001.

Scott, Janny. "A Nation Challenged: The Portraits, Closing a Scrapbook Full of Life and Sorrow." *New York Times* 31 Dec. 2001: B6.

Seery, John. *Political Theory for Mortals: Shades of Justice, Images of Death*. Ithaca: Cornell UP, 1996.

Sontag, Susan. "Talk of the Town." *New Yorker* 24 Sept. 2001: 32.

Stow, Simon. "Pericles at Gettysburg and Ground Zero: Tragedy, Patriotism, and Public Mourning." *American Political Science Review* 101 (2007): 195–208.

Thucydides. *History of the Peloponnesian War*. Trans. Rex Warner. London: Penguin, 1972.

"Victims live in our hearts." Editorial. *Boston Herald* 1 Jan. 2002: 20.

Warner, David. "Fanfare for the Common Man." *Articles* 8 (2002): 72–85.

Williams, Linda. "Film Bodies: Gender, Genre, and Excess." *Film Theory and Criticism*. 6th ed. Ed. Leo Braudy and Marshall Cohen. New York: Oxford UP, 2004. 727–41.

———. "Porn Studies: Proliferating Pornographies On/Scene: An Introduction." *Porn Studies*. Ed. Linda Williams. Durham: Duke UP, 2004. 1–23.

Wills, Garry. *Lincoln at Gettysburg: The Words that Remade America*. New York: Simon & Schuster, 1989.

Zinn, Howard. *Terrorism and War*. New York: Seven Stories, 2002.

12 Theater after 9/11

Robert Brustein

In an ominous coincidence, the terrorist attacks on the World Trade Center and the Pentagon occurred around the beginning of the Second Millennium, a time traditionally associated with Apocalypse. In a slightly less apocalyptic synchronism, September 11 also coincides with the beginning of every new theater season. Not that Broadway wants to know. Rather than acknowledge the threats and fevers of our times, the terror that now enshrouds our lives, the commercial stage has been conscientiously devoted to manufacturing escapism and obscurantism, through witless entertainments and irrelevant revivals. In September alone, with the war in Iraq in its third year and Hurricane Katrina continuing to dominate the headlines, the *New York Times* Arts and Leisure section announced new musicals about "trailer trash singing show tunes" (*The Great American Trailer Park*), about "a single guy looking for sex" (*Slut*), about a romance between "a musician with Tourette's syndrome and a journalist with an obsessive-compulsive disorder" (*In My Life*), about "a love triangle involving [Alfred Kinsey], his wife and his lab assistant" (*Dr. Sex*), plus another edition of Elaine Stritch's favorite show tunes. Revivals of *The Fantasticks, The Odd Couple, The Pajama Game, The Caine Mutiny Court-Martial, Carrie,* and *Peter Pan,* among other choice tidbits from our showbiz past, are some of the blockbusters promised in the future.

I am as fond of nostalgia and escapism as the next guy, but it is a pity that the commercial stage is failing its opportunity to provide some understanding of our predicament. You would think that Broadway could stir itself over the catastrophe of Hurricane Katrina more vigorously and imaginatively than those worthy curtain speeches by stars asking patrons for disaster relief. As an example of how deftly theater can adapt itself to current events, I refer you to the recently closed revival of *Two Gentlemen of Verona* (the musical version in Central Park) where John Guare, changing only twenty-nine words of the Duke's "Bring All the Boys Back Home" number, transformed it into a rousing commentary on Bush's military and economic failures ("If we didn't have a war / Then where / Would we spend our money / Where / Welfare, Clean Air, Child Care"). It made us aware how some of those failures now poison the flotsam in the flooded streets of New Orleans.

Since the theater is a barometer of how people behave and feel at any given moment in history, I suppose even mindless entertainment says something about how the events of September 11, the Iraq War, and now the disasters in Louisiana and Mississippi have affected the American mind. What it tells us is that when Bush comes to shove, we want to bury our heads in warm sand. It is often noted that the modern stage is out of touch with the deeper concerns and impulses of the society. Even our theater's "serious" themes, notably sexual, ethnic, and racial identity, are of less immediate concern to the theatergoing public (those in blue states included) than to people who work in the profession. How else do we explain the large number of one-person shows by gays and lesbians, and their preoccupation with their not-so-private parts?

This disjunction between stage and audience may help to explain why public interest in the stage is dwindling. At the same time that Broadway, when not recycling popular movies in musical form (*The Lion King, The Producers, Monty Python's Spamalot*), is busy pondering the tribulations of gay baseball players and teenage spelling bee nerds, the rest of the country is worrying about terrorism, body counts, the environment, nuclear proliferation, poverty, the mismanagement of the economy, the futility of the Iraq War, and all the other pressing issues botched by Bush.

Luckily, there is a dramatic world elsewhere, namely not-for-profit theater venues. These are proving somewhat more hospitable to new plays examining significant national themes. And we should be encouraged by a detectable rise in the quality, ambition, and pertinence of the American theater during the time of our many trials. It is true that the resident theater movement, once the great hope for a more adventurous alternative to the commercial stage, lost some of its original spunk after the evisceration of the National Endowment for the Arts caused a precipitous drop-off in public and private funding. It is also true that too often off-Broadway, instead of discovering exciting new talent, seems to be looking for ways to move safe products to the Great White Way.

Still, these last three years were a period when there were as many intelligent and gifted artists writing for the stage as ever before in our history: Tony Kushner, August Wilson, Craig Lucas, Paula Vogel, Suzan-Lori Parks, Richard Nelson, Charles L. Mee, Jr., John Patrick Shanley, Sarah Ruhl, Rebecca Gilman, Doug Wright, Stephen Adly Guirgis, Paul Rudnick, Adam Rapp, Tracy Letts—this is a partial list. And they were fashioning plays that were not just limited domestic dramas, but sometimes deep probes into the social and political issues of the time.

It was also a period when American directors, led by Robert Wilson, Andrei Serban, Anne Bogart, Robert Woodruff, and many others—following in the footsteps of the great European auteurs like Peter Brook and Ingmar Bergman—were continuing their audacious investigations of great classical and modern drama. (And, sadly, it was also a time when we lost some of our most valued artists, notably Arthur Miller and August Wilson in playwriting,

Marlon Brando in acting, Susan Sontag, who both directed and wrote for the stage, and Arnold Weinstein, a great librettist and lyricist.)

It is often said that the Al Qaeda attacks on September 11, 2001, created a national trauma as profound as any event in our history. The last several years of American theater have directly or indirectly exposed that psychic wound through its choice of themes, characters, and mood. Unlike Pearl Harbor, which unified the country and stimulated an outburst of anti-Axis sentiment, most American playwrights have been slow to confront directly the repercussions of September 11. In the 1940s, all our leading Broadway dramatists—Robert Sherwood (*There Shall Be No Night*), Lillian Hellman (*Watch on the Rhine*), Maxwell Anderson (*The Eve of St. Mark*), S. N. Behrman (*No Time For Comedy*), among others—were rushing to compose patriotic plays in support of the war effort. And there were innumerable Hollywood movies promoting it as well, usually starring John Wayne and Ronald Reagan. The Al Qaeda attacks produced a lot of bumper stickers and the Patriot Act. Although they initially unified the nation, those attacks did not produce a lasting form of patriotism, largely because of growing doubts about the credibility of our enterprise in Iraq. As for the American theater, this traditionally liberal arena has remained deeply suspicious of the present administration and its propaganda apparatus, especially after it became clear that Iraq had no weapons of mass destruction or any links with Al Qaeda (that is, until the invasion turned Iraq into a breeding ground for terrorism).

Perhaps it is for that reason that the theater did not show much interest in the conduct of the Iraq War. As for Hollywood, it has produced nothing about the present conflict as cogent as, say, David O. Russell's movie *Three Kings*, in 1999, which dramatized the tragic results of America's broken promises during the first Iraqi invasion. Where the war gets most attention is on the television comedy circuit, particularly in the monologues of Jon Stewart, Bill Maher, and Lewis Black.

But a handful of playwrights are just now beginning to examine the effects of September 11 on our national psyches. Tony Kushner wrote a play called *Homebody/Kabul* before the attacks even took place, which evoked the sense of rootlessness and displacement in Afghanistan. Another prescient work, *Terrorism*, by two Siberians called the Presnyakov Brothers, also written before the attacks on New York, extended the metaphor of terror to our daily lives. *Omnium Gatherum* by Theresa Rebeck and Alexandra Gersten-Vassilaros was the first play to focus on the victims of the World Trade Center attack, through the agency of an infernal dinner party, where the dead debate the motives behind September 11 and even invite a terrorist to join the conversation.

It was not long before other playwrights were taking the temperature of the United States following our incursion into Iraq and our brutal treatment of those interned in Guantanamo and Abu Ghraib. Sam Shepard's *The God of Hell* represented a powerful indictment of how our conduct toward prisoners abroad was influencing government behavior at home. (The British also weighed in with such entries as David Hare's *Stuff Happens* and *Guantanamo: Honor Bound to Defend Freedom.*) In short, after a long period when American political theater was primarily devoted to issues of social injustice and unequal opportunities regarding women, gays and lesbians, blacks, Latinos, and other minorities, it is now beginning to look outward as well, examining our responsibilities toward the world.

It is probable that the catastrophes on our native soil have encouraged us once again to think globally rather than locally. After September 11, we lost a lot of our innocence, not to mention our belief in American invincibility. After Abu Ghraib and Guantanamo, we lost a considerable amount of our moral authority, not to mention our certitude about the righteousness of our cause. After Hurricane Katrina, in a terrifying example of how bad policies can reinforce natural calamities, we lost more of our faith in our government. The American theater is perfectly positioned to chronicle this national unease. A play that provokes pity and terror is not incompatible with a night on the town.

(2006)

13 Real Planes and Imaginary Towers

Philip Roth's *The Plot Against America* as 9/11 Prosthetic Screen

Charles Lewis

History claims everybody.

—Philip Roth

Philip Roth's *The Plot Against America* (2004) is a counterfactual historical novel about Charles A. Lindbergh's 1940 presidential election defeat of Franklin Roosevelt. Although this work makes no reference to September 11, 2001, or its aftermath, Roth has given his reader an alternative past that, in both its divergence from historical fact and its resonance with the present, poses a number of intriguing questions about its connection with 9/11. This relation, in turn, not only speaks to what we might mean by post-9/11 literature more generally, but it also carries us even further beyond Ground Zero to the question of reading fiction in reference to any historical event or context. Roth's novel repeatedly and variously puts his reader on post-9/11 alert, as it were, and many of the early reviews of *The Plot Against America* pointed to its historical, thematic, and figurative evocations for the post-9/11 reader.[1] Just as intelligence gathering before and after 9/11 has sought to identify and interpret the evidence in the "chatter" regarding terrorist threats, the reader of Roth's novel can sift through the fiction to detect and decipher a pattern of signals linking the novel to 9/11 and the Bush administration's response to it in the ensuing years.

However, the novel's considerable achievement as a compelling and convincingly realistic depiction of America in the 1940s should caution us against reading this work as pasteboard allegory; indeed, instead of requiring us to choose between these seemingly incompatible claims, the novel challenges us to see that it is *because* of Roth's realistic rendering of an imagined history that the novel offers us a lesson about fiction's role as a conductor between one historical period and another. Many readers have sensed, as has Paul Berman, that it is "as if a second novel, something from our own time, had been locked inside and was banging furiously on the walls, trying to get out" (15), while J. M. Coetzee has similarly wondered, "So what is the relation of his story to the real world? What is his book 'about'?" (4). However, Berman's "something from our own time" is not necessarily the same thing as Coetzee's "real world," and when still another reader can argue (as has Walter Benn Michaels[2]) that the book is so convincing in part because those events *did* happen—not to Jews but to African-Americans—we can begin to see that this novel does indeed present us with a complex set of authorial intentions, historical facts, fictional formations, and reader responses.

The Plot Against America is very much a novel about fear and memory in relation to the traumatic events that Roth imagines occurring between 1940 and 1942. In the novel, Lindbergh wins the presidency on an isolationist platform, keeps America out of the war with Hitler, and presides over an administration whose domestic programs and policies increasingly echo the early years in Nazi Germany. The causes and consequences of these events, their historical resonance, and the appropriate response to them are all the subject of much anguish and debate among the family, friends, and neighbors of the young Jewish protagonist and narrator from Newark, Philip Roth. Their lives begin to fall apart as they navigate the gathering homeland storm of an anti-Semitism that becomes more overt (as in the Roth family trip to Washington) and then violent across the country (even to the point of precipitating the imposition of martial law). Jews begin to emigrate abroad and accept relocation at home, even as the characters continue to wonder: Could it happen here? Is it happening? How do we interpret these events in relation to what has happened before? These questions, however, constitute more than the very real and immediate dilemma for the characters in Roth's fiction. Nor are they just the stuff of counterfactual speculation about the distant past for the reader, insofar as the recurring theme of "never before" in the novel fictionally anticipates and even potentially revises our own understanding of 9/11. Indeed, the novel serves as a kind of 9/11 replacement narrative, in which the reader encounters a familiar topography projected onto the fictional screen, as it were, of an imagined past standing in for historical fact. We can detect and decipher this coincidental relation by exploring how the literal presence of prosthesis *in* the novel offers a trope for reading the novel *as* a prosthetic device.

Philip's cousin Alvin goes off to fight with the Canadians against the Nazis and returns with one leg missing, and Philip is variously horrified by and filled with wonder at Alvin's stump and his prosthetic limb. Alvin's loss and its replacement, as well as Philip's response to it, are part of a larger pattern in the novel in which the (mostly male) characters' experiences of humiliation, damage, or trauma are intricately bound up with novelistic formations of projection, displacement, and substitution. Sometimes these are novelistic conventions involving character doubling, as when Philip is terrified about having his hapless neighbor Seldon Wishnow wear his own clothes or Philip's father is variously linked to Little Robert, the legless beggar who loiters outside his father's office. This doubling is largely a function of Philip's finding himself shuttling between memories about the past and fears about the future, as the present becomes increasingly difficult for him to inhabit or understand. Characters, objects, and events start standing in for each other, most notably in his dreams and fevered illnesses, but also as real events accelerate around him, replacing or altering what he knows with something else he also knows, as when his stamp collection is transformed in his dreams into a series of Nazi inscriptions, he finds his brother Sandy's forbidden portraits of Lindbergh hidden under the bed, or he sees his own aunt on news footage at the Lindbergh White House.

Alvin's limb and this series of screenlike surfaces (stamps, drawings, and movie newsreels) together constitute a pattern of prosthetic substitution resulting from a traumatic relation to the real. In this way the novel offers a self-reflexive trope for reading its relation to 9/11: as a prosthetic screen, a substitute surface that both registers the traumatic consequence of that event and stands in as the projected realization of it. Instead of giving us a "real" 9/11 novel (in some literal or conventional sense), Roth has fabricated a replacement narrative manifestly attached to the stump of a distant historical past but whose connection to more recent events also suggests that the author's fictional "recollection" resembles one of the transmogrified "dream stamps" in the collection of his (identically named) protagonist.

Although not nearly so much as a novel like *Operation Shylock* and with a seemingly more conventional and realistic visage, *The Plot Against America* is nevertheless wrapped in a kind of historiographic scaffolding. Roth selects and then diverges from a pivotal event of twentieth-century world history, he gives us characters who are themselves given to discussions about the subject of history, and he offers various meditations on personal and collective memory. He uses his own name for his fictional protagonist, but he chooses to provide extensive historical documentation in the postscript to underscore the differences between fact and fiction. Like many of his postmodern peers (whose work is sometimes described as historiographic metafiction[3]), Roth directs our attention toward questions about history and fiction—even to the point of suggesting that at least in part the novel is significantly "about" them. Still, Roth's realistic texturing, psychological acuity, and even historical plausibility resist a reading that would portray the novel as either a telegraphed polemic about "History" or a transparent allegory about a particular historical event.

It is also important to note that Roth's realist narrative is itself stamped in what we might call dreamscaped dyes and textures—not only the literal dreaming in the novel (which is extensive), but also the way in which real events and Philip's response to them (especially the working of memory and fear) resemble dreamwork operations such as substitution, displacement, or projection. Although Philip's dreams are ostensibly bound to the counterfactual events fictionalized here, this imaginary past is itself analogously dredged up and forged out of memories and fears grounded in something more recent, for we are told at the outset that a "perpetual fear" (1) presides in the present-day mind of the adult narrator named Philip Roth. We learn almost nothing about this present fear, however, for the fears that infuse the dreams and memories of the novel are manifestly tied to the perspective and plight of childhood in Roth's use of a narrator whose point of view formally poses key questions about the relationship between the past and present (the adult narrator recollects a childhood memory) and between historical fact and novelistic fiction (the narrator is named Philip Roth).

Just as "fear" is the first word of the novel, "prosthesis" is the last, a figure not only for the narrator to describe himself in that final line, but also for the reader to grab hold of a novel that, although attached to the historical past of America in the 1940s, also stands in (what Art Spiegelman has called) "the shadow of no towers" and the trauma of our own time. For what might be described as a sort of "aftermath effect" of this novel is oddly prefigured not solely by the appearance of the "horrible wonder" of the Lindbergh story in Roth's imagination but by its *disappearance*. Although ostensibly the centerpiece of the narrative, Lindbergh's presence is ultimately denied us, as the phantom president vanishes into the air and this one nightmare of history collapses at the end of the novel and dissolves without a trace, except in the childhood memories of a contemporary narrator whose world looks just like ours. The traumatic events depicted here have no palpable lasting impact on world history since then, which suggests a kind of forgetting that resembles the absence of the absence, as it were, of more recent events that similarly seem to have made our own world not quite like itself. Unlike more conventionally or literally Ground Zero narratives about that day and its aftermath (or, conversely, their allegorical counterparts), Roth's novel suggests how artfully and powerfully fiction can variously realize a "sacrifice of relations" (to invoke Henry James) and yet register how "never before" can reverberate between a distant future and a recent past.

A prosthetic reading of *The Plot Against America* along these lines could draw on a rich and varied body of work in the areas of trauma, memory, and even disability studies.[4] And yet while we would expect that many interpretations of 9/11 literature would build on these critical frameworks, it is also important to consider how the latter might offer us a way to clarify—or complicate—the question of *which* literary works we might include under this 9/11 rubric. For the novel genre alone, the distinction between what we might mean by "9/11 literature" and "literature after 9/11" would seem to open up an expanse beyond Ground Zero as seemingly endless as the notion of a "war on terror." Since 9/11 we have witnessed the publication of dozens of novels whose readers have felt compelled to cite 9/11 as a point of reference. Admittedly, we would want to consider distinctions among, for example, the claim that a novel is "about" 9/11, the proposition that a novel has been influenced by 9/11, and the observation that readers might be interested in a novel because of 9/11.[5] Indeed, any inventory of 9/11 literature could be neither stable, exclusive, nor exhaustive, especially as that date becomes more distant and its consequences continue to unfold.

Put differently, while we might desire to assign some sort of definition or description of literary works in terms of their "proximity to" Ground Zero or identification as 9/11 literature, as with those color-coded terrorist alerts we now receive periodically, the notion of the designation itself also marks an important change we might not yet understand. Nevertheless, my analysis of Roth's novel is intended to suggest that even a work that makes no reference to 9/11 and whose historical subject precedes that event by over half a century can be read productively in relation to 9/11.

Beginning with its title, *The Plot Against America* echoes with a familiar set of evolving post-9/11 concerns: While the notion of a threat to America is of course nothing new, the idea of a set of secret sharers scheming to attack or undermine the United States would have a distinct resonance for the post-9/11 reader. Moreover, not only would our sense of the title arguably have been quite different on September 10, 2001, but also two days later, for by the publication of the novel in 2004 the notion of a "plot against America" had at least for some Americans broadened or even flipped to a growing concern about the threats from inside the American government as a result of its "war on terror." Roth's story, we should remember, is not just about an external scheme devised by fascists abroad whose strategies strike the reader as decidedly like those operating outside the nation-state model; it is also very much about the internal vulnerabilities, ideologies, and machinations of the American system.

The novel explores how these threats feed on each other, how difficult they can be to decipher, and how they pose complex challenges about the correct response. Is the president a fascist? Is he a dupe to his manipulative vice-president? How is the media complicit? Is the fight "over there" or here at home? Should we stay out of other countries' conflicts or is this isolationist naiveté or, worse, international complicity? What is the proper relation between key religious figures and government officials? What are we to make of the opposition party? All these familiar questions and others like it fill the novel—and therefore pose a kind of "cut-paste" effect for the contemporary reader. The fierce debates about American isolationism and exceptionalism, the complex negotiation between national identity and ethnic difference, the tensions between national security and civil rights, the uncertainty about how to interpret events or how to act, and even the sense of living at an unprecedented moment in history—all these familiar topics permeate this novel. From the public outcry about national relocation programs to the kitchen table arguments about whether the government would ever go so far as to read the Roth family mail, the reader follows the characters' struggles to interpret events around them that are far removed from our own, yet their observations and exclamations can cause the reader to either shudder or smile in recognition, as when Philip asks his father who might be "willing to speak out against Lindbergh's kissing Hitler's behind": "'What about the Democrats?' I asked." To which the father replies, "Son, don't ask me about the Democrats. I'm angry enough as it is" (101). The many references in the novel to the phrase *Never Before* invoke the Holocaust, yet they also resonate with reactions to the 9/11 attacks—both the disbelief and the resolution ("Never Again") hinged around this historical pivot point. But the phrase does more than underscore how this imagined past anticipates the present, for the novel also provides a version of "before" that disturbs or revises or even provisionally nullifies our claims about our own historical moment—never before. Conversely, the novel has a density or thickness that resists turning its alterity into allegory. Roth cross-wires the analogizing circuits that might serve as conductors for easy comparisons between Lindbergh and Bush; for example, Lindbergh attempts to keep America out of any alliances that might bring war with the Nazis, whereas Bush reversed course from his "modest" isolationism as a candidate to an ambitious course of action in the "war on terror" in Afghanistan and Iraq. Roth is careful to complicate things so that those who might be tempted to read the novel reductively as a broadbrushed connect-the-dot indictment of the Bush administration get tripped up on this isolationist theme.[6] In the same way, the flip involving Jews and Muslims as domestic and foreign perpetrators and victims creates a similarly re-routed circuitry between the events depicted in the novel and our current historical moment.

Yet even if Roth did not have George W. Bush in mind in his depiction of Lindbergh, it is nevertheless difficult for a reader encountering this fictionalized portrait not to recollect Bush's infamous May 2003 flight suit appearance aboard the aircraft carrier *U. S. S. Abraham Lincoln* and his declaration there, "Mission Accomplished." Lindbergh's persona as a plain-speakin' pilot-of-state, the patriotic populisms of his administration's major programs (as in the Just Folks and Homestead 42 initiatives), the machinations of a far-right vice-president lurking behind the scenes, and the administration's close affiliations to religious figures such as the historical Father Coughlin and the fictional Rabbi Bengelsdorf—all of these have led readers like Berman to describe the resistance or failure to see some connection to Bush as "dim-witted" (15), even as others like Coetzee have granted that although the "similarities . . . are hard to brush over. . . . [i]n any sensible reading, *The Plot Against America* is 'about' the presidency of George W. Bush in only the most peripheral way" (4).

But this last point is something of a straw man, for Roth's story is not quite just about Lindbergh, either. Nor, of course, would this novel need to be "about" George W. Bush to be productively described as 9/11 literature. I refer here not only to the broader parallels between these two presidencies and their respective historical and social frameworks, but again to the clue in the opening line of the novel that "[f]ear presides over these memories" (1). As critics have struggled to say what this book is "about" or have attempted to describe the correspondences or connections between past and present—or between fact and fiction—they have repeatedly echoed Berman's claim that fear is "finally . . . the rumbling engine that keeps *The*

Plot Against America securely aloft and chugging forward—the emotion that Roth has allowed himself to feel, luxuriously and at length" (28).[7]

Roth has himself weighed in on the question of his intentions in writing this book. In a *New York Times* essay published before the release of the novel, Roth worried that "readers are going to want to take this book as a roman clef [*sic*] to the present moment in America. That would be a mistake" (4). Yet his repudiation of such a reading would seem to be grounded primarily in his concern that if cast as allegory, his novel would not be credited as a fully realized or convincing depiction of the past:

> I set out to do exactly what I've done: reconstruct the years 1940–42 as they might have been if Lindbergh, instead of Roosevelt, had been elected president in the 1940 election. I am not pretending to be interested in those two years—I am interested in those two years. . . . My every imaginative effort was directed toward making the effect of that reality as strong as I could, and not so as to illuminate the present through the past but to illuminate the past through the past. (4)

For Roth, historical allegory is both too flat-footed and rather heavy-handed for the sorts of fictional renderings and registrations of reality in which he was interested as an artist. While granting that "[l]iterature is put to all kinds of uses, public and private," Roth insists that "one oughtn't to confuse those uses with the hard-won reality that an author has succeeded in realizing in a work of art" (4). Yet even in this essay, Roth's own insistence that "[h]istory claims everybody, whether they know it or not and whether they like it or not" (4) is perhaps ironically borne out in such a way as to suggest that recent events have somehow made their claim on this work after all:

> And now Aristophanes, who surely must be God, has given us George W. Bush, a man unfit to run a hardware store let alone a nation like this one, and who has merely reaffirmed for me the maxim that . . . all the assurances are provisional, even here in a 200-year-old democracy. We are ambushed, even as free Americans in a powerful republic armed to the teeth, by the unpredictability that is history. May I conclude with a quotation from my book? "Turned wrong way round, the relentless unforeseen was what we schoolchildren studied as 'History,' harmless history, where everything unexpected in its own time is chronicled on the page as inevitable. The terror of the unforeseen is what the science of history hides, turning a disaster into an epic." (5)

Here Roth has paradoxically suggested that the "terror of the unforeseen" might be not only what "the science of history hides" but also another sort of presence not entirely or so easily recognized in his fiction. What we can see in this work is more than a remedy to the problem of historical hindsight, for the novel does not simply reverse our gaze by inviting us to look, as it were, through the other end of the lens at events as they unfold and are experienced in "real time" by his characters. Also "turned wrong way round" is a more recent and similarly unforeseen terror.

Roth's use of a contemporary adult narrator named Philip Roth to recollect events from his childhood formally bundles these questions about the relationship between past and present, as well as between fact and fiction. For example, the young Philip tells us,

> Israel didn't yet exist, six million European Jews hadn't yet ceased to exist, and the local relevance of distant Palestine . . . was a mystery to me. . . . [W]e'd already had a homeland for three generations. I pledged allegiance to the flag of our homeland every morning at school. . . . Our homeland was America. (4–5)

At one level, this reference might be seen as just an anachronistic wink, for although the notion of a "homeland" is invoked here in reference to the desire for a Jewish homeland in Palestine (which again presents links to the current situation), most of Roth's American readers arguably had never encountered a reference to the United States as a "homeland" until invoked by Bush after 9/11.[8] This more recent usage returns home, so to speak, to an earlier imaginary past. Perhaps more importantly, in projecting this memory both through the lens and upon the surface of childhood—and then refracting it through the perspective of contemporary adulthood—Roth signals he is up to something more than just historical rhyming. As a result, the operations of memory and fear suggest that the narrator's predicament is replicated in the reader's experience of an uncanny sense of reencounter with a proximate past by way of a fictionalized distance.

Roth has managed to evoke the dreamlike confusion, nightmarish effect, and vertiginous sense of dislocation that informs our own historical moment in a pervasive dream motif that is framed literally with Philip and his brother falling asleep on the evening of the Republican convention and awakening to the fictional reality that the party has nominated Lindbergh (14–15). Indeed, the rupture of the narrator's childhood innocence by the "nightmare" of Lindbergh (whose sightings in the skies over Washington are themselves rendered in cartoonish, dreamlike images) has an uncanny feel that prefigures the experience of seeing the planes hit the towers and watching them collapse, as well as what some would call the unprecedented changes in America since then: it couldn't happen here, we thought—or were told we did. But it did, it was happening here, and we struggled to make sense of it, much as do the characters in Roth's novel, especially the young protagonist but also his father and all those who are supposed to be in charge. Dreaming is linked to his brother Sandy's drawings, Philip's repeated nightmares and fevered reveries about Seldon Wishnow and Alvin, the Dante-like journey of Sandy and his father to Kentucky, and even Roth's attempt to put the novel back on the historical rails by hav-ing Roosevelt return to the presidency and America manage to enter the war more than two years later and help defeat the Axis powers as if the "nightmare" never happened. But Roth is offering us more than a sort of coincidental version of the "nightmare of history," in that the dreams are themselves the novelistic realization of the prosthetic connection between two historical frameworks.

This dream motif continues throughout the novel, perhaps most impor-tantly linked to the recurring depiction of stamp collecting, which is cast repeatedly as the subject of dreams and whose surface is rendered in images that suggest dreamwork: "It was a nightmare all right, and it was about my stamp collection. Something had happened to it. The design on two sets of my stamps had changed in a dreadful way without my knowing when or how" (41). In the dream, Philip is walking with his friend and fellow col-lector, Earl Axman. Philip has his stamp album clutched to his chest when someone shouts his name and begins chasing him. Philip hides to check the stamps in his album that "might have come loose from their hinges" because he has stumbled and dropped the album where he regularly plays a game called "I Declare War" with other children. When he checks his 1932 Washington bicentennials, he is "stunned" to see Hitler's image and name substituted for Washington's (42–43). He is similarly horrified to discover that the stamps in his 1934 National Parks series, depicting "everything in America that was the bluest and the greenest and the whitest and to be preserved forever in these pristine reservations," have been stamped with a black swastika (43).[9]

Like the dreams, the stamps suggest a sort of metonymic trope for the novel's connection to a 9/11 framework, in which the stamps do more than serve as the surface upon which many of Philip's fears are projected; they also appear as miniature screens that mimetically resemble and prosthet-ically stand in for the dreamlike texture and plotting of the real events depicted in the novel. In the same way, the much larger screens of the increasingly surreal newsreel montages at the Newsreel Theater rupture the distinction between dreamwork image and daytime reality. When "his-tory's next outsized intrusion" arrives as "an engraved invitation" from the Lindberghs for Rabbi Bengelsdorf and his wife, Evelyn, (Philip's aunt) to attend a state dinner for the Nazi von Ribbentrop, to which they wish to bring his brother Sandy, Philip's confusion at these "loosening hinges" is complete: "It was barely possible to accept that Evelyn could herself have stepped overnight from our local little society into 'March of Time' celeb-rity, but now Sandy as well?" (184–85). The "horrible wonder" of seeing von Ribbentrop and his wife at the White House along with his own aunt is too much for Philip to resist, however, and he sneaks unaccompanied by an adult into the theater to witness alone this collective nightmare in a packed theater (echoing the more recent experience of watching the towers fall on television). Roth shifts here to a news montage of war images ("[p]icture after picture of misery without end"), until the "beheaded babies bubbling blood" give way abruptly, as if in a dream, to the bucolic images of the White House: "A twilit spring evening. Shadows falling across the lawn. Blooming bushes. Flowering trees" (200).

Like the stamps and movies, Philip's dreams and fevered reveries about Alvin's prosthetic leg (as well as the other dreams, nightmares, and fevers linked to traumatic loss) prefigure not just the counterfactual replacement of the historical facts in Roth's fiction, but also the projection of something more recent onto the canvas of a realistic fictional past that itself retains the texture of a dream. These aspects of the novel together constitute what I am referring to as its form, and they function as a prosthetic screen, which suggests Freud's concept of a screen memory: an imagined and therefore more tolerable artificial memory of a childhood experience that substitutes for another (and typically more recent) memory too painful to recall and render accurately. Realizing Roth's desire to right the sense that history is experience "turned wrong way round," the prosthetic play of misremembering the past is more than the stuff we find *in* the novel; it is also a way to think *about* the novel in relation to 9/11.

These prosthetic screens are closely tied to the pervasive and varied depictions of injury and illness in the story. Philip's being sick upon encountering Alvin's scab prefigures his more serious illness later in the book, an intense fever and complete collapse tied not only to the dream motif in the novel but also to the traumatic breakdown of any epistemological grounding about what is real and true and right. This occurs shortly after a critical substitution occurs, when Philip comes home and believes his father is dead, only to discover it is the neighbor, Mr. Wishnow, who has perhaps hanged himself. Philip's fear, combined with his sense that he no longer can know anything with any confidence, leads to his collapse: "I didn't seem to know whether my own father . . . was really alive or pretending to be alive. . . . I didn't know anything. . . . I felt woozy and thought I was going to faint (171–72). At this point Philip again vomits and collapses, believing that his "leg had been blown off." He remains in bed with a high fever for six days with a disease he describes as "that not uncommon childhood ailment called why-can't-it-be-the-way-it-was" (172).

Indeed, in a novel whose canvas is given over to catastrophe on such a large national and even international scale, much attention is given to the more immediately personal world of family, friends, and neighborhood, especially with respect to Philip's cousin Alvin. Both the stump and the prosthesis are a key source of curiosity and terror for Philip (Roth even names Chapter 4 "The Stump") in what could be described as a novelistic trauma ward of mostly male damage rendered as various sorts of impotence, emasculation, or castration. It is notable, for example, that the chapter entitled "The Stump" opens with an inventory and analysis of Jewish manhood in America, in which Philip compares more successful men like Abe Steinheim or his Uncle Monty with his father. This boyhood observation frames

Philip's first doubts about his father: "I began to wonder if my father knew what he was talking about" (125). Much later in the story, this doubt is rendered as paternal and professional impotence: "my father's authority as a protector had been drastically compromised if not destroyed. . . . Shockingly enough, my father had been rendered impotent by his company's having obediently joined hands with the state. There was nobody left to protect us except me" (209).

Alvin's return home as an amputee recalls for Philip the still more gruesome case of "Little Robert," a man "with no legs at all, a man who began at the hips and was himself no more than a stump" (127). It is significant that Philip always sees him on the sidewalk outside his father's downtown office, a man whose "colossal freakishness" Philip tries to describe or imagine but can't quite because "the fear of gaping merged with the terror of seeing to prevent me from ever looking long enough to register what he wore" (128). Indeed, Roth sets up this anecdote as an odd set of mirrored exchanges that links Robert to both his father and himself insofar as Robert is linked in Philip's mind to the father's workplace and the son's name (128). Much later, the connection between Robert and his father resurfaces in a scene almost overloaded with images of male trauma and damage. When Philip returns home one day and believes it is his own father and not Mr. Wishnow who has committed suicide in the closet, he has two recollections: first, he remembers what Alvin had told him was his last memory of his own father closing a car door on his finger as a little boy; second, he compares this memory with one of his own father, whose exchanges with Little Robert, the "stump of a man," suggest for Philip a kind of specular encounter of similarly damaged men (169). This pattern of damage to male digits and limbs is even portrayed as a kind of phallic loss in Alvin in the associations involving his leg, penis, and mouth. Alvin's dental woes plague him with a rot and decay likened to the infection that sets in when the "stump goes bad" (135), and Alvin's mouth later appears to Philip to discharge more than bad breath when Philip observes Alvin masturbating in the basement; Philip takes Alvin's moans "to be anguish at his no longer himself having two legs to walk on" (148). Philip retreats, but later returns to the basement to discover but not understand what he is seeing: "I didn't know what to think, except that it was something terrible. In the presence of a species of discharge as yet mysterious to me, I imagined it was something that festered in a man's body and then came spurting from his mouth when he was completely consumed by grief" (148).

Both the stump and the prosthesis together suggest a painful absence and presence, succinctly described by Alvin when he speaks of the pain "that grabs you and won't let you go. . . . There's pain where you are . . . and there's pain where you ain't. I wonder who thought that up" (154). So central is this motif that it would seem to be more than just a figuration of phallic loss (much as we would not be satisfied with such observations about the World Trade Center). It is as if memory stands in a sort of prosthetic relation to the real, which the stump conveys as both a presence and an absence: "What I saw was what the word 'stump' describes: the blunt remnant of something whole that belonged there and once had been there" (136). Philip says that it "resembled the elongated head of a featureless animal, something on which Sandy, with just a few well-placed strokes, could have crayoned eyes, nose, and mouth, teeth, and ears, and turned it into the likeness of a rat" (136). This linkage between the stump and the artist's canvas echoes the connection between Lindbergh and his brother Sandy's drawings: the completion of Lindbergh's famous transatlantic flight coincides with the day Philip's mother discovers herself pregnant with Sandy, and he "would later record this moment with a drawing illustrating the juxtaposition of these two events" (5).

Like the stamps, this drawing, completed by Sandy "at the age of nine and smacking inadvertently of Soviet poster art," feels much like a description of the novel itself, whose same juxtapositions are also rendered in a realistic mode through the lens of a child. But while Sandy's many illustrations celebrate Lindbergh (even as they remain hidden under a bed), Lindbergh becomes for Philip "the first famous living American whom I learned to hate" (7), and he therefore attempts to take possession of a very different sort of figure—the wounded Alvin. At one point he wraps the bandage from Alvin's stump on his own leg, discovers a dislodged scab there, and vomits. Philip, however, doesn't shy away for long, and in a week he is bandaging Alvin's stump. While the stump heals, the artificial leg remains in the closet, "largely hidden from sight. . . . Except for its eerily replicating the shape of the lower half of a real lower limb, everything about it was horrible, but horrible and a wonder both" (142). Philip goes on to describe the prosthesis in great detail, and his depiction offers an interpretive schematic for a novel that can be described in similar terms. The lower region of this artificial limb is the familiar and realistic portion, a mimetic reproduction of the real, whereas the upper section, which is both stranger and the site of attachment, is "horrible and a wonder." As a counterfactual depiction of America in the 1940s, then, the novel is not unlike this artificial leg, capable of "eerily replicating" the real historical one, for the story is convincingly and conventionally rendered historical fiction that keeps its pants and shoes on, so to speak, and its mechanisms of attachment comparatively hidden. At the same time, however, the narrator ventures past this illusion, variously and almost compulsively going down to the basement, into the closet, through the drawers, and up the leg to view the stump, handle the straps, wrap the bandages around himself, and even confront the displaced scab from Alvin's wound. These acts work as an invitation for readers to do the same.

When we arrive at the last lines of the novel, the fictional child narrator is explicitly linked to his own narrative: "There was no stump for me to care for this time. The boy [Seldon Wishnow] himself was the stump, and until he was taken to live with his mother's married sister in Brooklyn ten months later, I was the prosthesis" (362). This prosthetic aspect of the novel is indeed a "horrible wonder," but what joints exactly might we be encountering here? For while we might be tempted to propose that it is Roth's ability to conjoin the historical facts with the artifice of his imagination about this period in American history, what are we then to make of the final part of the book, in which the nightmare ends, Lindbergh disappears, and this leg of the narrative is seemingly lopped off or left behind in the faux-dustbin of counterfactual history? What remains? It is something more than (or different from) the *frisson* of "what if it could have happened here then?"

Readers such as Coetzee have noted this problem, for the "what if" aspect of counterfactual history typically engages in some sort of speculation about a kind of "butterfly effect" of events in which even the smallest of changes at a point in time will have a large impact on the course of history later. Clearly, something as significant as the Lindbergh presidency depicted here and the long delay of America getting into the war against Germany and Japan would have had considerable, if not monumental, consequences up through the present day. Roth, however, simply reinstalls Roosevelt in office two years later and places the narrative needle back into the groove of history where it more or less left off, as if it had been in a kind of holding pattern, flying in circles and going nowhere. But it is not the domino-like correspondence between two distant historical periods which Roth is interested in tracking—at least not in that direction.

As Alvin reminds us, "there's pain where you are . . . and there's pain where you ain't," and only part of the eerie ache of the phantom limb is caused by the amputation of the Lindbergh story. For in having the central plotline literally fall out of the sky and disappear into thin air, Roth commits neither literary gaffe nor historiographical error, for the absence left there is a gaping space that prefigures the sensation of standing in the ever-lengthening shadow of no towers. Perhaps Roth's notion of the "terror of the unforeseen" suggests that we do not yet know what we will come to mean by "9/11 literature." Yet the stamped swastika on the jacket of Roth's novel, like the emblematic cover art of Spiegelman's *In the Shadow of No Towers,* suggests that the absent towers might be a presence we can sometimes detect only by virtue of the sheen made possible by the truth-telling slant of light on a differently textured surface in an alternative dye of ink. *The Plot Against America* is an instance of such a space apart, where fiction sometimes stands in.

2004

NOTES

1. See, for example, Berman, Charles, Coetzee, Kakutani, and Morrison.
2. Michaels examines how Roth's novel serves a different kind of contemporary displacement and suppression—how by functioning as a "placeholder for

prejudice of all kinds" (298), the novel reflects neoliberalism's nostalgic need for (anti)-racism in order to ignore current social inequities.

3. See Hutcheon.

4. See, for example, Caruth, Landsberg, Mitchell and Snyder, Sturken, and Wills.

5. This list could include not only stories that refer to the attacks directly or centrally, but also those that, although written *before* 9/11, address terrorism in relation to the World Trade Center, such as Jennifer Egan's *Look At Me* and Don DeLillo's *Mao II*. They are at least prophetic works, and it is an odd sensation indeed to read them with our images of the planes in the sky now cut-pasted into our reading experience. Novels that are arguably being read *because* of 9/11 and the war on terror might include works as varied as Alice Sebold's *The Lovely Bones* (which, while making no reference to those events, has been described by some as expressing a "post-9/11" desire to deal with the whereabouts of the dead) and Khaled Hosseini's *The Kite Runner* or even Azar Nafisi's novelistic memoir *Reading Lolita in Tehran,* two foreign works whose domestic popularity has been seen by some as neoconservative self-congratulation and whose bestselling visibility in airports and airplanes everywhere speaks to an ironically evocative bit of cultural work. Finally, a novel like William Gibson's *Pattern Recognition* not only refers to the 9/11 attacks extensively but also pursues a sort of running inquiry about reading, semiotics, and the interpretation of historical events that can itself be read as a 9/11 component of the novel, which is nicely reflected in having the protagonist (Cayce Pollard) described as the CPU of the novel, processing the data and trying to make meaning out of it.

6. Several critics have commented on this point. See, for example, Rothberg (306) on this issue in response to Michaels.

7. Coetzee similarly claims that "one of the things that *The Plot Against America* is about is, precisely, paranoia" (4). Miller also notes that "*The Plot Against America* is a book about fear" (2).

8. See Pease for a discussion of the Bush administration's rhetorical deployment of this particular term. Pease frames his analysis in the broader context of those "master narratives" that function as "regulatory fictions through which government policymakers exercise normative control over the population" (1).

9. This particular image is nicely rendered in the design of the book jacket by Milton Glaser, which seems especially fitting as a 9/11 link, as he was the graphic designer who created the "I Love New York" logo. One might also wonder if this reference to the despoiling of the national parks is even intended to echo (if on another frequency) critiques of the fate of the national park system under the Bush administration.

WORKS CITED

Berman, Paul. "What if It Happened Here?" Rev. of *The Plot Against America,* by Philip Roth. *New York Times Book Review* 3 Oct. 2004: 1+.

Caruth, Cathy. *Unclaimed Experience: Trauma, Narrative, and History.* Baltimore: Johns Hopkins UP, 1996.

Charles, Ron. "Lucky Lindy, Unfortunate Jews." Rev. of *The Plot Against America,* by Philip Roth. *The Christian Science Monitor* 28 Sept. 2004. 21 Dec. 2006 http://www.csmonitor.com/2004/0928/p15s02-bogn.html.

Coetzee, J. M. "What Philip Knew." Rev. of *The Plot Against America,* by Philip Roth. *The New York Review of Books* 18 Nov. 2004: 4–6.

DeLillo, Don. *Mao II.* New York: Penguin, 1991.

Egan, Jennifer. *Look at Me*. New York: Nan A. Talese-Doubleday, 2001.

Freud, Sigmund. "Screen Memories." *The Standard Edition of the Complete Psychological Works of Sigmund Freud*. Vol. 3. Trans. James Strachey. London: Hogarth, 1961.

Gibson, William. *Pattern Recognition*. New York: Putnam, 2003.

Hosseini, Khaled. *The Kite Runner*. New York: Riverhead, 2003.

Hutcheon, Linda. *A Poetics of Postmodernism: History, Theory, Fiction*. New York: Routledge, 1988.

Kakutani, Michiko. "A Pro-Nazi President, A Family Feeling the Effects." Rev. of *The Plot Against America*, by Philip Roth. *New York Times* 21 Sept. 2004. 21 Dec. 2006 http://query.nytimes.com/gst/fullpage.html?res=9B02E4D71539F93 2A1575AC0A9629C8B63.

Landsberg, Alison. *Prosthetic Memory: The Transformation of American Remembrance in the Age of Mass Culture*. New York: Columbia UP, 2004.

Michaels, Walter Benn. "Plots Against America: Neoliberalism and Antiracism." *American Literary History* 18 (2006): 288–302.

Miller, Laura. "*The Plot Against America* by Philip Roth." *Salon.com Books* 29 Sept. 2004. 21 Dec. 2006 http://dir.salon.com/story/books/review/2004/09/29/ roth/index.html.

Mitchell, David T., and Sharon L. Snyder. *Narrative Prosthesis: Disability and the Dependencies of Discourse*. U of Michigan P: Ann Arbor, 2001.

Morrison, Blake. "The Relentless Unforeseen." Rev. of *The Plot Against America*, by Philip Roth. *Guardian Unlimited Books* 2 Oct. 2004. 21 Dec. 2006 http:// books.guardian.co.uk/review/story/0,,1317026,00.html.

Nafisi, Azar. *Reading Lolita in Tehran*. New York: Random House, 2003.

Pease, Donald E. "The Global Homeland State: Bush's Biopolitical Settlement." *boundary 2* 30.3 (2003): 1–18.

Roth, Philip. *The Plot Against America*. Boston: Houghton Mifflin, 2004.

———. "The Story Behind *The Plot Against America*." *New York Times Book Review* 19 Sept. 2004. 21 Dec. 2006 http://query.nytimes.com/gst/fullpage. html?res=9500E7DB1338F93AA2575AC0A9629C8B63.

Rothberg, Michael. "Against Zero-Sum Logic: A Response to Walter Benn Michaels." *American Literary History* 18 (2006): 303–11.

Sebold, Alice. *The Lovely Bones*. New York: Little, Brown & Co., 2002.

Spiegelman, Art. *In the Shadow of No Towers*. New York: Pantheon, 2004.

Sturken, Marita. *Tangled Memories: The Vietnam War, the AIDS Epidemic, and the Politics of Remembering*. Berkeley: U of California P, 1997.

Wills, David. *Prosthesis*. Stanford: Stanford UP, 1995.

14 Precocious Testimony
Poetry and the Uncommemorable

Jeffrey Gray

1.

The widely circulated view of September 11, 2001, as a watershed moment for American society poses problems for an understanding of both geopolitical events and their representations. What is in doubt is not only what the date divides (by some literary-critical accounts, as I note below, a trivial, ludic, or aestheticized postmodernist poetry on one side, and an engaged, collectively-based poetry, animated by casstastrophe, on the other) but also the location and stability of the watershed itself, which, on inspection, appears far less determinate in time and space than it may have appeared in 2001. In what sense, for example, could the assault on 9/11 be "the absolute event, the 'mother' of all events," as Jean Baudrillard claims in *The Spirit of Terrorism?* (4). In what sense was it "The Day America Changed," to use the headline of newspaper accounts across the country echoed in poem titles such as Stanley Plumly's "The Morning America Changed" and Joy Harjo's "When the World As We Knew It Ended"?

One instance of the watershed view was the poet Lawrence Ferlinghetti's prediction in October 2001 that poetry from now on would be divided into two categories: B.S. and A.S., Before September 11 and After. Ferlinghetti's reckoning does something beyond dividing time into Before and After. The play on "B.S." invites us to see pre-9/11 poetry (of the United States, presumably) as irrelevant, trivial, or false. Thus,

> Only a rich capitalist consumer society such as ours before 9/11 can afford artists and poets that basically present only their own private concerns in works that have little relation to the world around them and nothing important to say about that world. . . . If 9/11 spelt the death of the postmodern, among other myriad deaths, perhaps it was high time that artists and poets got a Wake Up call, as America itself got one. ("Prophecy")

Around the same time, the feminist editor Daniella Gioseffi remarked, "I've had it with *ennui* and the school of abstract expressionist, French nihilism! It is dead for me, especially since 9/11." The terms are both dated and conflicted, but Gioseffi seems to mean, on the one hand, postmodern irony, or playful, experimental, autotelic writing in general; and, on the other (suggested by "*ennui*"), solipsistic, confessional, angst-ridden writing—two polar opposites by most accounts. Neither would be satisfactory from a certain engaged standpoint, one that demands fidelity to *collective* realities, especially collective suffering, and to a language of relative transparency.

Even if one were to accept these broad if not caricatured categories of undesirable poetry, the alternatives are far from clear. Are we asking for a faithful language, a language of immediacy, of presence, a language in which nothing will be figurative? Does the dream of a faithful language mean that one should "steer clear of the sublime," as Ulrich Baer advises, lest the literary representation efface the event? (30). Does the post-9/11 ethos demand engagement, so that poems, say, should entail reference to deprivation and injustice, indictment of those thought responsible, help for those victimized? Should engaged poems be allegorical, as Frederic Jameson once recommended Third World literature should be? The dream at times seems almost to demand a representation co-extensive with what it represents. Marco Abel, writing of literature after 9/11, entertains this possibility (or impossibility) when he writes that we must reject analogy or simile, since figurative language "reduces the irreducible to the familiar . . . without marking that this knowledge has been cast in representational terms" (1245). By contrast, he says, an adequate response "begins *in* the event. Language immanently inheres and subsists in the event's variability or seriality" (1245). This idea, and the idea that language should be, as Abel suggests, involved in something besides "representation as resemblance," suggests a language like that imagined by the Argentine idiot-savant Funes in Jorge Luis Borges' story "Funes, the Memorious." Brilliant and paralyzed, Funes imagines a world of signs specific to events or things, and a vocabulary sufficient not only to every "leaf of every tree of every wood" but also to every moment that every leaf is perceived (Borges 66). It is not only difficult for him to imagine that the word "dog" stands for many species and for millions of individual animals, but it bothers him that the word should stand for the *same* dog at different times of day, in different positions. Funes' dream, as Borges showed, is one of insatiable specificity, the dream of someone who could name but could not think.

Finally, isn't the dream of faithfulness—mimetic, figurative, or not— exactly what Theodore Adorno feared when he made his famous remark that to write poetry after Auschwitz would be barbaric? Before he died in 1969, Adorno retracted this remark, conceding that "Suffering has as much right to be represented as a martyr has to cry out. So it may have been false to say that writing poetry after Auschwitz is impossible" (*Negative* 365).[1] The retraction—with its substitution of "impossible" for "barbaric"—suggests that the danger lies not in writing about disaster but in the pretense of understanding it. Adorno writes that "the aesthetic principle of stylization makes an unthinkable fate appear to have had some meaning . . . something of its horror is removed. This alone does an injustice to the victims" (*Negative* 365). But the alternative of silence—of supposing that the event is beyond representation—runs the risk of privileging and idealizing the unspeakable. No doubt, in his retraction, Adorno recognized this danger and saw the need to decanonize silence. Thus he wrote, "It is now virtually in art alone that suffering can still find its voice, consolation, without immediately being betrayed by it" ("Commitment" 312).

Two examples from film, discussed by Cathy Caruth in *Unclaimed Experience: Trauma, Narrative, and History,* help us understand some of the problems inherent in the dream of a faithful representation. During the eleven years it took to make the eight-hour documentary *Shoah,* Claude Lanzmann said that refusing to understand was his "iron law." The attempt to portray an impossibility was made possible, he said, by scrupulous avoidance of "the absolute obscenity in the very project of understanding" ("Hier est kein Warum," in *Au Suject de Claude Lanzmann,* by Bernard Cuau et al [Paris: Belin, 1990]. qtd. in Caruth 123–24, n. 13).

Similarly, Alain Resnais, when asked to make a documentary on Hiroshima, refused to use archival footage (though he had done so to make his earlier *Night and Frog* about the Nazi concentration camps). Only through the fictional story *Hiroshima, Mon Amour* were Resnais and Marguerite Duras able to suggest the event's historical specificity—a "faithful" history evoked by means of a rigorous indirectness (Caruth 27).

These examples help us to identify two dangers, which seem to correspond to Adorno's first and second thoughts on poetry after Auschwitz: 1. the pretense of assimilating and being true to traumatic experience, and therefore committing the obscenity of understanding, as Lanzmann calls it; and 2. the idealizing of trauma as untouchable and therefore transcendent. It is the second danger that trauma theorists such as Caruth and Shoshana Felman sometimes seem to court and to which Linda Belau calls attention. We need, Belau argues, to see the trauma as *part* of the symbolic, not beyond it. To place trauma beyond language is to lose track of the ethical dimension. Indeed, Belau writes, only through language can there be an "unspeakable."[2]

2.

In a lecture at Oxford in 1895, the poet Stephane Mallarmé spoke about the formal changes taking place in the French verse of his time. In giving this account, he suggested that he was speaking before he was ready ("Il convient d'en parler déja"), before he had grasped the situation. Shoshana Felman, who discusses the lecture at length, writes that

> such precocious testimony in effect becomes, with Mallarmé, the very principle of poetic insight and the very core of the event of poetry,

which makes precisely language—through its breathless gasps—*speak ahead of knowledge and awareness* and break through the limits of its own conscious understanding. ("Education" 21; emphasis mine)

Felman suggests that it is in this way that poetry speaks *"beyond its means"* (21) and thus testifies to "the ill-understood effects and to the impact of *an accident whose origin cannot precisely be located* but whose repercussions, in their very uncontrollable and unanticipated nature, still continue to evolve even in the very process of the testimony" (21–22; emphasis mine).

It is this temporal dislocation, as I said at the outset, that I would like to explore in order to question the view of 9/11 as a discrete event for which one can discover a corresponding and adequate language. The conditions of representation are inextricably located in both past and future, out of synchronic time. Particularly in the poem, as Christopher Lane remarks, "the issue of what happens where and when is subordinated . . . to how the mind anticipates, recalls, and transforms events (461). When, just after September 11, Jean Baudrillard said, "We have dreamt of this event," he reminded us that conditions of representation, outward and inward, depend far less on a material event "out there," confined to a discreet moment, than is often imagined (5). The events are also *in here;* we have dreamed of them and continue to dream of them. (And we *have* seen the events before, as the hijackers also had: both in American movies and in documentary footage of the 1993 attack on the WTC.)[3] Testimony is precocious because the event is always the missed event; traumatic experience itself, as Felman, Caruth, Belau, and others have explained, is necessarily a missed experience, "neither chronologically linear nor diachronically constituted" (Belau). Lacan writes that "the missed encounter that organizes the temporality of trauma is an encounter with the timeless real" (Book XI 55; qtd. in Belau). In place of a faithful language addressing a stable traumatic event, then, I would like to substitute an inadequate and ill-prepared language, always precocious, engaging an event that is missed, a "timeless real." A precocious mode of witnessing will be not so much representational as performative, proceeding diachronically and, at times, by blessings, imprecations, rhythms, and curses; it is an art that does not compromise what happens by pretending to know what happened.

In the context of this reality—that events are not discrete in time and space, and that, with the errancy that practically defines poetry, our representations of them necessarily wander from verisimilitude—that I want to notice some directions in contemporary poetry that run counter to the dream of a faithful language. I suggest that another direction is being taken, drawing on ancient sources of poetry in divination, repetition, and prophecy, performing Rimbaud's "alchemy of the word" (193) by tapping into those archaic modes in order to answer to the missed event of the trauma.

I should note that of course the "timeless" is a highly suspicious category in an era of historicist critique. It is particularly suspect when it is framed not in Lacanian terms—or, for that matter, religious terms (the idea of a time outside of linear *chronos*)—but in those of the New Criticism, where it was often invoked to wrench texts out of their time in order to look at their internal dynamics, as if the dynamics themselves were not responses to those times. In what follows, I'd like to rescue the idea of an atemporal poetry from that New Critical context in order to observe that much of poetry's power resides precisely in its atemporal slippage and that, lacking this slippage, poetry can become predictable and indeed negligible.

Poetry answers most to the needs induced by loss when it least imitates the reportorial illusion of access to prior realities. Poetry's performative and magical elements, its roots in divination, incantation, and prophecy are evident even or especially at its most unsubjective, even when it is least personal and most linguistically determined—here I refer to any writing practice that inhibits reflex, that frustrates the usual resources from which a writer is prompted to draw, and that takes the writer instead into areas where little or nothing is known. In speaking of the poetry that emerged following 9/11, I must first to trace the broader, more visible contours of the response—in poems that seem to me to demonstrate that dream of immediacy, of understanding—before turning to some alternative possibilities.

3.

The list of poets who wrote poems explicitly about the attacks of September 11 includes Ai, David Baker, Amiri Baraka, Daniel Berrigan, Charles Bernstein, Frank Bidart, Fred Chappell, Lucille Clifton, Andrei Codrescu, Billy Collins, Robert Creeley, Diane di Prima, Stephen Dunn, Lawrence Ferlinghetti, Tess Gallagher, Albert Goldbarth, Deborah Garrison, Kimiko Hahn, Sam Hamill, Joy Harjo, Pierre Joris, X. J. Kennedy, Galway Kinnell, Steve Kowit, Michael McClure, W. S. Merwin, D. Nurkse, Alicia Ostriker, Jay Parini, Robert Pinsky, Stanley Plumly, David Ray, C.K. Williams, and Al Young.[4] Thousands of other lesser known poets also responded to the event, the bulk of them on websites within the first few weeks after September 11 or on public non-virtual posting sites such as that of Union Square, Manhattan, during the first week after. The overwhelming response among the poets—striking a balance with the high-volume outrage of some radio and television commentators—was guilt. The "we-had-it-coming" case had been made in prose first, almost immediately after the collapse of the towers—in Baudrillard's article, later a book, cited above; in Susan Sontag's much-discussed comments in the *New Yorker*; in the popular book *9/11* put together in a few days by Noam Chomsky and his editors; and in prose remarks by Wendell Berry, among many others. But poets' responses followed quickly.[5] David Meltzer's poem "26:ix:01" reads:

sayonara
bad architecture

evil enterprise
innocents remain
complicit regardless

Michael McClure writes, in "Black Dahlia":

> THE CUPS WE DRINK FROM ARE THE SKULLS OF ARABS
> AND THIS SILK IS THE SKIN OF BABIES.
> . . .
> WE ITCH LIKE SCABIES
> FOR THE RAPE OF THINGS. (141)

Diane di Prima's "Notes toward a Poem of Revolution" reads in part,

> What did we in all honesty expect?
> That fascist architecture flaunting
>   @ the sky
> . . .
> While we mourn & rant for years
> over our 3000   how many
>
>   starve
> thanks to our greed. (41)

Pamela Hale, in "Poem for an Iraqi Child in a Forgotten News Clip" (quoted in the film *Poetry in Wartime*), writes,

> I'm sorry that your mom was killed
> When a missile struck your home. . . .
> That missile came in my name
> Paid for by my tax dollars.

Alicia Ostriker, who put online a collection of 9/11 poems, offers her own, titled "the window, at the moment of flame," which, after contrasting her wealth with the misery of people elsewhere in the world, concludes

> and all this while I have been shopping, I have
>
> been let us say free
> and do they hate me for it
>
> do they hate me[6]

The same consensus and the same clear sense made of the event characterize much of Sam Hamill's *Poets Against the War*, which consists of 260 poems quickly solicited and published in response to an invitation from Laura Bush for a poetry symposium at the White House. (The invitation was declined and the book inscribed "For Laura Bush.") Eleven thousand poets responded, says Hamill. Those chosen for the volume, and no doubt many of those not chosen, share the theme cited above; indeed, the binary oppositions set out in Ostriker's poem are even starker in the poems of this group.[7] Eleanor Wilner in "Found in the Free Library" describes how the nefarious 'They' functions in our lives: "they stole our pensions, poured their smoke / into our lungs, . . . beat our ploughshares / into swords. . . ." (224). Jim Pearson's "kunishi ridge 2nd bn. first marines" sets out the choices in alternating stanzas: one stanza describes women's hair and women's voices in the wind, singing to their children; the next describes the killing power of 155 mm howitzers (173). Marge Piercy, in a poem explicitly called "Choices," asks

> Would you rather have health insurance
> you can actually afford, or bomb Iraq?
> Would you rather have enough inspectors
> to keep your kids from getting poisoned
> by bad hamburgers, or bomb Iraq? (179).

Arthur Sze in "The Aphrodisiac" says that Henry Kissinger doesn't care for the song of an oriole or for a handicapped woman but only for death and destruction: he has no use for

> a campesino
> dreaming of spring.
> He revels in the instant
> before a grenade explodes (224–5).

It is not the falsehood of the choices that is disheartening (and they are sometimes false: Americans have little right to complain about costly health insurance or unclean food compared with conditions in much of the world) but rather the fact that they are so familiar. As with politicians' "Save the Children" campaigns, who will disagree with the choices of children over bombs, peasants over bombs, or orioles over bombs? The binarisms in such poems are at least as clear-cut as those of George W. Bush. The problem with the poems then is not that they are "engaged" but that we are offered a world *tout connu*. Nothing is defamiliarized. Moreover, the subjects speaking in such poems are completely stable: they *know*.

4.

Certain elements still discernible, even obvious, in poetry—as I have said above, ancient (indeed Paleolithic), incantatory, prophetic, ceremonial—

may in the end perform the opposite of what we think of as "commitment," drawing upon and spreading their effects diachronically *through* history rather than reflecting an historical moment, applying to startlingly diverse situations beyond the context of a poem's original impetus.[8] While it is a subject too large to explore here, I would note the western mystical concept of *kairos*, a sacred time that contains and transcends secular time, constituting the participation of the eternal *in* time. To invoke such ideas is not to skirt, much less to ignore, "events." When Bruno Latour remarks that "The question was never to get *away* from facts but [to get] *closer* to them" (231), he distinguishes between "matters of fact" and "matters of concern." Some poems—I will now suggest alternative examples—allow us to understand and approach matters of concern in a way that an allegiance to matters of fact too often precludes. I do not present *all* of these examples as aesthetically superior—on the contrary some are deeply flawed—but I do think they reveal a different energy and a different level of engagement, an attention to the problems of making, often a notably different diction, and in most cases an approach that entails a diachronic spread through time rather than a synchronic emphasis. (The latter point, with which I began this chapter, is worth repeating: the isolation of a traumatic event risks obscuring larger forces at work over long stretches of historical time.) They are not identical responses, but all differ sharply from the poetics of the poems I've discussed above.

I will refer in what follows to two overlapping categories: on the one hand, the poetry of discourse and abstraction that has developed during the past quarter of a century and that has attained a surprising power at the end of an age that prized the flat and concrete mode over all others; and, on the other hand, the poetry, never gone for long, that draws on mnemonic and archaic, magical elements. While I will try to discuss these categories separately, the fact is they have much in common. An artificial rather than a naturalistic diction, for example, is conventional in ceremonial, performative, and repetitive actions such as curses and blessings, as I will indicate below. But most of all, both of these modes implicitly repudiate that flat, "natural" or direct address I have been discussing as characteristic of a great deal of twentieth-century writing, particularly writing after the mid-century.

I will first consider two poems from the first category: "Curse," by Frank Bidart, and "War," by C.K. Williams. Frank Bidart is a poet famous for opening up psychologies uncomfortable to witness, much less to inhabit. I can think of no contemporary poem that requires more caution than the following, and it may be several years too soon to read it at all. I quote it in full:

May breath for a dead moment cease as jerking your

head upward you hear as if in slow motion floor

collapse evenly upon floor as one hundred and ten

floors descend upon you.

May what you have made descend upon you.
May the listening ears of your victims their eyes their

breath

enter you, and eat like acid
the bubble of rectitude that allowed you breath.

May their breath now, in eternity, be your breath.

         *

Now, as you wished, you cannot for us
not be. May this be your single profit.

Of your rectitude at last disenthralled, you
seek the dead. Each time you enter them

they spit you out. The dead find you are not food.

Out of the great secret of morals, *the imagination to enter
the skin of another,* what I have made is a curse.[9]
    (*Star Dust* 25–26; emphasis Bidart's)

Of all the perspectives that attend a situation, it is Bidart's burden to
find the one whose pathologies and dreads run rawest. An early narrator of his, "Herbert White," is a serial child killer and necrophiliac, and
while the poem is set in quotation marks ("Curse" is not), a real Herbert
White did exist, just as the unnamed speaker of "Curse" exists, literally,
with a vengeance. Bidart locates that perspective, hears its accents, and
inhabits it. In contrast to postmodernism's purported turn toward linguistic play and dispersion of the Subject, Bidart's personae are irredeemably
subjective. What does it feel like to hate this way? To desire this way? Or
perhaps "feeling" is not the best word, since, in an interview, Bidart once
remarked that his poetry was "necessary thought" (Halliday 232). When
we read "Curse," in spite of the iteration of the "May you . . ." generic to
both curses and blessings, we find the language is not that of emotion but
of careful, long-nursed *thought*. (See also Bidart's "Luggage": "may what
was not // rise like grief before you" [*Star Dust* 16].) This hater's diction
is grand, distilled, and apocalyptical. "Now that you've been freed from
your self-righteousness," one might have written, but the more elaborate

and archaic "Of your rectitude at last disenthralled" has the scale of Scripture, the pronouncement not of a paranoid terrorist but of a thinker who has pondered his retribution. "Curse" is, in fact, so liturgical that it may be seen as issuing not from a human being at all but from God, not far-fetched when we consider that this is the poet who translated chapters of Genesis into his own pulse and prosody. The prayer of "Curse" is that its bearer will find nowhere, ever, to turn for solace.

At this point in my first writing of these comments, I realized that I had completely misread the poem. Perhaps the error was pardonable: Could this *not* be the voice of a terrorist, hurling his apocalyptic curse against the great Satan with its countless victims and its until-now unassailable rectitude, the Great Power whose citizens will find no rest even in the afterlife? Could this poem not be a curse that found its target—that is, a curse written before rather than after the fact? If so, it is a devastating poem.

Because this misreading still seems strong and necessary, I will let it stand while I turn to what seems a more obvious reading of the poem as a version of the Biblical "eye for an eye": may you who have perpetrated this horrible deed upon 3,000 innocents experience in turn what they experienced. (In a note, Bidart confirms that "The poem springs from the ancient moral idea [the idea of Dante's *Divine Comedy*] that what is suffered for an act should correspond to the nature of an act" [83].) May your sense of righteousness be eaten away by the sufferings you have inflicted. The one profit you have reaped is that now we can never ignore you: you have our undivided attention. Indeed, only now do you fully exist for us.

What I credit Bidart with is precisely *"the imagination to enter / the skin of another,"* a feat he has performed often, most famously in his long poem about the anorexic Ellen West. But, according to my second, "right" reading, he has entered that skin not to level this "curse" against the United States but rather to admit that this entering-into has produced not sympathy (in his note to the poem, Bidart quotes Shelley's *Defense of Poetry:* "the great secret of morals is love" [83]) but hatred. This is "Frank Bidart" speaking, still a persona but one closer to home than Herbert White, Ellen West, or an unnamed terrorist. The ending is an admission of failure, but in that failure lies the whole import of the poem, the poet's allowance that this is the pass to which he has been brought, that this is the only place to which these reflections can lead.

This second reading seems all the more clear in view of Bidart's concerns during the past decade, culminating in the publication in 2005 of *Star Dust.* The poem titled "Advice to the Players," for example, is written in the mode and, at the end, the style, of Hamlet's speech. It consists of bare, terse statements separated by asterisks. "We are creatures who need to make," says this advisor, and "Making is the mirror in which we see ourselves" (10). "Making" means not only books and business but also "being," even "the shape we give this afternoon, a conversation between two friends, a meal." Crucially, however, the speaker says, "Without clarity about what we make, and the choices that underlie it, the need to make is a curse, a misfortune" (11). This is repeated later in the poem as "Without clarity, a curse, a misfortune" (11) and still later, in italics: "*Without clarity, a curse, a misfortune*" (12).

Thus, the poem "Curse" suggests a failure, *our* failure as *homo faber*, to achieve the clarity that would turn our words in a direction other than that of a curse. A final implication of this second reading, then, in which the curse has been leveled at Osama bin Laden and his ilk, suggests that the curse also—or chiefly—inheres in the burden of the making, the burden of having to make when one has not clarity (to alter I Corinthians 13 by one phoneme). So that to the poet's last words, "what I have made is a curse," should be added, "on myself."

Curses, imprecations, blessings, sacrifices, speculations on and efforts to influence the gods and the afterlife draw upon the most ancient roots of magic, divination, prophecy, and poetry. (See several such poems in Bidart's work, including "Heart Beat" with its prayer for "*less life less life*" [*Star Dust* 19].) To speak of the breath of the dead being now *your* breath is to speak out of linear time. To speak of coming into and out of existence in accordance with the perspective of the perceiver is also atemporal. To speak of "eternity" or of the terrorists in the future being spat out by the dead, to wish, performatively ("May you"), that the victims' now presumably demolished perceptions should enter you, the terrorist, and destroy you—all of this is to employ elements that are among the earliest constituents of poetry as they are also of magic and indeed of human community.

5.

C. K. Williams's poem "War" appeared in the *New Yorker* two months after the attacks of September 11. Williams's work, while distinct from Bidart's, nevertheless resembles it in two important regards: neither poet seems to have had, as Bidart says, "a romance with verse" (Halliday 234), and both suggest, against the teaching of poetry workshops over the past four decades, that there is a place for an abstract, rhetorical, and even, by most measures, archaic kind of diction. This latter point needs to be situated in the context of a poem that is a meditation as much on time as on catastrophe.

"War" is composed of three numbered sections, each of four long-lined tercets. At the outset, the poem's diction is flatter than that of "Curse" or other of Bidart's recent poems. Williams's first lines are incidental, casual: "I keep reading an article I found recently" (*Collected* 599), an article concerning ancient Mayan scribes who were customarily tortured and put to death when their side lost a war. The warrior class saw no more importance in their deaths—so the glyphs suggest—than bomber pilots see in a blip on their radar screens.

Following the latter comparison come two others: first, "the Greek and Trojan gods," who would mercilessly desert the beings they had created, and, second, "the god we call ours," also a deserter. In all periods, the warriors fought "until nothing remained but rock and dust and shattered bone," and in all periods, the scribes watched as their best formulations of a spiritual life, "('Do unto, Love, Don't Kill')," were "garbled to canticles of vengeance and battle prayers" (599).

With this last line—whether we think of Islam, Christianity, or Judaism—we are brought up to the present, the subject of the poem's third part. Now the heightened language and elegiac conventions come forward, placing us in the fall of the year, evoking the fall, also, of the Twin Towers. Then the aftermath, the news we all know, and finally, in italics, the commentary. In spite of the routine cycles of nature, the poem says, this has happened, and this, the italicized stanzas argue, is how we must see it:

> Fall's first freshness: strange, the season's ceaseless wheel,
> starlings starting south, the leaves annealing, ready to release,
> yet still those columns of nothingness rise from their own ruins,
>
> their twisted carcasses of steel and ash still fume, and still,
> one by one, tacked up by hopeful lovers, husbands, wives, on walls,
> in hospitals, the absent faces wait, already tattering, fading, going out.
>
> *These things that happen in the particle of time we have to be alive,*
> *these violations which almost more than any altar, ark, or mosque,*
> *embody sanctity by enacting so precisely sanctity's desecration.*
>
> *These broken voices of bereavement asking of us what isn't to be*
> *   given.*
> *These suddenly smudged images of consonance and peace.*
> *These fearful burdens to be borne: complicity, contrition, grief.* (600)

Crucial to the temporal slippage in "prophetic" poetry is the diachronism we see in Williams's poem. "War" does not deny eventness; we live, Williams writes, in a "particle of time." But, amid the elegiac and rhetorical echoes and allusions ("fall's first freshness" as if out of Hopkins), the "yet still" and "still" structure inscribes the insistence on memory in the face of an ongoing rhythm. The "season's ceaseless wheel" suggests the non-linearity not only of the seasons but of the catastrophe at the heart of the poem, which is something ongoing: the "columns of nothingness" that "still . . . rise from their own ruins," the twisted structures "still fum[ing]," the faces of the victims "still . . . wait[ing] . . . fading, going out."[10]

The catalogues of diminution—"starlings starting south, the leaves annealing" or "already tattering, fading, going out"—and the accretion of the closing anaphora of "These things that happen . . . these violations

. . . These broken voices . . . These suddenly smudged images . . . These fearful burdens. . . ."—all contribute to the mourning of ephemera, a sense in larger part determined by the tracing of nature's rhythms, worked out in conventionally poetic and musical phrases (again, the "season's cease-less wheel" and "starlings starting south") even while the colossal absence is still hanging in the air, just as those "absent faces" hang there, not yet fallen back or merged into the larger order of movement and decay.

I began this discussion of Bidart and Williams with the question of a return to the powers of discursiveness, abstraction, and rhetoric (in a non-pejorative sense) after almost a century of flat style. At this late date, the plausibility and effectiveness of a latinate, polysyllabic diction may seem anomalous. This is a language that exerts little effort to condense, framing a response to things that a twentieth-century ethos thought inappropriate if not impossible in serious poetry—the diction of "sanctity," "bereave-ment," "rectitude," and "complicity, contrition, grief."

6.

Two conspicuous long poems were written in response to 9/11: Galway Kinnell's "When the Towers Fell" and Amiri Baraka's "Somebody Blew Up America." The history of the American long poem reveals its strengths to be double: it can retain the startling line-by-line juxtapositions that char-acterize modern poetry in general while also allowing the diachronic sweep that we see in Whitman, Pound, Eliot, Williams, or Olson. Thus, I wish to use the Kinnell and Baraka poems to return to the subject of diachronism with which I began this essay, where I argued that the more "transparent" writing was weakened by a synchronic emphasis.

Baraka's poem, coming as it did just after he had been appointed poet laureate of New Jersey, and containing as it did vituperative accusa-tions against the Israelis (claims wildly popular in France and of course throughout the Arab world), attracted a level of attention unusual for any contemporary poet; indeed, Baraka's may be the only instance in an entire century of a contemporary poem receiving front-page press and prime-time television notoriety. Certainly the attention dwarfs that received by Pound's Bollingen Award in 1948, the only comparable scandal (and one in which anti-Semitism was also at issue). The poem is 95 strophes broken into three main sections. The battle lines, as usual in Baraka, are drawn up along clear Manichaean lines; indeed, Baraka has this one element in common with poems I quoted much earlier: he knows. (This is why, as John R. O. Gery comments, we always know where we are in a Baraka poem.) The poem is Whitmanian but even more Ginsbergian in its dozens of anaphora—indeed the *same* anaphora ("who") as in *Howl*, but here used to introduce separate rhetorical questions. Since the lines lack ques-tion marks, when one reads

> Who got fat from plantations
> Who genocided Indians
> Tried to waste the Black nation
> . . .
> Who created everything
> Who the smartest
> Who the greatest
> Who the richest
> Who say you ugly and they the goodlookingest (42)

the clauses work both ways—that is, as rhetorical questions and as relative clauses, as interrogations and as points of transition. Ginsberg was describing a cultural situation; his accusations come into play principally in the "Moloch" sequence. Baraka, on the other hand, knows the answer to every one of his questions: the answer to "who" is of course the white man (the Wasp, the Jew, the mainstream, the media, the moneyed, the empowered). Nevertheless, media interest or public indignation were roused not by these particular lines, which I quote to characterize the poem's style, but by the suggestion that somebody (the same somebody who "got fat from plantations"?) *knew* the event was going to happen:

> Who knew the World Trade Center was gonna get bombed
> Who told 4000 Israeli workers at the Twin Towers
> To stay home that day
> Why did Sharon stay away? (49)

In the fury immediately following the poem's appearance, no one thought to ask Baraka whether he actually thought that the Jews or the media or the establishment knew the attack was imminent. Did he think that "They" planned it and executed it? Connie Chung asked instead if Baraka didn't think that, as New Jersey poet laureate, he shouldn't write more "uplifting" poems, a question that Baraka easily parried by saying that allegiance to truth and beauty, not good cheer, is the poet's duty, and by insisting that his critics had dwelt on this one anti-Semitic passage to the exclusion of other questions, such as

> Who put the Jews in ovens,
> who helped them do it
> Who said 'America First'
> and ok'd the yellow stars (48)

or

> Who killed Malcolm, Kennedy & his Brother
> Who killed Dr. King, Who would want such a thing?
> Are they linked to the murder of Lincoln?[11]

It would be impossible to de-historicize a poem like this, to apply a merely formal analysis, but to look at trauma is to look at *both* event and response: the blunt or contrived rhymes ("linked" and "Lincoln," and many others) and hip-hop aesthetic are no less relevant than the performance elements, particularly the incantatory momentum, gradually building to the cry of a great screech owl—not a mammalian howl, as in Ginsberg, but an avian and equally oral but pre-semantic "Whoooo": "Who and Who and WHO who who / Whoooo and Whoooooooooooooooo!" (50) Meanwhile, the diachronic view reminds us that there is an important echo here, earlier than that of *Howl*. Baraka is writing back to Vachel Lindsay's infamous and, after its publication in 1914, very popular poem "Congo" (subtitled "A Study of the Negro Race"). Section One of that poem, called "Their Basic Savagery," repeats sounds such as "boomlay boomlay boomlay BOOM," variations on "hoo doo" and "voo doo" and notably:

> BOOM, steal the pygmies,
> BOOM, kill the Arabs,
> BOOM, kill the white men,
> HOO, HOO, HOO. (4)

Lindsay was, by his own account, trying to restore poetry to its oral sources, from vaudeville back to the Greeks. The poem's third and last section, quoting the "Congo tune," reads, "'Mumbo-Jumbo will hoo-doo you, / Mumbo-Jumbo will hoo-doo you. / Mumbo . . . Jumbo . . . will . . . hoo-doo . . . you.'" (7). In Baraka's live performances of "Somebody Blew up America," the re-writing of Lindsay becomes even clearer, since he uses a muted "boom" sound at the outset and slows down at the end, as Lindsay's ellipses also direct a reader to do, so that the final repeated "hoooo" (the same sound as in Lindsay with the same number of repetitions) becomes a hoarse cry, more performative than denotative.

The bulk of Baraka's poem consists of a long list of crimes across the centuries, particularly the twentieth. In one sense, Baraka's defense, cited above, is cogent: September 11 is not an "event" but part of a much greater, many-layered continuum. Perhaps Connie Chung intuited this when the "fact" somehow slipped her mind, in the context of Baraka's appointment as poet laureate by a governor who had almost certainly never read him and of the enormous catalogue of atrocities in which, once one had read the poem, the day of 9/11 was virtually buried.

Poems at this level of formalism tap into human rhythms as deeply embedded as the sleeping and waking we perform as heliotropic organisms. The pre-semantic archaism of sound (in this case the whooooooing of the poem) underplays denotation and resonates at lower strata of memory. In the Baraka poem, more than in most, one sees the political dimension of returning to the alchemy of the word not only in the obvious thematic attack on hegemony but in the implicit attack on instrumental language.

7.

Much of Galway Kinnell's long "When the Towers Fell" also suggests a dia-chronic approach and sensibility and also catalogues enormities like those listed by Baraka. The poem has its own Whitmanian echoes (along with pas-sages quoted from Whitman, Villon, Celan, Hart Crane, Aleksander Wat) and perhaps echoes of Pound—"Some with torn clothing, some bloodied, / some limping at top speed like children . . ." [53]). When the Holocaust is introduced, the poet notes, "This is not a comparison but a corollary, / *not a likeness but a lineage* / in the twentieth-century history of violent death—" (54; emphasis mine). The poem as later collected in Kinnell's volume *Strong is Your Hold* is slightly reworked, so that the diachronic aspect of this pas-sage is explicit: "They come before us now not as a likeness / but as a cor-ollary, a small instance in the immense / lineage of the twentieth century's history of violent death" (40).[12] These lines form a helpful gloss on Abel's discussion, earlier, of the inappropriateness of figuration. Likenesses and corollaries, *pace* Abel, reveal contours and patterns in time. "Lineage" is not linearity but resonance and affinity.[13] The "lineage" that Kinnell offers parallels C.K. Williams's connections to Mayan scribes and Indian gods and Baraka's litany of global horrors. Kinnell catalogues

> black men in the South castrated and strung up from trees,
> soldiers advancing through mud at ninety thousand dead per mile,
> train upon train headed eastward made up of boxcars shoved full to
>   the corners with Jews and Gypsies to be enslaved or gassed,
> state murder of twenty, thirty, forty million of its own . . . (54)

While this comes close to description and "account," the spread of events across time again suggests lineage and legacy: the "black omens, that the last century dumped into this one" are "our futures . . . our own black milk crossing the sky . . ." (53).[14] (The "black milk" is from Paul Celan's refrain in "The Death Fugue": "Black milk of daybreak.") Once again, the power of the poem does not inhere in its historical specificity as much as in its sweep and its webbing of poetry, prophecy, and his-tory.[15] At the poem's end, four tercets describe the collapse of the towers, which then condense into a "black hole," "infinitesimally small: mass / without space, where each light / each life, put out, lies down within us" (54). What these lines trace is the claustrophobic, annihilating condensa-tion of space, collapsing as if down to a single cell, the space *in us*. The image of *im*plosion rather than *ex*plosion is an image of our time as of no

earlier time—in part, because of the now general understanding of astro-
nomical black holes, vortices so dense that they swallow even light, but
also because the demolition of buildings has become a familiar spectacle,
carefully staged and televised. Even the destruction of the Twin Towers
was not centrifugal *ex*plosion, where debris flies in all directions. The
towers *descended,* slamming down "floor by floor into themselves"; what
one saw (despite the smoke and debris that flew for blocks around at the
bottom, "rolling outward") was vertical collapse. This is the image in
Bidart's 'Curse' as well. First impact; then the intense heat and smoke;
then the collapse downward of one hundred and ten floors. The poet
David Rigsbee has written in a similar vein:

> There is no inwardness like this:
> floor after human floor collapsing,
> pipes and fittings, miles of artifice
> melted into the original mash of being,
> selves exiled into the surrounding wood.

*Ex*plosion, whether in the Big Bang, in a population, or in an economy
(a "boom") often suggests a beginning. Implosion can only suggest annihilation. Thus implosion functions as a sign of a contemporary paradigm, centripetal and associated with postmodern commodification and
instant cooptation of peripheral forces. Implosion is what happens after
history is over; it suggests interiority, the condition (or the pathology) of
a new century.

8.

I have suggested here some symptoms of a "prophetic" mode in contemporary poets that is at odds with the aesthetics and poetic practice of most
of the past century, especially the past half century, and certainly, as I
indicated earlier, with that dream of a faithful and immediate language
that resurfaced after 9/11.[16] Often this prophetic mode entails the tapping
of dream in the other sense—not as a wished-for ideal but as an eruption
of unconscious phenomena. "We have dreamt of this event," as Baudrillard
remarked (5). We know that dream and poetry have had close relations
through history and do so even to the present. The poet of the following
lines, the last that I'll quote, labored to find the language that inhabits
dreams and that shapes our fears and deepest affinities. His approach was
based in part on the work of Carl Jung, who was particularly influential
among the generation that came of age in the 1960s and 1970s, and on
Jung's belief in timeless patterns of the collective unconscious—indeed,
patterns intact from five million years ago. The passage reads as follows:

> I saw it in a dream
> Coming bigger and closer till almost
> The size of the earth it crashed
> Into the Atlantic—
> I watched it from the point of Manhattan.
> The earth took it with a tremendous jolt—
> Impact and penetration. Next thing
> The moon was inside the earth,
> Cramming its phosphor flames
> Under the scabby humped pelt of the prairies.
> And above me the towers of Manhattan
> Swayed like curtains of ash. (83)

The lines are from Ted Hughes's "The Badlands," from his final book *Birthday Letters,* published in 1998 but addressing an experience several decades before: a trip across America taken by Hughes and his wife Sylvia Plath. The scene shares neither time nor place with September 11 (the young couple are driving through North Dakota) but is as apocalyptical and apparently specific as if it *had* been written about that event. The speaker establishes the source of the scene ("a dream"), the viewpoint (the "point of Manhattan"), and the vocabulary of catastrophe: "impact and penetration," two of the words used repeatedly in news media reporting the events of 9/11. The poem sweeps outward, westward, to include "the scabby humped pelt of the prairies," conflating the "Badlands" of the title and New York City. (The attack was not on the towers, presumably, but on the United States) Most striking of all is that "the towers of Manhattan"—a phrase that evokes the poetic history of skyscrapers in Crane, Auden, Eliot, Ginsberg, and O'Hara—should reveal their extreme frailty moments before their collapse, by "swaying" as if they had been softened into hanging fabric, the word "curtains" not only suggesting the end of a spectacle but the end (as in "of ash") of life.

No matter how much we insist that poetry answer socio-historical purposes, it often slips free of temporal limits, at the very least in the sense that it applies to more than one time, as well as to times as yet unimagined—indeed, that is the way that it *does* answer to socio-historical purposes.[17] Consider a poetic strategy that we find in the Kinnell, Baraka, and Hughes poems alike—the technique of collapsing multiple times and locales within a few poetic lines. The effect is not only of tracing transgeographical, transcultural lineages and webs of knowledge but also of tracing the action of the mind, at once synchronic and diachronic.[18] (Writing of the brain's processing of images, Antonio R. Damasio oberves that "[i]mages of something that has not yet happened and that may in fact never come to pass are no different in nature from the images you hold of something that has happened. They constitute the *memory of a possible future* rather than of the past that was" [97, emphasis mine].) It is not technique or any single device (incantation, archaism, high diction, prophetic tone, etc.) that I wish to emphasize so much as a movement of the mind that follows the logic of the missed encounter. This is the movement traced in "The Badlands," a poem that now seems extraordinarily precocious, and a poem that animates a reality much more than it describes one.

In the first quarter of the twentieth century, the baby of archaic, prophetic, and magical forces—which always lay in the subsoil of poetry—was thrown out with the bathwater of predictable, sentimental Victorian imagery and themes. Rhythm and rhyme, were seen, as the century progressed, as ornament, without any constitutive function. (When, much later, those elements did return, as secular and unthreatening "New Formalism," they seemed staler than before.) This century-old "freedom" from verse forms is *still* being celebrated by poets who imagine themselves throwing off the shackles of the "Western tradition." But perhaps the first decades of the 21st century will not be about the end of irony, so often proclaimed after the 9/11 attacks, so much as about the end of a bland, desacralized, conversational poetry, whether "engaged" or not. In its place—as some of my preceding examples suggest—we may see poetry drawing again on ancient incantatory and performative forces—at times violent, at times ceremonial, seldom anecdotal or reportorial. Lest I begin to endorse the very kind of before/after view that I repudiate at the outset of this chapter, I would predict that all possible modes and approaches will continue to coexist, as they did through the twentieth century, but that the freshness deep down things that Hopkins celebrated will come from deep sites indeed. The poetry that rises from those strata seems unlikely to be of the kind I examine in the early sections of this chapter, the kind, that is, that predominated in the last half of the century now gone.

What constitutes the witness, as both Mallarmé and Freud testified, is not the fact of *reporting* the accident but rather the readiness to become "a medium of the testimony—and a *medium of the accident*" (Felman, "Education" 24; emphasis Felman's). In *The Interpretation of Dreams* (Chapter 2), Freud stressed the importance of unconscious testimony, arguing that one does not have to possess the truth in order to bear witness to it. One need not envision a Victorian parlor with Madame Blavatsky channeling the pharaohs of Egypt, but it is worth noting that vatic utterances, on the one hand, and poems in which language is allowed to write itself, on the other, are not the opposites they seem. Both concern the "medium"—in the two senses of spiritualistic and linguistic/semiotic. Both involve a poetry that is written out of an inability to understand, out of a willingness not to understand, out of an awareness that the appointment with the real is always missed. With such a stance toward the world, a poet has a chance of offering not merely a version of events but a performance of the timeless real.

NOTES

1. The original remark is from "Cultural Criticism and Society"; the "retraction" appears in *Negative Dialectics*. For a discussion of the frequent misinterpretations of the "After Auschwitz" remark, as well as a catalogue of its many citations, see Rothberg. Rothberg suggests, both in this remark and its retraction, that Adorno has not been well served by his translators.

2. It would be well at this point to define a term. The American Psychiatric Association's *Diagnostic and Statistical Manual of Mental Disorders* defines "trauma" both in terms of the specific types of events that cause it (the controversial "category a") and in terms of symptomatic responses, which are not explicitly tied to specific kinds of events (Caruth 115, n. 5). While these two views continue to be debated within the psychiatric field, Caruth, favoring the second set of terms, sees trauma as "the response to an unexpected or overwhelming violent event or events that are *not fully grasped as they occur,* but return later in repeated flashbacks, nightmares, and other repetitive phenomena" (115, n. 5; emphasis mine). We should remember Freud's going back and forth between the psychic and the historical or cultural in his own thoughts on trauma in both *Beyond the Pleasure Principle* and *Moses and Monotheism.*

3. A good deal has been written about the foreshadowing of September 11 in popular art but also about September 11 itself *as* "art," specifically as an instance of performance art enabled by the collusion of television. See particularly the controversy surrounding the troubling remarks of Karleinz Stockhausen, treated at length in Lentricchia and MacAuliffe.

4. Of this list, those not discussed in this article may be found in my works cited, except for Albert Goldbarth, Jay Parini, and D. Nurkse, whose poems appeared in the September 2002 issue of *Poetry*, and Billy Collins's "The Names," which was read to a joint session of Congress on September 11, 2002.

5. While I first encountered most of the following poems on the Internet, several of them now have a history—from website, to thematic anthology (e.g., *Poets Against the War, enough, An Eye for an Eye Makes the Whole World Blind,* and *September 11, 2001: American Writers Respond*), to poet's book. I've listed the print appearances in the works cited, followed by the website where they first appeared.

6. This poem was later collected in *September 11, 2001: American Writers Respond* and still later in the author's volume *No Heaven*.

7. Pamela Hale's poem, cited above, was also included in *Poets Against the War* (84–86).

8. I am using "prophetic" to mean not so much the idea of the past seeing the future but (as in religious *kairos* as well as in post-relativity science) a state of simultaneity.

9. I wish to thank the poets Frank Bidart and Stanley Plumly for sending me two (at the time) unpublished poems, "The Curse" and "The Morning America Changed," respectively. "The Curse" later appeared in the *Threepenny Review,* and then in Bidart's book *Star Dust.* Plumly's poem later became a prose commentary, collected in *September 11, 2001: American Writers Respond.*

10. Baudrillard, more prosaically, echoes this ongoing quality of the destruction: "Even in their pulverized state, they have left behind an intense awareness of their presence. No one who knew them can cease imagining them and the imprint they made on the skyline" (48).

11. Baraka later answered his accusers at length in a statement, "I Will not Apologize, I Will not Resign." Regarding Israeli foreknowledge of the World Trade

Center bombing, Baraka says that "not only was the US warned repeatedly by Germany, France, Russia, England, but also Israel . . . Michael Ruppert of the Green Party [stated] clearly . . . 'the Israel Mossad knew that the attacks were going to take place,' they knew that the World Trade Center were [*sic*] the targets . . . the entire Imperialist world knew and warned the US CIA in advance, but no action was taken." Similarly, Jean Baudrillard in *The Spirit of Terrorism* does not distance himself from popular Arab and French theories about plots; indeed, he seems to endorse them when, in a discussion of a collusion between terrorism and World Order, he writes, "A small step, then, to imagine that if terrorism did not exist, the system would have invented it. And why not, then, see the September 11 attacks as a CIA stunt?" (53–54).

12. Kinnell revises the poem substantially in the book version, dropping whole sections, adding lines ("Some were pushed" in the book follows "Some burned, their very faces caught fire"), and reversing lines. He also drops the English translations of the Villon, Celan, and Wat passages.

13. Recently, Theresa de Lauretis compared the current U.N. to the League of Nations and the current issuing of gas masks to old smudged photos of World War I, commenting, "This is not to say that history repeats itself, but rather that states of emergency have the capacity to collapse history and to suspend the logic of linear temporality" (367–68).

14. These lines are dropped in the book version.

15. See also, for a very similar technique, Robert Hass's "Bush's War," which, rather than delving into the synchronous event of 9/11 or even the years-long war in Iraq, instead diachronically spreads out across twentieth-century history, cataloguing the body counts while setting the poem in contemporary Berlin in the beauty of springtime. From Berlin, the poem flashes forward, not back, reminding us that—as quantum physics teaches—the terrain stretches equally either way ("it is a trick of the mind / That the past seems just ahead of us"): thus, "Flash forward: the firebombing of Hamburg, / Fifty thousand dead in a single night," "Flash forward: / Firebombing of Tokyo, a hundred thousand / in a night," and "Flash: / Two million Vietnamese . . . "

16. Other instances of the approaches I have mentioned would include Robert Bly's *The Insanity of Empire: A Book of Poems Against the Iraq War*, which includes several poems that offer repetitive, apocalyptical, and "precocious" modes, including "Call and Answer" and "Let Sympathy Pass" (a title derived from Whitman).

17. A number of canonical poems, for example, notably Emily Dickinson's "Because I Could Not Stop for Death," found a new life in memorial gatherings following 9/11. But it was W.H. Auden's "September 1, 1939" that became the most-quoted poem of this period, not only for its images of wartime apocalypse but for its New York setting, the poet speaking from "one of the dives / on 52nd Street" and alluding to "the blind skyscrapers" and to "[t]he unmentionable odour of death / [that] offends the September night." Auden repudiated the poem, in part since he no longer believed in its last line ("We must love one another or die"), but those who revisited the poem following September 11 were particularly alert to the lines "I and all the public know / What all schoolchildren learn / Those to whom evil is done / Do evil in return."

18. In "Traveling Poetries," Jahan Ramazani reminds us of other dense collage-like poetic juxtapositions, including the beginning of Pound's "Canto 81," Frank O'Hara's "The Day Lady Died," and Langston Hughes's "I've Known Rivers," all instances of covering multiple places and times within a few lines. Novels have other strengths and strategies, Ramazani suggests, but this is what poetry can do.

WORKS CITED

Abel, Marco. "Don DeLillo's 'In the Ruins of the Future': Literature, Images, and the Rhetoric of *Seeing* 9/11." *PMLA* 118 (2003): 1236–50.

Adorno, Theodore. "Commitment." *The Essential Frankfurt School Reader*. Ed. Andrew Arato and Eike Gebhardt. New York: Continuum, 1982. 300–18.

———. "Cultural Criticism and Society." *Prisms*. Trans. Samuel Weber and Shierry Weber. Cambridge: MIT, 1983. 17–34.

———. *Negative Dialectics*. Trans. E. B. Ashton. New York: Continuum, 1973.

Ai. *Dread*. New York: Norton, 2003.

Baer, Ulrich. "A Crisis of the Imagination: September 11 and Telling the Stories of Loss." *American Letters and Commentary* 14 (2002): 28–32.

Baker, David. "Late Blooming Roses." In Heyen, William, ed. *September 11, 2001* 33–34.

Baraka, Imamu Amiri. "I Will Not Apologize, I Will Not Resign." *ChickenBones: A Journal for Literary and Artistic African-American Themes*. www.nathanielturner.com/barakaonwhoblewupamerica.htm. 2 October 2002.

———. *Somebody Blew Up America and Other Poems*. St. Martin: House of Nehesi, 2003.

Baudrillard, Jean. *The Spirit of Terrorism*. Trans. Chris Turner. New York: Verso, 2003.

Belau, Linda. "Trauma and the Material Signifier." *Postmodern Culture* 11.2 (2001). http://www3.iath.virginia.edu/pmc/.

Bernstein, Charles. *Girly Man*. Chicago: U Chicago P, 2006.

Berrigan, Daniel. "After." Cohen and Matson 78–79.

Berry, Wendell. "Thoughts in the Presence of Fear." 10 November 2001. *Orion Online*. 12 June 2002 www.oriononline.org/pages/oo/sidebars/America/Berry.

Bhabha, Homi. "Statement for the *Critical Inquiry* Board Symposium." *Critical Inquiry* 30 (2004): 342–49.

Bidart, Frank. *Star Dust*. New York: Farrar, 2005.

Bly, Robert. *The Insanity of Empire: A Book of Poems Against the Iraq War*. St. Paul: Ally Press, 2004.

Borges, Jorge Luis. "Funes the Memorious." *Labyrinths*. New York: New Directions, 1962. 59–66.

Caruth, Cathy. *Unclaimed Experience: Trauma, Narrative, and History*. Baltimore: Johns Hopkins UP, 1996.

Chappell, Fred. "The Attending." In Heyen, William, ed. *September 11, 2001* 72–73.

Chomsky, Noam. *9/11*. New York: Seven Stories, 2001.

Clifton, Lucille. "9/11/01–9/17/01." In Heyen, William, ed. *September 11, 2001* 80–84.

Codrescu, Andrei. "9/11." *it was today*. Minneapolis: Coffee House, 2003. 142–43.

Cohen, Allen and Clive Matson, eds. *An Eye for an Eye Makes the Whole World Blind: Poets on 9/11*. Oakland: Regent, 2002.

Collins, Billy. "The Names." www.divinestra.com/names.html. September 11, 2002.

Creeley, Robert. "Ground Zero." Cohen and Matson150.

Damasio, Antonio R. *Descartes' Error: Emotion, Reason, and the Human Brain*. New York: Grosset/Putnam, 1995.

de Lauretis, Theresa. "Statement Due." *Critical Inquiry* 30 (2004): 365–68.

di Prima, Diane. "Notes Toward a Poem of Revolution." In Cohen and Matson, eds. *An Eye for an Eye Makes the Whole World Blind*, etc. [see item under Cohen] 40–43.

Dunn, Stephen. "To a Terrorist." *Between Angels.* New York: Norton, 1989. 79–80. (also appeared in *Alicia Ostriker: Poems for the Time [An Anthology].* www.mobylives.com/Ostriker.)

Felman, Shoshana. "Education and Crisis, on the Vicissitudes of Teaching." In Felman and Laub, *Testimony* [see item under Felman and Laub] 1–56.

———. "The Return of the Voice: Claude Lanzmann's *Shoah.*" Felman and Laub 204–83.

Felman, Shoshana, and Dori Laub, eds. *Testimony: Crises of Witnessing in Literature, Psychoanalysis, and History.* New York: Routledge, 1992.

Ferlinghetti, Lawrence. "History of the Airplane." In Cohen, etc. 15–16.

———. "Poetry as Prophecy." 16 October 2001 pbs.org/newshour/bb/poems/july-dec01/ferlinghetti.

Freud, Sigmund. "Remembering, Repeating and Working-Through." *The Standard Edition of the Complete Psychological Works of Sigmund Freud.* Vol. 12. Trans. James Strachey. London: Hogarth, 1917–19. 147–56.

———. *The Interpretation of Dreams.* New York: Barnes & Noble, 1994.

Gallagher, Tess. *Dear Ghosts.* Saint Paul: Graywolf, 2006.

Garrison, Deborah. "I Saw You Walking." *New Yorker.* 22 October 2001. 56.

Gery, John R. O. Personal Interview. 29 December 2006.

Gioseffi, Daniela. "Poetry and Politics After 9/11." users.tellurian.com/wisewomensweb/PoetsUSA/Gioseffi_Ed.html. 11 September 2002.

Hahn, Kimiko. "Four Poems." In Heyen, William [see full info under Heyen.] 164–66.

Hale, Pamela. "Poem for an Iraqi Child in a Forgotten News Clip." In Hamill, Sam [see full info under Hamill] et al. 84–86.

Halliday, Mark. "Interview." *In the Western Night: Poems 1965–1990.* Frank Bidart. New York: Farrar, Straus & Giroux, 1990. 230–42.

Hamill, Sam. "The New York Poem." Cohen and Matson 26–63.

———, et al., eds. *Poets Against the War.* New York: Thunder's Mouth, 2003.

Harjo, Joy. "When the World as We Knew it Ended." Heyen 168–69.

Hass, Robert. "Bush's War." *American Poetry Review* 35.2 (Mar/Apr 2006): 64.

Heyen, William, ed. *September 11, 2001: American Writers Respond.* Silver Springs: Etruscan 2002.

Hughes, Ted. "The Badlands." *Birthday Letters.* New York: Farrar, 1998. 82–83.

Jameson, Frederic. "Third World Literature in the Era of Multinational Capitalism." *Social Text* 15 (1986): 65–88.

Joris, Pierre. "9/11/01." *enough.* Ed. Rick London and Leslie Scalapino. Oakland: O Books, 2003. 22.

Kennedy, X.J. "September Twelfth, 2001." In Heyen, William [see under Heyen] 221.

Kinnell, Galway. "When the Towers Fell." *New Yorker* 16 September 2002: 51–54.

———. *Strong is Your Hold.* New York: Houghton Mifflin, 2006.

Kowit, Steve. "The Equation." In Heyen, William [see under Heyen] 224.

Lacan, Jacques. *The Seminar of Jacques Lacan: the Four Fundamental Concepts of Psychoanalysis.* Vol. 11. Trans. Alan Sheridan. Ed. Jacques-Alain Miller. New York: Norton, 1978.

Lane, Christopher. "The Poverty of Context: Historicism and Nonmimetic Fiction." *PMLA* 118 (2003): 450–69.

Latour, Bruno. "Why Has Critique Run Out of Steam? From Matters of Fact to Matters of Concern." *Critical Inquiry* 30 (2004): 225–48.

Lentricchia, Frank, and Jody McAuliffe. *Crimes of Art and Terror.* Chicago: U Chicago P, 2003.

Lindsay, Vachel. *The Congo and Other Poems.* New York: Dover, 1992.

McClure, Michael. "Black Dahlia." In Cohen and Matson, eds. *An Eye for an Eye Makes the Whole World Blind: Poets on 9/11*. 141–42.

Meltzer, David. "26:ix:01." www.bigbridge.org/issue7/warpeace.htm.

Merwin, W.S. "To the Words." In Heyen, etc. 3–4.

Ostriker, Alicia. "the window, at the moment of flame." In Heyen, etc. 294–95.

Pearson, Jim. "kunishi ridge 2nd bn. first marines." In Hamill, "The New York Poem." Cohen and Matson 173.

Piercy, Marge. "Choices." In Hamill, "The New York Poem." Cohen and Matson 179.

Pinsky, Robert. "9/11." *Washington Post* 8 September 2002: W26

Plumly, Stanley. "The Morning America Changed." Unpublished poem. (for prose version see Heyen 307–09.)

Ramazani, Jahan. "Traveling Poetry." *Modern Language Quarterly* 68 (2007): 281–303.

Ray, David. "Six Months After" and "The Dilemma." In Cohen, etc. 138–40.

Rigsbee, David. *Sonnets to Hamlet*. Columbus: Pudding House, 2004.

Rimbaud, Jean-Arthur. *Complete Works, Selected Letters*. Trans. Wallace Fowlie. Chicago: U Chicago P, 1966.

Rothberg, Michael. "After Adorno: Culture in the Wake of Catastrophe." *New German Critique* 72 (1997): 45–81.

Sontag, Susan. Qtd. in "Talk of the Town." *New Yorker* 24 September 2001.

Sze, Arthur. "The Aprodisiac." In Hamill, etc. 224–25.

Williams, C. K. "War." *Collected Poems*. New York: Farrar, 2006. 599–600. (The poem first appeared in the *New Yorker* 5 November 2001. 80–81. It later appeared also in Hamill et al.)

Wilner, Eleanor. "Found in the Free Library." In Hamill, "The New York Poem." Cohen and Matson 224.

Young, Al. "Held Captive." In Cohen, etc. 88–89.

Afterword
Imagination and Monstrosity

Robert Pinsky

Monstrous events resemble mutations.

Whether from natural disaster or act of war or terrorism, lethal shock at a certain scale deflects culture into directions beyond ordinary imagining, yet undetectable at first.

The Japanese movie monster *Godzilla* first appeared in 1954, nine years after atom bombs fell on Hiroshima and Nagasaki. A prehistoric reptile, Godzilla is somehow also a mutant caused—explicitly—by atomic radiation. His lethal breath is not only fiery but radioactive. The creature has persisted for decades now, through many films and offshoots, along with countless theories attempting to comprehend Godzilla's relation to the attacks that killed approximately two hundred thousand people, mostly civilians.

The comparison is one of reaction: the mystery and force, the bizarrely folded variety, of cultural response to national wounds that are sustained intimately, by ordinary citizens. The creature, the enduring science-fiction lizard, embodies the unforeseen and unforeseeable relation between trauma and culture.

After the first violent calamity, the deflection develops along its unanticipated course. The preposterous atomic dinosaur destroys and redeems, punishes and atones, exhaling the bewildering fires of re-enactment. It apologizes and it accuses. It rages and it sublimates. Ludicrous, vulgar, disturbing, at once crude and enigmatic—imagination takes forms that could not be dreamed up by rhetoric, incarnations almost beyond understanding

Like the lurid monster, culture itself mutates unpredictably. Its responses to historical extremes of violence include the outrageous. The bombs themselves were code-named—with sardonic humor, or mere understatement?—"Little Boy" and "Fat Man." The names with their surface insouciance may have served secrecy, but nevertheless they suggest an ironic awareness of the extreme nature of the weapons. It is possible to imagine them as a way of dispelling awe. Like language in a dream, or like the ambiguous movie dragon, the phrases acknowledge a difficult reality by cloaking it. Understatement, grotesquerie, comedy can be means to contain what has gone beyond previous limits.

Laboring to deal with extremes, imagination makes itself a riposte to outrage. *Outrage* is a word that in its origins turns out to have nothing to do with "rage"—it is cognate with "ultra" and "outré," a going-beyond, as by outlandish inventions gestated in the fitful sleeps and startled awakenings of reason. The association of the word with anger is another cultural creation. We users of English, in our communal forge, have joined the idea of rage to outrage, anger to excess.

If *outrage* suggests a going-beyond, crashing heedlessly beyond reasonable limits, the word *monster* involves a perceptible warning: it is related to "demonstrate" and "monstrance"—a caution flag or logo of danger, or something to show or to be seen or heeded. I associate it with carnival and peep-show, an emphasis on sensation, maybe a little detached or mechanical. Along with the still and moving images, actual or recreated, the journalistic reports, the political exploitation, the speeches and moralizing, punditry and investigation—as our aggregate account of the monstrous event forms and reforms, expands and reconfigures like a crystal colony in its chemical bath—other, more organic processes rise from the dream-depths: other means of perception, other definitions of rage, permutations of empathy.

An example is poetry, the art that arranges the sounds of language, a physical reality, to imitate expressively an emotional and intellectual reality. A poem can work on a more intimate scale than cinematic images and with an emotional reality more immediate than scholarship: integrating emotional, intellectual, even bodily responses. Here is a poem first published in the *Threepenny Review* in Spring 2002:

Curse

May breath for a dead moment cease as jerking your

head upward you hear as if in slow motion floor

collapse evenly upon floor as one hundred and ten

floors descend upon you.

May what you have made descend upon you.
May the listening ears of your victims their eyes their

breath

enter you, and eat like acid
the bubble of rectitude that allowed you breath.

May their breath now, in eternity, be your breath.

*

Now, as you wished, you cannot for us
not be. May this be your single profit.

Of your rectitude at last disenthralled, you
seek the dead. Each time you enter them

they spit you out. The dead find you are not food.

Out of the great secret of morals, *the imagination to enter
the skin of another,* what I have made is a curse. (Bidart 25–26)

"Curse," by Frank Bidart, with its title and final word, establishes the primal immediacy, but also the ancient genre, of cursing. A curse can be an ejaculation, and it can be a ritual, and, as the poem demonstrates, the malediction can be simultaneously immediate and traditional.

With the kind of primary emotional response that reporting, punditry, and rhetoric tend to pass over or ignore, Bidart begins from a fundamental, nearly primordial response: anger. In the way of lyric poetry, he refines and elaborates that response. As the word *lyric* implies, the poem involves a kind of dialogue between the individual voice and the cultural instrument that is in one's hands, and handed-down.

Thus, Bidart presents a personal, vocal rage at "the bubble of rectitude," the suicide-killers' delusional carapace of divine approval. The indictment of those killers, and the imagining of them "disenthralled" and confronting their victims in an afterlife, leads to the introspective, self-reflective final sentence. The loathing for self-righteousness, the rejection of those who feel assured of divine approval, is not diminished or even tempered by the final realization, "what I have made." The curse remains a curse, though its ironic relation to empathy is acknowledged.

Bidart's poem, true to a moment of apprehension early in the monstrous event's history, retains the immediate reality's emotional force. I think "Curse" survives its moment in time by considered attention to that moment: the authority of immediacy joined to the authority of reflection.

In a rather different process, perhaps the reverse, some works of art anticipate an event; many of the best poems about the event may be written long before the event: the authority not of immediacy but perspective. For example, the truism that a great event is transformative demands a viewpoint that corrects grandiosity. William Butler Yeats in "Easter 1916" tempers the repeated proposition that "all is changed, changed utterly" by including a stanza where bombast is contrasted with quiet, fanaticism with the flow of life:

Hearts with one purpose alone
Through summer and winter seem

Enchanted to a stone
To trouble the living stream.
The horse that comes from the road,
The rider, the birds that range
From cloud to tumbling cloud,
Minute by minute they change;
A shadow of cloud on the stream
Changes minute by minute;
A horse-hoof slides on the brim,
And a horse plashes within it
The long-legged moor-hens dive,
And hens to moor-cocks call.
Minute by minute they live:
The stone's in the midst of all. (74)

By invoking the authority of the ordinary, Yeats makes the idea of historic transformation credible.

Politicians and poets have asserted that the September 11 attacks were transformative—with the truth in the proposition sometimes undermined by political or emotional manipulation, or by a quality of mere rhetoric. The muddled, compelling communal dream of the monster Godzilla, a creature formed in the depths by trauma, a being vengeful yet benign, in its way also touches ordinary life, but with only a gestural sense of the ordinary: with images that echo the trauma—cities on fire, vehicles upended, panic and destruction in the streets. That strange, muddled, but compelling popular dream more or less omits both the large scale of history and the small scale of domestic life. The monster-movie reality leaves the past as hazy and unspecified as the intimate, substituting the hypnotic storm of special effects.

Yeats imagines a more detailed, intimate social texture: his conspirators come—unlike the poet—from "counter or desk." He greets them with polite nods, he says, then jokes about them with his friends "around the fire at the club." The difference in social class, like the natural details of cloud, stream, moor-hen, and horse, embodies a world apart from the sudden, large-scale violence. By adding perspective, these two kinds of quiet, the nod of greeting on the street and the passing cloud, give reality to the contrasting and clangorous element of transformation.

That effect of perspective suggests how a successful poem about a communal trauma may be written long before the event. Here is Mark Strand's translation of a poem by the Brazilian poet Carlos Drummond de Andrade (1902–1987):

Souvenir of the Ancient World

Clara strolled in the garden with the children.
The sky was green over the grass,

the water was golden under the bridges,
other elements were blue and rose and orange,
a policeman smiled, bicycles passed,
a girl stepped onto the lawn to catch a bird,
the whole world—Germany, China—
    all was quiet around Clara.

The children looked at the sky: it was not forbidden.
Mouth, nose, eyes were open. There was no danger.
What Clara feared were the flu, the heat, the insects.
Clara feared missing the eleven o'clock trolley,
She waited for letters slow to arrive,
She couldn't always wear a new dress. But she strolled in the garden,
    in the morning!
They had gardens, they had mornings in those days! (22)

Here the idea of utterly transformative catastrophe—in some sense what rhetoric calls "a commonplace"—takes on a memorable embodiment that omits the large scale except by implication. Here is the opposite of special effects, reversing the disaster movie's cursory treatment of actual life. The stroke of the concluding lines is extreme without bombast.

Yet global scale is not omitted. The rather objective, even cold voice that notes "other elements" and enumerates the everyday concerns of a modest, civilian life, also incorporates "the whole world—Germany, China."

The central idea of sudden, drastic change is not only a rhetorical commonplace, it is one of the primary and persistent responses to the September 11 attacks. That conceptual handhold, the idea of irrevocable transformation, a harsh awakening, has been exploited with great efficiency by politicians—which does not invalidate the concept. Strand's version of Andrade's poem, perhaps in some measure restorative beyond those manipulations, gives that concept the dignity of a felt truth. The world that once was, the world of mild ordinary anxieties, has been lost or feels lost. The poem includes the known and the unknown in recognizable, convincing proportions. That the ancient world is recent becomes an epiphany, a way of recognizing the creatures that rise above the surface—actual monstrosities with unforetold imaginings in reaction to them, with proportions and qualities of disruption still unrevealed.

Another truism or frequent assertion is that other countries—"Germany, China" perhaps?—have a more first-hand or ripened acquaintance with disaster, hatred, or violence than the Americans. Counter to the perceived or actual lack of historical understanding, counter to an alleged or actual anti-intellectual element in American culture, the work of study proceeds, striving to comprehend before and after, the ancient world and the present, information and phantasm. The chapters gathered here bring the patient attention of scholarship to monstrosity and outrage. The reflective work of the scholar, cool by old principle and ardent by conviction, takes its own place in the tangled and still-unfolding tapestry of nightmare, myth, and perception.

WORKS CITED

Bidart, Frank. "Curse." *Star Dust.* New York: Farrar, 2005.

Strand, Mark, trans. *Looking for Poetry: Poems by Carlos Drummond de Andrade and Rafael Alberti and Songs from the Quechua.* New York: Knopf, 2002.

Yeats, W.B. *Yeats's Poetry, Drama, and Prose.* Ed. James Pethica. New York: Norton, 2000.

Contributors

Paul Atkinson teaches in the Communications and Writing program at Monash University. His research focuses on the relationship between materiality and corporeality in Henri Bergson's writings on science, with emphasis on the relationship between immanent change and extended movement. He is currently working on a series of articles that explore the relationship between processual theories of time, aesthetics, and narrative.

Robert Brustein is the founding Director of the Yale and American Repertory Theaters, creative consultant to the A.R.T., Senior Research Fellow at Harvard University, and Distinguished Scholar in Residence at Suffolk University. In addition to his work as a critic for the *New Republic,* he is the author of five plays, twelve adaptations, and fifteen books of essays on theater in American culture, most recently *Millennial Stages: Essays and Reviews 2001–2005* (Yale 2006). He is a member of the American Academy of Arts and Letters and has received Fulbright and Guggenheim awards. Twice winner of the George Jean Nathan Award, he was recently inducted into the Theatre Hall of Fame.

Rebecca Carpenter, Associate Professor of English at McDaniel College, has published articles on D. H. Lawrence, Joseph Conrad, and popular culture. She is currently working on a book about representations of male failure and British decline in the twentieth- and twenty-first centuries.

Simon Cooper, Senior Lecturer in Communications at Monash University, is the author of *Technoculture & Critical Theory: In the Service of the Machine?* (Routledge 2003).

Laura Frost is Associate Professor of English at Yale University, where she teaches twentieth-century literature and culture. Her publications include *Sex Drives: Fantasies of Fascism in Literary Modernism* (Cornell 2002) and articles on James Joyce, D. H. Lawrence, Virginia Woolf,

Aldous Huxley, Sylvia Plath, and Kathryn Harrison, as well as pieces on contemporary culture, such as photography at Abu Ghraib.

Richard Glejzer, Professor of English at North Central College, is the author of *Between Witness and Testimony* (SUNY 2001) and has co-edited two collections, *Witnessing the Disaster: Essays on Representation and the Holocaust* (Wisconsin 2003) and *Rhetoric in an Antifoundational World* (Yale 1998).

Jeffrey Gray, Professor of English at Seton Hall University, is the author of *Mastery's End: Travel and Postwar American Poetry* (Georgia 2005) and editor of the five-volume *Greenwood Encyclopedia of Poets and Poetry* (Greenwood 2006). His articles and poetry have appeared in the *Atlantic Monthly, Callaloo, Profession, American Poetry Review, Contemporary Literature,* and many other journals. He is a two-time Fulbright recipient, and has lived and taught in Central America, the South Pacific, Asia, and Europe.

Mitchum Huehls, visiting Assistant Professor of English at UCLA, has published articles in *Contemporary Literature, Cultural Critique,* and elsewhere. His book, *Qualified Hope: A Postmodern Politics of Time,* is forthcoming from the Ohio State University Press.

Ann Keniston, Associate Professor of English at University of Nevada, Reno, is the author of *Overheard Voices: Address and Subjectivity in Postmodern American Poetry* (Routledge 2006) and *The Caution of Human Gestures: Poems* (David Robert 2005).

Charles Lewis, Associate Professor of English and director of the writing program at Beloit College, is author of *A Coincidence of Wants: The Novel and Neoclassical Economics* (Garland 2000) and articles on various American authors.

Stephanie Li, Assistant Professor of English at the University of Rochester, has published essays in *Callaloo* and *American Literature* and is completing a book titled *'Something Akin to Freedom': The Politics of Sexual Agency in Narratives by African American Women.*

Nancy K. Miller is Distinguished Professor of English and Comparative Literature at the Graduate Center, CUNY. Her most recent books are *But Enough about Me: Why We Read Other People's Lives* (Columbia 2002) and the co-edited anthology *Extremities: Trauma, Testimony, and Community* (Illinois 2002).

Robert Pinsky, who teaches in the graduate creative writing program at Boston University, was named U.S. Poet Laureate in 1997. His new book of poetry is *Gulf Music* (Farrar 2007). His previous collections include *Jersey Rain* (Farrar 2000) and *The Figured Wheel: New and Collected Poems 1966–1996* (Noonday 1996), awarded the 1997 Lenore Marshall Poetry Prize. His translation of *The Inferno of Dante* won the Los Angeles *Times* Book Award in poetry. He is poetry editor of *Slate.*

Jeanne Follansbee Quinn, Director of studies for the Program in History and Literature at Harvard University, has published essays on James Agee and Walker Evans, Richard Wright and American pragmatism and is completing a book tentatively titled *Democratic Aesthetics: Popular Front Anti-Fascism.*

Michael Rothberg is Associate Professor of English and Comparative Literature and Director of the Unit for Criticism and Interpretive Theory at the University of Illinois, Urbana-Champaign. He is the author of *Traumatic Realism: The Demands of Holocaust Representation* (2000) and co-editor, with Neil Levi, of *The Holocaust: Theoretical Readings* (2003). He is currently completing a book tentatively titled *Multidirectional Memory: The Holocaust, Decolonization, and the Legacies of Violence.*

Lance Rubin, chair of Humanities at Arapahoe Community College, is completing a book titled *"Remembering is Hell": William Dean Howells and the Politics of Memory,* has a forthcoming essay on Philip Dick, and is currently co-editing *Beyond* Fight Club: *Reading Chuck Palahniuk.*

David Simpson is Professor of English at the University of California at Davis. He is the author of numerous books, most recently *The Academic Postmodern and the Rule of Literature: A Report on Half-Knowledge* (Chicago 1995), *Situatedness; or Why We Keep Saying Where We're Coming From* (Duke 2002), and *9/11: The Culture of Commemoration* (Chicago 2006).

Simon Stow, Associate Professor of Government at the College of William and Mary, is the author of *Republic of Readers?: The Literary Turn in Political Thought and Analysis* (SUNY Press 2007) as well as numerous articles on the intersection of philosophy and literature.

Index

7 World Trade Center, 181–182
9–11—Artists Respond, 60–61, 72–78
9/11 Commission Report, 46, 188
9/11 Memorial, 1, 239
24 (TV), 171
102 Minutes: The Untold Story of the Fight to Survive Inside the Twin Towers. See Dwyer, Jim, and Flynn, Kevin

A

A Moment of Silence, 60, 67
Abel, Marco, 262, 276
Abu Ghraib, 214–215, 244, 245
Acheson, U.S. Secretary of State Dean, 143, 155
Adorno, Theodore, 262–263
Afghanistan: war in, 44, 73, 139, 144, 238, 244, 251; causalities in, 37
Al Jazeera, 109, 215
Al Qaeda, 2, 151–152, 165, 168, 244
Amazing Spider-Man. See Spider-Man.
An Eye for an Eye Makes the Whole World Blind: Poets on 9/11, 3
Anderson, Benedict, 228
Anderson, Maxwell: *"The Eve of St. Mark,"* 244
Andrade, Carlos Drummond: "Souvenir of the Ancient World," 288–289
Anker, Elisabeth, 233
Apter, David, 166
Arendt, Hannah, 126, 224–225, 238
Aristotle: *Nicomacheane Ethics,* 24
atrocities: in Rwanda, 68; in Cambodia, 68
Auschwitz, 106, 117, 262, 263
Auster, Paul, 226

B

Baetens, Jan, 67
Baer, Ulrich, 189, 262
Baker, David, 265
Baraka, Amiri: "Somone Blew Up America," 265, 273–276, 278
Barneuve, Julien, 209
Baudrillard, Jean: 8, 170–171, 216, 264–265, 277; *The Spirit of Terrorism,* 10, 108, 261
Barthes, Roland: 25, 35; *Camera Lucinda,* 25, 189
Batchen, Geoffrey, 37
Behrman, S.N.: *No Time For Comedy,* 244
Beigbeder, Frederic: 5, 183; *Windows on the World,* 4, 194, 200, 220
Belau, Linda, 263–264
Bell, Steve, 146
Berger, James, 84
Berger, John: "Horror Pictures," 28
Bergman, Ingmar, 243
Berman, Paul, 246–247, 251
Bernard-Donals, Michael, 117
Bernstein, Charles, 265
Berrigan, Daniel, 265
Berry, Wendell, 265
Bidart, Frank: 2, 265; "Curse," 4, 268–271, 277, 286–287
Biennial, Whitney, 183
Big Brother. *See* Orwell, George
Bin Laden, Osama, 73, 112, 145, 168, 271
Bird, John, 66
Blair, Cherie, 146
Blair, Tony, 143–150, 153–154, 156
Blanchot, Maurice, 111, 116, 118
Bogart, Anne, 243
Bogdanski, Jack, 231

Borges, Jorge Luis: "Funes, the Memorious," 262
Borradori, Giovanna, 61
Brando, Marlon, 244
Brogan, Kathleen, 87
Brook, Peter, 243
Brooker, Peter, 75
Burroughs, William S., 169
Bush, George W.: philosophy, declarations, and criticisms thereof, 11, 43, 46, 53, 77, 129, 168, 224, 242–243, 251, 267; and administration, 2, 46, 60, 107, 143, 144, 230, 238–239; as character, 54, 58, 70, 146–150, 156
Bush, Laura, 267
Busiek, Kurt, 69

C
Campbell, J. Scott, 71
Captain America, 68, 69, 77
Caruth, Cathy: 99, 199, 263–264
Celan, Paul, 276
Chan, Paul, 183, 194
Chappell, Fred, 265
Chen, David, 35
Cheney, Dick, 54, 146–149
Cheney, Lynne, 168
Chung, Connie, 274–275
Churchill, Ward, 224, 233
Clarke, Jonathan, 167
Clemens, Valdine, 162
Clifton, Lucille, 265
Codrescu, Andrei, 265
Cody, Cornelia, 93
Cold War, 46
Collins, Billy, 265
Coetzee, J.M., 246–247, 251, 258
Cohen, Allen, 3
Collateral Damage (film), 108, 110
Colossus of New York, The. See Whitehead, Colson
Coughlin, Father Charles, 251
Coulter, Ann, 229, 231
Creeley, Robert, 265
Croft, Stuart, 167
"Curse." *See* Bidart, Frank

D
Damasio, Antonio R., 278
Danto, Arthur, 199
Davidson, James, 232–233
Davison, Al: "Ground Zero: A dream I had on Sep 9, 2001," 74

De Certeau, Michel, 86–87
DeLillo, Don: 2, 4–5, 183, 199; *Falling Man*, 4–5, 183, 199; "In the Ruins of the Future: Reflections on Terror and Loss in the Shadow of September," 9, 45, 124, 128–131; *Mao II*, 9, 10, 11, 123–131, 134
Derrida, Jacques, 61–62, 212
Di Prima, Diane: "Notes toward a Poem of Revolution," 265, 266
Die Ziet, 43
Dixie Chicks, The, 168
Douglass, William, 166
Drew, Julie, 144
Drew, Richard, 191
Dunn, Stephen, 265
Duras, Marguerite, 263
Dwyer, Jim: *102 Minutes*, 4, 213

E
Earle, Steve, 168
Eco, Umberto, 60
Egan, Jennifer: "Elements of Tragedy," 95
Eichmann, Adolf, 225
Eisner, Will: "The Real Thing," 67; "Reality 9/11," 67
Emperor's Children, The. See Messud, Claire
Empire State Building, 67, 188
Espiritu, Karen, 102
Euben, Peter, 237–238
Extremely Loud & Incredibly Close. See Foer, Jonathan Safran

F
Falling Man. See DeLillo, Don
Feinberg, Kenneth, 35
Felman, Shoshana, 263–264
Ferlinghetti, Lawrence, 261, 265
Fischl, Eric: *Tumbling Woman*,182
Fish, Stanley, 61, 74–75
Fleischer, Ari, 168
Flight 93 (film), 188
Flynn, Kevin: *102 Minutes*, 4, 213
Foer, Jonathan Safran: 56, 201, 214; *Extremely Loud & Incredibly Close*, 7, 10, 11, 42–53, 56, 183–199, 201, 214, 220, 221
Foucault, Michel, 169, 237
Franklin, Ruth, 193

Freedman, Mira, 72
Freedman, Samuel G., *Lettes to a Young Journalist*, 231
Freud, Sigmund: on *Nachträglichkeit*, 7, 42; *Project for a Scientific Psychology*, 42; *Beyond the Pleasure Principle*, 139; on screen memory, 255; *The Interpretation of Dreams*, 279
Fridolfs, Derek, 75
Friedrich, Jörg: *The Fire*, 211

G

Gabriel, Barbara, 87
Gallagher, Tess, 265
Garrison, Deborah, 265
Gersten-Vassilaros, Alexandra. *See* Rebeck, Theresa
Gery, John R.O., 273
Gioseffi, Daniella, 261–262
Ginsberg, Allen, 273–275
Glover, Carol, 234
Gluck, Louise, 2
Godzilla, 285
Gorer, Geoffrey, 237
Goldbarth, Albert, 265
Grass, Günter: *The Tin Drum*, 185; *Crabwalk*, 211, 213
Greenberg, Judith, 195
Gebbie, Melinda, 73, 78
Giuliani, Mayor Rudolph, 26, 70, 168
Gilman, Rebecca, 243
Guantanamo Bay, 46, 244, 245
Guirgis, Stephan Adly, 243
Guy Fawkes, 72

H

Hahn, Kimiko, 265
Hale, Pamela: "Poem for an Iraqi Child in a Forgotten News Clip," 266
Halper, Stefan, 167
Hammad, Suheir: "first writing since," 9, 124, 131, 132, 134–138
Hamill, Sam: 265; *Poets Against the War*, 4, 266, 267
Hare, David: 11, 156, 245; "Stuff Happens," 4, 146–150; *Guantanamo*, 245.
Harjo, Joy, 265
Harris, Larry: *Totems of the Fall*, 31
Haynes, Rob, 77
Helmers, Marguerite, 111
Heller, Terry, 162, 177

Hellman, Lillian: *Watch on the Rhine*, 244
Heroes, 60, 66, 68
Hill, Charles, 111
Hiroshima, 186, 221, 238, 263, 285
Hiroshima, Mon Amour (film), 263
Hirsch, Marianne, 108–110, 189–190
Hoffman, Jan, 22, 25, 235
Holland-Toll, Linda, 162
Holocaust: 55, 68, 100–101, 111, 117, 199, 200, 209, 218, 221, 251, 276; Memorial Museum, 28
Holzer, Jenny, 181, 200
Hortsch, Dan, 226
Hughes, Langston, 90
Hughes, Ted, 278
Hustler, 234
Hustvedt, Siri, 67
Huyssen, Andreas, 68

I

In the Shadow of No Towers. See Spiegelman, Art 1, 6–7, 8, 42–44, 53–58, 258
Iñárritu, Alejandro Gonzalez, 183
Iraq: war in, 2, 11, 38, 43, 44, 143, 145–156, 164, 166, 174, 212, 220, 238, 242–244; casualties in, 37; "The Face and Voice of Civilian Sacrifice in Iraq," 37, 215; relation to Vietnam, 58
Iwo Jima, 72, 111

J

Jackson, Kenneth T., 226
Jameson, Fredric, 174, 262
Jameson, Wendell, 234, 235
Janet, Pierre, 87
Jarecki, Eugene: *Why We Fight*, 238
Jenkins, Simon, 62
Joris, Pierre, 265
Jung, Carl, 277
Junod, Tom: "The Falling Man," 186, 191

K

Kant, Emmanuel, 124
Kakoudaki, Despina, 238
Kaplan, E. Ann: 182; *Trauma Culture*, 86
Katrina, Hurricane, 242, 245
Kaufmann, Walter, 230
Kelley, Tina, 234, 235

Kellner, Tatana: *Requiem for September 11,* 28–32
Kendrick, Walter, 231, 232, 234, 236
Kennedy, X.J., 265
King, Stephen: 95, 162, 183; "Elements of Tragedy," 95; "The Things They Left Behind," 183
Kinnell, Galway: 265, 278; "When the Towers Fell," 4, 273, 276–277
Kirkman, Robert, 75
Kirn, Walter, 49, 52
Kissinger, Henry, 267
Kosovo, 68
Kowit, Steve, 265
Kozloff, Max, 189
Kubiak, Anthony, 170
Kushner, Tony: 243; *Homebody/Kabul,* 244

L

Lacan, Jacques, 110, 264
LaCapra, Dominick, 102, 117, 136
Lane, Anthony, 180
Lane, Christopher, 264
Langewiesche, William, 225
Lanzmann, Claude, 200, 263
Latour, Bruno, 268
Laub, Dori, 117, 200
Leach, Neil, 82
LeCarre, John, 143
Ledig, Gert, 210: *Payback,* 212
Lee, Paul, 74
Letts, Tracy, 243
Levinas, Emmanuel, 100–101, 110, 117
Levine, Anne-Marie: "Four November 9ths," 9, 124, 131–134, 140
Levitz, Paul: "Tradition," 62
Lin, Maya, 226, 238
Lincoln, Abraham, 227–228
Lindsay, Vachel, 275
Lockett, Christopher, 171
Loraux, Nicole: *Mothers in Mourning,* 228–229, 230; *Divided City,* 238
Lovell, Jarret, 61
Lucas, Craig, 243
Lyotard, Jean-Francois, 165

M

Maher, Bill, 145, 167–168
Mallarmé, Stephane, 263, 279
Mallon, Thomas, 226, 231, 234
Matson, Clive, 3
McClatchy, J.D.: "Jihad," 4

McClure, Michael: "Black Dahlia," 265, 266
McDonald, Brian, 73
McDonald, Christie, 36
McEwan, Ian: 2, 11; *Saturday,* 146, 150–156, 220.
McGlothlin, Erin, 55
McGruder, Aaron, 168
McKinley, President William, 56, 114
Mee, Charles L., 243
Meltzer, David: "26:ix:01," 265
Merwin, W.S., 265
Messud, Claire: *The Emperor's Children,* 2, 12, 215–218, 220–221
Michael, George, 145
Miller, Arthur, 243
Milletti, Christina, 162
Moon, Reverend Sun Myung, 126–127
Moore, Alan, 73, 78
Moore, Tony, 75
Moriarty, Pat, 75
Müller, C.O., 232

N

Nagasaki, 285
National Commission on Terrorist Attacks Upon the United States, 36
Nayak, Meghana, 145
Neal, Arthur G.: *National Trauma and Collective Memory,* 82–83
Nelson, Anne: "The Guys," 4, 24
Nelson, Richard, 243
New Criticism, 265
New Formalism, 279
Niles, Steve, 74
Nossack, Hans Erich, 210, 211, 212
Novak, Lorie, 31–34
Nurkse, D.: "October Marriage," 9, 124, 131, 132, 138–140, 265

O

O'Connell, Brian, 73
O'Rourke, Megan, 194
Oates, Joyce Carol, 199–200
Oklahoma City Bombing, 226
Olsen, Jimmy: *9–11—The World's Finest Comic Book Writers & Artists Tell Stories to Remember,* 69
Orwell, George, 169
Osterweil, Ara, 235
Ostriker, Alicia, 265, 266

P

Pacheco, Carlos, 69
Pachoumis, Peter, 74
Palahniuk, Chuck: *Lullaby,* 11, 161–179;
    Fight Club, 161; *Survivor,* 161.
Palumbo-Liu, David, 49
Parini, Jay, 265
Parks, Suzan-Lori, 243
Patriot Act, 244
Patterson, Zabet, 235
Paz, Sharon: *11'09"01,* 183
Pearl Harbor, 62, 244
Pears, Iain: 209–210, 213; *The Dream
    of Scipio,* 209
Pearson, Jim, 267
Pentagon, the, 1, 31, 133, 144, 227, 239
Petit, Philippe, 198
Piercy, Marge, 267
Pinsky, Robert: 2, 15, 265; "Anniver-
    sary," 4
Plot Against America, The. See Roth,
    Philip
Plumly, Stanley: "The Day America
    Changed," 261, 265
Poets Against the War. See Hamill, Sam
*Poets on 9/11. See An Eye for an Eye
    Makes the Whole World Blind:
    Poets on 9/11*
"Portraits of Grief," 3, 8, 13, 19–41,
    200, 213, 216, 224–241
Posner, Richard, 46. *See also 9/11 Com-
    mission Report*
Powel, Eric, 74
Presnyakov brothers: *Terrorism,* 244
Prosser, Jay, 37

R

Radstone, Susannah, 145
Raines, Howell, 21–22, 227, 235
Rapp, Adam, 243
Ray, David, 265
Reagan, Ronald, 244
Rebeck, Theresa: *Omnium Gatherum,*
    244
Resnais, Alain, 263
Reynolds, Richard, 70
Rice, Condoleezza, 43
Rich, Frank, 236
Rigsbee, David, 277
Romita, John Jr., 63
Roth, Philip: *The Plot Against America,*
    2, 3, 246–260; *Operation Shy-
    lock,* 248.
Rouleau, Duncan, 70

Rudnick, Paul, 243
Ruhl, Sarah, 243
Rumsfeld, Donald, 46, 146–149
Rushdie, Salman: *The Satanic Verses,*
    123
Russell, David O: *Three Kings* (film),
    244

S

Sale, Tim, 71
Salecl, Reneta, 84
Saturday. See McEwan, Ian
Scanlan, Margaret, 166, 171
Schor, Naomi, 25
Schwarzenegger, Arnold, 108. See also
    Collateral Damage
Scott, Janny, 21, 24, 227, 231, 235
Seagle, Steven T.: "Unreal," 70
Sebald, W.G., 210–212, 215, 218, 221
Self, David, 77
Serban, Andrei, 243
Seuss, Diane, 183
Shanksville, PA, 1, 31, 213, 216
Shanley, John Patrick, 243
Shepard, Sam: *The God of Hell,* 244
Shepherd, Laura, 144
Sherwood, Robert: *There Shall Be No
    Night,* 244
Shoah (film), 263. *See also* Lanzmann,
    Claude
Silver Surfer, 68
Silverstein, Larry, 181, 183, 200
Singer, Alan, 35
Sontag, Susan, 25, 180, 189, 193, 231,
    235, 244, 265
Sowd, Aaron, 70
Spiegelman, Art: 2, 46, 99–119, 168,
    183, 200; *In the Shadow of
    No Towers,* 1, 6–7, 8, 42–46,
    53–58, 258; *Maus,* 6, 55,
    100–102, 106; *Maus II,* 55,
    106, 109, 111.
Spider-Man, 8, 9, 60–71, 78
Spirit of Terrorism, The. See Baudril-
    lard, Jean
Stone, Oliver, 200
Straczynski, J. Michael. *See* Spider-Man
Strand, Mark, 288–289
"Stuff Happens." *See* Hare, David
Sturken, Marita, 200
Suez Crisis, 146–147
Superman, 60, 61, 69, 70, 71
Sze, Arthur, 267
Szymborska, Wisława, 180–182

T

Terrorist, The. See Updike, John

Thor, 69

Thucydides, *History of the Pelopone-
    sian War,* 228

Townsend, Tim, 77

Twin Towers, 4, 36, 57, 62, 66, 67, 71,
    82–97, 139, 165, 195, 212, 217,
    231, 272, 277. *See also* World
    Trade Center

Two Gentlemen of Verona (play), 242

U

United 93 (film), 77, 171, 188

Updike, John: 2; *The Terrorist,*12,
    215–221

U.S.S. Abraham Lincoln, 251

V

Victim Compensation Fund, 35

Vietnam: War, 28, 46, 58; Veterans'
    Memorial, 226, 238

Vogel, Paula, 243

W

Wachs, Eleanor, 93

Warner, David, 234, 239

Wayne, John, 244

Weinstein, Arnold, 244

What We Saw (film), 185

White, E.B., 83

Whitehead, Colson: *The Colossus of
    New York,* 8, 82–98; "Lost and
    Found," 82–83, 85.

Willems, Mo: "Walking the Williams-
    burg Bridge to Work," 67

Williams, C.K., 265, 276; "War," 268,
    271–273

Williams, Linda, 234, 236

Wills, Garry, 228

Wilner, Eleanor, 267

Wilson, August, 243

Wilson, Robert, 243

Windows on the World. See Beigbeder,
    Frederic

Woodruff, Robert, 243

World Trade Center (WTC), 1, 4,
    6,23, 26, 36, 37, 38, 56, 60,
    66, 68, 73, 75, 83–87, 92–94,
    96–97, 101, 111–112, 116,
    125, 133, 135, 136, 144,
    180, 181, 182, 183, 185,
    187, 193, 194, 197–198,
    199, 224, 225, 239, 242,
    244, 256, 264, 274

World Trade Center (film), 77, 171,
    200. *See also* Stone, Oliver

Wright, Doug, 243

Y

Yaeger, Patricia, 87

Yeats, William Butler: "Easter 1916,"
    287–288

Young, Al, 265

Z

Zelizer, Barbie, 68, 189, 190

Zinn, Howard, 37, 226

Zircher, Patrick, 75

Žižek, Slavoj: 10, 61, 66–67, 116,
    170; *Welcome to the Desert
    of the Real: Five Essays on
    September 11 and Related
    Dates,* 10

Zukin, Sharon, 82

Zulaika, Joseba, 166

Ba = 620488

0096802333

Lightning Source UK Ltd.
Milton Keynes UK
UKOW06f1827040216

267735UK00029B/693/P

9 780415 883986